A Chronology of
Noteworthy Events
in American Psychology

A Chronology of Noteworthy Events in American Psychology

Warren R. Street

AMERICAN PSYCHOLOGICAL ASSOCIATION
WASHINGTON, DC

Published by
American Psychological Association
750 First Street, NE
Washington, DC 20002

Copies may be ordered from
APA Order Department
P.O. Box 2710
Hyattsville, MD 20784

In the UK and Europe, copies may be ordered from
American Psychological Association
3 Henrietta Street
Covent Garden, London
WC2E 8LU England

Typeset in Goudy by Techna Type, Inc., York, PA

Printer: Braun-Brumfield, Inc., Ann Arbor, MI
Cover Designer: Minker Design, Bethesda, MD
Technical/Production Editor: Susan Bedford

Library of Congress Cataloging-in-Publication Data
Street, Warren R.
    A chronology of noteworthy events in American psychology / Warren R. Street.
        p.   cm.
    Includes bibliographical references and indexes.
    ISBN 1-55798-267-8 (case).—ISBN 1-55798-261-9 (paper)
    1. Psychology—United States—History.   2. American Psychological
Association—History.   I. Title.
BF108.U5S77   1994
150'.973—dc20   94-29690
                                                                                    CIP

British Library Cataloguing-in-Publication Data
A CIP record is available from the British Library

Printed in the United States of America
First Edition

CONTENTS

Introduction vii

I.   BEFORE 1892: DIVERSE TRADITIONS............................ 1
II.   1892–1919: THE FIRST GENERATION 73
III. 1920–1939: BETWEEN THE WARS: CONSOLIDATION
      AS AN INDEPENDENT SCIENCE.................................... 145
IV.   1940–1949: POSTWAR DIVERSITY AND EXPANSION............ 201
V.   1950–1969: PSYCHOLOGY COMES OF AGE........................ 225
VI.   1970–1985: A PARTNERSHIP OF SCIENCE AND
      PRACTICE... 293
VII. 1986–PRESENT: THE SECOND CENTURY........................ 343

Name Index.. 367
Subject Index.. 387
Calendar Index.. 409
APA Division Index.. 417
About the Author.. 425

INTRODUCTION

The exact dates of historic political events, such as important battles, treaties, coronations, and elections, have been recorded carefully and their anniversaries are often noted publicly, sometimes by national holidays. The history of psychology, like the histories of nations, is made up of countless discrete events, each occurring at some fixed time in the past. Although it is unlikely that any of these events will ever be the occasion for a national holiday, a chronological record of important events presents an interesting perspective on the story of the development of contemporary psychology.

This volume contains brief descriptions and exact dates of 2,827 noteworthy events in the history of psychology, with particular attention given to American psychology and the American Psychological Association (APA). The collection includes dates of birth; publication of important books, articles, and mental tests; passage of influential legislation; events in the histories of psychological associations and institutions; court decisions, research announcements, and awards; and scores of other events not easily categorized. Each event has been numbered in chronological order, beginning with Entry 1, the reported date of the birth of Plato, and ending with Entry 2827, the appearance of Sigmund Freud on the cover of *Time* magazine for the fourth time.

The collection has been compiled from biographies and autobiographies, public archives, history texts, journal articles, biographical dictionaries, association archives, contemporary newspaper reports, and correspondence with psychologists who were present when the events took place. A complete source citation for each event exceeds the scope of this volume, but a description of frequently used sources is appropriate. Among the most useful general books have been

American Psychiatric Association. (1944). *One hundred years of American psychiatry*. New York: Columbia University Press.

Ayd, F., & Blackwell, B. (Eds.). (1984). *Discoveries in biological psychiatry*. Baltimore: Ayd Medical Communications.

Beighton, P., & Beighton, G. (1986). *The man behind the syndrome*. New York: Springer-Verlag.

Bremner, R. H. (Ed.). (1970–1974). *Children and youth in America: A documentary history*. Cambridge, MA: Harvard University Press.

Ellenberger, H. F. (1970). *The discovery of the unconscious: The history and evolution of dynamic psychology*. New York: Basic Books.

Epstein, R. (Ed.). (1980). *Notebooks, B. F. Skinner*. Englewood Cliffs, NJ: Prentice Hall.

Evans, R. B., Sexton, V. S., & Cadwallader, T. C. (Eds.). (1992). *The American Psychological Association: A historical perspective*. Washington, DC: American Psychological Association.

Fancher, R. (1990). *Pioneers of psychology* (2nd ed.). New York: Norton.

Freud, S. (1953–1966). *The standard edition of the complete psychological works of Sigmund Freud*, (J. Strachey, Ed. and Trans., Vols. 1–23). London: Hogarth Press.

Herrnstein, R. J., & Boring, E. G. (Eds.). (1965). *A source book in the history of psychology*. Cambridge, MA: Harvard University Press.

Hilgard, E. R. (1987). *Psychology in America: A historical survey*. San Diego, CA: Harcourt Brace Jovanovich.

Hothersall, D. (1984). *History of psychology*. Philadelphia: Temple University Press.

Hurd, H. M. (Ed.). (1916). *The institutional care of the insane in the United States and Canada*. Baltimore: Johns Hopkins University Press.

Jones, E. (1953–1957). *The life and work of Sigmund Freud* (Vols. 1–3). New York: Basic Books.

Kane, J. N. (1981). *Famous first facts: A record of first happenings, discoveries, and inventions in American history* (4th ed.). New York: H. W. Wilson.

Kanner, L. (1964). *A history of the care and study of the mentally retarded*. Springfield, IL: Charles C Thomas.

Kimble, G. A., Wertheimer, M., & White, C. (Eds.). (1991). *Portraits of pioneers in psychology*. Hillsdale, NJ: Erlbaum; and Washington, DC: American Psychological Association.

McGuire, W. (Ed.). (1974). *The Freud/Jung letters: The correspondence between Sigmund Freud and C. G. Jung*. Princeton, NJ: Princeton University Press.

Napoli, D. S. (1981). *Architects of adjustment: The history of the psychological profession in the United States*. Port Washington, NY: National University Publications, Kennikat Press.

The NDA book (Vol. 2). (1990). Rockville, MD: FOI Services.

Pate, J. L., & Wertheimer, M. (1993). *No small part: A history of regional organizations in American psychology.* Washington, DC: American Psychological Association.

Peterson, J. J. (1983). *The Iowa testing programs: The first fifty years.* Iowa City: University of Iowa Press.

Puente, A. E., Matthews, J. R., & Brewer, C. L. (Eds.). (1992). *Teaching psychology in America: A history.* Washington, DC: American Psychological Association.

Ridenour, N. A. (1961). *Mental health in the United States: A fifty-year history.* Cambridge, MA: Harvard University Press.

Rieber, R. (Ed.). (1980). *Wilhelm Wundt and the making of a scientific psychology.* New York: Plenum Press.

Rosenzweig, S. (1992). *Freud, Jung, and Hall the king maker: The historic expedition to America.* Göttingen, Germany: Hogrefe & Huber.

Shipley, T. (Ed). (1961). *Classics in psychology.* New York: Philosophical Library.

Sneader, W. (1985). *Drug discovery: The evolution of modern medicines.* New York: Wiley.

Sokol, M. M. (Ed.). (1981). *An education in psychology: James McKeen Cattell's journal and letters from Germany and England, 1880–1888.* Cambridge, MA: MIT Press.

Valenstein, E. S. (1986). *Great and desperate cures: The rise and decline of psychosurgery and other radical treatments for mental illness.* New York: Basic Books.

Weintraub, F. J. (Ed.). (1976). *Public policy and the education of exceptional children.* Reston, VA: Council for Exceptional Children.

Zusne, L. (1987). *Eponyms in psychology: A dictionary and biographical sourcebook.* New York: Greenwood.

It is common for other references to have contributed only one or two entries to the collection. Hundreds of articles, obituaries, award citations, and news entries in the *American Psychologist*, the *Journal of the History of the Behavioral Sciences*, and early volumes of *Psychological Bulletin* and the *American Journal of Psychology* contributed entries. Various editions of the *APA Membership Directory*, *American Men of Science*, *American Men and Women of Science*, and the *Dictionary of American Biography* have been helpful in establishing some birth dates.

Many events related to the APA were found in issues of the *APA Monitor* and in materials available in the APA Library, including the APA Council of Representatives agendas, APA convention programs, and newsletters of state associations and APA divisions. Founding documents of APA divisions were located in the APA Division Affairs office.

Publication dates of books, journals, journal articles, films, television shows, and radio broadcasts were found in the copyright card catalog of the Library of Congress, with occasional excursions into the original copyright registers. Unfortunately, many major psychological journals were not registered in the copyright office in the first years of their publication, and their initial publication dates have been lost. In a few cases, a date was retrieved by inspecting the actual first issue of the journal placed on deposit at the Library of Congress. It should be noted that the publication date of a journal usually is not the same as the issue date. Sometimes, several months may pass before an issue with a given nominal date is actually published.

References to court decisions were typically verified by reference to U.S. Supreme Court reports or to state and regional reports. Dates of federal legislation were obtained from *Statutes at Large*, which are the published volumes of Acts of Congress, or by reference to the histories of legislation published in the *U.S. Administrative Code and Congressional News*. Many dates of incorporation of state psychological associations were obtained through correspondence with secretaries of state of individual states. Dates of psychologist licensure legislation in each state were obtained from state association newsletters and correspondence with state university law libraries.

I referred to several sources when choosing which individuals to include. I tried to include all Americans and major Europeans cited by Zusne (1984), who based his selection on rankings of eminence reported by Annin, Boring, and Watson (1968). In addition, to the extent that I could identify their birth dates, I included winners of major APA awards, figures described in obituaries in the *American Psychologist*, APA presidents and chief executive officers, and Nobel prize winners whose research relates to psychology. Thus, many living psychologists have been included. Readers should understand that many outstanding psychologists have not been included in this chronology and that no critical evaluation of one's contributions is implied.

In choosing among books and articles, I referred to several reviews of the literature in psychology that selected noteworthy publications on the basis of expert opinion, citation counts, textbook bibliographies, and compilations of recommended reading lists. The following is a list of the more helpful sources in choosing individuals, books, and articles for inclusion:

Annin, E. L., Boring, E. G., & Watson, R. I. (1968). Important psychologists, 1600–1967. *Journal of the History of the Behavioral Sciences, 4,* 303–315.

Garfield, E. (1978, August 7). The 100 articles most cited by social scientists, 1969–1977. *Current Contents,* pp. 5–12.

Garfield, E. (1978, September 11). The 100 books most cited by social scientists, 1969–1977. *Current Contents*, pp. 5–16.

Garfield, E. (1992, November). Most-cited papers, 1986–1990. *APS Observer*, 5(6), 8–9.

Guthrie, R. V. (1976). *Even the rat was white: A historical view of psychology*. New York: Harper & Row.

Harvard list of books in psychology (4th ed.). (1971). Cambridge, MA: Harvard University Press.

Higbee, K. L. (1975). Psychological classics: Publications that have made lasting and significant contributions. *American Psychologist, 30*, 182–184.

McCollom, I. N. (1973). Psychological classics: Older journal articles frequently cited today. *American Psychologist, 28*, 363–365.

O'Connell, A. N., & Russo, N. F. (1983–1988). *Models of achievement: Reflections of eminent women in psychology* (Vols. 1–2). New York: Columbia University Press.

Solso, R. (1979). Twenty-five years of recommended readings in psychology. *American Psychologist, 34*, 703–705.

Sternberg, R. J. (1992). *Psychological Bulletin*'s top 10 "hit parade." *Psychological Bulletin, 112*, 387–388.

Stevens, G., & Gardner, S. (1982). *The women of psychology* (Vols. 1–2). Cambridge, MA: Schenkman.

Zusne, L. (1984). *Biographical dictionary of psychology*. Westport, CT: Greenwood.

This chronological history of psychology was begun more than 20 years ago as a product of personal curiosity and was reinforced by describing historic events to classes, corresponding with colleagues, and discovering an occasional odd or humorous event. Colleagues Ludy Benjamin, Jr., David Cole, Donald Dewsbury, Raymond Fancher, Paul Mountjoy, Phil Tolin, and Max Zwanziger contributed several dates of events in the early stages, and the Central Washington University small grants and faculty development programs have supported some aspects of the project throughout its development.

The APA became interested in the chronology prior to its centennial celebration in 1992 and has generously supported the expansion of the collection, enabling it to almost quadruple in size over the past 4 years. With the passing of the centennial year, work on the collection has continued under the aegis of the APA Historical Database Project. Gary VandenBos, Julia Frank-McNeil, and Susan Bedford, all of APA Publications, have provided constant encouragement and advice. They have extended the APA's prestige and stable support to the project, making it possible to gather information on more than a casual basis. Rick Sample and Laura Dworken, of the APA Library, have pointed out valuable sources and tolerated widening circles of opened volumes in library areas of two buildings.

My graduate assistants are regularly recruited for the project, even though the work barely falls within the scope of their master's degrees in counseling or school psychology. David Billings, Devin Gaenz, Lori Dunkel, Karen Patnode, Martine Robbins, and Shobhna Wadhwa all have taken up residency in the library at one time or another for this reason. Lara Nesselroad, of the University of Oregon Library, has responded helpfully to many electronic mail requests for information.

My greatest debt is to my wife and colleague, Libby Street. She has been a thorough and gently critical editor of each entry in this book. She has tolerated side trips to libraries during vacations, endured the crisis of a hard disk crash, and waited patiently while I cleared up "one last inconsistency" and made a backup. Libby has listened with apparent interest to obscure histories of drugs, mental hospitals, licensure legislation, and schismatic associations of psychologists with Byzantine originating motives. Altogether, quite a gift.

Any inaccuracies in these records are due to my own oversights. Additions or corrections to the APA Historical Database are welcome and may be sent to Warren R. Street, Professor of Psychology, Central Washington University, Ellensburg, WA 98926-7575, or to my electronic mail address, WARREN@CWU.EDU (Internet).

I

BEFORE 1892
DIVERSE TRADITIONS

The conceptual and practical elements of contemporary Western psychology were crafted by philosophers, biologists, humanitarians, physicians, and educators in the centuries before the founding of the American Psychological Association (APA) in 1892. These elements have been enclosed within the membrane of modern psychology, but allegiances to their parent disciplines have been maintained—like ethnic groups uneasily committed to nationhood, but committed nonetheless. This chapter traces events before scientists and practitioners recognized in the late nineteenth century that they were related by membership in the new discipline of psychology.

We are left with the sparest records of actual events that later have been recognized as influential in the history of psychology: the births of prominent figures, the foundings of a few institutions, and an occasional date of publication or scholarly presentation. The sparseness of the records of the earliest actual events is illustrated by the position of John Locke's birthday in this chronology. Locke's empiricism grafted the observational methods of William Harvey (Entry 12) and Isaac Newton (Entry 20) onto a stock of philosophical problems traditionally approached by means of logic and correct alignment with religious belief. His views are thought of as relatively modern contributions to psychology, yet only 17 entries precede his birth in this chronology.

Locke is joined in this chapter by other Europeans often cited in the first pages of introductory textbooks and the first paragraphs of histories of psychological specializations: René Descartes (Entry 14), who proposed the dualism of mind and body and the mechanical nature of behavior; James Mill (Entry 58) and John Stuart Mill (Entry 100), explicators of associationism; Hermann Ebbinghaus (Entry 196), systematic investigator of learning and memory; Wilhelm Wundt (e.g., Entries 139, 223, 275, and 361), founder of the first laboratory of experimental psychology (Entries 390 and 396); and Alfred Binet (e.g., Entry 242), whose intelligence tests opened the door for the mental testing movement.

These names evoke images of stiff portraits in histories and texts of psychology. Other listings of events before 1892 also bring to mind photographs and drawings seen by every beginning student of psychology. Who is not familiar with a photograph of a steel bar resting in the skull of Phineas Gage, the unfortunate railroad worker whose personality was transformed after he survived an explosion on the job (Entry 191)? Franz Joseph Gall's (Entry 51) phrenology reminds us of images of neatly mapped heads, with each cranial area associated with a different personal trait. And Franz Anton Mesmer's (Entries 39 and 64) *baquet*, charged with animal magnetism and the placebo effect, lives on in introductory psychology textbooks.

Most of the events of this chronology before 1892 are associated with philosophical psychology and what was to become experimental psychology. Fewer events are related to the practice of psychology, although this inequality will be found to be reversed in later chapters. The history of the practice of psychology is represented by such early events as the founding of facilities for people with mental illness (e.g., Entries 3, 10, 22, 24, 61, and 221) and mental retardation (e.g., Entries 181, 185–186, and 193) that varied in the quality of care extended to their clients. The careers of Philippe Pinel (Entries 42 and 84–86), Jean Itard (Entries 65 and 95), Dorothea Dix (Entries 99, 210, and 221), and Henry H. Goddard (Entry 296) are prominently linked to the practice of psychology in institutional settings, as Sigmund Freud's (e.g., Entries 228, 471, and 480), Alfred Adler's (Entry 321), and Carl Jung's (Entry 359) are to individual psychotherapy.

By the last half of the nineteenth century, the elements of contemporary psychology were present and were assembled by such pioneers as Wilhelm Wundt, Ernst Weber (Entry 88), and Gustav Fechner (Entries 96 and 202) into a coherent discipline. In 1869, before James McKeen Cattell (Entry 267) was 9 years old, the work of Fechner and Wundt was noted in the United

States (Entry 308), stimulating the thought and work of Charles Peirce (e.g., Entries 154 and 373), William James (e.g., Entries 163 and 440), and James's student G. Stanley Hall. In 1878, Hall earned the first American PhD in psychology (Entry 381) and left America to study in Europe, where he became Wundt's first American student. Hall returned to the United States in 1880, the year Cattell left the United States to study in Europe (Entry 406). Cattell started working in Wundt's laboratory in 1883 (Entry 441) and returned to Pennsylvania with his doctoral degree in 1887 (Entry 503). He became the first American professor with the title *professor of psychology* in 1889 (Entry 520).

This first chapter ends just prior to the founding of the APA, but a review of its last entries reflects a discipline ready to recognize itself: The first textbooks of psychology were being published (e.g., Entries 496, 505, 531, 550, 553, and 560), communication was established through scholarly journals (e.g., Entries 349, 504, and 555), university laboratories were founded (Entries 436 and 440), and the first International Congress of Psychology was convened in Paris (Entry 529).

May 22, 427 BCE (1)
Plato was born. Plato founded the Academy of Athens, where his metaphysics, epistemology, nativism, and social philosophy found expression and came to pervade Western thought. Plato was a dualist, separating the physical world from the world of true forms. His assertion that reality is known through reason was not challenged until the rise of empiricism.

November 13, 354 (2)
Aurelius Augustinus (St. Augustine) was born. Augustine's views stemmed from introspection and phenomenology. He described several faculties of the soul, including reason, memory, will, and imagination.

February 24, 1409 (3)
The founding of the world's first mental hospital was inspired. On this day in Valencia, Spain, Father Juan Gilabert Joffre came upon a crowd harassing a "madman." Wealthy citizens responded to a sermon calling for a hospital for the insane. The Hospital de Nuestra Doña Santa Maria de los Inocentes was founded later in the year and is still in operation.

February 19, 1473 (4)
Nicolaus Copernicus was born. Copernicus argued for a heliocentric view of the universe instead of a geocentric one, demoting humans to a peripheral position in

the universe and promoting objectivity in the study of human affairs. A scientific psychology rests on the assumptions generated by the Copernican revolution.

December 9, 1484 (5)

Pope Innocent VII issued the papal bull "Summis Desiderantes Affectibus." It appointed Heinrich Kramer and Johann Sprenger to be inquisitors in northern Germany. Kramer and Sprenger's *Malleus Maleficarum* (*The Witch Hammer*) became the standard guide to the diagnosis, behavior, trial, and punishment of witches for two centuries. It presents a comprehensive theory of behavior.

March 6, 1492 (6)

Juan Luis Vives was born. Vives was a humanist whose works on education advocated learning through induction and experience and emphasized a functional analysis of mental events, mental associations, memory, and emotions.

October 28, 1538 (7)

The first university in the Americas was founded in what is now Santo Domingo, in the Dominican Republic. This city was chosen as the site of the first Interamerican Congress of Psychology in 1953.

January 22, 1561 (8)

Francis Bacon was born. Bacon vitalized and articulated the modern philosophy of empiricism, the foundation of all modern science, including experimental psychology.

February 15, 1564 (9)

Galileo Galilei was born. Galileo is recognized as the founder of the modern scientific method. His reliance on controlled observation to reveal the course of natural events produced important discoveries in physics and astronomy. Of importance to psychology was his discovery that the pitch of a sound is related to vibrations at its source.

November 2, 1566 (10)

Work began on the first mental hospital in Mexico. The Hospital y Aliso de Convalescietes de San Hipolito was founded by Bernardino Alvarez and was formally inaugurated on January 28, 1567.

December 27, 1571 (11)

Johannes Kepler was born. A by-product of Kepler's study of planetary motion and optics was an understanding of the optics of vision. Kepler proposed that the retina, not the lens, was the site of visual reception.

April 1, 1578 (12)

William Harvey was born. Harvey is famous for establishing that blood circulates in the body. He also properly identified the brain as an information processing and coordinating center.

April 5, 1588 (13)

Thomas Hobbes was born. Hobbes's social philosophy proposed that people are motivated by self-interest, later called *psychological hedonism*. Hobbes was an early empiricist who asserted that physical events produce mental experiences. He supposedly was born prematurely because his mother was frightened by news of the approach of the Spanish Armada.

March 31, 1596 (14)

René Descartes was born. Descartes was the first great thinker to break with the scholasticism of the Middle Ages. He proposed that the mind and body were separate but interacting entities. Descartes attempted to define the basic qualities of mind, studied properties of the nervous system, and wrote on the optics of vision.

October 10, 1605 (15)

King James I of England examined Anne Gunther, a supposed victim of witchcraft. Gunther's behavior, resembling the symptoms of conversion disorder, had attracted widespread attention. James found her "perfectly cured from her former weakness by a potion given unto her by a phisitian, & a tablet hanged about her neck."

November 10, 1619 (16)

A three-part dream by René Descartes inspired analytic geometry and the application of mathematical rationalism to other fields of knowledge.

June 19, 1623 (17)

Blaise Pascal was born. Pascal was a pioneer in discovering the laws of probability, which allowed the statistical prediction of uncertain natural events, including human behavior.

August 29, 1632 (18)

John Locke was born. Locke was the founder of empiricism in England, laying the foundation for scientific psychology. His *An Essay Concerning Human Understanding* proposed that ideas are derived from sense experience, not from innate or divine sources.

November 24, 1632 (19)

Baruch de Spinoza was born. Spinoza's philosophy proposed a parallelism of mind and body, that is, that both mental and physical phenomena are expressions of the same divine source. His view was also completely deterministic, positing that free will is an illusion created when one thinks of the determined course of action.

December 25, 1642 (20)

Sir Isaac Newton was born on this day, in the same year Galileo died. Newton's work in vision and optics, and his deterministic philosophy of science, have strongly influenced psychology.

July 1, 1646 (21)

Gottfried Wilhelm Leibniz was born. Leibniz was a mathematician and philosopher who promoted a theory of reality that was based on irreducible elements of activity called *monads*. The theory strongly affected early conceptions of perception and the nature of consciousness.

April 27, 1654 (22)

The Salpêtrière asylum was founded in Paris. The asylum initially housed "undesirables" of all kinds but became, by the early 1800s, a site for the systematic and humane care of people with mental illness and mental retardation.

November 23, 1654 (23)

A dream by Blaise Pascal inspired his laws of probability. Pascal, a playboy until this day, reported that God appeared in a dream with the theme of "certitude." Pascal reformed and devoted his life to the search for the laws of certitude.

May 1, 1657 (24)

The Salpêtrière asylum was opened in Paris. It originally housed "undesirable" individuals of all kinds and, in the 1830s, was the site of some of the first humanitarian reforms in care of people with mental illness.

November 28, 1660 (25)

A group of 12 experimental philosophers met in the London quarters of Lawrence Rook. The group founded a "Colledge for the promoting of Physico-Mathematicall Experimentall Learning," which soon became Great Britain's Royal Society.

July 15, 1662 (26)

The first charter of Great Britain's Royal Society was sealed in London. This is usually cited as the formal founding date of the Society.

December 22, 1666 (27)

The first official meeting of France's Royal Academy of Sciences was held in the private library of Louis XIV on rue Vivienne, Paris. The first public meeting was on April 29, 1699, at the Louvre.

March 12, 1685 (28)

George Berkeley was born. Berkeley, the Bishop of Cloyne, was an early associationist whose principle of "subjective idealism" asserted the primacy of mind over matter. Berkeley proposed that sensations and ideas are the fundamental units of reality and are reflections of the mind of God.

December 31, 1691 (29)

Christian Thomasius, a German philosopher and jurist, published an early work on personality assessment with the title "New Discovery of a Well-Grounded and For the Community Most Necessary Science of the Knowledge of the Secrets of the Heart of Other Men from Daily Conversation, Even Against Their Will."

August 30, 1705 (30)

David Hartley was born. Hartley founded the school of associationism, stressing contiguous brain vibrations as the cause of learning, forgetting, imagination, and perception. Contiguity remains a central explanatory principle of these phenomena.

September 7, 1707 (31)

George Louis Buffon was born. Buffon was a naturalist whose pre-Darwinian theory of evolution retained the notion of divine creation but proposed the capacity for organic change in response to the environment.

December 25, 1709 (32)

Julien La Mettrie was born. La Mettrie pioneered a mechanistic view of humans, asserting that the physical being is the only being, thus providing a starting point for modern objective psychologies. Against the background of his times, La Mettrie's controversial views heightened his impact on the intellectual community.

April 26, 1710 (33)

Thomas Reid was born. Reid was the first proponent of the Scottish school of philosophy. His philosophy was an attempt to reconcile a belief in the divine origin of ideas with mounting evidence favoring empiricism. He contended that knowledge of objects and the faculties for mental activities are innate properties of the soul, but that they are activated by experience.

May 7, 1711 (34)

David Hume was born. Hume was an empiricist and associationist whose *An Enquiry Concerning Human Understanding* is a classic treatise on the relation between sense experience and ideas, the role of contiguity in relating ideas, and the nature of the idea of causation.

June 28, 1712 (35)

Jean-Jacques Rousseau was born. Rousseau is best known as an author and moral philosopher, but his book *Emile* promoted the formation of developmental psychology. The book presented a conception of childhood as a series of naturally ordained stages. The role of parenting and education was to facilitate the emergence of natural growth.

October 5, 1713 (36)

Denis Diderot was born. Diderot was a French empiricist and promoter of the scientific method. His *Encyclopedie*, one of the great works of the Enlightenment, contained an entry on psychology that disseminated the idea among educated people that behavior could be scientifically studied.

September 30, 1715 (37)

Etienne de Condillac was born. Condillac introduced Locke's empiricism to France and argued that sensation is the source of mental life.

April 22, 1724 (38)

Immanuel Kant was born. Kant championed the nativistic view of epistemology. He asserted that mental processes have no substance and therefore cannot be scientifically studied.

May 23, 1734 (39)

Franz Anton Mesmer was born. In the 1700s, Mesmer popularized the use of suggestion, which he called *animal magnetism*, to bring about physical cures. A French royal commission later concluded that animal magnetism was nonexistent and that suggestion alone produced Mesmer's cures. The use of hypnotism in psychotherapy can be traced to mesmerism.

September 9, 1737 (40)

Luigi Galvani was born. Galvani discovered how nerves affect muscles and first described the electrical nature of nervous transmission.

August 1, 1744 (41)

Jean Lamarck was born. Lamarck's theory of inheritance of acquired traits was an early brand of evolutionary theory that continues to intrigue biologists and psychologists.

April 20, 1745 (42)

Philippe Pinel was born. With his appointment in 1793 to the directorship of the Bicêtre insane asylum, Pinel began modern, humane treatment of institutionalized mental patients. He was one of the first to act on the belief that abnormal behavior was the result of natural causes instead of moral degeneration or demonic possession.

January 12, 1746 (43)

Johann Heinrich Pestalozzi was born. Pestalozzi was a founder of modern methods of education and child study. His approach to education involved carefully observing the child's capabilities and tailoring learning activities to those capabilities.

February 15, 1748 (44)

Jeremy Bentham was born. Bentham was a social philosopher whose philosophy of government promoted the greatest happiness for the greatest number of people. Psychology derived the principle of hedonistic motivation from Bentham's proposals concerning the relation of the individual to the state.

March 23, 1749 (45)

Pierre Simon Laplace was born. Laplace is responsible for applying the concept of the normal distribution to scientific observations in general, instead of only to isolated phenomena. This assumption of generality has formed the backbone of traditional inferential statistics.

June 11, 1749   (46)

Physiologist Jacob Pereire reported to the French Academy his program of successfully training a deaf–mute person to read and speak, one of the first recorded programs of special education.

August 28, 1749   (47)

Johann von Goethe was born. Although he is best known as an author, Goethe's studies of color vision were some of the first phenomenological studies in the modern scientific tradition. His writing might also have influenced Freud's concept of libido.

November 22, 1753   (48)

Dugald Stewart was born. Stewart popularized the Scottish school of faculty psychology, which argued for a divine source of knowledge and human mental abilities.

April 11, 1755   (49)

James Parkinson was born. Parkinson was an English naturalist and medical doctor whose tract *An Essay on the Shaking Palsy* (1817) first described the neurological condition that bears his name. The name *Parkinson's disease* was coined by Jean-Martin Charcot and was not adopted by the British for several decades.

June 5, 1757   (50)

Pierre Cabanis was born. A French physician, Cabanis studied the physical nature of mental events. In 1795 he was asked to study whether a person was still conscious after being guillotined. He concluded that the answer was no.

March 9, 1758   (51)

Franz Joseph Gall was born. Gall was a medical doctor who identified the functional differences between white and gray matter in the brain. He later developed his suspicions about the relation between head shape and personality into systematic phrenology. Although largely a pseudoscience, phrenology spurred interest in the study of brain localization.

August 26, 1760   (52)

Gregor Feinaigle was born. Feinaigle was a German mnemonist who gave exhibitions and instruction on memory throughout Europe. He applied his methods to education in several schools in Ireland.

May 19, 1762   (53)

Johann Fichte was born. Fichte, a follower of Kant, asserted that concepts of time and space were innate.

February 14, 1766   (54)

Thomas Robert Malthus was born. Malthus's observation that population increases faster than the food supply stimulated theories of social and biological competition. Darwin's theory of natural selection was the most prominent of these.

August 23, 1769 (55)

Baron Georges Cuvier was born. Cuvier was a French comparative anatomist who studied relations between anatomical form and function. Despite the importance of these relations to the theory of evolution, Cuvier remained a creationist.

November 11, 1771 (56)

Marie François Xavier Bichat was born. Bichat was the founder of modern histology. He was responsible for the identification of similar tissues in organs throughout the body and proposed that tissue types be considered the basic anatomical unit.

February 5, 1772 (57)

Pierre Laplace presented his first paper on probability to the French Academy of Sciences.

April 6, 1773 (58)

James Mill was born. Mill was a pioneer of association psychology. His philosophy contended that sensations create ideas that may associate with each other. Complex ideas are compounds of these constituent elements.

June 13, 1773 (59)

Thomas Young was born. Young was an English physicist who applied Newton's work on the spectrum to the problem of color vision. Because all colors can be produced by red, blue, and green light, Young proposed that there are three color receptors in the retina. This idea was expanded by Hermann von Helmholtz and became known as the Young–Helmholtz theory.

July 20, 1773 (60)

Luigi Rolando was born. Rolando carried out early explorations of localization of brain functions and was among the first to electrically stimulate the brain. Many of his functional assignments are now known to be incorrect, but his influence guided research in productive directions.

October 12, 1773 (61)

The first U.S. state mental hospital, the Publick Hospital for Persons of Insane and Disordered Minds, opened in Williamsburg, Virginia. The first "keeper" was James Galt, and the first patient was Zachariah Mallory. The hospital was closed during the American Revolution, raided by both sides in the Civil War, burned in 1885, moved in the 1960s, and continues today as Eastern State Hospital.

January 23, 1774 (62)

Tuscany, Italy, passed the first public ordinance providing for hospitalization of people with mental illness.

April 19, 1774   (63)
An African American woman named Charity was admitted to the Hospital for the
Insane at Williamsburg, becoming the first African American person admitted to
a mental institution in the United States.

July 28, 1774   (64)
Franz Mesmer performed his first supposed cure using "animal magnetism." His
patient was a Fräulein Osterlin, who had 15 hysteric (conversion disorder) symptoms.

April 24, 1775   (65)
Jean Itard was born. Itard's interest in special education began with the study of
Victor, the "Wild Boy of Aveyron," and led to work with deaf persons. His
individualized methods form the basis of modern special education techniques.

November 14, 1775   (66)
Paul Feuerbach was born. Feuerbach was a German jurist who advocated intimi-
dation through punishment as a deterrent to crime. Feuerbach's methods were
based on an early functional approach to behavior.

May 4, 1776   (67)
Johann F. Herbart, the founder of educational psychology, was born. Herbart
developed the concept of *apperceptive mass*, defined as the accumulation of experiences too weak to stimulate conscious awareness but strong enough to enhance
or interfere with the effects of later experiences.

December 31, 1776   (68)
Johann Spurzheim was born. Spurzheim popularized Gall's theory of phrenology
in England, France, and the United States in the early 1800s.

April 30, 1777   (69)
Johann Karl Friedrich Gauss was born. Gauss formulated the theory of the normal
curve and established its ubiquity in measurements of natural phenomena. He is
also responsible for the least squares method of curve fitting.

May 2, 1777   (70)
Franz Mesmer was expelled from the practice of medicine in Vienna. The precip-
itating incident was Mesmer's treatment of a Fräulein Paradies, a 17-year-old pianist
who had been blind since the age of 3. Mesmer claimed that his use of "animal
magnetism" had restored her sight, but only when she was alone with him.

January 9, 1778   (71)
Thomas Brown was born. Brown was a Scottish school philosopher who first
distinguished between the processes of sensation and perception.

October 15, 1783 (72)

François Magendie was born. Magendie is primarily known for his discovery of the differentiation of sensory and motor spinal nerves. Magendie made this discovery after, but independently of, Charles Bell. His studies advanced the experimental study of the physiology of behavior.

March 4, 1784 (73)

King Louis XVI appointed a royal commission to study Franz Mesmer's cures using "animal magnetism." The commission, formed at Mesmer's urging, was chaired by Benjamin Franklin, included chemist Antoine Lavoisier, and was charged with examining the scientific validity of Mesmer's methods.

July 22, 1784 (74)

Friedrich Wilhelm Bessel was born. Bessel was an astronomer made curious by the circumstances of David Kinnebrook's dismissal at the Greenwich Observatory. He found that Kinnebrook's errors were caused by differences in individual reaction times. This began the search for the "personal equation" and the study of individual differences.

August 11, 1784 (75)

Benjamin Franklin submitted the report of his royal commission on mesmerism and "animal magnetism" to King Louis XVI. The report was also signed by astronomer Jean S. Bailly; Joseph I. Guillotin, the physician who invented the guillotine; and chemist Antoine L. Lavoisier. Ironically, the guillotine was later used to execute both Bailly and Lavoisier.

September 10, 1785 (76)

The first documented use of the term *social science* occurred on this date in a letter written by John Adams, later president of the United States.

December 17, 1787 (77)

Jan Purkinje was born. Purkinje was a physiologist who contributed work in visual neurology, perception, and the phenomenology of vision. He reported the apparent shift of hue accompanying decreases in illumination, now called the *Purkinje shift*.

February 22, 1788 (78)

Arthur Schopenhauer was born. Schopenhauer contributed an early theory of color vision but is best known for his theory of the primacy of the will as the determinant of individual behavior.

March 8, 1788 (79)

Sir William Hamilton, the Scottish philosopher, was born. Hamilton's concept of *redintegration* accounted for memory of associated events.

February 18, 1790 (80)

Marshall Hall was born. Hall was a pioneer in the study of reflex physiology. He identified reflexes as unconscious, involuntary functions mediated entirely by the spinal cord.

September 22, 1791 (81)

Michael Faraday was born. Faraday's discovery of electromagnetic induction made possible the experimental study of the functional nature of the nervous system and contributed the idea of force fields to Gestalt theory. He also invented the stroboscope.

October 29, 1791 (82)

John Elliotson was born. Elliotson promoted the use of mesmerism in England and provoked scientific studies of its effectiveness. He continued to believe in "magnetism" despite the disapproval of the scientific and medical establishment.

November 28, 1792 (83)

Victor Cousin was born. Cousin was a French philosopher whose contention that experiences were built from sensations led to an ontology that considered God the prime cause of all events. Cousin's *Elements of Psychology* (1834), as translated by Caleb S. Henry, was the first book published in the United States with the word *psychology* in its title.

August 25, 1793 (84)

Philippe Pinel was appointed director of the Bicêtre asylum, the site of his later reforms in the treatment of people with mental illness.

September 2, 1793 (85)

Philippe Pinel released the first mental patients from their chains at the Bicêtre asylum. About 50 were released on this day and another 30 were released the next day.

September 11, 1793 (86)

Philippe Pinel formally assumed his post as director of Bicêtre asylum. Pinel had been drawn to psychiatry when a friend became mentally ill, ran away, and was killed by wolves. Pinel instituted the first modern humane care of mental patients at the Bicêtre and later at the Salpêtrière asylum.

April 1, 1794 (87)

Pierre J. M. Flourens was born. Flourens introduced the method of extirpation to study brain functions, established the gross functional divisions of the central nervous system, and found evidence for cerebral "mass action," the principle that the brain acts as a whole.

June 24, 1795   (88)

Ernst Weber was born. Weber is best known for his work on the sense of touch, leading to the discovery of the *just-noticeable difference* in sensation and *Weber's law* of psychophysics.

August 2, 1795   (89)

Great Britain's Astronomer Royal Nevil Maskelyne first detected errors in his assistant David Kinnebrook's time estimates. Kinnebrook was fired, but astronomer Friedrich Bessel's investigation of the errors led to the systematic study of reaction time, individual differences, and mental chronometry as a measure of cognitive processes.

January 19, 1796   (90)

David Kinnebrook made his last observation at Greenwich Observatory. Kinnebrook was later fired for observations disagreeing with those of the Astronomer Royal, Nevil Maskelyne. Repercussions of this incident led to Bessel's study of individual reaction times and the founding of the psychological field of individual differences.

February 22, 1796   (91)

Adolphe Quételet was born. Quételet was a probability theorist who applied the "law of deviation from an average," now called the *normal curve*, to biological and social attributes. He coined the term "statistics."

January 20, 1797   (92)

The Maryland legislature authorized the first mental hospital in the state and only the second in the United States. Originally built on land now occupied by Johns Hopkins University, its functions were later moved to Spring Grove Hospital in Catonsville.

January 19, 1798   (93)

Auguste Comte was born. Comte was a French social philosopher who contended that individual behavior is largely a product of social forces. Comte coined the term *sociology* to describe the objective study of this process.

July 16, 1798   (94)

The earliest U.S. federal public health service was created. The services were originally extended only to merchant seamen.

July 25, 1799   (95)

Victor, the "Wild Boy of Aveyron," was captured. Victor was later studied by Jean Itard, a pioneer in special education.

April 19, 1801 (96)

Gustav Theodor Fechner was born. His theory relating stimulus energy to sensory experience marked the beginnings of scientific psychology and the field of experimental psychophysics. Fechner's personal eccentricity and the fact that he recorded the date of his psychophysical insight (October 22, 1850) has resulted in Fechner Day celebrations in some psychology departments.

July 14, 1801 (97)

Johannes Müller was born. Müller explained the *law of specific nerve energies* and applied it to his work in sensation. He was a founder of modern experimental psychology.

October 14, 1801 (98)

Joseph Antoine Ferdinand Plateau was born. Plateau proposed an early version of the power law of psychophysics. His research also touched on color vision and visual movement aftereffects.

April 4, 1802 (99)

Dorothea Lynde Dix was born. Dix helped found 32 hospitals for people with mental illness and 15 training schools for people with mental retardation. During the Civil War she organized and ran the military nurse service. Her work began when, as a student, she cared for a few mentally ill convicts in miserable circumstances at the House of Correction in Cambridge, Massachusetts.

May 20, 1806 (100)

John Stuart Mill was born. Mill extended the philosophy of associationism by proposing that simple elements combine to form wholly new experiences that are not merely additive products of their constituent parts. This concept was a precursor of Gestalt psychology.

January 16, 1807 (101)

Psychiatrist Isaac Ray was born. Ray was among the first to promote the insanity defense in criminal trials. His *Medical Jurisprudence of Insanity* (1838) was the first American book on the subject. Ray was also one of the founders of the Association of Medical Superintendents of American Institutions for the Insane (1844), a precursor of the American Psychiatric Association.

February 12, 1809 (102)

Charles Darwin was born. Darwin's theory of evolution by natural selection opened all human qualities to scientific inspection, gave rise to comparative psychology, and strongly influenced developmental psychology.

April 9, 1810 (103)

Pierre Laplace presented the *central limit theorem* to the French Academy of Sciences. The theorem is the basis for drawing inferences about the characteristics of populations from sample data and forms the cornerstone of modern inferential statistics.

January 20, 1812 (104)

Edouard O. Séguin was born. Séguin founded the world's first "school for the feeble-minded" in Paris in 1839. He used environmental stimulation and structured exercises to develop the potential of his students. He was one of the organizers of the School for Mental Defectives at Randall's Island, New York (1849).

April 14, 1813 (105)

The first private psychiatric hospital in the United States was founded in Philadelphia. The hospital was called The Asylum for the Relief of Persons Deprived of Their Reason and was administered by the Religious Society of Friends (Quakers). In 1914 its name was changed to Friends Hospital.

July 12, 1813 (106)

Claude Bernard was born. Bernard was an experimental physiologist whose work on the internal environment anticipated the concept of homeostasis.

August 16, 1816 (107)

Johann Jacob Guggenbuhl was born. Guggenbuhl founded the first residential treatment facility for people with mental retardation at Abendberg, Switzerland.

April 15, 1817 (108)

The first school for deaf persons in the United States opened in Hartford, Connecticut. Thomas Hopkins Gallaudet was the founder and served as superintendent until 1830.

May 21, 1817 (109)

Rudolf Lotze was born. Lotze wrote the first text in what could be called physiological psychology (1852). His "theory of local signs" related sensory information to conscious experience. An explanation of the phenomenon of three-dimensional spatial perception from two-dimensional information was a noteworthy application of this theory.

April 14, 1818 (110)

The U.S. Army Medical Corps was founded, with physician Joseph Lovell as its surgeon general.

May 5, 1818 (111)

Karl Marx was born. Marx's social philosophy centered on the economic nature of social behavior and the orderly progression of economic and social change.

May 27, 1818 (112)
Franciscus Cornelius Donders was born. Donders was one of the early researchers in mental chronometry, using reaction time as an index of mental processes and individual differences.

June 11, 1818 (113)
Alexander Bain was born. Bain bridged the eras of philosophical associationism and experimental psychology. He founded the first philosophical psychology journal, *Mind*, in 1876. The journal is still being published.

November 7, 1818 (114)
Emil Du Bois-Reymond was born. His work on the electrical nature of nervous transmission was important in the development of neuropsychology.

June 6, 1819 (115)
Ernst Wilhelm von Brücke was born. One of Freud's teachers, Brücke was a physiologist and antivitalist who required his students to take an oath to use only common physical and chemical forces as explanatory principles.

April 27, 1820 (116)
Herbert Spencer was born. Spencer devised a pre-Darwinian theory of evolution and coined the phrase *survival of the fittest*. He applied his evolutionary concepts to all human mental and behavioral phenomena, presaging American functionalism and behaviorism.

December 16, 1820 (117)
Königsberg astronomer Friedrich Bessel made the first of his "personal equation" observations on this night. Intrigued by the dismissal of British astronomer David Kinnebrook for observations disagreeing with those of Kinnebrook's superior, Bessel found individual differences in reaction times and began the study of reaction times and mental chronometry that continues today.

August 31, 1821 (118)
Hermann von Helmholtz was born. The breadth of Helmholtz's expertise made him one of the greatest scientists of the nineteenth century. He was the first to measure the speed of nervous conduction and made equally important contributions to understanding visual and auditory physiology, spatial perception, and color vision.

February 16, 1822 (119)
Sir Francis Galton was born. Galton's research interests ranged widely over the study of individual differences, heritability of traits, statistics, and the invention of psychometric apparatuses. He is often cited as a founder of systematic methods of psychological measurement.

July 22, 1822 (120)
Gregor Johann Mendel was born. Mendel founded modern genetics, providing psychology with a mechanism to explain and predict the biological transmission of physical characteristics affecting behavior.

January 8, 1823 (121)
Alfred Russel Wallace was born. Wallace was stimulated by reading Malthus's *Essay on the Principle of Population* to develop a theory of evolution at the same time as Darwin. Receipt of Wallace's manuscript, "On the Tendency of Varieties to Depart Indefinitely from the Original Type" in June 1858 spurred Darwin to make public his own theory of evolution.

December 21, 1823 (122)
Jean Henri Fabre was born. Fabre was a French high school teacher with a passion for the study of insect ethology. His detailed papers reported the natural behavior of insects observed close to his home and served as models for a later generation of professional ethologists.

June 16, 1824 (123)
The Society for the Prevention of Cruelty to Animals was founded in London. It became the Royal Society in 1840 at the command of Queen Victoria. The Society was an early embodiment of the movement for humane treatment of animals that continues to provoke controversy and procedural reforms in experimental psychology.

June 28, 1824 (124)
Paul Broca was born. Broca was the first to identify a brain location associated with a specific behavior, the speech centers of the left frontal cortex (1861). The area is now named for Broca.

July 24, 1824 (125)
The first American public opinion poll was published in the Harrisburg *Pennsylvanian* and the Raleigh *Star*. The poll predicted the outcome of the presidential race among John Quincy Adams, Henry Clay, and Andrew Jackson. Modern advances in social science methodology have markedly increased the accuracy of public opinion polling.

January 22, 1825 (126)
The Virginia legislature authorized Western State Hospital in Staunton. This was the nation's fifth public mental hospital and opened on July 25, 1828.

May 4, 1825 (127)
Thomas Henry Huxley was born. Huxley was a popular promoter and defender of Darwinism and the scientific method. He coined the term *agnosticism* to mean that nothing could be known without physical demonstration.

November 29, 1825 (128)

Jean-Martin Charcot was born. Charcot was a pioneer of modern neurology best known to psychologists for his investigations of hypnosis and hysteria and his influence on Freud. Charcot believed hysteria to be the cause of hypnotic behavior. Charcot was honorary president of the First International Congress of Psychology in 1889.

June 15, 1826 (129)

British surgeon James Wardrop reported to the Royal Society that he had created an artificial pupil for a woman who had been born blind. His paper described the perceptual problems caused by the patient's new visual ability.

January 29, 1827 (130)

The first federal law relating to services for people with disabilities was passed. The law provided land for the Deaf and Dumb Asylum of Kentucky.

November 18, 1828 (131)

John Langdon Down was born. In 1866, Down first described the syndrome of physical and mental abnormalities that now bears his name. He called it "Mongolism" and integrated it into an ethnic theory of abnormality.

June 7, 1829 (132)

Eduard Pflüger was born. Pflüger explored the electrical stimulation of motor nerves and the functions of the spinal cord. He contended that spinal reflexes were conscious functions because they were purposeful.

August 1, 1829 (133)

Ivan M. Sechenov was born. Sechenov proposed that all mental processes and behavior operate as reflexes of the brain, arising through contiguous association. His reduction of cognitive processes to neural origins was farsighted but little known outside of his native Russia. Pavlov's thinking was influenced by Sechenov.

March 30, 1831 (134)

The Salpêtrière asylum of Paris began a program of treatment of "idiotic" women.

September 1, 1831 (135)

Charles Darwin's father reluctantly gave him permission to sail on the *Beagle*. Arguments by both Darwin and his uncle, Josiah Wedgwood, were needed.

September 5, 1831 (136)

Charles Darwin was interviewed by Captain Fitzroy of the *Beagle* for the position of ship's naturalist. Fitzroy almost rejected Darwin because of the shape of Darwin's nose.

December 27, 1831   (137)

The *Beagle* departed England with Charles Darwin aboard as ship's naturalist.

August 4, 1832   (138)

Phrenologist Johann Gaspar Spurzheim arrived in the United States for a public lecture tour. Spurzheim died during this tour, on November 10, 1832. Phrenology enjoyed widespread popular acceptance as a personality assessment tool in nineteenth-century America.

August 16, 1832   (139)

Wilhelm Wundt was born. He gathered introspective reports of elementary visual, auditory, and other experiences to study how selective attention and the will construct conscious experience from them. Wundt founded the world's first functional psychology laboratory (1879) at the University of Leipzig, and his students were the primary founders of experimental psychology.

August 26, 1832   (140)

Wilhelm Wundt was baptized by his father.

October 27, 1832   (141)

William Ireland was born. Ireland wrote the first well-organized and medically oriented text on mental retardation, *On Idiocy and Imbecility*.

August 5, 1834   (142)

Ewald Hering was born. Hering proposed a theory of color vision based on three types of receptors operating by opponent processes to detect black–white, yellow–blue, and red–green differences in stimulation. Hering's theory strongly influenced modern theories of color vision.

December 4, 1834   (143)

Carl Lange was born. Lange offered a theory of emotion similar in content and contemporaneous with that of William James. The James–Lange theory of emotion asserts that emotions are the results, not the causes, of visceral changes.

April 4, 1835   (144)

John Hughlings Jackson was born. Jackson studied the neurology of epilepsy, aphasia, and paralysis. *Jacksonian epilepsy* is named for him. He emphasized that hierarchical relations between evolutionary levels of the brain were more important than the search for exact locations of functions.

November 14, 1835   (145)

The first mental hospital in Canada opened. The institution was the Provincial Asylum in St. John, New Brunswick.

November 18, 1835   (146)
Cesare Lombroso was born. Lombroso contended that criminal behavior resulted from genetic degeneration and could be detected by facial features typical of more primitive stages of human development.

October 2, 1836   (147)
Darwin returned to England on the *Beagle* after a 5-year voyage.

January 16, 1838   (148)
Franz Brentano was born. Brentano's psychology, essentially a rational analysis of the mind's activities while experiencing external events, provided an alternative to the content psychology of Wilhelm Wundt and to physiological reductionism.

February 6, 1838   (149)
Eduard Hitzig was born. With Gustav Fritsch, Hitzig established the electrical excitability of the brain and located some of the areas associated with motor behavior.

February 18, 1838   (150)
Ernst Mach was born. Mach was a physicist whose book *The Analysis of Sensations* (1886) strongly influenced psychology. The book laid down a foundation for scientific positivism and a theory of form perception that presaged Gestalt psychology.

March 5, 1838   (151)
Gustav T. Fritsch was born. Fritsch and a colleague, Eduard Hitzig, were the first to establish the electrical excitability of the brain and thus to establish correspondence between some brain locations and motor responses.

September 28, 1838   (152)
Charles Darwin read Thomas Malthus's essay on population. Malthus's ideas on species survival revealed the concept of natural selection to Darwin. He wrote, "It at once struck me that under these circumstances favourable variations would tend to be preserved and unfavourable ones to be destroyed. The result would be the formation of new species."

June 10, 1839   (153)
The first county asylum in New York, on Blackwell's Island, received its first patients. They had previously been housed in the basement and first story of the Manhattan State Hospital, the nation's fourth mental institution, founded in 1825.

September 10, 1839   (154)
Charles Peirce was born. Peirce is best known for founding American pragmatism, but, by many accounts, Peirce was the first American empirical psychologist. His experimental work examined color vision and difference thresholds. He was the first psychologist elected to the National Academy of Sciences.

December 18, 1839 (155)

Théodule Armand Ribot was born. Ribot was instrumental in introducing dynamic psychology in France. His major contributions were in the areas of affect and mental disorders. In 1885 Ribot was appointed to teach the first course in experimental psychology offered by the Sorbonne, at the University of Paris.

April 4, 1840 (156)

Henry Bowditch was born. Bowditch opened the first American physiological laboratory, at Harvard University in 1871. He demonstrated the all-or-none firing of heart muscle fibers and proposed that nerves cannot be fatigued.

April 17, 1840 (157)

Hippolyte Bernheim was born. Bernheim was a French neurologist and hypnotist who explored the connections among suggestibility, mental illness, and psychotherapy.

May 7, 1841 (158)

Gustave Le Bon was born. Le Bon was a sociologist who influenced social psychology through his theory of the "crowd mind" as an explanation of the shared and uninhibited behavior of individuals in large groups.

June 13, 1841 (159)

The second mental hospital in Canada, the Provincial Asylum in Toronto, was opened.

July 4, 1841 (160)

Wilhelm T. Preyer was born. Preyer's contributions were in the areas of color vision and child development. Preyer wrote the first book that specifically addressed child psychology, *The Mind of the Child* (1881).

August 9, 1841 (161)

Johann F. Herbart, often cited as the founder of educational psychology, gave his last lecture at the University of Göttingen.

November 13, 1841 (162)

James Braid saw his first demonstration of mesmerism. He was convinced that mesmerism was fraudulent but that it produced real effects. He coined the term *hypnotism* for the phenomenon, believing that it was a heightened state of attention.

January 11, 1842 (163)

William James was born. James founded the first demonstration laboratory of psychology equipment in America (1875) and wrote the classic *Principles of Psychology*. His approach stressed the adaptive qualities of thought and behavior, presaging functionalism and behaviorism. APA President, 1894 and 1904; President, American Philosophical Association, 1906.

January 15, 1842 (164)

Josef Breuer was born. Breuer was Freud's first collaborator and helped to develop the methods of free association and emotional catharsis.

January 19, 1842 (165)

George Trumball Ladd was born. Ladd was an early functionalist. His *Elements of Physiological Psychology* was the first book in English on the subject. Ladd was a founder of the APA and served as its president in 1893.

October 29, 1842 (166)

The New Hampshire Asylum for the Insane opened in Concord. This was the state's first mental hospital and the nation's 13th.

November 1, 1842 (167)

The *Asylum Journal* became the first regular newspaper printed in and issued from a mental hospital, the Vermont Asylum for the Insane, in Brattleboro. It was begun by a 17-year-old printer admitted as a patient on July 15, 1842. The paper's motto was "Semel insanivimus omnes," or "We have all, at some time, been mad." Publication ended in 1847 with the printer's discharge.

January 13, 1843 (168)

Sir David Ferrier was born. Ferrier discovered the visual and sensory cortex areas of the brain and mapped the functions of much of the cortex through electrical stimulation and ablation. He founded the journal *Brain*.

January 20, 1843 (169)

A British mechanic named Daniel M'Naghton shot Edmund Drummond, private secretary of Prime Minister Sir Robert Peel, thinking Drummond was Peel. M'Naghton was later acquitted of murder because it was judged that his paranoid mental condition rendered him incapable of judging right from wrong. The M'Naghton rule is a landmark precedent of the modern insanity defense.

March 6, 1843 (170)

The case of Daniel M'Naghton was debated in the House of Lords soon after he was acquitted of murder by the British court. The case established the M'Naghton rule, that individuals whose mental illness rendered them incapable of judging right from wrong were not guilty of a crime, on grounds of insanity. Queen Victoria was incensed by the verdict.

March 11, 1843 (171)

Harald Höffding was born. Höffding maintained that all mental events were physical in nature, to be studied through introspection. He identified the recognition of similar elements as the determinant of transfer of training. Höffding wrote the first Danish psychology text in 1882.

March 12, 1843 (172)
Gabriel Tarde was born. Tarde was a sociologist whose theory of imitation, a related theory of crowd behavior, and writing on economic psychology make him an important figure in the history of social psychology.

April 1, 1843 (173)
The first magazine for mental patients, *The Illuminator*, began publication at the Pennsylvania Hospital in Philadelphia. The first issue was 24 pages in length.

July 7, 1843 (174)
Camillo Golgi was born. Golgi was a neurologist who first identified axons and dendrites and their functions. He also identified the sense receptors of muscular sensations. Nobel prize, 1906.

February 1, 1844 (175)
Granville Stanley Hall was born. Hall founded several psychological journals and, in 1892, founded the APA. Hall's research interest was child development, which he took to be an analog of human evolution. APA President, 1892 and 1924.

September 28, 1844 (176)
In an article published on this date, physician Thomas Laycock applied the reflex concept to the entire central nervous system.

October 15, 1844 (177)
Friedrich Wilhelm Nietzsche was born. Nietzsche developed a theory of human motivation that emphasized the primacy of instinct, repressed and disguised by reason.

October 15, 1844 (178)
The plans for the American Psychiatric Association were discussed in the home of Thomas S. Kirkbride of Philadelphia, one of the founders. The formal founding took place the next day at the Jones Hotel, also in Philadelphia. The original name of the organization was the Association of Medical Superintendents of American Institutions for the Insane.

October 16, 1844 (179)
The American Psychiatric Association was founded by 13 physicians at the Jones Hotel in Philadelphia. The organization was first called the Association of Medical Superintendents of American Institutions for the Insane, became the American Medico-Psychological Association in 1894, and adopted its current name in 1913. Samuel B. Woodward was elected president at this meeting.

January 14, 1847 (180)
Johannes Orth was born. Orth was a founder of the Würzburg School, which stressed the obscure, "imageless" nature of thought and conscious processes.

May 1, 1847 (181)

The first German government-sponsored facility for children with mental retardation was founded in a former convent at Mariaberg.

September 20, 1847 (182)

At its annual meeting in Boston, the American Association of Geologists and Naturalists voted to become the American Association for the Promotion of Science. By the time of the next annual meeting, the name had changed to the American Association for the Advancement of Science.

December 1, 1847 (183)

Christine Ladd-Franklin was born. The focus of her work was color vision. The theory that bears her name describes the nature and evolutionary emergence of black–white, red–green, and blue–yellow photoreceptors. She and Mary Whiton Calkins were the first two women members of the APA.

April 21, 1848 (184)

Carl Stumpf was born. Stumpf was an early experimental psychologist interested in the study of spatial perception, audition, and the scientific study of music.

April 26, 1848 (185)

The Highgate Asylum for Idiots was established. This was England's first formal institution for people with mental retardation and was sponsored by the Duke of Cambridge.

May 8, 1848 (186)

The Massachusetts legislature created the first U.S. school for people with mental retardation, allotting $2,500 for a trial year with "ten indigent idiots." The school, called the Massachusetts School for the Idiotic and Feeble-Minded Youth, opened under director Gridley Howe on October 1, 1848. The first superintendent was Walter E. Fernald, for whom the school is now named.

May 10, 1848 (187)

The American Association for the Advancement of Science was founded by a constitution committee of members of the American Association of Geologists and Naturalists. Mathematician–astronomer Henry D. Rogers chaired the committee.

May 20, 1848 (188)

George John Romanes was born. Romanes is considered to be the founder of comparative psychology, although his tendency to anthropomorphize was avoided by later students of animal behavior.

May 25, 1848 (189)

The New Jersey State Lunatic Asylum opened in Trenton. This was the state's first and the nation's 17th public mental institution.

September 1, 1848 (190)

August Forel was born. Forel is remembered primarily for his early studies of the social behavior of ants and other insects. He also published studies in legal psychiatry, mental health, and hypnotism.

September 13, 1848 (191)

Dynamite blew a tamping iron through the brain of Phineas P. Gage, a 25-year-old foreman of the Rutland and Burlington Railroad. The incident is often cited in psychology texts because Gage survived the accident, but the brain injury radically altered his personality. He became indifferent to others, impulsive, and at times grossly profane. Gage died on May 21, 1861.

September 20, 1848 (192)

The first meeting of the American Association for the Advancement of Science was held in Philadelphia. William Redfield presided over the 87 scientists in attendance.

October 1, 1848 (193)

The first American residential facility for people with mental retardation admitted its first resident. The experimental facility was a wing of the Perkins Institution for the Blind in Boston. Gridley Howe was director of the program and Walter E. Fernald the first superintendent. The original annual budget was $2,500.

September 26, 1849 (194)

Ivan Pavlov was born. Pavlov brought one of the fundamental processes that alter behavior, the conditioned reflex, to the attention of the scientific community. He identified its functional elements and extensively studied its characteristics. Pavlov won the Nobel prize in 1904 for his work in digestion.

January 22, 1850 (195)

The General Assembly of Virginia passed an act providing free care for African American mental patients at the mental institution at Williamsburg.

January 24, 1850 (196)

Hermann Ebbinghaus was born. Ebbinghaus carried out exhaustive pioneering studies in learning and recall, using himself as the subject. He developed several measures of recall, the nonsense syllable, and curves of learning and forgetting.

February 16, 1850 (197)

John B. Dods lectured the U.S. Senate on "electrical psychology," Dods's version of mesmerism.

April 5, 1850 (198)

Francis Galton gave up the life of the idle rich and sailed with an expedition to southwest Africa, thus beginning his life as a scientist.

April 9, 1850 (199)
Physician George S. Huntington was born. After observing an illness in a Long Island, New York, family, Huntington was the first to describe the syndrome of familial nervous degeneration now known as Huntington's disease or Huntington's chorea. He described the condition in a paper titled "On Chorea," published on April 13, 1872.

July 20, 1850 (200)
Georg E. Müller was born. Müller conducted the first experimental study of attention (1873), investigated psychophysics through systematic studies of weight judgments, developed a theory of color vision, and discovered the importance of internal processes (e.g., preparatory set) that affect memory.

August 26, 1850 (201)
Charles Richet was born. Richet was responsible for a rebirth of interest in hypnotism and parapsychology in the early 1900s. He coined the term "ectoplasm" to denote the substance related to psychic abilities. His career in more conventional physiology focused on hypersensitivity to proteins and resulted in his winning the Nobel prize in 1913.

October 22, 1850 (202)
Gustav Fechner received an insight into the mathematical nature of the mind–body relation. Both Fechner's law and the semireligious nature of his revelation are described in many histories of psychology.

January 1, 1851 (203)
Patients at the Utica State Asylum in Utica, New York, began publication of the nation's second regular newspaper produced at a mental institution. Its motto was "Devoted to Usefulness."

May 19, 1851 (204)
Standards for the construction of mental hospitals were adopted by the American Psychiatric Association. Among the provisions was the recommendation that there should be no more than 250 patients housed in each building.

July 7, 1851 (205)
Lillien Jane Martin was born. Martin worked with G. E. Müller in psychophysics and founded the world's first mental health clinic for normally functioning children and elderly individuals. She managed the psychology laboratory at Stanford University and was a founder of the Indiana Academy of Science.

July 28, 1851 (206)
Theodor Lipps was born. Lipps promoted a theory of aesthetics that was based on an empathic relation between perceiver and object.

February 6, 1852 (207)

C. Lloyd Morgan was born. Morgan was an important comparative psychologist who applied the principle of parsimony to explanations of behavior. *Morgan's canon* directs psychologists to prefer the simplest adequate explanation for a behavior.

May 1, 1852 (208)

Santiago Ramón y Cajal was born. Ramón y Cajal was a histologist and neuroanatomist who was the first to recognize that neurons are separate morphological units of the nervous system, not nodes in a nervous net.

July 22, 1852 (209)

Henry R. Marshall was born. Marshall was an architect by profession but his work in aesthetics, emotion, consciousness, and instinct allied him to early American psychologists. APA President, 1907.

August 31, 1852 (210)

Congress authorized building the first federal mental hospital, the Government Hospital for the Insane in Washington, DC. Mental health reformer Dorothea Dix selected the site, which Congress purchased for $25,000, overriding President Pierce's veto. The hospital, later known as St. Elizabeth's Hospital, officially opened on March 3, 1855.

November 16, 1852 (211)

Maximilian von Frey was born. Frey provided the first comprehensive information about the cutaneous senses. He confirmed the existence of locations for heat, cold, pressure, and pain reception and studied differential sensitivities to each. He suggested a sensory receptor for each modality, but later work showed these identifications to be incorrect.

February 10, 1853 (212)

The Pennsylvania Training School for the Feebleminded, the third American institution of its kind, was founded. The school was incorporated on April 7, 1853, but not opened until 1855 in Germantown. James B. Richards was the first principal. The school has since moved to Elwyn and is known as the Elwyn Training School.

July 17, 1853 (213)

Alexius Meinong was born. Meinong was strongly influenced by Franz Brentano and Brentano's empirical approach to philosophical psychology. Meinong founded the first Austrian experimental psychology laboratory at the University of Graz in 1884. His philosophy influenced the school of form-quality in psychology.

October 6, 1853 (214)

Johannes von Kries was born. Kries's work in the physiology of vision led to the correct identification of the functions of the rods and cones of the retina. He did some of the first experimental studies of color perception and identified and named the different varieties of color blindness.

November 15, 1853 (215)

The *Asylum Journal*, a publication of the Association of Medical Officers of Asylums and Hospitals for the Insane, was first published. John C. Bucknill was the editor of this British journal.

May 15, 1854 (216)

The first treatment facility for alcoholism in the United States was organized. Called the United States Inebriates Asylum, the Binghamton, New York, institution was established "for the reformation of the poor and destitute inebriates." Its cornerstone was laid on September 24, 1858.

June 15, 1854 (217)

Hermann von Helmholtz published his work on the speed of nervous conduction in an article titled "On the Velocity of Some Processes in Muscles and Nerves." Helmholtz estimated the speed of nervous conduction to be 90 ft/s (27 m/s).

September 8, 1854 (218)

The cornerstone was laid for the State Asylum for Idiots in Syracuse, New York, the first building in the United States expressly built for the care and training of people with mental retardation and developmental disabilities. The program itself, directed by Harvey B. Wilbur, had begun in 1851.

December 21, 1854 (219)

Morton Prince was born. Prince promoted the use of scientific methods in the study of abnormal personality and is best known for a pioneering study of multiple personalities. Prince founded the *Journal of Abnormal Psychology* (1906), now titled the *Journal of Personality and Social Psychology*, and established the Harvard Psychological Clinic (1927).

February 14, 1855 (220)

Ernst Ewald was born. Ewald was a sensory physiologist whose pressure-pattern theory of hearing proposed different patterns of basilar membrane response to combinations of intensity and frequency of sound.

March 3, 1855 (221)

Congress officially founded the first federal mental hospital, the Government Hospital for the Insane in Washington, DC. The legislation, written by reformer Dorothea Dix, called for "the most humane care and enlightened curative treatment of the insane of the Army and Navy and of the District of Columbia." After 1916 the hospital was named St. Elizabeth's Hospital.

October 30, 1855 (222)
Gilles de la Tourette was born. Tourette is remembered for identifying the syndrome of tics, explosive outbursts, and "astonishing and imaginative profanity" that bears his name. He was shot in the head by a paranoid client in 1896. He recovered but suffered a progressive bipolar disorder, and became strident, bizarre, and theatrical. He died in a mental hospital in 1904.

November 10, 1855 (223)
Wilhelm Wundt received his MD degree, summa cum laude, at the University of Heidelberg. His doctoral thesis was on touch sensitivity in hysterical patients. He subsequently placed first in the state medical board examination.

November 20, 1855 (224)
Josiah Royce was born. Royce was a philosopher with a strong interest in the problems of psychology. His papers addressed consciousness, imitation, extrasensory perception, invention, consulting, self-consciousness, and mental disorders. APA President, 1901.

December 3, 1855 (225)
William Burnham was born. Burnham directed work in educational psychology and community mental health at Clark University under G. Stanley Hall. He was one of the founders of the mental hygiene movement of the early 1900s. His book *The Normal Mind* was especially influential.

January 6, 1856 (226)
Hermann von Helmholtz published his research on the physiology of stereoscopic vision.

February 15, 1856 (227)
Emil Kraepelin was born. Kraepelin was a founder of modern psychiatry and psychopharmacology. He devised an early nomenclature for mental disorders, including new terms such as *manic–depressive* and *paranoid*.

May 6, 1856 (228)
Sigmund Freud was born. Freud is the most widely cited psychologist of the twentieth century. His concepts of psychological determinism and unconscious and emotional motivation, and his psychoanalytic method of treatment have been enduring contributions. This traditional birth date differs from town records, which give March 6, 1856, as Freud's birth date.

May 14, 1856 (229)

Hermann von Helmholtz published his work on the electrical stimulation of frog muscles.

May 14, 1856 (230)

In response to the urging of geologist Charles Lyell, Charles Darwin began to write a book on his theory of speciation. He first planned a "very thin and little volume," but later envisioned a long work that included all of his evidence. In the end, the brief book *The Origin of Species by Means of Natural Selection* was published in 1859.

January 20, 1857 (231)

Vladimir M. Bekhterev was born. Bekhterev brought extensive study of the nervous system to bear on an understanding of conditioned responses, with special emphasis on psychiatric problems. He named his science "reflexology." Bekhterev founded the first psychological laboratory in Russia, at the University of Kazan in 1886.

February 5, 1857 (232)

Franz (Carl) Müller-Lyer was born. Müller-Lyer was primarily a sociologist but, in 1889, he devised the visual illusion with which his name is usually associated.

March 7, 1857 (233)

Julius Wagner von Jauregg was born. Wagner von Jauregg won the Nobel prize in 1927 for his work in psychiatry. He discovered that malaria causes improvement in syphilitic psychosis and injected mental patients with the malaria parasite.

March 27, 1857 (234)

Karl Pearson was born. Pearson is one of the founders of modern statistics. He developed the widely used product–moment correlation coefficient (r) and the chi-square statistic.

April 10, 1857 (235)

Lucien Lévy-Bruhl was born. Lévy-Bruhl pursued the study of mental processes in primitive humans with the intent of demonstrating differences between civilized and primitive mentality. Lévy-Bruhl's theories, although mistaken, provided information about non-Western thinking.

April 17, 1857 (236)

The fourth U.S. institution for people with mental retardation was founded by the state of Ohio. It was located at Columbus but was destroyed by fire in 1881. The first superintendent was G. A. Doren. The Ohio Institution at Columbus was reputedly the most generously endowed of the early state institutions.

April 30, 1857 (237)

Eugen Bleuler was born. Bleuler introduced Freudian thought to psychiatry and coined the word *schizophrenia* in 1908.

May 10, 1857 (238)

Hendrick Zwaardemaker was born. Zwaardemaker studied hearing and the sounds of speech, but did his most important work on the sense of smell. He developed several apparatuses for controlled experiments, searching unsuccessfully for the nature of that which makes substances odorous. He proposed a scheme of nine basic odors.

May 11, 1857 (239)

Sir Charles Locock first described potassium bromide therapy for epilepsy. Locock believed that epilepsy was caused by masturbation and knew that bromide reduced libido. The drug worked, but not for Locock's reasons. In the late 1930s, Tracy Putnam and Frederick Gibbs at Boston City Hospital showed that epilepsy was accompanied by synchronous nervous discharge in the brain.

May 12, 1857 (240)

Henry Donaldson was born. Donaldson was a prominent neurologist whose thorough studies of the brain were published as a book, *The Brain*, in 1895. At the Wistar Institute, Donaldson introduced the albino rat as an experimental subject and developed the Wistar rat strain later used in many psychological studies.

July 8, 1857 (241)

Frank Angell was born. Angell did most of his work in psychophysics and founded the experimental laboratories at Cornell University (1891) and Stanford University (1893).

July 11, 1857 (242)

Alfred Binet was born. Binet is best known for the development of modern conceptions of, and tests for, intelligence. He was also interested in suggestibility and general experimental psychology. He was a cofounder of the psychology laboratory at the Sorbonne.

November 17, 1857 (243)

Joseph Babinski was born. Babinski was a French neurologist who discovered several reflexive signs for diagnosing impairment of the central nervous system. The *Babinski reflex* of the toes in infants is often used in introductory psychology texts as an example of an innate reflex that disappears with growth of the nervous system.

November 27, 1857 (244)

Sir Charles S. Sherrington was born. Sherrington's studies of neural and synaptic physiology, reflexes, the motor cortex, and reciprocal innervation form the foundation of modern physiological psychology. Nobel prize, 1932.

April 15, 1858 (245)

Emile Durkheim was born. Durkheim was a French sociologist best remembered by psychologists for his theory of the social causes of suicide. Durkheim tended to emphasize the separation between sociology and psychology.

April 15, 1858 (246)

Millicent Washburn Shinn was born. Shinn was the first woman to earn the PhD at the University of California. She was best known for her observational studies of a single infant, her niece, first published in 1893 and later as a popular book, *The Biography of a Baby* (1900).

May 8, 1858 (247)

Wilhelm Wundt was offered the post of assistant professor to Hermann von Helmholtz at the Physiological Institute at Heidelberg. Wundt, then 27, accepted.

June 18, 1858 (248)

Charles Darwin received a manuscript from Alfred Russel Wallace titled "On the Tendency of Varieties to Depart Indefinitely from the Original Type" and realized that Wallace had discovered the principle of natural selection. This realization spurred Darwin to publish *The Origin of Species by Means of Natural Selection* before Wallace published his work.

July 1, 1858 (249)

Charles Darwin read Alfred Wallace's paper on evolution to the Linnaean Society along with portions of Darwin's own long-withheld manuscript of *The Origin of Species by Means of Natural Selection*. This was the first public announcement of Darwin's theory.

July 9, 1858 (250)

Franz Boas was born. Boas was a revolutionary figure in the study of the interaction of culture and individual behavior. He inaugurated the first American longitudinal study of growth in 1891. *The Mind of Primitive Man* (1911) is his most important book for psychologists.

November 10, 1858 (251)

Harry Kirke Wolfe was born. Wolfe studied under Hermann Ebbinghaus and Wilhelm Wundt, earning his degree at the University of Leipzig in 1886. He established the experimental psychology laboratory at the University of Nebraska in 1889, founding a program that has produced many presidents of the APA. He was an inspirational teacher and pioneering researcher in child and educational psychology.

December 29, 1858 (252)

Alfred Georg Ludwig Lehmann was born. Lehmann was a Danish student of Wilhelm Wundt whose major works dealt with color aesthetics and superstition. He began the first experimental laboratory in Denmark, at the University of Copenhagen.

February 2, 1859 (253)

Henry Havelock Ellis was born. Ellis wrote some of the first objective works on human sexual behavior. He introduced the terms *autoeroticism* and *narcissism.*

February 27, 1859 (254)

Bertha Pappenheim, Josef Breuer and Sigmund Freud's "Anna O.," was born in Vienna. The treatment of Anna O.'s hysterical symptoms by the cathartic method strongly influenced the development of psychoanalysis.

April 7, 1859 (255)

Jacques Loeb was born. Loeb applied the concept of orienting responses of plants, called *tropisms*, to animal behavior, resulting in a mechanistic explanation of animal behavior. His work was summarized in his books *The Mechanistic Conception of Life* (1912) and *Forced Movements, Tropisms, and Animal Conduct* (1918). Comparative psychology was strongly influenced by Loeb's work.

April 8, 1859 (256)

Edmund Husserl was born. Husserl coined the term *phenomenology.* Husserl contended that because consciousness synthesizes a meaningful reality from the objective data it is given, phenomenological observation of subjective experiences is essential to the understanding of being. Husserl's thought has influenced humanistic psychology.

May 30, 1859 (257)

Pierre Janet was born. Janet was a French psychopathologist remembered for his dissociation theory of hysteria and hypnosis. He introduced the words *dissociation* and *subconscious* into psychological terminology.

June 20, 1859 (258)

Christian von Ehrenfels was born. Ehrenfels was an Austrian philosopher who proposed in 1890 that form quality (*Gestaltqualitat*) is an independent element of perception. The idea set the stage for Gestalt psychology.

August 18, 1859 (259)

George S. Fullerton was born. Fullerton's experimental work focused on psychophysics, especially the perception of small differences between stimuli. APA President, 1896.

September 28, 1859 (260)
The first public school class for children with mental retardation was proposed to the Halle, Germany, school board.

October 18, 1859 (261)
Henri Bergson was born. A Nobel laureate, Bergson asserted that the phenomena of mind could not be understood by the methods of science.

October 20, 1859 (262)
John Dewey was born. Dewey was an early functionalist, best known for his impact on educational reform by promoting learning by doing. His influential article on the reflex arc concept in psychology emphasized functional relations and adaptation as the proper focus of psychology. APA President, 1899.

November 10, 1859 (263)
Edmund Clark Sanford was born. Sanford earned his degree under G. Stanley Hall at Johns Hopkins University and went with Hall to Clark University, where he supervised the psychology laboratory. He produced several studies of reaction time and wrote a widely used laboratory manual (1892). APA President, 1902.

November 11, 1859 (264)
Hermann von Helmholtz published his work on color blindness.

November 24, 1859 (265)
Charles Darwin's *The Origin of Species by Means of Natural Selection* was published. All 1,250 copies of the first printing were sold on the first day of sale.

January 6, 1860 (266)
George F. Stout was born. Stout was primarily known for his psychology textbooks, especially his *Manual of Psychology* (1899), and for the doctrine of conation, a theory of mental processes that incorporated thinking, feeling, and motivational factors.

May 25, 1860 (267)
James McKeen Cattell was born. He studied mental testing and individual differences. Cattell edited *American Men of Science*, *Psychological Review*, and the journal *Science*. He was the first American professor of psychology, founded the psychology laboratory at the University of Pennsylvania in 1888, founded the Psychological Corporation, and was APA President in 1895.

June 30, 1860 (268)
A famous debate was held between Thomas Henry Huxley and Bishop Samuel Wilberforce of the Church of England on the subject of Darwin's theory of evolution by natural selection.

November 1, 1860 (269)

William Bryan, experimental psychologist and administrator, was born. With the purchase of a chronoscope, Bryan founded the fourth psychology laboratory in the United States at Indiana University in 1888. The university celebrated the founding with the Bryan Symposium in Psychology on October 21, 1939. APA President, 1903.

December 19, 1860 (270)

Hermann von Helmholtz presented work on the relation between violin string motions and hearing.

January 12, 1861 (271)

James Mark Baldwin was born. Baldwin was an early developmental and theoretical psychologist who founded the *Psychological Review*, *Psychological Monographs*, and, with James McKeen Cattell, *Psychological Bulletin*. APA President, 1897.

April 11, 1861 (272)

An aphasic patient named Leborgne entered Paul Broca's surgical ward at the Bicêtre asylum. Leborgne was called "Tan" because, except for occasional curses, it was his only word. He died on April 17, giving Broca the opportunity to do the critical autopsy that resulted in identification of the language centers of the brain.

April 18, 1861 (273)

Paul Broca performed an autopsy on a person who had been aphasic and who had died the previous day. Broca found a lesion originating in the third frontal convolution of the left hemisphere, an area now named for Broca and known to be associated with language functions in most people.

August 4, 1861 (274)

Sir Henry Head was born. Head was a neurologist who established that peripheral nerves can regenerate by cutting two nerves in his own arm. He was the first to trace the path of sensory impulses from the receptor to the cortex. Research late in his career focused on aphasia.

September 18, 1861 (275)

Wilhelm Wundt read a paper on individual differences in visual and auditory reaction times to a congress of German scientists meeting in Speyer. This was Wundt's first report of what would become experimental psychology. Wundt was assistant to Helmholtz at Heidelberg at the time.

August 3, 1862 (276)

Oswald Külpe was born. Külpe used systematic introspection to study thought processes and founded the Würzburg school of imageless thought.

August 29, 1862 (277)

Ernst Meumann was born. Meumann did some early introspective work on sensation but is most noted for becoming the founder of experimental pedagogy.

January 30, 1863 (278)

Joseph Jastrow was born. He earned the first doctorate from the first formal PhD program in psychology in the United States, at Johns Hopkins University under G. Stanley Hall in 1886. His writing presented a scientific view of psychology to the general public, and he organized the psychology pavilion at the Columbian Exposition in Chicago in 1893. APA President, 1900.

February 27, 1863 (279)

George Herbert Mead was born. Mead was a social philosopher important to psychology because of his view that the sense of self arises from the consequences of social interaction. This social behaviorism brought Mead's approach close to that of behavior analytic psychologists.

March 3, 1863 (280)

The charter of the National Academy of Sciences was signed by President Abraham Lincoln.

March 30, 1863 (281)

Mary Whiton Calkins was born. Calkins invented the paired-associate method of measuring learning and memory. She promoted psychology as the science of the self for most of her career. Calkins founded the psychology laboratory at Wellesley College in 1891, the 13th to be founded in the United States. APA President, 1905.

June 1, 1863 (282)

Hugo Münsterberg was born. Münsterberg came to the United States in 1892 to direct William James's laboratories at Harvard University. He was one of the first applied psychologists, extending research and theory to industrial, legal, medical, clinical, educational, and business settings. APA President, 1898; President, American Philosophical Association, 1908.

June 16, 1863 (283)

Friedrich Schumann was born. Schumann's studies of part–whole relations in sensation and perception were forerunners of Gestalt psychology.

September 10, 1863 (284)

Charles E. Spearman was born. By studying correlations of intelligence task scores, Spearman proposed two factors: general intelligence (*g*), and specific abilities (*s*). The existence and nature of factors of intelligence continue to interest psychologists. He developed the Spearman rank-order correlation coefficient and the Spearman-Brown reliability coefficient.

September 25, 1863   (285)

Edmund Delabarre was born. Delabarre was a general experimental psychologist who founded the laboratory at Brown University in 1892 and was one of the founders of the APA.

May 21, 1864   (286)

Edward Wheeler Scripture was born. Scripture's early research focused on reaction time and hearing and was typical of the Wundtian physiological psychology of the day. Later work took Scripture into experimental phonetics and speech research. Scripture was one of the founding members of the APA.

June 14, 1864   (287)

Alois Alzheimer was born. In 1907, Alzheimer first described the syndrome of behavioral and physical degeneration in aging adults that now bears his name.

September 15, 1865   (288)

Matataro Matsumoto was born. Matsumoto earned his doctoral degree at Yale University under Edward W. Scripture, then returned to Japan, where he introduced applied experimental psychology and helped to train the senior generation of Japanese experimental psychologists. In addition to applied psychology, he wrote about the psychology of art.

September 26, 1865   (289)

George Stratton was born. Stratton is remembered primarily for the first studies of the effects of prolonged inversion of the visual field, finding that he readily adapted to this distortion and later suffered disorientation when his inverting lenses were removed. He also studied aesthetics and social behavior. APA President, 1908.

September 29, 1865   (290)

Frederick Batten was born. Batten identified a syndrome of progressive intellectual deterioration and physical symptoms that now bears his name. He has been called the "father of pediatric neurology."

January 28, 1866   (291)

Carl Emil Seashore was born. Seashore founded the second psychological clinic in the United States and helped to found the Iowa Child Welfare Research Station. His studies centered on educational psychology and the psychology of music and art. Seashore's true family name was Sjostrand, which means *seashore* in Swedish. APA President, 1911.

February 20, 1866   (292)

Edwin Starbuck was born. Starbuck pioneered the study of the psychology of religion and offered some of the first university courses in tests and measurements and educational psychology.

March 6, 1866 (293)

Georges Dumas was born. Abnormal psychology was his focus. Dumas's encyclopedic *Traite de Psychologie* (1923) was a medically oriented, systematic summary of experimental psychology.

April 21, 1866 (294)

The American Society for the Prevention of Cruelty to Animals (ASPCA) was founded by Henry Bergh. The ASPCA and more militant animal rights advocates set the stage for the adoption of codes of ethical procedures in experimental psychology and other sciences.

July 9, 1866 (295)

Ivan M. Sechenov was indicted by a Russian court for the materialistic explanations of psychic phenomena contained in his book *Reflexes of the Brain* (1863). Frogs were used in many of Sechenov's studies, and he proposed letting a frog testify in his defense.

August 14, 1866 (296)

Henry H. Goddard was born. Goddard was the first psychologist at the Vineland Training School (1906), originally called the New Jersey School for Feeble-Minded Boys and Girls. He is also known for the Kallikak family study, which he took as evidence for the genetic foundation of intelligence.

September 13, 1866 (297)

Adolph Meyer was born. Meyer was the most prominent American psychiatrist of his time. His holistic approach recommended that the organic, psychological, and social factors affecting the patient must all be considered in diagnosis and treatment. He suggested the appropriateness of the term *mental hygiene*.

January 11, 1867 (298)

Edward Bradford Titchener was born. Titchener promoted his interpretation of Wundtian experimental psychology, *structuralism*, in the United States. Psychology, for Titchener, was the systematic analysis of mental experience through introspection.

June 12, 1867 (299)

Howard C. Warren was born. Warren's principal contribution was establishing, editing, and publishing many early journals of American psychology. He founded the *Journal of Experimental Psychology* and owned and edited *Psychological Bulletin*, *Psychological Review*, and *Psychological Monographs*. APA President, 1913.

June 28, 1867 (300)

Lightner Witmer, experimental and clinical psychologist, was born. Witmer founded the first psychology clinic, at the University of Pennsylvania in 1896, and coined the term *clinical psychology*.

October 12, 1867   (301)
Boris Sidis was born. Sidis, a personality and abnormal psychologist, was one of the first American psychologists to study the unconscious motivation of behavior. He emphasized the importance of social context in the definitions of normal and abnormal behavior and did early work in multiple personality and hypnosis.

March 2, 1868   (302)
Eleanor Achison McCulloch Gamble was born. Gamble earned her degree under E. B. Titchener at Cornell University in 1898 and spent her career at Wellesley College. She was the most prominent early researcher on the sense of smell.

April 8, 1868   (303)
Herbert S. Jennings was born. Jennings was a comparative psychologist who focused on the behavior of lower organisms. He avoided mentalistic explanations for animal behavior.

April 9, 1868   (304)
James Leuba was born. Leuba had broad interests, concentrating on the psychology of religion, perception, comparative psychology, and motivation. Leuba founded the psychology laboratory at Bryn Mawr College in 1898.

June 2, 1868   (305)
The American Psychiatric Association adopted a "project of law" describing the association's standards regarding legal rights of the insane, including commitment and discharge procedures and protection from civil and criminal prosecution.

October 6, 1868   (306)
Charles Herrick was born. Herrick was a physiologist who studied the structure of the brain and found that the structures of lower animals form the basis of the human brain.

January 20, 1869   (307)
William Healy was born. Healy was a child psychiatrist whose work with delinquent children led to founding the first American child guidance clinic, the Juvenile Psychopathic Institute (1909) in Chicago. With Grace M. Fernald, Healy devised the Healy-Fernald series of performance tests for intelligence.

March 18, 1869   (308)
The first published reference in the United States to the experimental psychology of Gustav Fechner and Wilhelm Wundt was made by philosopher Charles S. Peirce. Peirce's article, a review of Noah Porter's *The Human Intellect*, appeared in *The Nation*. Peirce judged Fechner and Wundt's contributions "to be of more value than all the others put together."

April 29, 1869 (309)

The first article on neurasthenia, by George Beard, was published. The article appeared in the *Boston Medical and Surgical Journal.*

May 1, 1869 (310)

Walter Dill Scott was born. Scott was a pioneer in industrial and business psychology, as it was then called. He chaired a committee that devised the first personnel classification tests for the U.S. Army and wrote on advertising, efficiency, and motivation. APA President, 1919; Chair, American Council on Education, 1927.

May 8, 1869 (311)

James R. Angell was born. Angell was the most prominent early spokesperson for American functionalism. He viewed behavior and mental processes as mediators between the organism and its environment. He created Yale University's Institute of Human Relations. APA President, 1906.

May 19, 1869 (312)

James Crichton Browne sent the first of many photos of people with mental illness to Charles Darwin. Brown was a psychiatrist and amateur photographer whose photos provided evidence used by Darwin in his book *The Expression of the Emotions in Man and Animals.*

May 21, 1869 (313)

John Wallace Baird was born. Baird conducted early studies of the roles of convergence and accommodation in depth perception. APA President, 1918.

August 31, 1869 (314)

Karl Marbe was born. Marbe's work in psychophysics contributed to the Würzburg school of imageless thought. Later in his career he contributed studies in industrial aptitude testing, accident-prone behavior, and other areas of industrial and applied psychology.

October 17, 1869 (315)

Robert S. Woodworth was born. Woodworth was one of the first to consider the motivational state of the organism to be a critical intervening variable. His experiments in motivation and physiological psychology led to influential texts in general, systematic, and experimental psychology. APA President, 1914; American Psychological Foundation Gold Medal, 1956.

November 24, 1869 (316)

A special Committee of Investigations began 11 days of investigation of Charles H. Nichols, the first superintendent of the Government Hospital for the Insane in Washington, DC, later named St. Elizabeth's Hospital. Among the charges was that of "rebel proclivities." Nichols served in his post from 1852 to 1877.

December 17, 1869 (317)

The military commander of the Union forces occupying Virginia, Major General Canby, authorized the first U.S. institution for the exclusive care of African American mental patients. Howard's Grove Asylum, later named Central State Hospital, was opened in April 1885 near Petersburg.

December 23, 1869 (318)

German biochemist Friedrich Miescher mailed a report announcing his discovery of "nuclein" to the *Medical-Chemical Journal*. Nuclein was later named *nucleic acid* by Richard Altmann (1889) and even later was found to be composed of DNA and RNA. Miescher was the first to identify this substance and confirm that it was found in the nuclei of all cells.

January 19, 1870 (319)

Eduard Hitzig presented the first account of electrical stimulation of the human brain in a report to the Medical Society of Berlin. Hitzig induced eye movements through brain stimulation. Nonhuman subjects were further studied by Hitzig, Gustav Fritsch, and David Ferrier. American physician Roberts Bartholow conducted further studies of human participants, first reported in 1874.

January 24, 1870 (320)

William Alanson White was born. White conceived of mental illness as a social, biological, and psychological process involving the whole organism. White promoted the humane and kind treatment of people with mental illness. He coined the term *mental hygiene*. President, American Psychiatric Association, 1924.

February 7, 1870 (321)

Alfred Adler was born. Adler was an early associate of Sigmund Freud. His theory of "individual psychology" stressed the need for superiority. His terms *inferiority complex* and *style of life* have become part of everyday language.

April 11, 1870 (322)

Oliver Munsell's book *Psychology, the Science of Mind*, an early American work, was published.

April 29, 1870 (323)

William James, after reading an essay by French philosopher Charles Renouvier, decided that "My first act of free will shall be to believe in free will." This brought an end to a personal crisis of depression and marked the beginning of James's own brand of psychology.

June 18, 1870 (324)

Madison Bentley was born. Bentley, whose initial work was in the area of mental imagery, was a prolific book reviewer and served as the consulting psychologist to the Library of Congress. APA President, 1925.

August 24, 1870 (325)

Willard S. Small was born. Small was the first person to use the behavior of rats in mazes as a measure of learning.

August 31, 1870 (326)

Maria Montessori was born. Montessori pioneered a system of early childhood education that was based on a graduated series of direct experiences and exploration. Montessori was the first woman to be awarded the MD degree by an Italian university (1896).

December 8, 1870 (327)

Ernst Moro was born. Moro discovered that the startle reflex in infants could be used to diagnose abnormal development of the central nervous system.

February 18, 1871 (328)

George Yule was born. Yule's work in statistics resulted in the concepts and computational methods of partial correlation, multiple regression, and the contingency coefficient.

February 20, 1871 (329)

Raymond Dodge was born. Dodge's experimental work focused on the effects of alcohol on motor performance and studies of vestibular reactions, visual perception, and personnel selection. He was the first to study eye movements during reading. APA President, 1916.

April 29, 1871 (330)

L. William Stern was born. Stern is best known for the concept of the intelligence quotient, but also did work in applied, developmental, and differential psychology. He coined the term *applied psychology* in 1903.

June 22, 1871 (331)

William McDougall was born. McDougall developed theories of social and personality psychology that were based on instincts. He was a founder of the British Psychological Society and the *British Journal of Psychology*.

July 25, 1871 (332)

Margaret Floy Washburn, an animal psychologist, was born. Washburn was the first woman granted a PhD in psychology by an American university and she was the second woman elected to the National Academy of Sciences (1931). APA President, 1921.

October 19, 1871 (333)

Walter B. Cannon was born. His area of concentration was the physiology of emotion. Cannon's theories, later elaborated by Philip Bard, were first thoroughly treated in Cannon's book *Bodily Changes in Pain, Hunger, Fear, and Rage* (1915).

October 29, 1871   (334)
Narziss K. Ach was born. Ach was one of the founders of the Würzburg school of imageless thought.

March 17, 1872   (335)
George Coghill was born. Coghill was a developmental psychobiologist whose work focused on the role of prior behavior in shaping reflexes.

July 21, 1872   (336)
Walter B. Pillsbury, a general experimental psychologist and textbook author, was born. Pillsbury's *The Essentials of Psychology* (1911), *The Fundamentals of Psychology* (1916), and *History of Psychology* (1929) were well-known. APA President, 1910.

August 1, 1872   (337)
Francis Galton published a statistical analysis of the efficacy of prayer. He compared recovery rates at Roman Catholic hospitals with those at public hospitals and found no difference, despite the fact that Catholic patients probably were prayed for more often.

January 20, 1873   (338)
Clara Ellen Fowler, the "Sally Beauchamp" of Morton Prince's study of multiple personalities, was born.

February 20, 1873   (339)
Charles H. Judd was born. Judd's experiments on transfer of training discredited the traditional concept of formal discipline in education and substituted a more modern theory of identical elements. APA President, 1909.

March 3, 1873   (340)
The first federal antiobscenity law, the "Comstock law," was passed. The law was intended for the welfare of children. A later court test (*U.S. v. Bennett*) upheld the law and produced the "Hicklin rule" for obscenity: "Whether the tendency of the matter is to deprave and corrupt the morals of those whose minds are open to such influences."

March 13, 1873   (341)
Charles S. Myers was born. Myers was a founder of the *British Journal of Psychology* and was a pioneer in British applied and industrial psychology.

March 24, 1873   (342)
Edouard Claparède was born. Claparède wrote on sleep, neurology, and animal psychology, but his principle contributions were in child psychology. His *Psychology of the Child and Experimental Pedagogy* (1909) was a landmark volume in the field and influenced the work of Jean Piaget. With Théodore Flournoy, Claparède founded the *Archives de Psychologie* (1901).

April 30, 1873 (343)

Harvey A. Carr was born. Carr is best known as the standard-bearer of American functionalism in the 1920s. Psychology was to be the study of the functions that connected psychological antecedents to their consequences. Carr's experimental work focused on comparative psychology, learning, and visual space perception. APA President, 1926.

May 21, 1873 (344)

Hans Berger was born. Berger was a psychiatrist who invented the electroencephalogram, first tried it on his son, and named the pattern of brain activity during rest and meditation the *alpha rhythm*.

June 15, 1873 (345)

Max F. Meyer was born. Meyer promoted a vision of psychology that resembled and preceded Watson's behaviorism but did not attract Watson's following. His experimental work was primarily in the area of acoustics.

July 10, 1873 (346)

Theodore Simon was born. With Alfred Binet, Simon produced the first intelligence test, and he continued to promote its appropriate use—while working to rectify its misuse—after Binet's death. Simon also developed an intelligence scale for infants and created the first psychological consultation service for juvenile delinquents.

August 21, 1873 (347)

Edwin B. Holt was born. Holt combined a behavioral focus with an emphasis on intentions, wishes, and goals.

September 14, 1873 (348)

Edwin B. Twitmyer was born. Twitmyer used methods of classical conditioning to condition the knee-jerk reflex to the sound of a tone. His work preceded Pavlov's but was indifferently received by the American psychological community. His career was in speech therapy. He was the first director of the first special speech clinic in the United States, at the University of Pennsylvania.

February 26, 1874 (349)

The Library of Congress received its copy of the first issue of the *Journal of Nervous and Mental Disease.*

April 21, 1874 (350)

Oskar Pfungst was born. Pfungst was a self-taught comparative psychologist best known for his methodical examination of Clever Hans, a performing horse. The Clever Hans phenomenon was a prototypical case of experimenter expectancy effects.

May 27, 1874 (351)

Shepherd Ivory Franz was born. Franz pioneered studies of cortical localization of learned behaviors. Through extirpation of brain tissue, Franz showed that impaired abilities could be regained and that the amount of impairment was not closely related to the site or amount of lost brain tissue. APA President, 1920.

August 31, 1874 (352)

Edward Lee Thorndike was born. Thorndike's research in learning and educational psychology resulted in the laws of effect and exercise. His studies of cats learning to escape from "puzzle boxes" are especially well-known. With Irving Lorge, he compiled the Thorndike–Lorge lists of word frequency. APA President, 1912.

October 12, 1874 (353)

Abraham A. Brill was born. Brill was the first to translate many of Sigmund Freud's works into English for American readers. He also wrote several books of his own in which he promoted psychoanalysis. He founded the New York Psychoanalytic Society in 1911.

November 6, 1874 (354)

Helen Bradford Thompson Woolley was born. Woolley was a child clinical psychologist who was a codeveloper of the Merrill-Palmer Scales for children. She was the first director of the Child Development Institute at Teachers College, Columbia University (1926).

November 27, 1874 (355)

Egas Moniz was born. Moniz was a Portuguese surgeon who performed the first modern operations on the frontal lobes for treatment of mental disorders. He received the Nobel prize in 1949 for this work and for the invention of the arteriograph.

January 3, 1875 (356)

Katharine Cook Briggs was born. Briggs's interpretation of Jungian personality theory formed the basis of the Myers-Briggs Type Indicator, constructed by her daughter, Isabel Myers.

June 6, 1875 (357)

Grace Kent was born. The Kent-Rosanoff Free Association Test is the best known product of Kent's work in clinical psychology. She is also responsible for several other clinical assessment instruments.

July 13, 1875 (358)

June Etta Downey was born. Downey's contributions were in the areas of clinical psychology and personality assessment. Her Downey Will-Temperament Tests (1919) received some research attention in the 1920s. She founded the psychology laboratory at the University of Wyoming in 1900.

July 26, 1875 (359)

Carl Gustav Jung was born. Once allied with Sigmund Freud, Jung later proposed a theory of personality that deemphasized sexual motives and posited opposing forces of introverted–extraverted and rational–irrational personality types. Jung's concepts of the collective unconscious and archetypes and his interest in symbolism linked psychology to anthropology, religion, and art.

October 1, 1875 (360)

Wilhelm Wundt joined the faculty at the University of Leipzig.

November 20, 1875 (361)

Wilhelm Wundt gave his first lecture at the University of Leipzig. The lecture was titled "The Influence of Philosophy on the Experiential Sciences."

November 21, 1875 (362)

Knight Dunlap was born. Dunlap's experimental work focused on visual perception, abnormal and social psychology, and the psychology of religion. His theoretical positions insisted on a psychology of observable responses that did not rely on introspection or instinct for data or explanation. APA President, 1922.

December 2, 1875 (363)

The Society for the Protection of Animals Liable to Vivisection, or the Victoria Street Society, was founded in England by Frances Power Cobbe, an early animal rights activist. The society adopted a militant program of prevention of cruelty to animals, especially animals used in research. The research ethics of experimental psychologists have been strongly affected by animal rights groups.

December 28, 1875 (364)

The New York Society for the Prevention of Cruelty to Children, an important early organization for child welfare advocacy, held its first meeting. John D. Wright was the group's first president. The organization was inspired by public attention to the case of 8-year-old Mary Ellen Wilson, who had been beaten by her adoptive parents and sold into servitude.

March 6, 1876 (365)

Charles S. Peirce purchased a notebook in Cologne and recorded his first set of color vision observations. Intermittent observations were made until February 15, 1877, and reported in the April 1877 issue of the *American Journal of Science*. Peirce was the first psychologist elected to the National Academy of Sciences (1877).

March 30, 1876 (366)

Clifford Beers was born. A former mental patient, Beers was the founder of the mental hygiene movement. His popular book, *A Mind That Found Itself: An Au-*

tobiography, described the inhumane treatment he had received in the asylums of the day. The mental hygiene movement emphasized community programs of prevention, early diagnosis, and humane treatment.

May 26, 1876 (367)

Robert M. Yerkes was born. With John D. Dodson, Yerkes developed the Yerkes–Dodson law relating motivation to performance. Mainly a comparative psychologist, Yerkes studied chimpanzee behavior. As APA president in 1917, Yerkes was instrumental in shaping the response of psychologists to the demands of World War I, the first large-scale program of applied psychology.

June 6, 1876 (368)

The American Association on Mental Deficiency was founded. The original name of the group was The Association of Medical Officers of American Institutions for Idiots and Feeble-Minded Persons. Edouard O. Séguin was elected president.

June 7, 1876 (369)

The American Association on Mental Deficiency held its first meeting in Media, Pennsylvania.

June 12, 1876 (370)

Guy Whipple was born. Whipple's interests were in educational psychology and testing. He published an early guide to mental measurements in 1910 and was an advocate of training standards for test administrators and interpreters. Whipple was a founder of the *Journal of Educational Psychology* (1910) and designed the Whipple tachistoscope.

June 13, 1876 (371)

William S. Gosset was born. Writing under the name "Student," Gosset originated and described the *t* test. His employer, the Guinness Brewery, prohibited him from publishing under his own name.

January 15, 1877 (372)

Lewis M. Terman was born. Terman was a student of G. Stanley Hall. He developed the Stanford Revision of the Binet-Simon Intelligence Scale in 1916 and is also known for his longitudinal studies of a group of exceptionally intelligent children. APA President, 1923.

April 18, 1877 (373)

Charles S. Peirce was elected to the National Academy of Sciences. He was the first psychologist so honored.

May 3, 1877 (374)

Karl Abraham was born. Abraham, a German psychoanalyst, proposed that adult personality could be traced to childhood experiences and fixation at early developmental stages.

July 6, 1877 (375)

Robert Ogden was born. Ogden, an early Gestaltist, was instrumental in disseminating Gestalt ideas in the United States and in inviting influential German Gestalt psychologists to come to the United States. His book, *Psychology and Education* (1926), was the first Gestalt-oriented book by an American psychologist.

September 29, 1877 (376)

Naomi Norsworthy was born. Norsworthy was one of the first psychologists to be involved with the mental testing movement, especially as applied to the assessment of children with mental deficiencies. She was the first woman graduate student at Columbia University.

November 27, 1877 (377)

Vivian Henmon was born. Henmon's research touched on individual differences, teacher placement, aptitude testing, language functions, and other subjects in educational psychology. He also constructed the Henmon-Nelson Test of Mental Ability.

January 9, 1878 (378)

John Broadus Watson was born. Watson's behaviorism defined psychology as an objective, experimental branch of natural science, shunning mentalism. APA President, 1915.

February 8, 1878 (379)

Martin Buber was born. Buber was a Christian existentialist philosopher whose description of the intimate "I–Thou relationship" with God influenced humanistic theories of personality and psychotherapy.

May 24, 1878 (380)

Lillian Moller Gilbreth was born. Gilbreth was an industrial psychologist who pioneered the use of time-and-motion studies to improve industrial productivity. Gilbreth's book, *Cheaper by the Dozen*, popularized her efficiency-oriented family life. Gilbreth is the only psychologist ever to have appeared on a U.S. postage stamp (1984).

June 26, 1878 (381)

G. Stanley Hall earned his PhD in psychology from Harvard University. His was the first PhD in psychology granted by an American institution.

June 26, 1878 (382)

Aaron Rosanoff was born. Rosanoff was a psychiatrist who studied genetic and physiological factors in psychosis. The Kent-Rosanoff list of free association word response frequencies (1901) was compiled with Grace Kent and has been used in learning studies and in psychological assessment.

July 19, 1878 (383)

Walter Dearborn was born. Dearborn was an educational psychologist who supervised the Harvard Growth Study, a longitudinal study of 1,533 children from 1922 to 1934. Utilizing the Dearborn Group Tests of Intelligence, the study described patterns of physical growth but failed to find correlates with intellectual growth.

September 8, 1878 (384)

Joseph Peterson was born. Peterson did early work in auditory and visual perception, learning, intelligence testing, and the transfer of training. APA President, 1934.

November 6, 1878 (385)

Kurt Goldstein was born. Goldstein was a neurologist specializing in brain injuries when he was influenced by Gestalt psychology. Gestalt holism led Goldstein to a distributed functions theory of brain activity. Goldstein developed tests of concept formation and brain injury.

December 9, 1878 (386)

Géza Révész was born. Révész and David Katz were founders of the journal *Acta Psychologica* (1935). Révész's areas of research concentration were sensation and perception.

January 1, 1879 (387)

(Alfred) Ernest Jones was born. Jones was an early associate of Sigmund Freud, becoming a part of Freud's inner circle after the defections of Carl Jung and Alfred Adler. He introduced psychoanalysis in England and wrote the standard English-language biography of Freud's life and work.

January 28, 1879 (388)

Julia Bell was born. Bell conducted some of the first systematic studies of familial diseases, including color blindness and hemophilia. One familial disease, X chromosome-linked mental retardation, or Martin–Bell syndrome, is named for her.

March 15, 1879 (389)

Henri Wallon was born. Wallon was a French psychopathologist and developmental psychologist. He founded an early children's clinic in 1921. His approach emphasized the effects of the social and physical environment on the individual behavior of children.

March 24, 1879   (390)
Wilhelm Wundt submitted a petition to the Royal Saxon Ministry of Education requesting funds to establish a "collection of psychophysical apparatus." Because the petition was denied for lack of funds, Wundt established the first psychological laboratory with his personal equipment.

May 27, 1879   (391)
Karl Bühler was born. Bühler, a member of the Würzburg school of imageless thought, studied introspective accounts of complex problem solving. His studies of child development with Charlotte Bühler were among the first systematic studies in developmental psychology.

July 24, 1879   (392)
Herbert S. Langfeld was born. Langfeld proposed that consciousness does not exist in isolation from motor acts. His research was in action, inhibition, aesthetics, and emotional expression. He promoted an international arena for American psychology. APA President, 1930.

August 16, 1879   (393)
Charles Wilfred Valentine was born. Valentine, an educational psychologist, founded the *British Journal of Educational Psychology* and wrote several texts on early education and intelligence testing in children. In addition, his text on experimental aesthetics was a standard for 40 years.

September 15, 1879   (394)
Albert Paul Weiss was born. Weiss was an early behaviorist who advocated that psychology abandon the concepts of consciousness and mental life in favor of observed behavior as the proper object of study. Weiss applied his behaviorism to practical behavioral problems such as automobile driving.

November 29, 1879   (395)
Grace Maxwell Fernald was born. Fernald developed the visual–auditory–kinesthetic–tactile system of teaching reading to readers with disabilities. With William Healy, she administered the pioneering Juvenile Psychopathic Institute in Chicago and developed the Healy-Fernald performance tests of intelligence.

January 17, 1880   (396)
Max Freidrich collected the first publishable data in Wilhelm Wundt's laboratory. G. Stanley Hall was one of the participants in Freidrich's study.

April 15, 1880   (397)
Max Wertheimer was born. Wertheimer was a founder of Gestalt psychology and is remembered for investigating the phenomenon of apparent movement known as the *phi phenomenon*, for describing the Gestalt laws of perceptual organization, and for introducing the study of cognitive processes in his book, *Productive Thinking*.

May 26, 1880 (398)

Harry Hollingworth was born. Hollingworth viewed himself as a systematic psychologist but is best remembered for his applied studies, including experiments on the effects of caffeine, used by Coca-Cola to defend against a federal lawsuit in 1939, and for studies of shell shock in World War I soldiers. APA President, 1927.

June 18, 1880 (399)

Wilhelm Wundt wrote a letter of recommendation for G. Stanley Hall, whom he called "a man of comprehensive philosophical knowledge, great scientific interests and solid independent judgment." Hall used the letter to secure his appointment at Johns Hopkins University.

June 21, 1880 (400)

Arnold Gesell was born. Gesell undertook monumental work in establishing age norms for the physical and motor development of children. His "ages and stages" approach had great popular appeal for parents. The Gesell Institute of Child Development carries on Gesell's work.

July 1, 1880 (401)

The National Association for the Protection of the Insane and Prevention of Insanity, an early advocacy group, was founded in Cleveland, Ohio. Harvey B. Wilbur was the first president.

July 3, 1880 (402)

The first issue of the "old series" of the journal *Science* was published. The journal was founded by inventor Thomas A. Edison and journalist John Michaels and was originally titled *Science: A Weekly Journal of Scientific Progress*. This series ceased publication in 1882 and was succeeded by the "new series" on February 9, 1883.

July 18, 1880 (403)

This is the date of the snake hallucination that resulted in the hysterical symptoms of "Anna O.," a patient of Josef Breuer and Sigmund Freud.

August 1, 1880 (404)

The second mental institution in the United States for African American patients only, the Eastern Asylum for the Colored Insane, was opened in Goldsboro, North Carolina.

August 19, 1880 (405)

Adelbert Ames, Jr., was born. Ames was a ophthalmologist whose research focused on visual sensation and perception. His "transactional functionalism" emphasized the interactions between person and environment as determinants of perception. The distorted room apparatus and rotating trapezoidal window apparatus were among the demonstration stimuli invented by Ames.

October 18, 1880 (406)

James McKeen Cattell enrolled at the University of Göttingen and studied under Rudolf Lotze. Cattell went to Leipzig and worked under Wilhelm Wundt after Lotze died in 1881.

October 20, 1880 (407)

Walter Van Dyke Bingham was born. Bingham was a pioneer of industrial psychology, personnel selection and guidance, and accident reduction, consistently basing his work on experimental findings. He founded the first university department of applied psychology at the Carnegie Institute of Technology (1915) and helped develop the first military personnel placement tests.

December 11, 1880 (408)

Josef Breuer began his treatment of 21-year-old "Anna O." Breuer's treatment of Anna O.'s symptoms marked the starting point of the psychoanalytic method, refined and elaborated by Breuer's partner, Sigmund Freud.

December 26, 1880 (409)

Elton Mayo was born. Mayo was responsible for the Hawthorne studies of industrial and social behavior.

January 10, 1881 (410)

Hanns Sachs was born on this day in 1881 and died on this day in 1947. An early Freudian, Sachs was the first training analyst and founded the *American Imago*.

February 5, 1881 (411)

At a public Harvard Lecture in Boston, G. Stanley Hall presented data linking adolescence and religious conversion. This early observation might have been the first reported evidence in the scientific study of the psychology of religion.

March 27, 1881 (412)

Sir Godfrey Thompson was born. Thompson was one of the statisticians that developed the technique of factor analysis in the 1930s. He also devised the Northumberland Tests, now called the Moray House Tests, used in Great Britain for educational placement.

March 31, 1881 (413)

Sigmund Freud received his MD degree from the University of Vienna. His dissertation topic was the reproductive system of eels. As a student, Freud discovered the analgesic properties of cocaine.

July 18, 1881 (414)

Henri Piéron was born. Piéron was a versatile and prolific French psychologist. He promoted a behaviorally oriented psychology through research in sensation, individual differences, applied psychology, physiological psychology, and comparative psychology. He established the Institut de Psychologie at the University of Paris (1920).

July 22, 1881   (415)
Augusta Fox Bronner was born. Bronner and her husband, William Healy, were instrumental in founding the first child guidance clinic, the Juvenile Psychopathic Institute, in Chicago in 1909.

October 6, 1881   (416)
The preface to the first book devoted specifically to child psychology, Wilhelm T. Preyer's *Die Seele des Kindes* (*The Mind of the Child*), was written.

October 13, 1881   (417)
Albert Edward Michotte was born. His focuses were perception, Gestalt psychology, and causality. Michotte's best remembered studies were ones in which the perception of causality was varied by systematic alterations in the relations between two moving bodies. Michotte believed that causality was not a product of learning but was directly perceived from the environment.

November 16, 1881   (418)
The trial of Charles Guiteau, assassin of President James Garfield, began. Guiteau's insanity defense was a cause célèbre of the day. Eight experts testified that he was insane. Fifteen others testified that he was sane, despite Guiteau's assertion that the murder was justified because God had ordered him to do it.

January 2, 1882   (419)
Jean-Martin Charcot was appointed to the newly created Chair of Nervous Diseases at the Salpêtrière, the first formal recognition of neurology as a separate medical discipline.

February 13, 1882   (420)
Jean-Martin Charcot presented "On the Various Nervous States Determined by Hypnotization in Hysterics" to the French Academy of Science in Paris.

March 30, 1882   (421)
Melanie Klein was born. Klein was an important child psychoanalyst who developed the technique of play therapy.

April 21, 1882   (422)
Percy Williams Bridgman was born. A Nobel laureate, Bridgman founded *operationism*, a branch of logical positivism.

May 1, 1882 (423)

G. Stanley Hall was appointed to the post of lecturer at Johns Hopkins University. He established the first research laboratory in psychology in the United States at Johns Hopkins University in 1883. Hall was given the title of Professor of Psychology and Pedagogics on April 7, 1884.

June 7, 1882 (424)

Josef Breuer treated "Anna O." for the last time. Soon afterward she was admitted to a sanitorium in Kreutzlingen, Switzerland. Records there show her far from cured of her symptoms.

June 27, 1882 (425)

Eduard Spranger was born. Spranger generated an early trait theory of personality that was based on religious, scientific, social, aesthetic, economic, and political types. In addition to these psychological elements, Spranger posited human physical and spiritual dimensions. He is considered a forerunner of humanistic psychology because of his spiritual emphasis.

July 2, 1882 (426)

Marie Bonaparte was born. Bonaparte used her wealth and influence to benefit Sigmund Freud and psychoanalysis. She paid the Nazis $4,824 to allow Freud to leave Austria in 1938.

July 12, 1882 (427)

"Anna O." was transferred from Josef Breuer's care to the Sanatorium Bellevue in Kreutzlingen, Switzerland.

August 3, 1882 (428)

Congress charged the secretary of the treasury with prohibiting the immigration of "lunatics, idiots, and people likely to become a public charge." On March 3, 1891, Congress added a $1,000 penalty for violations of this law.

October 4, 1882 (429)

James McKeen Cattell took hashish for the first time, in Baltimore. His diary records, "I have found a new world." Cattell experimented widely with drugs as a young man.

October 29, 1882 (430)

"Anna O." was discharged from the Bellevue Sanatorium in Kreutzlingen, Switzerland. She had been admitted on July 12, 1882, after 18 months of treatment by Josef Breuer that proved to be a cornerstone of the psychoanalytic method but not a satisfactory end of Anna's psychological problems.

November 18, 1882 (431)

Josef Breuer first told Sigmund Freud about "Anna O.'s" cathartic "talking cure," 5 months after Breuer's final visit with Anna O. Freud made the cathartic method the foundation of psychodynamic therapy.

February 9, 1883 (432)

The first issue of the "new series" of the journal *Science* was published. This series has continued to the present day. The journal was financially supported by Alexander Graham Bell and Bell's father-in-law, Gardiner Greene Hubbard, and edited by Samuel H. Scudder.

February 25, 1883 (433)

Herbert Woodrow was born. Woodrow's interests were in developmental and clinical psychology, with special attention given to individual differences in mental abilities. APA President, 1941.

February 26, 1883 (434)

Erich R. Jaensch was born. Jaensch was a German psychologist who is best known for his studies of eidetic imagery. This work was later corrupted by shaping it to the requirements of Nazi ideology. Jaensch published hundreds of articles on visual and spatial perception.

March 3, 1883 (435)

Sir Cyril Burt was born. Burt was the first psychologist to be knighted by a British monarch (1946). His work on mental tests, educational psychology, and factor analysis was well known. Charges that he fabricated or altered data in studies of kinship patterns of intelligence have tarnished his record.

March 8, 1883 (436)

The first formal psychology research laboratory in the United States was founded. The trustees of Johns Hopkins University allocated $250 for space and equipment for G. Stanley Hall's use. Interestingly, campus politics led the trustees to prohibit Hall from adopting the title *laboratory* for the facility.

April 24, 1883 (437)

Stanley D. Porteus was born. Porteus was the first practicing psychologist in Australia. His Porteus Maze Test, developed for testing children with retardation, was one of the first attempts at a nonverbal test of practical intelligence.

May 7, 1883 (438)

Mabel Fernald was born. Her work was in the area of mental deficiency, imagery, and memory.

May 23, 1883 (439)

Ivan Pavlov received the MD degree at Russia's Military-Medical Academy. His doctoral experiments were on the augmentor nerves of the heart.

November 20, 1883 (440)

William James wrote to the trustees of Harvard University to ask for a small room and $300 for a psychology research laboratory. The trustees allocated funds but did not dedicate space until two rooms in Lawrence Hall were assigned in the spring of 1885. James had earlier (1875) founded a demonstration laboratory to accompany his course on the "new" physiological psychology.

November 21, 1883 (441)

James McKeen Cattell reported for his first day of work gathering data in Wilhelm Wundt's laboratory.

January 26, 1884 (442)

Edward Sapir was born. Sapir was an anthropologist whose work related culture, language, and personality.

April 7, 1884 (443)

Bronislaw Malinowski was born. Malinowski's studies in cultural anthropology contributed to the psychological appreciation of the importance of social influences on behavior and moral judgment.

April 7, 1884 (444)

G. Stanley Hall was given the title of Professor of Psychology and Pedagogics by the trustees of Johns Hopkins University.

April 22, 1884 (445)

Otto Rank was born. Rank was an early and close associate of Freud. He extended principles of psychoanalysis to art, creativity, and myth. His emphasis on the birth trauma as the cause of anxiety later separated Rank from the mainstream of Freudian thought.

April 22, 1884 (446)

Frederick Wells was born. Wells was a clinical psychologist who instituted the first mental hospital internships for clinical psychologists, at the Boston Psychopathic Hospital in 1913. He wrote some of the first articles about personal adjustment and authored a revision of the Army Alpha Test (1941).

May 24, 1884 (447)

Clark Leonard Hull was born. Hull is most frequently identified with his hypothetico–deductive learning theory, an attempt at a mathematically rigorous explanation of the causes of behavior, but his work in aptitude testing, hypnosis and suggestibility, and concept acquisition was also influential. APA President, 1936.

May 25, 1884 (448)
Truman Lee Kelley was born. Kelly was a statistician and psychometrician with special interests in factor analysis, canonical correlation, multifactor theories of intelligence, and educational testing.

August 12, 1884 (449)
Lucile Dooley was born. Dooley was both a psychologist and psychiatrist. She specialized in the psychology of women and bipolar disorders.

August 18, 1884 (450)
Edward K. Strong, Jr., was born. Strong is known for his work in the area of vocational interest testing. His Strong Vocational Interest Blank (SVIB) was published in 1943 and continues to be a commonly used vocational interest inventory. The SVIB compares the examinee's responses with those of successful practitioners of various professions.

August 31, 1884 (451)
George A. L. Sarton was born. Sarton has been called the "father of the history of science." Among his many books, *Introduction to the History and Philosophy of Science* (1921) and *The Study of the History of Science* (1936) are representative works.

September 29, 1884 (452)
James McKeen Cattell brought a Remington Model 4 typewriter to Leipzig. Wilhelm Wundt, fascinated, obtained one for himself and increased his already prodigious scholarly output.

October 1, 1884 (453)
David Katz was born. Nativistic themes were prominent in Katz's studies of color perception and lent support to early Gestalt theories. He also conducted phenomenological studies of touch and published a book on child psychology that was based on conversations with children. Katz and Hungarian psychologist Géza Révész were cofounders of *Acta Psychologica*.

October 9, 1884 (454)
Helene Deutch was born. Deutch was instrumental in founding the Vienna Psychoanalytic Institute in 1925 and was its director for the first 10 years.

October 25, 1884 (455)
James McKeen Cattell presented his dissertation proposal to Wundt. The title was "An Essay on Psychometry, or the Time Taken Up by Simple Mental Processes." Wundt's legendary assessment was "Ganz Amerikanisch," meaning "typically American."

November 8, 1884 (456)

Hermann Rorschach was born. Rorschach developed the famous inkblot-style projective personality test. The test is widely used despite questionable validity. The test is so well-known that it has become a popular icon for all of clinical psychology. Constructed in 1911, the test was not published until 1921. Rorschach's fraternity nickname, "Klex," means "inkblot" in German.

November 16, 1884 (457)

Rudolf Pintner was born. Pintner combined interests in mental measurements and education of people with disabilities. His performance assessment measures supplied half of the items of the World War I Army Beta Test.

December 18, 1884 (458)

The organizing meeting of the American Society for Psychical Research was held. William James was instrumental in founding the organization.

January 8, 1885 (459)

The American Society for Psychical Research was founded. The first president was Simon Newcomb, an astronomer at Johns Hopkins University.

January 21, 1885 (460)

The term *psychopath* first appeared in print in its modern meaning. An article in the *Pall Mall Gazette* said, in part, "beside his own person and his own interests, nothing is sacred to the psychopath."

February 15, 1885 (461)

Hans Henning was born. Henning's work was on the senses of smell and taste. He identified six primary scents and four primary tastes and identified chemical analogs of these primary perceptions.

March 29, 1885 (462)

Walter R. Miles was born. Miles studied human performance and adaptation to adverse conditions. His work on vision was responsible for the use of red lighting in World War II pilot night mission ready rooms. APA President, 1932; Society of Experimental Psychologists Warren Medal, 1947; American Psychological Foundation Gold Medal, 1962.

April 8, 1885 (463)

James McKeen Cattell completed running participants for his doctoral research on reaction times. Cattell studied under Wilhelm Wundt.

April 9, 1885 (464)

Rosa Katz, a developmental psychologist, was born. Her 1927 book, *Conversations With Children* (with David Katz), described "the child's world, the children's metaphysics, their dreams, their orientation in time, their categories of reality, and their magical thinking" from field observations, one of the first systematic applications of this method.

April 24, 1885 (465)

Alexander Bain toured Wilhelm Wundt's laboratory at the University of Leipzig. James McKeen Cattell, a graduate student at the time, was also present.

April 28, 1885 (466)

Karl Muenzinger was born. Muenzinger's careful experimental work with rats contributed many papers on learning that supported Edward Tolman's theory of purposive behaviorism.

June 5, 1885 (467)

Warder Clyde Allee was born. Allee's research focused on animal social behavior.

June 29, 1885 (468)

Philosopher Paul Janet proposed to the Faculty of Letters of the Sorbonne that its first course in experimental psychology be created and that Théodule Ribot be appointed to teach the course. Ribot's appointment was confirmed on July 31, 1885, and instruction began in December.

September 16, 1885 (469)

Karen Horney was born. Horney's neo-Freudian personality theory emphasized the role of childhood strategies for the reduction of basic anxiety as a precursor to adult neurosis. She promoted feminist goals in analytic theory as well as in the larger society. Horney founded the American Institute for Psychoanalysis.

October 11, 1885 (470)

Sigmund Freud left Vienna to study under Jean-Martin Charcot in Paris.

October 20, 1885 (471)

Freud first met Charcot during Freud's 20-week visit to Paris. The occasion was the first of Charcot's famous *Leçons du Mardi* at the Salpêtrière asylum. Over time, Freud grew close to Charcot and was strongly influenced by Charcot's demonstrations of the relation between hypnotic suggestibility and hysterical symptoms.

October 23, 1885 (472)

Albert T. Poffenberger was born. His interests were in applied and physiological psychology, with specialization in studies of gustation, fatigue, transfer of training, drug effects, and the speed of nervous conduction. He was the last president of the American Association for Applied Psychology and urged its unification with the APA to form the modern APA in 1945. APA President, 1935.

November 5, 1885 (473)

The first subject of Alfred Binet's studies of intelligence, his daughter Madeline, was born. Binet's first published account of infant development appeared in 1890.

November 30, 1885 (474)

Pierre Janet reported his first studies of "sleep provoked from a distance," later called hypnosis, to the Society of Physiological Psychology. A second group of studies was reported May 31, 1886.

December 25, 1885 (475)

In a Christmas letter to his parents from Leipzig, James McKeen Cattell, about to earn his PhD from Wilhelm Wundt, wrote, "I have, little as it is, done more for psychology than any American and have no reason to doubt that I can easily stand among the first in the future."

January 9, 1886 (476)

Edwin R. Guthrie was born. Guthrie's associationist theory of learning relied solely on contiguity of stimulus and response to form learned sets in one learning trial. APA President, 1945; American Psychological Foundation Gold Medal, 1958.

March 1, 1886 (477)

James McKeen Cattell passed his doctoral examinations at the University of Leipzig under Wundt.

March 18, 1886 (478)

Kurt Koffka was born. Koffka, recognized as one of the founders of Gestalt psychology, presented a complete statement of the theory in his book, *Principles of Gestalt Psychology* (1935). He applied Gestalt notions to development, learning, and innate behavior.

April 14, 1886 (479)

Edward C. Tolman was born. Tolman's "purposive behaviorism" merged cognitive elements such as expectations of reinforcement and cognitive maps into behavioral learning theory. Tolman won national admiration during the McCarthy era by organizing a protest against a state-mandated faculty loyalty oath. APA President, 1937; APA Distinguished Scientific Contribution Award, 1957.

April 25, 1886 (480)

Sigmund Freud opened his private medical practice at Rathausstrasse 7 in Vienna.

April 30, 1886 (481)

Graduation ceremonies were held for students of the first American training course for mental institution attendants. The course was conducted at Buffalo State Hospital, New York.

May 25, 1886   (482)
Leta Stetter Hollingworth was born. Hollingworth studied the nature, assessment, and treatment of mental retardation and giftedness in children. Her book *The Psychology of Subnormal Children* (1920) is an early classic in that field. Hollingworth was largely responsible for founding the American Association of Clinical Psychologists (1917).

June 13, 1886   (483)
Ludwig II, the psychotic king of Bavaria, jumped off a bridge into the Lake of Starnberg with his psychiatrist, Bernard von Gudden. Both men drowned. This obviously was before psychiatry learned to cope with transference.

August 6, 1886   (484)
Florence L. Goodenough was born. Goodenough was a child psychologist best known for the development of the Draw-A-Man Test. She was active in studies of intelligence, taking the position that intelligence is relatively fixed across the childhood years.

August 17, 1886   (485)
The doctoral dissertation of Harry Kirke Wolfe was approved by Wilhelm Wundt and others at the University of Leipzig. Wolfe was the second American, after Cattell, to earn a degree under Wundt. His dissertation topic was memory for tones. Wolfe returned to the United States, where he founded the psychology program at the University of Nebraska.

September 4, 1886   (486)
Christian Ruckmick was born. Ruckmick's research touched on the physiology of hearing, emotion, the galvanic skin response, and rhythm. In addition to his academic posts, Ruckmick was a sales manager for the Stoelting Company instrument manufacturing firm and Minister for Education in Ethiopia.

September 6, 1886   (487)
Edgar John Rubin was born. Rubin was a Danish Gestalt psychologist who invented the famous "vase/two faces" figure created by an ambiguous figure–ground relation. President, 10th International Congress of Psychology.

September 13, 1886   (488)
Sigmund Freud married Martha Bernays in Wandsbeck, Austria.

October 15, 1886   (489)
Upon returning to Vienna from Paris, Sigmund Freud gave his first public lecture on Charcot's proof of hysteria in males. Ridiculed by Viennese medical circles, Freud set out to find an actual case to present to the medical society.

October 20, 1886 (490)

Sir Frederick Bartlett was born. Bartlett studied the effects of prior experience on learning and memory. He was the first to hold the title of Professor of Experimental Psychology at Cambridge University and was knighted for his work in 1948.

October 23, 1886 (491)

Edwin Garrigues Boring was born. Boring worked in the areas of sensation, perception, and cognition, but he is best known as a teacher and historian of psychology. His book *A History of Experimental Psychology* has been a standard text and reference work since its publication in 1929. APA President, 1928; American Psychological Foundation Gold Medal, 1959.

November 20, 1886 (492)

Karl von Frisch was born. Von Frisch is best known for his ethological studies of communicative "dances" in honeybees, for which he won the Nobel prize in 1973.

November 26, 1886 (493)

Franziska Baumgarten-Tramer was born. Baumgarten-Tramer's contributions were in industrial, social, and developmental psychology.

January 21, 1887 (494)

Wolfgang Köhler was born. Köhler is best known for his studies of insightful problem solving in apes and his role in shaping the course of Gestalt psychology. He won the APA Distinguished Scientific Contribution Award in 1956, the first year it was awarded. APA President, 1959.

January 29, 1887 (495)

René Spitz was born. Spitz did landmark studies in orphanages, finding that environmental deprivation produced underdeveloped, apathetic infants, a condition he called "marasmus" or "hospitalism." He also studied the emergence of the smiling response in infants.

March 29, 1887 (496)

George T. Ladd's book *Elements of Physiological Psychology* was published.

April 11, 1887 (497)

Edward Alexander Bott was born. Bott's research concentrated on perception, rehabilitation, and military personnel assessment. He is best known, however, as an architect of organized psychology in Canada. He was a founder and the first president (1940) of the Canadian Psychological Association (CPA) and the first fellow of the CPA.

May 29, 1887   (498)
Louis L. Thurstone was born. Thurstone was an eminent psychometrician who brought mathematical methods to bear on problems of attitude scaling, factor analysis, psychophysics, and intelligence. APA President, 1933.

June 4, 1887   (499)
Samuel Fernberger was born. Fernberger was a psychophysicist who wrote several classic papers in the field. Other contributions included study of facial expression of emotion, professional psychology, and the history of psychology.

June 5, 1887   (500)
Ruth Fulton Benedict was born. Benedict was a cultural anthropologist whose writing on culture and personality has been important to psychologists. She presented evidence for cultural relativism in definitions of deviant behavior.

June 15, 1887   (501)
The first annual meeting of the Society of the Sigma Xi, the science honor society, was held. The first president was Henry S. Williams.

July 28, 1887   (502)
The Alabama Supreme Court decided *Parsons v. State*. The case established an important precedent in the insanity defense: that a person who could judge right from wrong was still not guilty if mental illness rendered him or her powerless to avoid the crime. This is sometimes known as the "irresistible impulse rule" in the history of the insanity defense.

August 13, 1887   (503)
This was the date of last entry in James McKeen Cattell's European diary, begun when he was a student on tour on July 13, 1880. Cattell cited his appointment to the faculty of the University of Pennsylvania and his marriage to Josephine Owen as "the two great events of the year."

September 30, 1887   (504)
The *American Journal of Psychology* was first published. The publisher and editor was G. Stanley Hall.

September 30, 1887   (505)
James Mark Baldwin's book *Elementary Psychology and Education* was published.

October 20, 1887   (506)
Karl Dallenbach was born. Dallenbach was a faithful student of Edward B. Titchener, whose many papers focused on sensation, perception, memory, and attention. He was the editor of the *American Journal of Psychology* for 42 years. American Psychological Foundation Gold Medal, 1966.

December 3, 1887 (507)

Carl Murchison was born. Murchison founded and edited many American psychology journals, including the *Journal of General Psychology* (1927) and the *Journal of Social Psychology* (1930). In the 1930s, he edited comprehensive handbooks of child psychology (1931), general experimental psychology (1934), and social psychology (1935).

January 9, 1888 (508)

James McKeen Cattell delivered his first university lecture, at Bryn Mawr College.

February 28, 1888 (509)

Francis Galton was measured at his own Anthropometric Laboratory. Some sample measurements include a right-hand squeeze strength of 80 lb (36 kg), head breadth of 6.15 in. (15.62 cm), and a 4.4-in. (11.2-cm) length of the middle finger of his left hand.

March 4, 1888 (510)

Howard Long was born. Long, an early African American psychologist, earned his PhD under G. Stanley Hall in 1916. He published several research monographs in educational psychology and was assistant superintendent for educational research for the Washington, DC, public schools for 23 years.

April 3, 1888 (511)

G. Stanley Hall was offered the first presidency of Clark University. The university opened its doors on October 2, 1889. Hall's first faculty included Franz Boas, Henry Donaldson, Edmund Sanford, and William H. Burnham.

April 22, 1888 (512)

Edmund Jacobson was born. Jacobson is best known for his methods of progressive relaxation, based on his instruments that measured muscle potentials in microvolts. He studied the covert behavior accompanying mental activity and developed what now is known as *biofeedback*. He was the founder of quantitative electromyography.

April 30, 1888 (513)

Maud Merrill James was born. As Maud Merrill, she was the coauthor, with Lewis Terman, of the 1937 revision of the Stanford-Binet test, an 11-year project. The test had two forms, initialed L and M after the first names of the collaborators. She was a child clinical psychologist, juvenile court consultant, and expert on delinquency.

April 30, 1888 (514)

John Dashiell was born. Dashiell began the psychology laboratories at the University of North Carolina and Wake Forest University. His own work was on perception, fatigue and efficiency, and learning. APA President, 1938; American Psychological Foundation Gold Medal, 1960.

August 8, 1888   (515)
Jacob Robert Kantor was born. Kantor was a prominent systematic psychologist who organized scientific values into a coherent system of psychology. For Kantor, both prescientific mentalistic issues and physiological events were alien to a science of behavior.

August 11, 1888   (516)
James McKeen Cattell was measured at Francis Galton's Anthropometric Laboratory in London. Among other measurements were an 89-lb (40-kg) right-hand squeeze and an upper limit of hearing of 19 kHz.

October 8, 1888   (517)
Ernst Kretschmer was born. Kretschmer's constitutional theory of personality classified people into asthenic, athletic, pyknic, and displastic types. He thought that bipolar disorder was associated with the pyknic type and schizophrenia with the asthenic and athletic types.

December 21, 1888   (518)
Anna Berliner was born. Berliner was Wilhelm Wundt's only female doctoral student. Berliner's specialties were visual perception, experimental optometry, and advertising psychology. She introduced applied experimental psychology to Japan during a 10-year sojourn there. She was forced to leave Germany in 1936 and finished her career in the United States.

December 28, 1888   (519)
Sidney Pressey was born. Pressey was an educational and developmental psychologist who was also active in professional organizations. He patented a machine for administering multiple-choice intelligence test items (1928) that later became the first teaching machine.

January 1, 1889   (520)
James McKeen Cattell was made professor of psychology at the University of Pennsylvania, becoming the first professor with that specific title in an American university.

March 13, 1889   (521)
Harvey Lehmann was born. Lehmann concentrated on studies of play in children and studies of causes of variation in the age of maximum achievement of different skills.

March 21, 1889   (522)
Dean A. Worcester was born. As an educational psychologist, Worcester's interests were in measurement and services for children of high intellectual abilities. He established the first psychology laboratory in New Mexico.

March 22, 1889 (523)

Walter S. Hunter was born. A comparative psychologist, Hunter used maze learning to investigate factors influencing behavior and invented the delayed reaction and double alternation tests for animals. He was also one of the founders of *Psychological Abstracts* (1937). APA President, 1931.

April 25, 1889 (524)

Delaware passed the first state law in which the state assumed responsibility for the care of people with mental illness and mental retardation.

April 26, 1889 (525)

Leonard Thompson Troland was born. Troland had many scientific and technical interests. In psychology, he published on optics, vision, emotion, and psycho-physiology. He was co-inventor of the Technicolor film process, and the basic unit of retinal illumination is named for him. The National Academy of Sciences' Troland Award is given annually for psychological research.

May 1, 1889 (526)

Freud began his treatment of "Emmy von N.," a case that resulted in the development of the cathartic method.

May 2, 1889 (527)

Edgar Doll was born. Doll's work in assessment extended from prison populations to children. He developed the Vineland Social Maturity Scale.

May 15, 1889 (528)

Charles-Édouard Brown-Séquard, a 72-year-old professor of medicine at the College de France, injected himself with an extract of guinea pig testicles. A month later he announced to the Societé de Biologie that he had found a drug to rejuvenate elderly men. Although Brown-Séquard had experienced a placebo effect, his report eventually led to the discovery of sex hormones.

August 6, 1889 (529)

The International Congress of Psychology first met, in Paris. Jean-Martin Charcot served as president. This meeting was titled the International Congress of Physiological Psychology; the present title was adopted in 1896 at the third congress.

August 8, 1889 (530)

The First International Congress on Hypnotism began in Paris. Attendees included Jean-Martin Charcot, Alfred Binet, Hippolyte Bernheim, Sigmund Freud, Joseph Babinski, Joseph Delboeuf, Ambroise-Auguste Liébeault, and William James.

September 5, 1889 (531)

Volume 1 of James M. Baldwin's *Handbook of Psychology* was published.

September 17, 1889 (532)

Sarah Carolyn Fisher was born. Fisher took a structuralist approach to her writing on systems of psychology, values and attitudes in family relations, and social psychology.

October 23, 1889 (533)

Frieda Fromm-Reichmann was born. Founder of the Psychoanalytic Institute of Southwest Germany, Fromm-Reichmann was the model for the therapist in the book *I Never Promised You a Rose Garden*, by a former patient, Hannah Green.

November 15, 1889 (534)

The first of a series of articles by Joseph Delboeuf appeared in *Revue de Belgique*, describing Pierre Janet's use of hypnosis to remove hysterical symptoms. The articles might have influenced Freud's treatment of "Emmy von N."

December 13, 1889 (535)

Stephan Polyak was born. Polyak was a prominent anatomist of the vertebrate visual system, with special attention given to the structure of the retina.

January 8, 1890 (536)

William James's academic title at Harvard University was changed to professor of psychology. James began his career at Harvard as an instructor (1872) and assistant professor (1876) of physiology. His title was later changed to assistant professor (1880) and professor (1885) of philosophy. On October 31, 1897, his title reverted back to professor of philosophy.

January 11, 1890 (537)

The first psychological laboratory at a Canadian university was inaugurated at the University of Toronto by James Mark Baldwin. Baldwin was at Toronto from 1889 to 1893 and was serving that appointment when he participated as a founder of the APA in 1892.

February 11, 1890 (538)

Heinz Werner was born. Werner's work in developmental psychology was best known, but he also contributed to the psychology of aesthetics and music, perception, and mental retardation. His *Comparative Psychology of Mental Development* elucidated his "orthogenetic" general laws of development.

February 17, 1890 (539)

Sir Ronald Fisher was born. Fisher was an agricultural statistician who developed the analysis of variance and coined the terms *null hypothesis*, *degrees of freedom*, and *randomized block design*. The analysis of variance F ratio is named for the initial of Fisher's name.

March 18, 1890   (540)
Carl Warden was born. Warden wrote extensively on comparative psychology and introduced simple mazes and the obstruction box into animal learning studies.

April 26, 1890   (541)
Harold E. Burtt was born. Burtt was a prominent teacher and author in the fields of industrial, consumer, legal, and aviation psychology. His research touched on aviator selection, lie detection, advertising effectiveness, and industrial efficiency.

May 1, 1890   (542)
Edna Heidbreder was born. Heidbreder's expertise in systematic psychology was reflected in her book *Seven Psychologies*, a widely used text. Other work included a series of studies of thinking. Heidbreder was active in many psychological associations.

May 20, 1890   (543)
Catherine Cox Miles was born. Miles is best known for her collaboration with Lewis Terman on longitudinal studies of the gifted and studies of gender differences in personality.

June 7, 1890   (544)
Karl S. Lashley was born. Lashley's theory of "equipotentiality" sprang from studies of brain extirpation that indicated that learning was more influenced by the amount of tissue removed than by the location of the tissue. APA President, 1929.

June 19, 1890   (545)
Abraham A. Roback was born. Roback was known for his writing on the psychology of character and as a historian of psychology, especially for books on American psychology, behaviorism, and psychiatry.

August 22, 1890   (546)
Floyd H. Allport was born. Allport was an early social psychologist who coined the term *social facilitation*. His work in social facilitation and conformity represented some of the first experiments in social behavior. APA Distinguished Scientific Contribution Award, 1965; American Psychological Foundation Gold Medal, 1968.

August 23, 1890   (547)
Lillian Gertrude Portenier was born. Her interests were in mental testing, mental health, and child psychology. Portenier served as president of the International Council of Psychologists and, at the University of Wyoming, was a central figure in state and regional psychological organizations.

August 30, 1890 (548)

The nation's oldest federal mental hospital, St. Elizabeth's Hospital in Washington, DC, was authorized by Congress to purchase additional land for expansion. The land acquired was known as the Oxon Hill Manor and overlooked the Potomac River about 3 miles (5 km) from the hospital.

September 9, 1890 (549)

Kurt Lewin was born. Lewin's field theory applied the principles of Gestalt perceptual theory to social, personality, and organizational psychology. Lewin and his students were pioneers of experimental social psychology and produced studies of cognitive dissonance, leadership, group cooperation and competition, conflict resolution, and group dynamics.

September 13, 1890 (550)

Volume 1 of William James's *Principles of Psychology* was published.

September 29, 1890 (551)

The Library of Congress received its two copies of the first volume of William James's *Principles of Psychology*.

October 1, 1890 (552)

Mary W. Calkins overcame Harvard University's prohibition against female students and was allowed to enroll in a physiological psychology class taught by William James and a class on Hegel taught by Josiah Royce. Calkins later became president of the APA (1905).

October 3, 1890 (553)

Volume 2 of William James's *Principles of Psychology* was published.

December 25, 1890 (554)

Gregory Zilboorg was born. A psychoanalyst, Zilboorg wrote articles and books on a variety of topics, including the psychology of suicide.

January 9, 1891 (555)

The first issue of G. Stanley Hall's *Pedagogical Seminary*, later titled the *Journal of Genetic Psychology*, was published.

January 22, 1891 (556)

Franz Alexander was born. Alexander and his Chicago Institute of Psychoanalysis promoted the expansion of psychoanalytic theory and practice to include important social, hereditary, and environmental factors. He helped to establish the field of psychosomatic medicine.

January 26, 1891 (557)

Wilder Penfield was born. Penfield was a neurosurgeon who carried out classic studies of the neurology of epilepsy. He also discovered that electrical stimulation of portions of the cortex could evoke vivid experiences of past events.

August 17, 1891 (558)

Abraham Kardiner was born. Kardiner was a cofounder of the first psychoanalytic training school in the United States, the New York Psychoanalytical Institute (1930). He applied psychoanalytic principles to cross-cultural studies.

October 19, 1891 (559)

Lois Meek Stolz was born. Stoltz was a developmental psychologist interested in early childhood education. She was a founder and first president of the National Association for Nursery Education (1929). At the time, there were only 80 nursery schools in the United States. She later helped to establish the Oakland Growth Study and developed indexes of adolescent growth.

October 23, 1891 (560)

Johann F. Herbart's *Textbook in Psychology* (Smith translation) was published in the United States.

October 27, 1891 (561)

The first of William James's Talks to Teachers was delivered at noon in the Upper Dane Hall Laboratory of Harvard University. There were 10 lectures in this series, sponsored by the Department of Pedagogy. The lecture series was repeated around the United States during the ensuing years and was published as a book in 1899.

December 14, 1891 (562)

William James's book *Psychology: Briefer Course* was published. The book served as a university text for decades and is still on most reading lists of great books.

II

1892–1919
THE FIRST GENERATION

The details of the founding (Entry 573) of the American Psychological Association (APA) and its first annual meeting (Entry 582) in 1892 are reported in many sources. At the second annual meeting in 1893 the first women members were admitted (Entry 601), although one of them, Mary Whiton Calkins, could not persuade Harvard University to recognize her status as a graduate student at that same time (Entries 552, 609, and 616).

The meetings of the APA expanded during the early years (Entries 656 and 1002), but expansion was accompanied by division, a continuing characteristic of the APA. The philosophical psychologists, being carried into increasingly unfamiliar territory by the new organization, were the first to break away (Entries 682 and 727). Regional psychological associations in the Midwest (Entries 729 and 1278), Southeast (Entries 774 and 798), and East (Entries 747, 1322, and 1460) were formed, complementing the APA. Finally, clinical psychologists left the APA, formed the American Association of Clinical Psychologists (Entry 1052), and later rejoined the APA as its Clinical Division (Entry 1091). The APA has always served as a center of gravity for scientist and practitioner psychologists, but the orbits of these two groups have sometimes diverged widely.

At the turn of the century, the proliferation of psychology courses and laboratories on university campuses prepared a route to careers for the first students to be born when psychology was an established discipline. The first generation of students trained as psychologists was equal to the opportunities provided by the open field. Scientific psychologists such as J. P. Guilford (Entry 640), J. J. Gibson (Entry 772), D. O. Hebb (Entry 786), Ernest R. Hilgard (Entry 787), Harry Harlow (Entry 812), S. S. Stevens (Entry 834), Kenneth Spence (Entry 848), B. F. Skinner (Entry 776), Neal Miller (Entry 894), Eleanor J. Gibson (Entry 925), Roger Sperry (Entry 966), Jerome Bruner (Entry 997), Eleanor Maccoby (Entry 1040), Leon Festinger (Entry 1082), and William K. Estes (Entry 1083) were all born in this period of less than three decades.

The practical applications of psychology have been promoted by others born during this short period. Anne Anastasi (Entry 877), Paul Fitts (Entry 946), Ernest J. McCormick (Entry 937), Kenneth Clark (Entry 981), Mamie Clark (Entry 1049), Nicholas Hobbs (Entry 986), Lee J. Cronbach (Entry 1011), Harry Stack Sullivan (Entry 565), Norma E. Cutts (Entry 576), Starke R. Hathaway (Entry 760), David Wechsler (Entry 623), Albert Ellis (Entry 968), and Gordon Derner (Entry 987) were among those to later mold the direction of applied psychology.

Many significant first events in the areas of applied and clinical psychology took place around the turn of the century. The first public school class for students with mental retardation was established (Entry 636), Binet and Simon's intelligence test (Entry 806) and Terman's Stanford revision (Entry 1046) appeared, and the first clients were seen in a psychological clinic (Entries 635, 637, and 756). The practice of psychology was promoted by the first mental health organization (Entry 867), the first psychologist in a military hospital (Entry 1059), and the first federal military rehabilitation program (Entry 1064). Each of these "firsts" has become an entire field of study and practice within the lifetimes of its earliest workers.

During this century two global wars stimulated the growth of scientific and applied psychology. In the first days of World War I, APA President Robert Yerkes volunteered the services of psychologists and gathered a committee of national leaders to organize the efforts of psychology in support of the American war effort (Entries 1028 and 1036). One outcome of the psychologists' involvement was the creation of the Army Alpha and Army Beta Tests (Entry 1051), mental and performance tests that were the forerunners of modern military and industrial aptitude classification instruments. Data from the Army Alpha Test also showed that racial differences in test scores varied across geographical areas of the country, providing evidence for the importance of environmental determinants of intellectual functioning at a time when a belief in genetic determinants provided a rationale for discriminatory social practices.

A more remote consequence of the war was the creation of the Psychological Corporation, publishers of psychological assessment instruments since 1921 (Entry 1119). The Psychological Corporation was founded by James McKeen Cattell with funds won from Columbia University in a suit following Cattell's dismissal from the faculty for his pacifism during the war (Entry 1048).

Finally, the early decades of the century were marked by contention between the great "schools" of psychology, explanatory systems that attempted to encompass all behavior. The struggle between the structural psychology of E. B. Titchener (e.g., Entries 298, 630, 771, and 777) and the functional psychology of William James, James Angell, and others (e.g., Entries 163, 311, and 343) dissolved into more restricted efforts by psychoanalysts (e.g., Entries 408, 572, 618, 680, 866, 899, and 967), behaviorists (e.g., Entries 755, 956, and 1090), and Gestalt psychologists born before the turn of the century (Entries 397, 478, 494, and 549) and not to influence American psychology until the World War II years.

January 18, 1892 (563)
Edmund Clark Sanford's *Laboratory Course in Psychology* was published.

February 8, 1892 (564)
Selig Hecht was born. Hecht discovered the processes of decomposition and regeneration of photopigments in the retina that transduce light energy into neural impulses. His work serves as a foundation of modern vision theory.

February 21, 1892 (565)
Harry Stack Sullivan was born. Sullivan's theory of personality stressed the social origins and social expression of personality. He asserted that personality is a quality not of an individual but of a relation between individuals. He developed a social milieu therapy for the treatment of schizophrenia.

February 28, 1892 (566)
Calvin P. Stone was born. Stone was a comparative and physiological psychologist who studied innate behavior, learning, and the effects of electroconvulsive shock in animals. He also offered the first regular U.S. university course on Freudian psychology at Stanford University in 1923. APA President, 1942.

March 9, 1892   (567)
Raymond Wheeler was born. Wheeler defended and modified Gestalt psychology.
With F. Theodore Perkins, he demonstrated stimulus relational set learning in
lower animals. Wheeler and Perkins's *Principles of Mental Development* (1932) was
a widely used educational psychology text in its day.

March 10, 1892   (568)
Samuel Renshaw was born. The Renshaw Training System for Aircraft and Ship
Recognition earned Renshaw an award from the U.S. Navy. His research was in
learning, perception, and memory. He wrote all 23 volumes of the journal *Visual
Psychology*. Renshaw helped found the Midwestern Psychological Association.

March 12, 1892   (569)
James M. Baldwin's *Psychology Applied to the Art of Teaching* was published.

May 24, 1892   (570)
William Crozier was born. Crozier's work with many species of lower animals led
to explanations of behavior based on tropisms, or innate orienting responses.

May 26, 1892   (571)
Paul Thomas Young was born. Young studied hedonic processes in behavior and
endeavored to give objective reference and experimental validity to the concept.
His research on preference showed the effect of experience in modifying accept-
ability. APA Distinguished Scientific Contribution Award, 1965.

June 29, 1892   (572)
Sigmund Freud first referred to the unconscious and to unconscious motivation in
a letter to Josef Breuer. Freud referred to a "second state of consciousness" that
participated in a "principle of constancy." He concluded that "the psychical experiences forming the context of hysterical attacks . . . are all of them impressions
which have failed to find adequate discharge."

July 8, 1892   (573)
The APA was organized in G. Stanley Hall's study at Clark University. There is
no precise roll of those in attendance, but 26 men had accepted membership in
the new organization and 5 more were invited at this organizational meeting.

July 18, 1892   (574)
Lightner Witmer passed his doctoral oral examination at the University of Leipzig
under Wilhelm Wundt, receiving the grade of magna cum laude. The degree was
formally awarded on March 29, 1893. Witmer was a founder of the APA and an
originator of modern clinical psychology.

August 28, 1892   (575)
Henry Turner was born. Turner first described the characteristics resulting from a
single X chromosome, affecting 1 in 2,000 females. Turner's syndrome is marked

by an absence of secondary sex characteristics, stunted growth, and webbing of the neck. Turner's syndrome, first described in 1938, is often cited in introductory psychology texts in discussions of inheritance.

September 23, 1892   (576)
Norma Estelle Cutts was born. Cutts was a leader in special education and school psychology, devoting her professional life to the improvement of services to children in the schools. She wrote *Practical School Discipline and Mental Hygiene* in 1941, several guides for parents in the 1950s, and resource books on disorderly students (1957) and individual differences in students (1960).

September 26, 1892   (577)
Honorio Delgado was born. Delgado introduced psychoanalysis and German concepts of experimental psychology to Latin America.

October 1, 1892   (578)
Horace English was born. English published many studies in educational psychology, learning, and memory, but he is best known for *A Comprehensive Dictionary of Psychological and Psychoanalytic Terms*, written with his wife, Ava C. English.

October 24, 1892   (579)
W. Horsley Gantt was born. Gantt was an American student of Ivan Pavlov who translated Pavlov's work into English and applied his methods to psychiatry.

November 8, 1892   (580)
Therese Friedman Benedek was born. Benedek was a psychoanalyst who specialized in the psychology of women, especially the physiology of the sexual cycle. Her book, *Psychosexual Functions in Women*, is a classic.

November 24, 1892   (581)
Franklin Fearing was born. Fearing was a physiological psychologist interested in the vestibular senses. His later teaching and writing focused on the social psychology of mass communication.

December 27, 1892   (582)
The first annual meeting of the APA was held at the University of Pennsylvania. The first address, given by G. Stanley Hall, was "History and Prospects of Experimental Psychology in America." The first annual budget was $63.

March 11, 1893   (583)
Lipot Szondi was born. Szondi developed a theory of the genetic origin of personality. His projective test of personality was based on the proposition that one would be attracted to the face of a person whose genetic type and, therefore, personality was similar to one's own.

April 11, 1893 (584)

Franz Brentano left the Roman Catholic priesthood. Brentano's empirical philosophy had put increasing distance between him and the church and finally led to an open split.

April 18, 1893 (585)

Edward Robinson was born. Robinson was a functionalist whose work on retroactive interference and transfer of learning was well-known.

May 9, 1893 (586)

William Moulton Marston was born. Marston was a colorful student of Hugo Münsterberg whose interest in the physiology of deception led to the development of the first "lie detector." Moulton promoted his machine tirelessly, even offering to test Bruno Hauptmann, the accused Lindberg baby kidnapper. Under the pseudonym of Charles Moulton, Marston created the comic strip "Wonder Woman."

May 13, 1893 (587)

Henry A. Murray was born. Murray assisted Morton Prince in founding of the Harvard Psychological Clinic (1927). His book *Explorations in Personality* (1938) was an early empirical study of personality. Murray developed his personality theory of needs and presses through work with the Thematic Apperception Test. APA Distinguished Scientific Contribution Award, 1961.

May 22, 1893 (588)

Coleman Roberts Griffith was born. Griffith was the first American psychologist to study the psychological aspects of sport, beginning in 1918 at the University of Illinois with observations of psychological factors involved in basketball and football. He directed the first athletic research laboratory in the United States (1925).

June 6, 1893 (589)

The first meeting of the American Medico-Psychological Association was held in Chicago. Judson B. Andrews was president. The group had been named the Association of Medical Superintendents of American Institutions for the Insane since 1844 and would become the American Psychiatric Association in 1913.

June 13, 1893 (590)

John E. Anderson was born. Anderson's research interests were primarily in experimental animal and child psychology. At the University of Minnesota he was director of the child welfare institute. APA President, 1943.

July 8, 1893 (591)

Fritz Perls was born. Perls was the founder, with Laura Perls, of Gestalt therapy, a humanistic psychotherapy popular in the 1960s. His book *Gestalt Therapy: Excitement and Growth in the Human Personality* (1951, with Ralph F. Hefferline and Paul Goodman) described the basis of his approach.

July 22, 1893 (592)

Karl A. Menninger was born. Menninger, with his father and brother, founded the Menninger Clinic in Topeka, Kansas. The clinic pioneered the use of psychologists in multidisciplinary psychiatric teams, and Menninger was a strong advocate for the independent professional standing of psychologists. He also developed a standardized battery of psychological assessment instruments.

July 29, 1893 (593)

Pierre Janet received his MD degree under Jean-Martin Charcot.

August 2, 1893 (594)

Psyche Cattell was born. A specialist in early childhood and measurement, Cattell constructed the Cattell Developmental Scales for measuring the mental abilities of young children. She was the founder and director of the Cattell School in Pennsylvania.

September 9, 1893 (595)

The *Wiener Medizinische Wochenschrift* (*Vienna Medical Weekly*) published Sigmund Freud's eulogy for Jean-Martin Charcot, who died on August 16, 1893. In the eulogy Freud likened Charcot's importance to that of Adam.

October 3, 1893 (596)

Clara Thompson was born. Thompson was a progressive figure in American psychoanalysis in the 1940s. She founded a training institute in 1943 that later became the William Alanson White Institute, which she headed until her death in 1958. She investigated the psychology of women, arriving at views that contradicted Freudian orthodoxy.

October 4, 1893 (597)

Edmund Clark Sanford's *Course in Experimental Psychology* was published. The text was one of the first laboratory manuals in American psychology.

October 16, 1893 (598)

G. Stanley Hall's *The Contents of Children's Minds on Entering School* was published. This was one of the first American books on child psychology and was based on data from questionnaires given to children.

December 11, 1893 (599)

The journal *Psychological Review* was first published. James McKeen Cattell and James Mark Baldwin were editors of the journal when it first appeared. This journal and three others were transferred to the APA by their owner, Howard C. Warren, by purchase and gift, in the years from 1925 to 1938.

December 20, 1893 (600)

Charlotte Malachowski Bühler was born. Bühler produced a humanistic theory of child development, the diary method of data collection, and several diagnostic instruments.

December 27, 1893 (601)

The second annual meeting of the APA was held at Columbia College. Mary Calkins and Christine Ladd-Franklin were elected to membership at this meeting. They were the first women members of the APA. The APA was the second American scientific society to admit women.

January 1, 1894 (602)

Jean Walker Macfarlane was born. Macfarlane directed the longitudinal Berkeley Guidance Study, begun in 1928. Major themes in her work were the variety of paths of normal development, complex interactions among factors influencing adjustment, and human resourcefulness.

January 27, 1894 (603)

Henry E. Garrett was born. Garrett's work was primarily in mental traits, learning, and mental organization. He served in editorial, consulting, and official capacities for many psychological associations. APA President, 1946.

February 20, 1894 (604)

Curt P. Richter was born. Richter studied human and animal behavior, with attention given to homeostatic mechanisms of motivation. APA Distinguished Scientific Contribution Award, 1957.

April 17, 1894 (605)

Rachel Stutsman Ball was born. Ball's contributions were in the fields of mental measurement of young children, personality development, and longitudinal studies of child development.

April 20, 1894 (606)

Carolyn Zachry was born. Zachry promoted the social adjustment and mental health missions of the schools, using psychological principles to accomplish those goals.

May 3, 1894 (607)

Phyllis Greenacre was born. Greenacre was a psychoanalyst with special interests in sublimation, transference, and fetishism.

June 23, 1894 (608)

Alfred C. Kinsey was born. Kinsey is best known for his large-scale surveys of human sexual behavior, but he was trained as an entomologist and was elected to the National Academy of Sciences for his work on gall wasp taxonomy.

October 29, 1894 (609)

Harvard University refused to admit Mary Whiton Calkins to doctoral candidacy, despite Hugo Münsterberg's testimony that she was the best student he had ever had at Harvard University. Harvard's refusal was based on Calkins's gender.

November 26, 1894 (610)

Norbert Wiener was born. Wiener pioneered the field of cybernetics, the application of information theory to the behavioral sciences. His first studies led to the development of a system for the rapid detection of antiaircraft fire.

December 7, 1894 (611)

James M. Baldwin's book *Mental Development in the Child* was published.

December 11, 1894 (612)

William Clark Trow was born. Trow applied psychology to the resolution of educational problems. His textbook *Educational Psychology* was the first to discuss the practical problems teachers faced in classrooms. Trow helped establish school psychology as a professional field in Michigan.

January 4, 1895 (613)

James McKeen Cattell purchased the failing journal *Science* in late 1894 and published its first issue under his editorship on this date. The journal had been founded in 1883 by Alexander Graham Bell and Gardiner Hubbard.

March 14, 1895 (614)

Phyllis Blanchard was born. Blanchard's career in clinical psychology was marked by a long association with the Philadelphia Child Guidance Clinic. Her books, *The Adolescent Girl* (1920) and *An Introduction to Mental Hygiene* (1930) are representative of her expertise.

April 3, 1895 (615)

Ruth Strang was born. Strang was an early leader of the school guidance movement and was especially influential in the 1950s and 1960s. Two areas of special interest in the schools were giftedness and reading research. Her *Educational Guidance: Its Principles and Practice* (1947) and *A Psychology of Adolescence* (1957) are books that reflect her interests.

June 10, 1895 (616)

Mary Whiton Calkins completed informal doctoral examinations at Harvard University. The university did not recognize her candidacy or formally award her degree because she was a woman. She later became president of the APA (1905). Later in her career, Calkins was offered a PhD degree from Wellesley College in lieu of her Harvard degree, but she refused to accept it.

July 8, 1895 (617)

Gardner Murphy was born. Murphy's broad interests were represented by experiments and familiar texts in social psychology, personality, and the history of psychology. APA President, 1944; American Psychological Foundation Gold Medal, 1972.

July 24, 1895 (618)

Sigmund Freud formed the theory that dreams represent wish fulfillments while dining at the Bellevue Restaurant in Vienna. He wrote that a plaque should be placed there to commemorate the occasion.

September 29, 1895 (619)

Joseph Banks Rhine was born. Rhine mounted a sustained attempt to raise psychical research to scientific standards. His research on extrasensory perception was widely known and always a topic of controversy.

December 3, 1895 (620)

Anna Freud was born. Sigmund Freud's youngest daughter was his constant companion and became a prominent child psychoanalyst. She refined and expanded the concept of defense mechanisms of the ego. She founded the Hampstead Child Therapy Center in England.

December 7, 1895 (621)

Francis Cecil Sumner was born. Sumner was the first African American to earn a PhD in psychology (1920). His many translations, book reviews, and abstracts reflected broad interests, with a focus on social psychology.

December 20, 1895 (622)

Suzanne Langer was born. Langer was a philosopher who contributed to psycholinguistics in her book *Philosophy in a New Key* (1942) and to aesthetics in *Feeling and Form* (1953).

January 12, 1896 (623)

David Wechsler was born. Wechsler's inclusion of motor performance items in intelligence tests broadened the generality and validity of measures of intelligence. The concept of deviation IQ is another of Wechsler's contributions. APA Distinguished Professional Contribution Award, 1973.

February 18, 1896 (624)

Fritz Heider was born. Heider applied the principles of Gestalt perceptual theory to social behavior, resulting in productive theories of attitude consistency, attitude change, and interpersonal perception. APA Distinguished Scientific Contribution Award, 1965.

March 30, 1896 (625)

The term *psychoanalysis* was first used in a paper by Sigmund Freud, published in French. The term was used in a paper published in Germany on May 15, 1896. Freud sent both papers to their publishers on the same day, February 5, 1896.

April 27, 1896 (626)

The first meeting of the New York Academy of Sciences Section on Psychology, Anthropology, and Philology was held. Sociologist Franklin H. Giddings was chair of the section, and psychologist–anthropologist Livingston Farrand was secretary. The first meetings of the New York Branch of the APA were held with the academy section's meetings, beginning in 1903.

May 2, 1896 (627)

Sigmund Freud presented his psychogenic theory of hysteria to the Society of Psychiatry and Neurology in Vienna. Psychiatrist Richard von Krafft-Ebbing declared, "It sounds like a scientific fairy tale." The paper was almost the last one Freud ever read in Vienna; the only other one was read 8 years later.

May 12, 1896 (628)

The New York legislature passed the first act establishing a state psychiatric institute. Ira van Gieson was the first director.

July 19, 1896 (629)

Samuel J. Beck was born. Beck's research, instruction, and publications centered on the reliability, validity, administration, and objective interpretation of the Rorschach Test.

July 28, 1896 (630)

Edward B. Titchener's *Outline of Psychology* was published.

August 9, 1896 (631)

Jean Piaget was born. Perhaps the most influential developmental psychologist of the twentieth century, Piaget described orderly stages of growth in the child's cognitive representation of the world and the effects of cognitive development on a broad range of related behaviors. APA Distinguished Scientific Contribution Award, 1969.

September 1, 1896 (632)

Mary Cover Jones was born. Jones was best known for her early studies of the elimination of fear responses through counterconditioning and for studies of differences between early and late-maturing girls. Jones also became a specialist in gerontology through her longitudinal studies at the Institute of Child Welfare at the University of California, Berkeley.

October 21, 1896   (633)

Boris M. Teplov was born. Teplov's early work was in military psychology, studying the diverse subjects of camouflage and leadership. After World War II, he turned to the psychology of music, individual differences, and, most significantly, to the study of the properties of the central nervous system.

November 5, 1896   (634)

Lev Semenovich Vygotsky was born. Vygotsky recast Soviet psychology in a mold consistent with Marxist thought. His special research interests were the social development of the child, especially as mediated by language, and the structure and function of consciousness and its relations to the unconscious. Vygotsky's life was cut short by tuberculosis at age 37.

November 26, 1896   (635)

The 23rd case at the world's first psychological clinic began. While the clinic's first case began in March of 1896, the 23rd was the first for which a record of a beginning date was kept. The clinic was founded at the University of Pennsylvania by Lightner Witmer.

November 30, 1896   (636)

The first American public school class for children with mental retardation opened in Providence, Rhode Island, under the auspices of Horace S. Tarbell, superintendent of schools.

December 29, 1896   (637)

In a presentation to the annual meeting of the APA, Lightner Witmer first used the term *psychological clinic*. Witmer's presentation, titled "The Organization of Practical Work in Psychology," described his psychology clinic, the first of its kind, at the University of Pennsylvania.

January 11, 1897   (638)

Carney Landis was born. Landis is best known for a paper with William A. Hunt describing the startle response, but he had wide-ranging interests in abnormal, developmental, physiological, and emotional psychology.

February 8, 1897   (639)

Rudolf Dreikurs was born. Dreikurs was a major interpreter of Adlerian personality theory, concentrating on the behavior of children and a functional analysis of misbehavior.

March 7, 1897   (640)

Joy Paul Guilford was born. Guilford's contributions were in the areas of quantitative methods in sensation, personality, psychophysics, and attention. APA President, 1950; APA Distinguished Scientific Contribution Award, 1964; American Psychological Foundation Gold Medal, 1983.

March 19, 1897 (641)

John G. Beebe-Center was born. Beebe-Center was one of the first to explore adaptation to affective states. He also studied the senses of taste and smell.

March 24, 1897 (642)

Wilhelm Reich was born. Reich was an associate of Sigmund Freud whose emphasis on sexual energy led to a split with conventional psychoanalysis. Reich later built devices to trap free sexual energy, or "orgone," and made extreme claims for the effects of concentrated orgone. His refusal to abandon the promotion and sale of orgone accumulators in the United States led to his imprisonment.

May 10, 1897 (643)

Margaret Schoenberger Mahler was born. Mahler's work focused on observation, diagnosis, and psychoanalytic treatment of psychotic children.

May 25, 1897 (644)

Heinrich Klüver was born. Klüver's studies on eidetic imagery and the effects of mescal were the first on these topics. Other studies investigated stimulus equivalence and the link between aggressiveness, hypersexuality, and the anterior temporal lobe (the Klüver–Bucy syndrome). American Psychological Foundation Gold Medal, 1965.

May 26, 1897 (645)

Katharine M. Banham was born. Banham's research focused on the social and emotional development of children and the rehabilitation of children with cerebral palsy. She was the first woman to earn the PhD at the University of Montreal and the first woman on the psychology faculty at Duke University, where she was a cofounder of the clinical psychology program.

June 10, 1897 (646)

In a letter to Harvard University president Charles W. Eliot, William James asked that his title be changed from professor of psychology to professor of philosophy. Hugo Münsterberg had become professor of psychology and James wrote, "psychology is not a big enough subject to be represented in the titles of two full professorships." The change became effective on October 31, 1897.

July 10, 1897 (647)

George M. Stratton's article "Vision Without Inversion of the Retinal Image" was published in *Psychological Review*. This study of adaptation to a world viewed through vision-inverting goggles is still cited in introductory psychology texts.

August 9, 1897 (648)

Lauretta Bender was born. Bender developed the Bender Visual Motor Gestalt Test for the diagnosis of neurological disorders. She was senior psychiatrist at New York's Bellevue Hospital from 1930 to 1956.

September 21, 1897 (649)

Albert Beckham was born. Beckham founded the psychology laboratory at Howard University, the first psychology laboratory at a predominantly African American institution for higher education. His specialty was clinical psychology and he was active in research, private practice, and consultation.

October 8, 1897 (650)

George Dinsmore Stoddard was born. Stoddard is known for his contributions to educational administration and leadership. His research focused on intelligence and environmental stimulation. He chaired the committee that restructured the postwar Japanese educational system and consulted with educational programs in Korea, East Africa, and Iran.

October 9, 1897 (651)

John A. McGeoch was born. McGeoch's research in learning concentrated on phenomena of human learning such as verbal learning, transfer of training, and retroactive inhibition. His book *The Psychology of Human Learning* (1942) was a comprehensive summary of the field.

October 18, 1897 (652)

Isabel Briggs Myers was born. Myers constructed the Myers-Briggs Type Indicator, which was based on the personality theory of Carl Jung as interpreted by Myers and her mother, Katharine Briggs.

October 23, 1897 (653)

Harold H. Anderson was born. Anderson conducted early studies of personality style, focusing on "dominative" and "integrative" styles in children and teachers. He was a pioneer of the field of clinical child psychology. With Gladys L. Anderson, he wrote the widely used *Introduction to Projective Techniques* (1951).

November 11, 1897 (654)

Gordon Allport was born. Allport's work in trait theory and humanistic psychology is reflected in his books *Personality: A Psychological Interpretation* (1937) and *Becoming: Basic Considerations for a Psychology of Personality* (1955). APA President, 1939; American Psychological Foundation Gold Medal, 1963; APA Distinguished Scientific Contribution Award, 1964.

December 11, 1897 (655)

Thelma Gwinn Thurstone was born. Thurstone's expertise was in mental testing. She collaborated with Louis L. Thurstone on the production of the Primary Mental Abilities Battery, the first application of factor analysis to the mental measurement of large groups.

December 28, 1897 (656)

The first simultaneous sessions at an APA annual meeting were held to accommodate diverging interests and an increasing number of presentations. One morning session was devoted to "discussion of physical and mental tests," whereas the other consisted of "psychological papers." The meeting was held at Cornell University.

December 29, 1897 (657)

The APA made its first financial commitment to an activity other than its own administration. The Committee on Physical and Mental Tests was given a budget of $100, a significant portion of the association's assets of $669.

January 12, 1898 (658)

The first meeting of the Childhood Society of Great Britain was held. Sir Douglas Galton, chairman of the society, presided over the meeting.

March 21, 1898 (659)

Morris Viteles was born. Viteles pioneered the field of industrial psychology with a study of streetcar motormen in Milwaukee in 1920, which led to some of the first industrial placement tests. Viteles's career focused on industrial training, aptitude testing, and organizational psychology. American Psychological Foundation Psychological Professional Gold Medal, 1988.

April 5, 1898 (660)

Clinical psychologist Morton Prince first hypnotized his patient, "Sally Beauchamp." He later found her to have three separate personalities. This was one of the first well-documented cases of multiple personality.

April 12, 1898 (661)

Eleanor Touroff Glueck was born. Glueck studied variables of family disruption and physique that predict juvenile delinquency.

April 30, 1898 (662)

Morton Prince discovered a second personality of "Sally Beauchamp."

May 18, 1898 (663)

Morton Prince first reported his "Sally Beauchamp" case of multiple personalities.

October 11, 1898 (664)

Frank Samuel Freeman was born. Freeman was an educational psychologist whose *Theory and Practice of Psychological Testing* (1949) was an influential book in that field.

November 9, 1898 (665)

Leonard Carmichael was born. His contributions were in the areas of child psychology and biopsychology, with special emphasis on the importance of genetic determinants of behavior. Carmichael's *Manual of Child Psychology* (1946) was a milestone in the scientific treatment of human development. APA President, 1940.

November 9, 1898 (666)

Harry Helson was born. Helson's best known studies were in the areas of color vision and *adaptation level theory*, a general proposal that judgments of experience are relative to a reference point that shifts with past experience and current background stimuli. Society of Experimental Psychologists Warren Medal, 1959; APA Distinguished Scientific Contribution Award, 1962.

November 19, 1898 (667)

William H. Sheldon was born. Sheldon's constitutional psychology was a system that related endomorphic, ectomorphic, and mesomorphic body types to normal and abnormal personality.

January 2, 1899 (668)

Fred S. Keller was born. Keller, an early radical behaviorist, is best known for the development of the personalized system of instruction (PSI), a self-paced method of instruction that is based on behavioral principles. He won the first American Psychological Foundation Award for Distinguished Teaching in 1970. APA Distinguished Scientific Award for Applications of Psychology, 1976.

January 11, 1899 (669)

Grete Lehner Bibring was born. Bibring was a prominent psychoanalyst and a training analyst at the Harvard Medical School.

January 28, 1899 (670)

The American Social Science Association was incorporated. The organization was a forerunner of the National Institute of Social Science, created in 1926.

February 22, 1899 (671)

Martha Guernsey Colby was born. Colby was an innovative researcher in the area of child development. Colby was the second woman to receive the PhD from the University of Michigan (1922).

April 22, 1899 (672)

William James's *Talks to Teachers* was published. This book consisted of a series of 10 lectures originally sponsored by Harvard University in 1891 and 1892. James arranged for the printing of the book, but Henry Holt marketed and distributed it.

June 3, 1899 (673)

Georg von Békésy was born. Von Békésy's work on the physiology of hearing resulted in the traveling wave theory of pitch perception. Society of Experimental Psychologists Warren Award, 1955; Nobel prize, 1961.

July 1, 1899 (674)

The Illinois legislature responded to the urging of women's groups and passed the first U.S. state law establishing separate court and detention facilities for juveniles. This development provided fertile ground in Illinois for early juvenile psychological clinics, such as William Healy's Juvenile Psychopathic Institute (1909).

August 1, 1899 (675)

Myrtle McGraw was born. McGraw was a developmental psychologist whose major interests included child development, maturation, and longitudinal studies of learning in twins. Her career development was extensively influenced by John Dewey.

September 9, 1899 (676)

Theodora Mead Abel was born. Abel's work focused on problems of mental testing, retardation, and clinical psychology.

September 28, 1899 (677)

Nancy Bayley was born. Bayley was a premier figure in developmental psychology. She initiated the longitudinal Berkeley Growth Study and developed the Bayley Scales of Infant Development. She was the first woman to receive the APA's Distinguished Scientific Contribution Award, in 1966. American Psychological Foundation Gold Medal, 1982.

November 1, 1899 (678)

John F. Fulton was born. Fulton was a neurophysiologist who discovered the receptors that are the source of the muscle senses. His careful studies of the effects of prefrontal lobotomy on affective behavior was of interest to psychologists.

November 2, 1899 (679)

Otto Klineberg was born. Klineberg was a social psychologist whose research and writing focused on race relations, international relations, and cross-cultural psychology. APA Award for Distinguished Contributions in the Public Interest, 1979; APA Award for Distinguished Contributions to the International Advancement of Psychology, 1991.

November 4, 1899 (680)

Sigmund Freud's book *Interpretation of Dreams* was first published. Six hundred copies were printed, and it took 8 years to sell them.

December 28, 1899 (681)

The first APA annual meeting session devoted to teaching psychology was presented by George S. Fullerton, Joseph Jastrow, H. Austin Aikins, and Charles H. Judd. The title of the presentation was "How Should Psychology Be Taught?" All of the speakers agreed that psychology must be taught as a science.

January 1, 1900   (682)

The Western Philosophical Association was founded in Kansas City. Philosophers and experimental psychologists were uncomfortable partners in the early APA, and this new independent philosophical association formalized the split. In 1901 the American Philosophical Association was formed in the eastern United States and merged with the western association in the 1910s.

January 5, 1900   (683)

Florence Halpern was born. Halpern was considered the "grandmother of psychology" in New York. Her interests were in clinical psychology, especially the assessment and treatment of children. She was part of a group that advocated the first certification bill for psychologists in New York.

February 20, 1900   (684)

Quinn McNemar was born. McNemar's expertise in statistics and psychometrics led to an influential text titled *Psychological Statistics* and many professional offices and consulting positions. President, Psychometric Society, 1951; APA President, 1964.

March 17, 1900   (685)

Helen Peak was born. Her field of expertise was in social psychology and social research methods. Peak published articles on the characteristics of Nazis, postwar problems in the reeducation of Germany, problems of objective observation, and attitude structure and change and her activation theory of motivation.

March 23, 1900   (686)

Erich Fromm was born. Fromm was a founder of the Frankfurt Psychoanalytic Institute, the William Alanson White Institute, and the Mexican Psychoanalytic Institute. Fromm's widely read books *Escape from Freedom* and *The Art of Loving* applied psychoanalytic theory to the relation between society and the individual.

March 25, 1900   (687)

Ruth W. Howard Beckham was born. Beckham was the first African American woman to earn the PhD in psychology, awarded to her at the University of Minnesota in 1934. Her research and consulting focused on the areas of mental retardation, child development, and family counseling. She directed the mental health and training programs of the National Youth Administration.

April 26, 1900   (688)

Ernst Kris was born. Kris modified traditional psychoanalysis by emphasizing ego functions and applied this approach to the study of art and the study of children's behavior.

May 3, 1900 (689)

Psychologist Gabriele Grafin von Wartensleben became the first woman to earn the PhD from the University of Vienna. In 1914, von Wartensleben published the first general description of Gestalt psychology.

June 6, 1900 (690)

Manfred Joshua Sakel was born. Sakel was a psychiatrist who discovered the effects of insulin shock therapy on schizophrenia.

June 10, 1900 (691)

Martin Scheerer was born. Scheerer was a Gestalt psychologist who worked with Kurt Goldstein to produce a series of tests of concept formation used in psychological assessment settings.

August 29, 1900 (692)

John Dollard was born. Dollard brought a background in sociology and psychoanalytic study to bear on the psychology of frustration and aggression, social learning and imitation, social stratification, and learning processes in psychotherapy.

September 9, 1900 (693)

Lucien Warner was born. Warner's studies in comparative psychology and animal learning and motivation contributed to successful methods for training seeing-eye dogs.

October 6, 1900 (694)

Margaret Altmann was born. Altmann was a pioneer in the descriptive ethology of large animals and is best known for studies of social behavior of elk in Wyoming.

October 9, 1900 (695)

Joseph Zubin was born. Zubin's most significant work was in experimental psychopathology and a theory of schizophrenia that was based on statistical analysis of objective measurements. He shared in the discovery of the P300 event-related brain potential. American Psychological Foundation Gold Medal Award for Life Achievement in the Applications of Psychology, 1990.

October 14, 1900 (696)

W. Edwards Deming was born. Deming devised statistical process control, an approach to industrial production and management psychology that contributed to the success of Japanese industry after World War II. Only later were Deming's methods studied and adopted in the United States.

November 9, 1900 (697)

Bluma Wulfomna Zeigarnik was born. The *Zeigarnik effect* is a principle of Gestalt psychology that describes the tendency for incomplete tasks to occupy one's attention.

November 17, 1900   (698)
The College Entrance Examination Board (CEEB) was founded. The tests of the
CEEB have been intended to provide objective measurements of academic achieve-
ment.

December 10, 1900   (699)
Carl Jung reported for duty at his first professional post at the Burghölzli Mental
Hospital in Zurich, Switzerland.

January 2, 1901   (700)
David Shakow was born. Shakow's research on thought disturbances in schizo-
phrenia was widely read. He was active in the development of modern professional
standards of clinical psychology. He headed the National Institute of Mental Health
Psychology Laboratory for many years. APA Distinguished Scientific Contribution
Award, 1975; APA Distinguished Professional Contribution Award, 1976.

February 5, 1901   (701)
Henry Nissen was born. A comparative psychologist, Nissen was the first to conduct
experimental studies of the chimpanzee, beginning in the 1920s. His studies on
sensory deprivation were among the first in that area and used chimpanzees as
subjects.

February 18, 1901   (702)
In an early study on dream behavior, John Mourly-Vold wrapped woolen tape
around the left ankles of 19 students and observed the effect of this treatment on
their dreams. He concluded that more active dream imagery was generated.

February 28, 1901   (703)
The National Herbart Society was reorganized as the National Society for the
Scientific Study of Education at the Auditorium Hotel in Chicago. Nicholas M.
Butler was elected president. In 1910, the organization assumed its current name,
the National Society for the Study of Education.

March 11, 1901   (704)
Willard S. Small's article "Experimental Study of the Mental Processes of the Rat
II" was published in the *American Journal of Psychology*. This was the first article
to report a study of maze learning in the rat and to use the term *psychobiology*.
Other articles in the series reported physical development and exploratory behavior
in the rat.

April 1, 1901   (705)
The London Psycho-Therapeutic Society was inaugurated. The society was dedicated to "the study of Mesmerism, hypnotism, and other psychic phenomena and
their adaptation to the cure and prevention of disease."

April 18, 1901 (706)

James McKeen Cattell became the second psychologist elected to the National Academy of Sciences.

June 4, 1901 (707)

Everet Franklin Lindquist was born. Lindquist was a pioneer in educational assessment who developed the Iowa Tests of Basic Skills and the Iowa Tests of Educational Development. During World War II, he developed a high school equivalency examination that has become the Test of General Educational Development (GED). His statistics text was a standard for many years.

June 4, 1901 (708)

Gregory Razran was born. Razran did extensive work in classical conditioning and served as an intermediary between American and Soviet psychologists.

June 17, 1901 (709)

The College Entrance Examination Board tests were first administered.

August 10, 1901 (710)

Noble H. Kelley was born. Kelley helped to inaugurate the graduate programs in clinical psychology at the University of Louisville and Southern Illinois University. In 1950 he began 20 years of service as the executive officer of the American Board of Professional Psychology. APA Award for Distinguished Professional Contributions, 1974.

September 4, 1901 (711)

Robert C. Tryon was born. Tryon completed well-known studies of behavior genetics by breeding generations of "maze-bright" and "maze-dull" rats. He formulated a theory of individual differences in maze learning. Tryon later focused on computerized cluster analysis and physical proximity of socially similar people in large urban populations.

September 9, 1901 (712)

Alexandra Adler was born. The daughter of Alfred Adler, she continued to refine the theory and applications of his individual psychology and to administer an Adlerian training center.

October 9, 1901 (713)

Herman George Canady was born. Canady was an African American social psychologist who was the first to study the race of the examiner as a possible source of bias in IQ testing.

October 24, 1901 (714)

The British Psychological Society was founded at University College of the University of London. The founding meeting was called by James Sully. Others in attendance were Sophie Bryant, William Halse, and Sir Robert Armstrong-Jones. The organization was first named The Psychological Society and changed to its present name in 1906.

November 6, 1901 (715)

George Katona was born. Katona's work in behavioral economics began with an article on the psychological effects of prewar German inflation. His work on consumer expectations and attitudes resulted in effective predictors of purchasing behavior. APA Distinguished Professional Contributions Award, 1977.

November 19, 1901 (716)

John B. Watson began his first psychology experiment as a graduate student at the University of Chicago. He studied maze learning in rats.

December 5, 1901 (717)

Milton H. Erickson was born. Erickson was the best known American practitioner of hypnotherapy in the twentieth century. He reached a wide audience through 50 years of research, publications, editing, lecturing, and teaching. Erickson was the founder and first president of the American Society of Clinical Hypnosis and initiated the *American Journal of Clinical Hypnosis*.

December 7, 1901 (718)

On a train trip with five other staff members of the Vineland Training School, director Edward R. Johnstone suggested forming a group to study the nature of intelligence and retardation. The group came to be called the Feeble-Minded Club in concert with the terminology of the day and evolved into the Vineland Laboratory by 1906.

December 16, 1901 (719)

Margaret Mead was born. Mead introduced the American public to cultural anthropology through her field studies of primitive societies. Her evidence on the cultural sources of personality, child rearing standards, and gender roles continues to influence developmental and social psychologists.

December 20, 1901 (720)

Walter Dill Scott gave an address on the potential application of psychological principles to advertising. This was a landmark in the early history of industrial psychology.

January 8, 1902 (721)

Carl R. Rogers was born. Rogers pioneered "nondirective" or "client-centered" therapy, which is based on the principles of humanistic psychology. He won the APA Distinguished Scientific Contribution Award in 1956 and the APA Distinguished Professional Contribution Award in 1972, the first years each of those awards was presented. APA President, 1947.

January 21, 1902 (722)

Georgene Hoffman Seward was born. Seward's work in clinical psychology was directed at studies of psychosomatic disorders and culture, personality, and psychotherapy. Special attention was paid to sexual behavior, gender roles, and the psychology of women.

January 24, 1902 (723)

Oskar Morgenstern was born. Morgenstern's book *Theory of Games and Economic Behavior* (1944), written with John von Neumann, revolutionized the study of decision making and stimulated hundreds of studies in social psychology, management, and economics on strategy, choice, negotiation, and cooperation and competition. The "prisoner's dilemma game" was a special focus for psychologists.

January 28, 1902 (724)

Andrew Carnegie endowed the Carnegie Institution with $10 million of U.S. Steel stock. The Carnegie Institution was founded to support scientific research, including psychological studies. A committee headed by James Mark Baldwin was formed to recommend worthy psychological projects. Baldwin filed his first report on October 31, 1902.

February 15, 1902 (725)

The first scientific papers were read to the British Psychological Society. James Sully presented "The Evolution of Laughter," William McDougall presented "Fechner's Paradoxical Experiment," and W. G. Smith presented "Pathological Changes in Immediate Memory and Association."

March 23, 1902 (726)

Lois Barclay Murphy was born. Her research interests included projective techniques, personality, child development, and the nature of sympathy. Murphy is known for helping to initiate Project Head Start.

March 31, 1902 (727)

The first annual meeting of the American Philosophical Association began. Many members of the new organization had represented the philosophical tradition within the APA. Their departure left the APA with a narrower empirical and applied focus.

April 15, 1902 (728)

James McKeen Cattell received the first grant by the Carnegie Institution to a psychologist. Cattell was given $1,000 to "prepare a list of the scientific men of the United States," a publication that became the modern *American Men and Women of Science*. The first grant for experimental psychology was made to Edward W. Scripture to study the sounds of human speech.

April 19, 1902 (729)

The Chicago Branch of the APA was formed on the campus of Northwestern University. This organization later became the Midwestern Psychological Association after many name changes and is the oldest regional psychological association affiliated with the APA.

May 14, 1902 (730)

Helen Flanders Dunbar was born. Dunbar was a psychoanalyst who specialized in psychosomatic medicine. She related "personality constellations" and situational factors to psychosomatic disorders.

May 14, 1902 (731)

William Stephenson was born. Stephenson was internationally known for his scientific approach to the measurement of subjective judgments, known as the "Q technique."

May 28, 1902 (732)

Tamara Dembo was born. Dembo brought Gestalt theory to bear on clinical, social, and developmental issues. She was an investigator in an often-cited study showing age regression behavior in frustrated children.

June 7, 1902 (733)

Edwin B. Twitmyer's dissertation was approved and he was recommended to the trustees of the University of Pennsylvania for the PhD degree. His dissertation reported classical conditioning of the knee-jerk reflex 3 years before Pavlov's studies of classical conditioning were published, but little note was taken of Twitmyer's work. His PhD was granted on June 18, 1902.

June 15, 1902 (734)

Erik H. Erikson was born. Erikson was a psychoanalyst trained by Anna Freud. His theory of development described psychosocial stages marked by focal crises at each stage, extending from infancy to old age. His writing was strongly influenced by field studies in cultural anthropology.

July 16, 1902 (735)

Aleksandr R. Luria was born. Luria was a prominent Russian psychologist whose early work on the objective study of affective states was followed by later studies of the functional organization of the brain, speech functions, memory, and rehabilitation. His work established the beginnings of neuropsychology.

July 17, 1902 (736)

Carl G. Jung was awarded the MD degree by the University of Zurich. His dissertation topic was the psychology and pathology of occult phenomena.

July 23, 1902 (737)

Theodore C. Schneirla was born. Schneirla was the foremost American comparative psychologist of the mid-1900s. His empirical work was based on observations of army ants. His "biphasic A-W theory" described behavior in terms of approach and avoidance of points in the environment. His *Principles of Animal Psychology* (1935, with N. R. F. Maier) was the leading text in its field.

September 9, 1902 (738)

Fritz Redl was born. Redl's career was devoted to the study of the behavior of delinquent children. Redl's views emphasized the primacy of the child's entire social and environmental milieu in both the etiology and treatment of unmanageable behavior. His *Children Who Hate* (1951) and *Controls From Within* (1952) were widely read summaries of his work at Detroit's Pioneer House.

September 11, 1902 (739)

Alice Bryan was born. Bryan analyzed the role of women in psychology, becoming one of the first to focus on women's issues within the discipline and profession of psychology. She promoted the formation of the National Council of Women Psychologists (1941), a response to the exclusion of women psychologists from war-related professional employment during World War II.

September 12, 1902 (740)

Karen Machover was born. Machover is best known for devising the Draw-A-Person Test, a projective personality assessment instrument.

October 10, 1902 (741)

Clark L. Hull began his "idea books." October 10, 1902, is the date of the second entry. The first was probably made on the 9th but is dated only "October, 1902." Hull recorded plans, theoretical ideas, research questions, and personal observations in his idea books throughout his life. His last entry, in his 73rd book, was made on April 21, 1952, 18 days before his death.

November 12, 1902 (742)

Norman Munn, a prominent developmental and comparative psychologist, was born. Munn's books *Handbook of Psychological Research on the Rat* (1950), *The Evolution and Growth of Human Behavior* (1955), and *The Evolution of the Human Mind* (1971) reflect his areas of specialization.

December 9, 1902 (743)

An earlier *Psychological Calendar* was published. It was "a collection of selections, teaching, through right use of words and power of will to direct thought so as to bring success, improve conditions—or whatever desired." The present calendar is confined to more modest purposes.

January 9, 1903 (744)

Donald W. MacKinnon was born. MacKinnon is best known for his extensive series of studies on creativity, performed at the Institute for Personality Assessment and Research at the University of California, Berkeley.

February 2, 1903 (745)

Karl Duncker was born. Duncker studied apparent movement, creativity, and problem solving. He originated the term *functional fixity*, denoting a common barrier to creative problem solving.

February 14, 1903 (746)

Carl Jung, ever the symbolist, married Emma Rauschenbach on Valentine's Day.

February 23, 1903 (747)

The first meeting of the New York Branch of the APA was held. Edward L. Thorndike chaired the meeting. This organization was the forerunner of the modern Eastern Psychological Association.

March 3, 1903 (748)

Congress expanded its immigration restrictions by prohibiting immigration of, to use its terms, feeble-minded persons, epileptics, insane persons, persons insane in the last 5 years, and persons with two or more episodes of insanity at any time in their lives.

March 18, 1903 (749)

Egon Brunswik was born. Brunswik's theory of "probabilistic functionalism" emphasized behavior as an adaptation to environmental conditions. His research with perceptual constancies served to confirm his theory. The related "lens model" of perceptual judgment has been expanded into a general model of human judgment.

March 31, 1903 (750)

Roger G. Barker was born. Barker's ecological psychology defined the "behavior setting" to be the determinant of many human behaviors. His 24-year longitudinal study of Oskaloosa ("Midwest"), Kansas, is an exemplary model of field observation. APA Distinguished Scientific Contribution Award, 1963.

April 10, 1903 (751)

Margaret Ives was born. She worked primarily in hospitals and courts, practicing psychotherapy with nurses and forensic patients and building internship and research programs.

April 17, 1903 (752)

John M. Stalnaker was born. Stalnaker's career revolved around aptitude and achievement assessment in educational settings. His research and administrative appointments included the College Entrance Examination Board, the Pepsi-Cola Scholarship Board, and the National Merit Scholarship Corporation.

April 22, 1903 (753)
Karl Zener was born. Zener wrote on problems of classical conditioning and motivation, but he is best known for work on the phenomenology of perception. He described six phases that intervene between the perceived object and processes in the cortex.

April 23, 1903 (754)
William James was elected to the National Academy of Sciences, the third psychologist so honored.

April 23, 1903 (755)
Ivan Pavlov presented "Experimental Psychology and Psychopathology of Animals" to the International Congress of Medicine at Madrid. This was the first public exposition of conditioned and unconditioned reflexes.

July 9, 1903 (756)
Lightner Witmer had his last clinical session with "Charles Gilman," the first client of the world's first psychological clinic at the University of Pennsylvania. Witmer began to treat Charles for a reading disorder in March 1896, inaugurating Witmer's pioneering methods in clinical psychology.

July 24, 1903 (757)
Theodore M. Newcomb was born. Newcomb's social psychological research focused on social influence, attitude development, community behavior, and small-group phenomena. His longitudinal studies of changing values in Bennington College students are especially well-known. APA President, 1956; APA Distinguished Scientific Contribution Award, 1976.

August 5, 1903 (758)
Rensis Likert was born. Likert studied attitude scaling, industrial psychology, and public opinion. Likert developed the familiar 7-point rating scale attitude measurement system that he called the *method of summated ratings*, but that is commonly called *Likert scaling*.

August 12, 1903 (759)
Laurance F. Shaffer was born. Shaffer's interests were in theories of personality and adjustment and in clinical psychology. Shaffer served as director of the Psychological Corporation for many years. APA President, 1953.

August 22, 1903 (760)
Starke R. Hathaway was born. Hathaway and J. Charnley McKinley developed the Minnesota Multiphasic Personality Inventory. His interests extended to medical

psychology, longitudinal studies of adolescents and crime, effects of mild aversive shock, hypnosis, lie detection, and modeling. APA Award for Distinguished Contribution for Applications in Psychology, 1977.

August 28, 1903 (761)
Bruno Bettelheim was born. Bettelheim was a survivor of Nazi concentration camps whose "milieu therapy" emphasized "structured permissiveness" as a therapeutic environment for psychotic and autistic children.

September 12, 1903 (762)
The first American book on child development, Irving King's *Psychology of Child Development*, was published.

November 7, 1903 (763)
Konrad Lorenz was born. Lorenz won the Nobel prize in 1973 for his work on innate behaviors, especially imprinting. The concept of critical periods of development and learning is derived from Lorenz's work.

November 10, 1903 (764)
William A. Hunt was born. Hunt was the first clinical psychologist in the U.S. Navy. He helped develop a 2-minute screening interview for navy applicants. A promoter of the scientist–practitioner model of clinical training, Hunt was a member of the first board of directors of the modern APA. APA Distinguished Professional Contribution Award, 1979.

November 30, 1903 (765)
Grace Heider was born. Heider was a developmental psychologist with a special interest in the process of language development in deaf children. Her book *Studies in the Psychology of the Deaf* (1940) reflects this interest. Her last book, *Vulnerability in Infants and Young Children*, was not written until 1973, testifying to her enduring productivity and interest in child development.

December 22, 1903 (766)
Magda Blondiau Arnold was born. Arnold is known for her work in the areas of emotion, neurophysiology, and perception and for refining the activation theory of emotion. Her book *Physiological Differentiation of Emotional States* summarized her research in these areas.

December 25, 1903 (767)
Mildred B. Mitchell was born. Mitchell worked with the Veterans Administration on a variety of research projects. She was the first clinical psychology examiner for the U.S. astronaut program. Mitchell participated in research and administration of U.S. Air Force contracts in bionics.

December 28, 1903 (768)
John von Neumann was born. Von Neumann was an outstanding mathematician who helped to develop the atomic bomb and the first electronic computers. With Oskar Morgenstern, he wrote *A Theory of Games and Economic Behavior*, the cornerstone of modern scientific theory and research in decision and choice behavior.

January 3, 1904 (769)
Harold Schlosberg was born. Schlosberg developed a theory of emotion that arranged emotions on bipolar scales of pleasant–unpleasant and attention–rejection. With R. S. Woodworth, he wrote *Experimental Psychology* (1954), a landmark text.

January 15, 1904 (770)
The journal *Psychological Bulletin* began publication under the editorship of James Mark Baldwin and Howard C. Warren. This journal and others were transferred by Howard C. Warren to the APA by purchase and gift from 1925 to 1938.

January 15, 1904 (771)
Edward B. Titchener, in a printed memo, invited selected psychologists to organize "an American society for the advancement of Experimental Psychology." The group eventually became the Society of Experimental Psychologists.

January 27, 1904 (772)
James J. Gibson was born. Gibson's research on perception showed that perceptual qualities are directly sensed from the environment, not built from simple sensory inputs. His book *The Senses Considered as Perceptual Systems* (1966) was a major summary of his work. APA Distinguished Scientific Contribution Award, 1961.

February 8, 1904 (773)
Edward F. Buchner of the University of Alabama wrote to prominent philosophers and psychologists regarding interest in a regional psychological association in the southeastern United States. The result was the organizing meeting of the Southern Society for Philosophy and Psychology, held in Atlanta, Georgia, on February 23, 1904.

February 24, 1904 (774)
The Southern Society for Philosophy and Psychology was founded at a meeting of the National Education Association in Atlanta. The organizer of the founding meeting was Edward Buchner. James Mark Baldwin was elected the first president of the society.

March 11, 1904 (775)
Hilde Bruch was born. Bruch was a psychiatrist whose specialty was studies of eating disorders, especially anorexia and obesity.

March 20, 1904 (776)

B. F. Skinner was born. Skinner's radical behaviorism provided a systematic analysis of the effects of consequences on behavior. His principles of instrumental conditioning affected nearly every field of psychology. APA Distinguished Scientific Contribution Award, 1958; National Medal of Science, 1968; APA Citation for Lifetime Contributions to Psychology, 1990.

April 4, 1904 (777)

Edward B. Titchener founded The Experimentalists, the club that became the Society of Experimental Psychologists in 1929, after Titchener's death. Women were excluded from membership until 1929, when Margaret Floy Washburn and June Etta Downey were admitted.

April 18, 1904 (778)

Zygmunt A. Piotrowski was born. Piotrowski wrote on many topics but is best known for his research on the Rorschach Test. He studied its use in assessing patients with schizophrenia and devised the approach to the Rorschach known as *perceptanalysis*. APA Distinguished Professional Contribution Award, 1980.

April 19, 1904 (779)

Carl G. Jung published his first studies on word association. The studies, carried out at the Burghölzli Hospital in Zurich, Switzerland, were interpreted by Jung as support for Sigmund Freud's theory of neurosis.

May 6, 1904 (780)

Elizabeth Duffy was born. Duffy initially formulated the arousal or activation theory of emotion, later brought to prominence by Magda Arnold and Donald Lindsley.

May 10, 1904 (781)

G. Stanley Hall's most influential book, *Adolescence*, was published.

May 14, 1904 (782)

Charles W. Bray II was born. Bray and E. G. Wever introduced and expanded the field of auditory electrophysiology. His interests were in hearing, experimental methods, and U.S. Air Force personnel selection and training. Bray and Wever won the first Howard C. Warren Medal of the Society of Experimental Psychologists in 1936.

May 16, 1904 (783)

Robert J. Wherry was born. Wherry was a quantitative industrial psychologist. His contributions in statistics included several factor-analytic methods and predictive procedures bearing his name. He also contributed to the literature in personnel selection and individual differences.

May 20, 1904   (784)
Frank A. Geldard was born. Geldard was a sensory psychologist with broad-ranging expertise. His *The Human Senses* served as a basic text for many years. During World War II he developed aviation training programs and continued to serve as a consultant to the military after the war. American Psychological Foundation Distinguished Teaching Award, 1974.

May 29, 1904   (785)
Robert H. Felix was born. Felix, a psychiatrist, was instrumental in the passage of the National Mental Health Act (1946) and the subsequent establishment of the National Institute of Mental Health, serving as its first director. He promoted interdisciplinary approaches to mental health issues and supported psychological research in that area.

July 22, 1904   (786)
Donald Olding Hebb was born. Hebb's book *The Organization of Behavior* constructed a system of behavior that was based on the physiology of the organism but extending to learning, motivation, perception, affect, and cognition. Hebb, a Canadian, was the only APA President (1960) who was not a citizen of the United States. APA Distinguished Scientific Contribution Award, 1961.

July 25, 1904   (787)
Ernest Ropiequet Hilgard was born. Hilgard's career has been marked by distinguished work across the entire range of modern psychology. Learning, hypnosis, child development, teaching of psychology, consciousness, and the history of psychology have been special focuses. APA President, 1949; APA Distinguished Scientific Contribution Award, 1967.

August 20, 1904   (788)
Anne Roe was born. Roe is best known for her work relating personality and vocational choice. Her book *The Psychology of Occupations* (1956) was the first thorough treatment of this topic. Her other interests included interviewing techniques, evolution and behavior, and creativity.

August 29, 1904   (789)
Ralph M. Stogdill was born. For 30 years, Stogdill was identified with leadership research, culminating with the *Handbook of Leadership* in 1974.

September 11, 1904   (790)
Martin David Jenkins was born. Jenkins conducted early research on race and intelligence scale scores. He found essentially equal intelligence levels and identified superior African American students, one of whom had the highest IQ score then on record. The behavioral science center at Morgan State College is named for Jenkins.

September 17, 1904 (791)

Oskar Pfungst began his examination of "Clever Hans," the horse supposedly endowed with human reasoning, reading, and mathematical abilities. Pfungst found that the horse's behavior was attributable to subtle cues from human observers. The case is often cited in discussions of experimenter expectancy effects.

September 25, 1904 (792)

Robert Ward Leeper was born. Leeper expanded on the work of Kurt Lewin, applying Lewin's field concepts to learning, personality, and emotions. His theories were precursors to cognitive learning theory.

November 4, 1904 (793)

Horace Mann Bond was born. Bond was an educational researcher and administrator whose studies of racial biases in testing and education were among the first empirical approaches to those topics. Bond's son Julian has been a prominent Georgia politician and civil rights activist.

November 28, 1904 (794)

Hans Wallach was born. Wallach's areas of research included the perception of form through motion, the organization of movement, and the use of perceptual learning or counteradaptation to reveal relations between perceptual information systems. APA Distinguished Scientific Contribution Award, 1983.

November 30, 1904 (795)

Max Wertheimer received the PhD degree at the age of 24 under Oswald Külpe at the University of Würzburg. Wertheimer became one of the founders of Gestalt psychology.

December 2, 1904 (796)

Willard L. Valentine was born. Valentine developed the introductory psychology course at Ohio State University, managed the APA journals program for many years, and served as treasurer of the APA.

December 12, 1904 (797)

Ivan P. Pavlov received the Nobel prize. The prize honored Pavlov's work in the physiology of digestion, but Pavlov mentioned his work with conditioned reflexes in his acceptance speech.

December 27, 1904 (798)

The first annual meeting of the Southern Society for Philosophy and Psychology was held at Johns Hopkins University. James Mark Baldwin was the first president of the association, which adopted its constitution at this meeting.

January 14, 1905 (799)

Florence Rockwood Kluckholn was born. She is known for her contributions in the areas of culture and personality and for her writing about women's issues.

February 11, 1905 (800)

Francis W. Irwin was born. Irwin's interests were in psychophysics, delay of reinforcement, and human decisions. He developed a theory of intentional behavior and motivation. In addition, he was a research consultant on military problems and chair of the board of editors of the APA.

March 3, 1905 (801)

Eugenia Hanfmann was born. Hanfmann's early work was in cognition, and her later work concentrated on personality assessment and counseling psychology. Her best known clinical research examined disrupted concept formation in patients with schizophrenia. She developed the Concept Formation Test.

March 20, 1905 (802)

Raymond B. Cattell was born. Cattell developed a factor-analytic theory of personality that led to the development of the Sixteen Personality Factor Questionnaire. In his work with the nature of intelligence, Cattell distinguished between "fluid" and "crystallized" intelligence. He produced one of the early culture-fair tests of intelligence.

April 19, 1905 (803)

Irving Lorge was born. Lorge gathered the first data on the effects of schooling on intelligence test scores. He and Edward L. Thorndike collaborated to produce the widely used book, *The Teacher's Word Book of 30,000 Words*, a list of the relative frequencies of appearance of English words in general literature.

April 24, 1905 (804)

John P. Seward was born. Seward's contributions included research on the habituation of the galvanic skin response, learning, tertiary conditioning, brain stimulation, reproductive behavior, gender differences in behavior and socialization, and the effects of hormones on behavior.

April 25, 1905 (805)

Henry C. Lavery patented the "phrenometer," a helmetlike device with adjustable probes for measuring the shape of the skull and giving a character assessment based on phrenology. Its success was mainly confined to county fairs.

April 28, 1905 (806)

Alfred Binet and Theodore Simon's first intelligence test and related research were presented to the International Congress of Psychology in Rome. Their paper, read by Henri-Étienne Beaunis, was titled "New Methods for Diagnosing Idiocy, Imbecility, and Moron Status."

April 28, 1905 (807)

George A. Kelly was born. Kelly developed the personal construct theory of personality and psychotherapy, emphasizing individual interpretations of a setting as the determinants of individual differences in behavior. Kelly's Role Repertoire Test was the basis of many studies of personality. APA President, 1955.

May 23, 1905 (808)

Roelof (Ralph) Gerbrands was born. Gerbrands was employed by Edwin G. Boring in September 1929 to make experimental equipment in the Harvard University shop. Gerbrands later went into business for himself, founding a company that became a major supplier of experimental psychology equipment, best known for its operant conditioning equipment.

June 14, 1905 (809)

Oscar Krisen Buros was born. Buros began assembling a list of mental measurements while still a student. The list grew into the *Mental Measurements Yearbook*, which appeared in frequent revisions and became the authoritative guide to psychological assessment instruments.

June 21, 1905 (810)

Jean-Paul Sartre was born. Sartre's philosophy and plays were major conduits of twentieth-century phenomenology and existentialism. His primary impact on psychology was that of existential psychoanalysis, a process of confronting individual values and choices described in Sartre's book *Being and Nothingness*.

September 1, 1905 (811)

Wayne Dennis was born. Dennis's field studies of the handicapping effects of environmental deprivation on physical, intellectual, and social development were landmarks in the field.

October 31, 1905 (812)

Harry F. Harlow was born. Harlow generated several lines of influential research. He is well-known for his studies of contact comfort and affectional bonds, learning set, curiosity motivation, and the effects of social isolation in primates. Society of Experimental Psychologists Warren Medal, 1956; APA President, 1958; APA Distinguished Scientific Contribution Award, 1960; National Medal of Science, 1967.

November 15, 1905 (813)

E. Lowell Kelly was born. Kelly's interests included clinical psychology, longitudinal studies of adult personality, marital compatibility, personality assessment, and training. APA President, 1955; American Psychological Foundation Psychological Professional Gold Medal Award, 1985.

December 30, 1905   (814)
Morton Prince published his book *The Dissociation of a Personality*, a classic case study of the multiple personalities of his patient "Sally Beauchamp."

January 6, 1906   (815)
Clarence H. Graham was born. Graham won the APA Distinguished Scientific Contribution Award in 1966 for his classic studies of color vision and studies of characteristics of achromatic vision such as critical flicker frequency, luminosity curves, and the area-intensity problem.

January 7, 1906   (816)
John Flanagan was born. Flanagan was an aviation psychology pioneer, the first psychologist in the U.S. Air Force (1941), and founder of the American Institutes for Research. He helped develop the critical incident technique of personnel selection and research-based programs of individual instruction. APA Distinguished Professional Contributions Award, 1976; American Psychological Foundation Gold Medal, 1993.

January 25, 1906   (817)
Molly Harrower was born. Harrower, a clinical researcher, developed the group Rorschach test, first described in her book *Large Scale Rorschach Techniques: Personality Change and Development, as Measured by the Projective Techniques* (1945, with Matilda Steiner).

February 12, 1906   (818)
Charles Roger Myers was born. Myers contributed to the development of Canadian psychology. His specialties were clinical psychology and the history of psychology. He was a founding member of the Canadian Psychological Association, its president in 1950, and its first executive officer (1970–1978). He was the first president of the Ontario Psychological Association.

March 4, 1906   (819)
Dorothea A. McCarthy was born. McCarthy was a child clinical psychologist with a special interest in language development in children. She devised the McCarthy Scales of Children's Abilities.

March 5, 1906   (820)
Dael Wolfle was born. Wolfle is a specialist in organizational psychology and scientific manpower who has held many administrative posts in scientific and technical organizations. He was the first executive secretary of the APA (1946–1950), holding office at the time of the modern reorganization of the APA and its rapid postwar growth in membership and scope.

March 12, 1906 (821)

Josephine Rohrs Hilgard was born. Hilgard's interests were in child psychiatry, especially the experience of "object loss" in children, hypnosis, and sibling rivalry and identification.

March 19, 1906 (822)

Joseph McVicker Hunt was born. Hunt was noted for his studies of the influence of early experience on intelligence and thinking. His interests extended to motivation, measurement, personality dynamics, psychotherapy, and social welfare. Hunt was the first president of the American Psychological Foundation (APF) in 1953. APA President, 1952; APF Gold Medal, 1979.

March 31, 1906 (823)

Marianne Frostig was born. She contributed to the areas of educational therapy, learning disorders, and assessment. Her Developmental Test of Visual Perception is well-known to workers in learning disabilities.

April 1, 1906 (824)

The *Journal of Abnormal Psychology* was first published by Morton Prince. It later became the *Journal of Abnormal and Social Psychology*, then was purchased by the APA in 1925, and resumed its original name in 1965.

April 11, 1906 (825)

The correspondence between Sigmund Freud and Carl Jung began with a letter from Freud thanking Jung for sending him a book of Jung's word association studies that supported Freud's theory of neurosis.

May 10, 1906 (826)

Leona E. Tyler was born. Tyler's *The Psychology of Human Differences* (1947) and *The Work of the Counselor* (1953) are significant works that reflect her principal teaching, research, and theoretical interests. APA President, 1973; American Psychological Foundation Gold Medal Award for Life Contribution by a Psychologist in the Public Interest, 1990.

June 12, 1906 (827)

Robert S. Woodworth delivered an invited address titled "Psychiatry and Experimental Psychology" to the 62nd Annual Meeting of the American Psychiatric Association in Boston. The address was a plea for the study of the problems of psychiatry with the methods of experimental psychology.

June 16, 1906 (828)

Hadley Cantril, Jr., was born. Cantril's research interests included attitude scaling, public opinion, and the influences of social factors on perception.

July 29, 1906 (829)

Muzafer Sherif was born. Sherif's "Robber's Cave" experiments were the best known of his many studies of social norms, attitude formation, social change, conflict resolution, and group processes. APA Distinguished Scientific Contribution Award, 1968.

September 1, 1906 (830)

Henry H. Goddard assumed his post as director of the Vineland Laboratory at the Vineland Training School in New Jersey. Under his direction, Vineland became a leader in the education of people with mental retardation. Goddard was succeeded by Stanley D. Porteus in 1919 and by Edgar Doll in 1925.

September 14, 1906 (831)

George M. Haslerud was born. Haslerud had a lifelong interest in creative transfer of prior training but contributed substantially to the study of primate aggression and the establishment of relations with Japanese psychologists. He was a cofounder of the New Hampshire Psychological Association.

September 15, 1906 (832)

The Vineland Laboratory was founded at the Vineland Training School in New Jersey, with Henry H. Goddard as its first director. The laboratory studied basic processes and applied methods in intelligence, retardation, and education.

October 4, 1906 (833)

George I. Sanchez was born. Sanchez was a specialist in mental measurements and bilingual education and a critic of culture bias in the intelligence tests of the day. He has been called the founder of Chicano psychology.

November 4, 1906 (834)

S. Smith Stevens was born. Stevens formulated the power law of psychophysics, devised direct scaling methods, extensively studied auditory perception, conveyed the philosophy of operationism to American psychology, and wrote many influential articles and books, notably the *Handbook of Experimental Psychology* (1951). APA Award for Distinguished Scientific Contribution, 1960.

November 23, 1906 (835)

James McKeen Cattell published the first of three papers in the journal *Science* on measuring eminence in scientists. The work grew into *American Men of Science* and, later, *American Men and Women of Science*. Cattell's work was supported in the beginning by the first Carnegie Institution grant made to a psychologist.

December 25, 1906 (836)

Nathan W. Shock was born. Shock was a life-span developmental psychologist who concentrated on gerontology. He founded the Baltimore Longitudinal Study of Aging in 1958 and was for 35 years head of the Gerontology Research Center of the National Institute on Aging.

December 27, 1906 (837)
The annual meeting of the APA coincided with the formal opening of Emerson Hall at Harvard University. The building was the first in the United States planned as a psychology facility and housed the psychology, philosophy, and sociology departments. It symbolized the permanence of psychology in American university curricula. Hugo Münsterberg presided over the ceremony.

December 27, 1906 (838)
An ad hoc committee of the APA recommended forming the APA's first committee on standards for apparatus, procedures, and results of group and individual tests. The resulting Committee on Measurement consisted of James R. Angell, Charles H. Judd, Walter B. Pillsbury, Carl E. Seashore, and Robert S. Woodworth.

January 23, 1907 (839)
Orval Hobart Mowrer was born. Mowrer was a learning researcher and theorist who extended a unified learning theory into interpretations of the phenomena of psychoanalysis. APA President, 1954.

January 24, 1907 (840)
Margaret Rioch was born. Rioch was primarily an individual psychotherapist. At the National Institute of Mental Health and at Children's Hospital of Washington, DC, she conducted training programs for mental health counselors.

January 26, 1907 (841)
Marie Jahoda was born. Jahoda's studies of prejudice and discrimination contributed to understanding anti-Semitism and authoritarianism. Her work on race relations included studies of desegregated housing and schools. APA Award for Distinguished Contributions in the Public Interest, 1979.

January 26, 1907 (842)
Hans Selye was born. Selye borrowed the term *stress* from physics to describe human and animal reactions to arousing environmental conditions. His work on the effects of stress and his general adaptation syndrome theory have generated hundreds of research articles on this subject.

February 26, 1907 (843)
John Bowlby was born. With the collaboration of Mary D. Salter Ainsworth, Bowlby's research and theory of the process of a child's attachment to a mother figure and the consequences of loss have exerted a significant influence on developmental psychology. APA Distinguished Scientific Contribution Award, 1989.

March 3, 1907 (844)
In Vienna, at 10 a.m. on this day, Carl Jung first met Sigmund Freud.

March 9, 1907 (845)
The first U.S. eugenic sterilization law was enacted by the Indiana legislature. The law provided for sterilization of "confirmed criminals, idiots, imbeciles, and rapists." The law was invalidated by the Indiana State Supreme Court in 1921 but replaced by another in 1923.

March 12, 1907 (846)
Marion A. Wenger was born. Wenger's interests were in human development and the function of the autonomic nervous system in emotional expression. Wenger's monograph "Studies of Autonomic Balance in Army Air Forces Personnel" is a classic in its field.

April 15, 1907 (847)
Nikolaas Tinbergen was born. Tinbergen earned the Nobel prize in 1973 with his ethological studies of innate behavior dispositions and their releasing stimuli. His later work included studies of childhood autism. APA Distinguished Scientific Contribution Award, 1987.

May 6, 1907 (848)
Kenneth Spence was born. Spence's exhaustive work defined the parameters of many factors influencing classically conditioned responses. He won the APA Distinguished Scientific Contribution Award in 1956, the first year it was awarded.

June 28, 1907 (849)
Edwin E. Ghiselli was born. Ghiselli helped establish the applied psychology center at the University of California, Berkeley. His interests were in individual differences, measurement, and industrial psychology. His book *Personnel and Industrial Psychology* has been used widely in the field. APA Distinguished Scientific Contribution Award, 1972.

August 12, 1907 (850)
Frederick A. Mote was born. Mote is best known for his studies on vision, including studies of adaptation to the dark and stereoscopic vision. He was involved in the development of selection tests for U.S. Navy personnel and studies of reinforcement and learning.

August 15, 1907 (851)
Clifford Beers's *A Mind That Found Itself: An Autobiography* was published. The book documented Beers's ineffective treatment by the mental health establishment and became the bible of the mental hygiene movement of the early 1900s.

September 2, 1907   (852)
Evelyn Hooker was born. Hooker performed a pioneering study in 1957 showing
that experienced clinicians using psychological tests could not distinguish between
homosexual men and heterosexual men. The study was evidence that homosexuality
is within the normal range of human behavior. APA Distinguished Contribution
to Psychology in the Public Interest Award, 1991.

September 2, 1907   (853)
The first International Congress of Psychiatry, Neurology, and Psychology began
in Amsterdam. Carl Jung, acting in Sigmund Freud's place, presented a paper on
Freud's theories. Jung met another admirer of Freud, Ernest Jones, for the first time
on this occasion.

September 14, 1907   (854)
Solomon Asch was born. Asch is well-known for his pioneering experimental
studies of conformity. The Asch line judgment paradigm established a standard
technique for studying factors influencing conformity. APA Distinguished Scientific
Contribution Award, 1967.

October 1, 1907   (855)
Sigmund Freud's treatment of Ernst Lanzer ("Rat Man") began. The case history
of Rat Man, an obsessive neurotic, augmented Freud's developing theories of the
symbolic expression of repressed sexual and aggressive impulses.

December 11, 1907   (856)
Herbert F. Wright was born. Wright was a pioneer in environmental psychology.
His early work with Roger Barker in Oskoloosa ("Midwest"), Kansas, established
the measurement units and research paradigms of ecological psychology. His later
independent work focused on the effect of community size on the development of
children.

December 23, 1907   (857)
Donald B. Lindsley was born. Lindsley is known for his research on the reticular
activating system and the activation theory of emotion. APA Distinguished Scientific Contribution Award, 1959.

December 26, 1907   (858)
John C. Eberhart was born. Through his career at the National Institute of Mental
Health, Eberhart promoted an environment of scientific freedom of inquiry in
clinical psychiatry, psychology, sociology, neurophysiology, biochemistry, and
pharmacology. He was an organizer of the Boulder Conference, resulting in the
scientist–practitioner model of clinical training.

January 7, 1908 (859)
Sigmund Freud's "Little Hans" (Herbert Graf) had his first phobic attack. Interviews with Little Hans led to Freud's theories of infantile sexuality and dreams as expressions of wish fulfillment.

March 3, 1908 (860)
John B. Watson accepted a faculty position at Johns Hopkins University. His starting salary was $3,000 per year.

March 15, 1908 (861)
Elsa Siipola was born. Siipola's areas of concentration were personality and projective techniques. She studied the effects of time pressure on perception, coping behavior, word association, and imagination.

March 30, 1908 (862)
Freud had his first session with "Little Hans." Hans's phobic reactions to horses led Freud to his theories of infantile sexuality and dreams as wish fulfillment. Hans was actually Herbert Graf, who later became an opera producer and director.

March 30, 1908 (863)
Howard Emery Wright was born. Wright's work in social psychology dealt with attitude measurement, effects of culture, and guidance techniques. Wright held many university administrative positions, finishing his career as acting chancellor of the University of Maryland.

April 1, 1908 (864)
Abraham Maslow was born. Maslow is best known for his studies of self-actualization and his hierarchial theory of motives. He strongly influenced the emergence of humanistic psychology in the 1950s and 1960s. Maslow was Harry Harlow's first doctoral student. APA President, 1968.

April 4, 1908 (865)
Fred McKinney was born. McKinney was known for the excellence of his introductory psychology course. His lectures were distributed through National Educational Television and the University of Mid-America. His research centered on counseling and learning. American Psychological Foundation Distinguished Contribution to Education in Psychology Award, 1977.

April 26, 1908 (866)
The First International Congress of Psychoanalysis was held in Salzburg, Austria. Forty-two Freudian psychologists attended.

May 6, 1908 (867)
The Connecticut Society for Mental Hygiene, the first voluntary mental health association in the United States, was established in the home of Clifford Beers in

New Haven. Beers, the author of *A Mind That Found Itself*, was a pivotal figure in the mental hygiene movement.

May 9, 1908 (868)

Edward H. Kemp was born. Kemp was primarily a human factors researcher whose work contributed to military training and equipment design. His academic research was in audition, and his applied research dealt with sonar and radar interpretation, motivation, fatigue, and attention.

June 22, 1908 (869)

Donald Marquis was born. Marquis's early research was in conditioning and learning. He took up applied work in industrial and organizational settings after studying personnel problems in World War II. His *Conditioning and Learning* (1940), written with Ernest Hilgard, was a classic textbook. APA President, 1948.

July 5, 1908 (870)

Pauline Snedden Sears was born. Sears's best known studies were of level of aspiration, self-esteem, achievement motivation, mathematics learning, and gender differences in children's behavior. American Psychological Foundation Gold Medal, 1980.

July 24, 1908 (871)

Thelma Alper was born. Her contributions include research in ego strength and achievement motivation. She devised the Psychological Insight Test and the Wellesley Role-Orientation Scale.

August 18, 1908 (872)

Else Frenkel-Brunswik was born. Frenkel-Brunswik's work on the psychology of prejudice contributed to the California F Scale for the measurement of the authoritarian personality. Authoritarianism was a dominant theme of the social psychology of the 1950s. She also coined the term *intolerance of ambiguity* to describe one authoritarian trait.

August 31, 1908 (873)

Robert R. Sears was born. Sears's work focused on the social development of the child, exploring antecedents of aggression, patterns of child rearing, and factors influencing self-esteem. APA President, 1951; APA Distinguished Scientific Contribution Award, 1975; American Psychological Foundation Gold Medal, 1980.

September 2, 1908 (874)

Dorothea Cross Leighton was born. Leighton was active in the fields of social psychiatry and testing, with a special interest in cross-cultural studies of Native Americans.

October 29, 1908 (875)

Louise Bates Ames was born. Ames was a developmental psychologist interested in child development, child-rearing practices, and gerontology. She was a cofounder of the Gesell Institute of Child Development.

December 15, 1908 (876)

G. Stanley Hall wrote to Sigmund Freud and Wilhelm Wundt, inviting each to deliver lectures as part of the 20th anniversary celebrations of Clark University in July 1909. Freud and Wundt both declined this invitation, but Freud accepted a later (February 16, 1909) invitation in which Hall changed the date to September and increased Freud's honorarium.

December 19, 1908 (877)

Anne Anastasi was born. Anastasi is best known for her influential publications about the nature, formation, and accurate measurement of psychological traits of the individual. APA President, 1972; APA Distinguished Scientific Award for the Application of Psychology, 1981; American Psychological Foundation Gold Medal, 1984; National Medal of Science, 1987.

December 22, 1908 (878)

The first White House Conference on Children was proposed to President Theodore Roosevelt by a group of eight national leaders of children's welfare organizations, headed by James E. West. West was a lawyer who had been raised in a Washington, DC, orphanage. President Roosevelt issued invitations on December 25, 1908, and the conference began on January 25, 1909.

December 31, 1908 (879)

Ward Halstead was born. Halstead's work on the brain and human behavior led to the Halstead Battery of Neuropsychological Tests, designed to diagnose brain damage. He was the first to suggest that RNA and protein molecules in brain cells may represent the memory engram.

December 31, 1908 (880)

The APA appointed its first committee to study methods of teaching psychology, the Committee on Methods of Teaching Psychology. The committee was chaired by Carl E. Seashore and included James R. Angell, Mary Whiton Calkins, Edmund C. Sanford, and Guy M. Whipple. The committee focused on the introductory course in psychology and reported its findings to the 1909 annual meeting of the APA.

January 17, 1909 (881)

Writing to Carl Jung, Sigmund Freud predicted that once Americans "discover the sexual core of our psychological theories they will drop us. Their prudery and their material dependence on the public are too great." On January 19, 1909, Jung replied, "I have noticed this prudishness, which used to be worse than it is now; now I can stomach it; I don't water down the sexuality any more."

January 18, 1909 (882)

Calvin S. Hall was born. Hall is best remembered as the coauthor, with Gardner Lindzey, of *Theories of Personality*, a classic text in that field. His research interests were behavior genetics, emotional behavior in animals, and dream analysis.

January 25, 1909 (883)

The first White House Conference on Children began with an address by President Theodore Roosevelt. The focus of the conference was the welfare of children dependent on the state. White House Conferences have been held every 10 years since this first meeting.

February 9, 1909 (884)

Norman Frederiksen was born. Frederiksen has specialized in applied studies of testing and problem solving in educational, organizational, scientific, and medical settings. Approaches to solving ill-structured problems were a special focus of his research. APA Award for Distinguished Professional Contributions, 1984.

February 19, 1909 (885)

The National Committee for Mental Hygiene was founded at the Manhattan Hotel in New York. The organization was a forerunner of the National Mental Health Association (NMHA). In its early years, the NMHA was also known as the Beers Society, named after Clifford Beers, the organizer of this founding meeting. William James helped to launch the society with a $1,000 loan.

March 27, 1909 (886)

David Krech (Isadore Krechevsky) was born. Krech's work emphasized the role of social factors in perception. He used the term "new look" to describe this approach. In later work, Krech and his colleagues produced a series of studies on brain chemistry and physical growth occurring in the brain as a consequence of learning. APA Distinguished Scientific Contribution Award, 1970.

April 5, 1909 (887)

The first American institute for research in nervous diseases, the Neurological Institute of New York, was incorporated. The institute opened on October 1, 1909, with Alexander Candlish as the first superintendent.

April 21, 1909 (888)

Rollo May was born. May's was the first PhD in counseling to be awarded by Columbia University (1949). His theories of therapy and personality were derived from existential philosophy and were one component of the humanistic "third force" movement. He spearheaded early resistance to efforts to make psychotherapy exclusively a medical profession.

May 10, 1909 (889)

Robert I. Watson was born. Watson was a historian of psychology whose *The Great Psychologists: Aristotle to Freud* was a primary text for many years. Watson was instrumental in founding APA's Division 26 (History of Psychology), the Archives of the History of American Psychology, the historical organization Cheiron, and the *Journal of the History of the Behavioral Sciences*.

May 30, 1909 (890)

Jerome D. Frank was born. Frank's career in psychology and psychiatry has been marked by his clear explanations of the therapeutic process and of aspects of psychological research that bear on the prevention of nuclear war. APA Award for Distinguished Contributions to Psychology in the Public Interest, 1985.

June 16, 1909 (891)

Volume 1 of Edward B. Titchener's A *Textbook of Psychology* was published.

July 6, 1909 (892)

The Child Conference for Research and Welfare began at Clark University in Worcester, Massachusetts. The conference was arranged by G. Stanley Hall as part of the university's 20th anniversary celebration. Sigmund Freud had been invited to deliver addresses on this occasion, but he declined. A second invitation, to deliver lectures in September 1909, was accepted.

July 7, 1909 (893)

The first surgical transplant of a human nerve was accomplished by Walter Jacoby of Munich. A 4.5-cm segment was transplanted into the hand of a 35-year-old manual laborer, Helmut Mitschke.

August 3, 1909 (894)

Neal E. Miller was born. Miller has made lasting contributions in motivation, aggression, social learning, and instrumental autonomic conditioning. APA Distinguished Scientific Contribution Award, 1959; APA President, 1961; National Medal of Science, 1964; APA Distinguished Professional Contributions Award, 1983; APA Outstanding Lifetime Contribution to Psychology Award, 1991.

August 19, 1909 (895)

Hedda Bolgar was born. Bolgar, a specialist in personality theory, psychoanalysis, and projective techniques, was a prominent trainer of clinical psychologists for 40 years.

August 21, 1909 (896)

Sigmund Freud and Carl Jung sailed from Bremen to attend a conference at Clark University. On the previous day, Freud had fainted in Jung's presence. Jung later attributed the incident to a conversation about corpses found in a peat bog and

Freud's inference that Jung's choice of topic symbolized the wish that Freud were dead. Freud attributed the event to fatigue and wine.

August 29, 1909 (897)
Sigmund Freud and Carl Jung arrived in New York aboard the steamer *George Washington* to attend the Clark University 20th anniversary celebrations convened by G. Stanley Hall. They stayed at the Hotel Manhattan in New York.

September 6, 1909 (898)
Clark University's 20th anniversary conference began. Arranged by Clark president G. Stanley Hall, the conference featured Sigmund Freud and Carl Jung among the speakers. This was Freud's only appearance in America. He called it "the first official recognition of our work."

September 7, 1909 (899)
Sigmund Freud gave the first of his five daily lectures at Clark University. In this lecture, Freud described Josef Breuer's case of "Anna O." and the "talking cure" used in her therapy.

September 9, 1909 (900)
William James met Sigmund Freud in the evening at G. Stanley Hall's home. James stayed to hear Freud's lecture the next day and walked with Freud to the railroad station in the evening. Freud later reported James's courage during an attack of angina pectoris during this walk.

September 10, 1909 (901)
The famous group picture of those attending the Clark University 20th anniversary conference was taken. The picture included Sigmund Freud, Carl Jung, William James, A. A. Brill, G. Stanley Hall, Bronislaw Malinowski, and Ernest Jones.

September 10, 1909 (902)
Sigmund Freud received an honorary Doctor of Laws degree from Clark University. This was the only honorary degree he ever received.

October 16, 1909 (903)
Arthur Benton was born. Benton has applied his studies of perceptual and cognitive deficits associated with brain lesion to neuropsychological assessment. The Benton Visual Retention Test is widely used in clinical settings. APA Distinguished Professional Contribution Award, 1978; American Psychological Foundation Gold Medal for Life Achievement in the Applications of Psychology, 1991.

October 20, 1909 (904)
The new U.S. Food and Drug Administration seized 40 barrels and 20 kegs of Coca-Cola syrup near Chattanooga, Tennessee, because Coca-Cola contained caf-

feine. Coca-Cola hired psychologist Harry Hollingworth to study the effects of caffeine on humans as part of its legal defense. Hollingworth's studies were models of experimental control across a broad range of conditions.

December 17, 1909 (905)
Annette Gillette was born. Gillette was an expert in school psychology, child clinical psychology, testing, and school adjustment.

December 28, 1909 (906)
Ivan Pavlov delivered his "Tower of Silence" lecture to the 12th Congress of Naturalists and Physicians in Moscow. The lecture emphasized the importance of experimental control and resulted some years later in a tower laboratory building actually erected in St. Petersburg to provide Pavlov the experimental isolation he required.

December 29, 1909 (907)
Robert M. Yerkes proposed to the APA annual meeting that the APA publish a journal of animal behavior, to be supported by a fee of $1 per member. This would have been the first APA journal, but the APA declined, feeling that competition with privately published journals would be inappropriate and unfair.

January 10, 1910 (908)
Marie Skodak Crissey was born. Crissey worked extensively with studies of mental retardation, testing, and child development, becoming well-known for her studies of environmental deprivation and enrichment on mental development. She helped develop special education, school psychology, and school social work programs in the public schools.

February 15, 1910 (909)
Ralph F. Hefferline was born. Hefferline was a behavior analyst whose work on operant conditioning of thumb movements demonstrated conditioning of behaviors without the participant's awareness. Hefferline also had an interest in Fritz Perls's Gestalt therapy. Popular psychologist Joyce Brothers completed her doctoral dissertation under Hefferline's supervision.

February 20, 1910 (910)
John G. Darley was born. Darley combined a career in research, writing, and practice in counseling psychology with administrative, editorial, and advocacy skills that made him a pivotal figure in the post-World War II development of the APA and modern professional psychology. APA Executive Officer, 1959–1962.

March 14, 1910 (911)
Oran Wendle Eagleson was born. Eagleson, an African American psychologist, earned his way from high school through the PhD by working in a shoe repair

shop. His research interests included racial and ethnic issues, problem solving, handwriting, music, and personality.

March 30, 1910   (912)
The International Psychoanalytic Association was formed in Nuremberg, Germany, with Carl Jung as the first president. Sándor Ferenczi gave the keynote address, "On the Organization of the Psychoanalytic Movement."

May 2, 1910   (913)
The founding meeting of the American Psychopathological Association was held at the Willard Hotel in Washington, DC, at the same time as the annual meeting of the American Neurological Association. Morton Prince was the first president of the American Psychopathological Association.

May 13, 1910   (914)
Peter A. Bertocci was born. Bertocci was a philosophical psychologist whose "personalism" encouraged confrontation with the moral, ethical, and emotional demands of being fully human. He actively promoted the roles of education and counseling in the pursuit of realizing one's human potential.

May 21, 1910   (915)
Shearley Oliver Roberts was born. Roberts contributed to psychology in the areas of child development, cultural differences, personality adjustment, and testing of intelligence, interest, and achievement. He established the psychology department at Fisk University (1951).

May 26, 1910   (916)
Ruth Hartley was born. Best known for her research in personality development and child psychology, Hartley also touched on educational psychology, the psychology of social roles, individual–group interactions, and feminist issues.

July 10, 1910   (917)
Donald E. Super was born. Super's longitudinal study of career development, the Career Pattern Study, began in 1951 and provided the first empirical information about lifetime changes in occupations. He served on the first APA committees on ethical standards and on test standards. APA Distinguished Scientific Award for the Applications of Psychology, 1983.

August 10, 1910   (918)
Angus Campbell was born. Campbell was known for his research on voting behavior. His book *The American Voter* greatly influenced American political science from a psychological perspective. He also studied racial attitudes and the subjective quality of life. APA Distinguished Scientific Contribution Award, 1974.

September 11, 1910 (919)

Leo M. Hurvich was born. Hurvich, with Dorothea Jameson, has been responsible for pioneering experiments on the opponent-process theory of color vision. Society of Experimental Psychologists Warren Medal, 1971; APA Distinguished Scientific Contribution Award, 1972.

September 19, 1910 (920)

Ledyard R. Tucker was born. Tucker developed three-mode factor analysis and interbattery factor analysis, and contributed to test theory, structural equation modeling, and individual-differences scaling models. APA Distinguished Scientific Contribution Award, 1987.

September 22, 1910 (921)

Robert L. Thorndike was born. Thorndike's career focused on personnel selection, psychometrics, and ability measurement. He was president of the Psychometric Society, the American Educational Research Association, and three divisions of the APA.

October 1, 1910 (922)

New Jersey State Psychological Services began when J. E. Wallace Wallin left the Vineland Training School to open a psychological laboratory at the New Jersey Village for Epileptics, near Princeton. This was the first state-supported psychological clinic in New Jersey.

October 13, 1910 (923)

Meredith P. Crawford was born. Crawford brought his skills as an experimental psychologist to bear on military problems during World War II. After the war, he became the first director of the Human Resources Research Organization (HumRRO) in 1951 and its first president when it became an independent corporation in 1969. APA Award for Distinguished Professional Contributions, 1983.

November 29, 1910 (924)

Edith Weisskopf-Joelson was born. Weisskopf-Joelson was a clinical psychologist with special interests in projective techniques and transcendental experiences. She developed widely used norms of responses to the Thematic Apperception Test.

December 7, 1910 (925)

Eleanor Jack Gibson was born. Gibson's work in perceptual development led to the APA Distinguished Scientific Contribution Award in 1968. Her "visual cliff" experiments are particularly well-known. She was the second female psychologist elected to the National Academy of Sciences (1971). National Medal of Science, 1992.

December 25, 1910 (926)
Erika Fromm was born. She was influenced by Gestalt psychologist Max Wertheimer. Her interests and research were in psychoanalysis and hypnosis. Typical of her efforts to combine the science and the practice of psychology was the establishment of a psychological laboratory in a Dutch hospital.

January 5, 1911 (927)
Gunnar Johansson was born. Johansson's studies of visual event perception have examined human interpretation of moving stimuli over time. Special topics have been perceptual vector analysis, perception of minimal events, biological motion, nonrigid motion, self-motion, and natural motion. APA Distinguished Scientific Contribution Award, 1986.

February 8, 1911 (928)
Freudians attacked the theories of Alfred Adler and his followers at a meeting of the Vienna Psychoanalytic Society. Adler resigned the presidency of the organization shortly afterward and founded his own society for individual psychology.

February 11, 1911 (929)
Joseph Peterson, instructor of psychology and the only PhD holder in the department at Brigham Young University, was among three psychologists warned by the Mormon General Church Council that they would be "dispensed with" if they did not discontinue their teaching of Darwinian theory. Peterson left at the end of the school year but went on to become president of the APA in 1934.

February 12, 1911 (930)
The first meeting of the New York Psychoanalytic Society was held. A. A. Brill was the founding president. This was the first association of psychoanalysts in the United States.

March 16, 1911 (931)
The trial of *U.S. v. 40 Barrels and 20 Kegs of Coca-Cola* began. The trial featured evidence from now-classic studies by Harry Hollingworth of the effects of caffeine on mental functions. Hollingworth began his research on February 3, 1911, and testified on March 27, 1911. The court acquitted Coca-Cola on June 13, 1914. Hollingworth was president of the APA in 1927.

April 13, 1911 (932)
Frank A. Beach was born. His areas of focus were comparative psychology and sexual behavior. Beach's provocative address, "The Snark was a Boojum" (1949), promoted the study of animals other than the rat in environments other than the laboratory. APA Distinguished Scientific Contribution Award, 1958; American Psychological Foundation Distinguished Teaching in Psychobiology Award, 1985.

April 19, 1911 (933)

The National Academy of Sciences Section on Anthropology was renamed the Section on Anthropology and Psychology. This was the first organizational accommodation to psychology by the National Academy of Sciences.

May 9, 1911 (934)

The American Psychoanalytic Association was founded in Baltimore. Ernest Jones convened the founding group of eight members. James J. Putnam was elected the first president of the organization.

June 4, 1911 (935)

Silvan Tomkins was born. Tomkins's early work explored personality assessment with the Thematic Apperception Test and the Tomkins-Horn Picture Arrangement Test. Later work focused on identifying a set of innate primary emotions and describing their features and development.

July 1, 1911 (936)

The nation's first mother's aid law took effect in Illinois. These laws were intended to aid widowed mothers and were the precursors of contemporary programs of aid to families with dependent children. There was strong opposition to mother's aid laws, citing the potential for creating dependency, usurping the responsibilities of families, and expense.

August 22, 1911 (937)

Ernest J. McCormick was born. McCormick was an industrial and organizational psychologist whose work dominated the areas of job analysis and human factors. He devised the widely used Position Analysis Questionnaire (1969) and wrote *Human Engineering* (1957), a landmark text.

September 29, 1911 (938)

Karl Lashley applied for admission to the graduate program in zoology at Johns Hopkins University. Lashley came in contact with zoologist Herbert S. Jennings and psychologist John B. Watson at Johns Hopkins, giving impetus to his interest in comparative psychology.

September 30, 1911 (939)

David Rapaport was born. Rapaport was a psychoanalytic psychologist who attempted a merger of psychoanalysis with mainstream psychology.

March 1, 1912 (940)

Walter B. Cannon and A. L. Washburn's article "An Explanation of Hunger," describing a classic study in which balloons were inflated in the stomach, was published by the *American Journal of Physiology*.

March 5, 1912 (941)

Isidor Chein was born. Chein was a social psychologist who brought skilled methodology to bear on social issues such as juvenile delinquency, drug addiction, intergroup relations, and ethnic group identification. APA Award for Distinguished Contributions in the Public Interest, 1980.

April 5, 1912 (942)

James A. Bayton was born. Bayton's research and consulting focused on consumer behavior in the area of commodity marketing. He served as a consultant to the National Association for the Advancement of Colored People and to the military on the effects of racism and segregation. American Psychological Foundation Distinguished Teaching in Psychology Award, 1981.

April 6, 1912 (943)

Dorothy Adkins was born. Adkins employed her expertise in factor analysis in studies of affect in children, curriculum design, and educational program evaluation. President, Psychonomic Society, 1950.

April 9, 1912 (944)

President Taft signed legislation establishing the U.S. Children's Bureau, the first federal agency to study and report on "all matters pertaining to the welfare of children and child life among all classes of our people." There was strong opposition to the Children's Bureau. Critics cited governmental meddling in family life and wasteful duplication of existing services.

April 16, 1912 (945)

Christian Ruckmick described the status of early experimental psychology in a presentation to the Society of Experimental Psychologists. He reported that the average annual salary of a full professor was $2,500 and that the wealthiest psychology department was that of Columbia University, with a total salary and operating budget of $13,549.

May 5, 1912 (946)

Paul Fitts was born. Fitts was a pioneer in human engineering psychology, aviation equipment design, and the application of information theory to visual stimuli.

May 12, 1912 (947)

Samuel B. Kutash was born. Kutash's interests were in clinical psychology, psychotherapy, and criminal behavior. He was a leader in the development of professional schools of psychology, helping to found the New Jersey School of Applied and Professional Psychology, the first independent, but university-related, program at Rutgers University (1974).

May 26, 1912 (948)

Sigmund Freud visited Ludwig Binswanger in Kreutzlingen, Switzerland. Carl Jung was 40 miles (64 km) away in Zurich, but Freud and Jung did not arrange to meet. In later letters, Jung referred to this as Freud's "Kreutzlingen gesture," taking it as an unconsciously motivated insult. The incident was the beginning of the end of the Freud–Jung relationship.

June 2, 1912 (949)

Bernard Berelson was born. Berelson's interests were communication and political behavior. He popularized the term *behavioral science* while at the Ford Foundation. With Gary Steiner, he wrote the book *Human Behavior: An Inventory of Scientific Findings* in 1964.

June 11, 1912 (950)

Lorrin A. Riggs was born. Riggs's research on human vision included studies of voluntary and involuntary eye movements, human color vision, afterimages, and pattern perception. His technical abilities have been responsible for the invention of several experimental instruments that are based on the contact lens. APA Distinguished Scientific Contribution Award, 1974.

June 12, 1912 (951)

Carl I. Hovland was born. Hovland's early work was on learning and motivation. He formulated the frustration–aggression hypothesis (1939) with John Dollard and others. During World War II, Hovland studied communication and later, with Irving Janis and Harold H. Kelley, wrote the classic book *Communication and Persuasion* (1949). APA Distinguished Scientific Contribution Award, 1957.

June 28, 1912 (952)

The New York State Hospital Commission, former Congressman William Bennett, and a consortium of steamship companies met and agreed to return 2,000 immigrant mental patients in New York hospitals to their countries of origin. There were 9,241 such patients in New York at the time, and it was widely believed that European countries were intentionally sending them to the United States.

July 22, 1912 (953)

Clyde H. Coombs was born. Coombs's research resulted in the development of the field of nonmetric scaling. His work has greatly influenced progress in mathematical psychology. APA Distinguished Scientific Contribution Award, 1985.

September 1, 1912 (954)

The Moscow Institute of Psychology was opened. Georgy Chelpanov, a student of Wilhelm Wundt and Carl Stumpf, was instrumental in its founding and was appointed first director.

November 12, 1912 (955)
Frederic M. Lord was born. Lord's seminal work, *Statistical Theories of Mental Test Scores* (1974), summarized his contributions to the theory and practice of psychological measurement. His item response theory has established methods of latent trait measurement, test equivalence, and analysis of errors of measurement. APA Distinguished Scientific Contribution Award, 1988.

February 24, 1913 (956)
John B. Watson gave his noteworthy lecture titled "Psychology as the Behaviorist Views It" to the meeting of the New York Branch of the APA at Columbia University. The lecture was also published in *Psychological Review* (1913).

April 15, 1913 (957)
Barbel Inhelder was born. Inhelder was Jean Piaget's primary collaborator and the successor to his chair at the University of Geneva and his lines of theoretical development. Her primary investigations have been in the child's understanding of conservation, conceptions of space and geometry, and the stage of formal operations.

April 17, 1913 (958)
Stuart W. Cook was born. Cook focused his research on the social problems of anti-Semitism, racism, desegregation, ethical treatment of human participants, resource conservation, and environmental protection. His career of socially responsible studies led to the APA Award for Distinguished Contributions to Psychology in the Public Interest in 1983.

May 25, 1913 (959)
After the defections of Alfred Adler, Wilhelm Stekel, and Carl Jung, Sigmund Freud formed a secret committee of loyal followers (Karl Abraham, Otto Rank, Ernest Jones, Hanns Sachs, and Sándor Ferenczi). Their first meeting was on this day. Freud gave each member a Greek intaglio to mount in a gold ring as a sign of membership.

May 26, 1913 (960)
John L. Kennedy was born. Kennedy was known for his work in applied experimental psychology and human engineering. With the Rand Corporation, he worked on designing air defense systems that included human factors considerations, using simulation as a comprehensive research tool.

May 27, 1913 (961)
Carl Pfaffmann was born. Pfaffmann's career was dedicated to careful and exhaustive exploration of the sense of taste and its physiology, neurology, and motivating properties. APA Distinguished Scientific Contribution Award, 1963.

June 6, 1913 (962)

Edward L. Thorndike's *Educational Psychology: Vol. 1. The Original Nature of Man* was published.

July 14, 1913 (963)

Mary Henle was born. Henle's major contributions have been thorough commentaries on the history and systems of psychology, with special attention given to the history of Gestalt psychology. She has also been an active investigator of the psychology of thinking and problem solving.

August 1, 1913 (964)

Wilhelm Wundt administered Anna Berliner's final oral examination, during which Berliner defended her doctoral dissertation, "Subjectivity and Objectivity of Sensory Impressions." Berliner was Wundt's only woman doctoral student.

August 14, 1913 (965)

Josef Brožek was born. Brožek has written extensively on the history and systems of psychology, especially Russian psychology. His other research has included work on nutrition and behavior.

August 20, 1913 (966)

Roger W. Sperry was born. Sperry's best known studies were of functional differences between the right and left cerebral hemispheres. He also studied neurospecificity through nerve regeneration and the functions of displaced organs. Society of Experimental Psychologists Warren Medal, 1969; APA Distinguished Scientific Contribution Award, 1971; Nobel prize, 1981; National Medal of Science, 1989.

September 7, 1913 (967)

Carl Jung presented his typology to the Fourth International Congress of Psychoanalysis in Munich and broke his ideological ties with Sigmund Freud.

September 27, 1913 (968)

Albert Ellis was born. Ellis has devised and promoted rational–emotive therapy, a cognitive–behavioral approach to psychotherapy that is based on exposing and confronting the irrational beliefs of the client. APA Distinguished Professional Contributions Award, 1985.

October 16, 1913 (969)

Raymond J. McCall was born. McCall's contributions were in philosophical and clinical psychology, especially in phenomenological approaches to personality and psychotherapy. He was a founder of the Wisconsin School of Professional Psychology (1980) and pivotal in the early growth of the Wisconsin Psychological Association.

December 1, 1913 (970)

Mary D. Salter Ainsworth was born. Ainsworth is known for her longitudinal naturalistic cross-cultural studies of mother–infant attachment and separation. She was strongly influenced by John Bowlby's theory of attachment. APA Award for Distinguished Professional Contributions, 1987; APA Distinguished Scientific Contribution Award, 1989.

December 5, 1913 (971)

The *Psychoanalytic Review* was first published.

December 5, 1913 (972)

Susan Walton Gray was born. Gray's research and professional activities promoted educational programs to overcome the social and environmental conditions of poverty. Gray and Rupert Klaus's Early Training Project provided a model for Project Head Start. She founded research and training programs in early childhood education, school psychology, and mental retardation.

January 26, 1914 (973)

Fillmore H. Sanford was born. Sanford's academic interests were in studies of leadership, attitudes, language, and mental health. As executive secretary of the APA (1950–1956), he promoted licensing and certification standards to fight quackery in psychological services.

February 18, 1914 (974)

Roger Kenton Williams was born. Williams's career was devoted to supervision of student research, general experimental psychology, and statistical applications of qualitative data.

March 1, 1914 (975)

Stella Chess was born. Chess's longitudinal studies of personality showed persistent, but weak, patterns of stable temperament from infancy to adulthood. Her book, *Origins and Evolution of Behavior Disorders: Infancy to Early Adult Life* (1984, with Alexander Thomas), summarizes this work. Chess also wrote authoritative books on child rearing for a general audience.

March 7, 1914 (976)

John T. Wilson was born. Wilson, an experimental psychologist, was the first director of National Science Foundation (NSF) programs in psychobiology, founded the NSF Program Analysis Office to assess national programs in science, and later directed the NSF Division of Biological and Medical Sciences. He won the first Distinguished Service Award ever given by the NSF.

April 3, 1914 (977)

Speaking to the annual meeting of the American Philosophical Society, E. B. Titchener delivered his assessment of behaviorism: "Elementary, my dear Watson!"

April 20, 1914 (978)
Reflecting his split with Sigmund Freud, Carl Jung resigned the presidency of the International Psychoanalytic Association.

May 25, 1914 (979)
The first convention of the Societies of Mental Hygiene was held at Johns Hopkins University. These local organizations later became affiliates of the National Mental Health Association.

July 23, 1914 (980)
Carlton Benjamin Goodlet was born. Goodlet directed his efforts as a behavioral scientist to fighting the effects of racism.

July 24, 1914 (981)
Kenneth B. Clark was born. Clark's work, with Mamie Phipps Clark, on the psychologically harmful effects of segregation was cited in the Supreme Court decision of *Brown v. Board of Education*. He was the first African American psychologist to serve as president of the APA (1971). APA Distinguished Contribution to Psychology in the Public Interest Award, 1978.

August 30, 1914 (982)
Roger W. Russell was born. Russell's academic interests have been in the biochemistry of behavior, psychopharmacology, the effects of environmental stressors on behavior, neurophysiology, and psychiatry. Executive Secretary of the APA, 1956–1959.

September 24, 1914 (983)
John B. Watson's *Behavior: An Introduction to Comparative Psychology* was published.

December 25, 1914 (984)
Thyroid hormone (*thyroxine*) was first isolated by Edward Kendall of the Mayo Clinic in Rochester, Minnesota.

February 28, 1915 (985)
Benton J. Underwood was born. Underwood extensively studied factors affecting verbal learning and memory, with special attention to distribution of practice, transfer, retroactive and proactive inhibition, and discrimination. APA Distinguished Scientific Contribution Award, 1973; American Psychological Foundation Distinguished Teaching in Psychology Award, 1987.

March 13, 1915 (986)
Nicholas Hobbs was born. Hobbs founded the nation's first mental retardation training program, stimulated Project Head Start, and founded programs for children with emotional disorders in homelike centers. APA President, 1966; APA Awards

for Distinguished Contributions in the Public Interest and Distinguished Professional Contributions to Public Service, 1980.

April 9, 1915 (987)
Gordon F. Derner was born. Derner's interests were in personality assessment, clinical psychology, and professional psychology. He was a pioneer in the development of professional schools of psychology, founding the early program at Adelphi University (1951). He also was the founding president of the National Council of Schools of Professional Psychology (1976).

April 11, 1915 (988)
John I. Lacey was born. Lacey's research, with Beatrice C. Lacey, has integrated neurophysiological and psychophysiological events and theories. The relation between cardiovascular activity, attention, and sensorimotor activity has served as the proving ground of their theories. APA Distinguished Scientific Contribution Award, 1976; American Psychological Foundation Psychological Science Gold Medal, 1985.

April 20, 1915 (989)
Joseph Wolpe was born. Wolpe developed and promoted behavioral techniques of psychotherapy. The method of systematic desensitization is attributed to Wolpe. His *Psychotherapy by Reciprocal Inhibition* (1958) and *The Practice of Behavior Therapy* (1969) were landmark books in the field. APA Distinguished Scientific Award for Applications of Psychology, 1979.

April 21, 1915 (990)
G. Stanley Hall was elected to the National Academy of Sciences, the fourth psychologist so honored.

April 23, 1915 (991)
Margaret Hubbard Jones was born. Her interests were perception, developmental psycholinguistics, cognitive development, and traffic safety. Jones applied theoretical approaches and rigorous methodology to social action programs.

May 20, 1915 (992)
Mary J. Wright was born. Wright's initial research was in child and social psychology, which she combined with teaching and community service. She then turned to administration, becoming the first woman to head a psychology department in Canada, at the University of Western Ontario. Wright was the first woman president of the Canadian Psychological Association.

May 22, 1915 (993)
Arthur H. Brayfield was born. Brayfield's interests have been in counseling and industrial/organizational psychology. APA Executive Officer, 1969–1975.

July 7, 1915   (994)
Sibylle Korsch Escalona was born. Escalona was a clinical child psychologist best known for her longitudinal studies of the correlation between measures of infant behavior and performance at later ages.

July 21, 1915   (995)
Clifford T. Morgan was born. Morgan's work focused on the physiological bases of behavior. His text *Physiological Psychology* (1943) was a standard for decades, and his introductory text was widely used. Morgan was a founder and the first president of the Psychonomic Society and founded and edited several of its journals.

September 24, 1915   (996)
Lillian E. Troll was born. Troll's research was primarily in development across the life span and interpersonal relations.

October 1, 1915   (997)
Jerome Bruner was born. Bruner has been a pivotal figure in modern cognitive psychology. His interests have been in cognitive development, "new look" studies in perception, educational reform, and social opinion formation and change. He helped found the Center for Cognitive Studies at Harvard University in 1960. APA Distinguished Scientific Contribution Award, 1962; APA President, 1965.

November 4, 1915   (998)
Herman Feifel was born. Feifel has focused on the psychology of death, dying, and bereavement. His 1959 book *The Meaning of Death* was a pivotal publication in the founding of his specialty, now called *thanatology*. APA Award for Distinguished Professional Contributions, 1988.

November 7, 1915   (999)
Lorraine Bouthilet was born. Bouthilet was the managing editor of *Behavioral Science* and the *American Psychologist*, prepared the first edition of the *Publication Manual of the APA*, and prepared the surgeon general's report, *Television and Behavior*. At the National Institute of Mental Health, she was research program specialist and clearinghouse director.

December 2, 1915   (1000)
Natalie Shainess was born. Shainess, a psychoanalyst, focused on the study of sexuality and society, the psychology of women, and personality development.

December 25, 1915   (1001)
James F. Bugental was born. Bugental was an early leader of the humanistic psychology movement of the 1960s and 1970s. He was the first president of the Association for Humanistic Psychology (1962). His existential orientation emphasized an "authentic" relation to one's world, leading to "organismic awareness."

December 29, 1915 (1002)

The first program committee for the APA annual meeting was appointed, "to avoid in the future congestion of the program due to an oversupply of titles." Madison Bentley, Robert Ogden, and Guy Whipple made up the committee.

December 29, 1915 (1003)

The APA passed a resolution reflecting early concern over practitioner standards. The APA discouraged "the use of mental tests for practical psychological diagnosis by individuals psychologically unqualified for this work."

January 4, 1916 (1004)

Sidney Siegel was born. Siegel was a statistician and decision theorist who provided, among other contributions, a widely used text in nonparametric statistics.

February 10, 1916 (1005)

Louis Guttman was born. Guttman devised a method of attitude scaling, *scalogram analysis*, derived from the cumulatively ordered preferences of the respondent.

February 11, 1916 (1006)

Bernice Levin Neugarten was born. Neugarten earned the first PhD in human development granted by a university, from the University of Chicago in 1943. Her major contributions have been in the psychology and sociology of adult development and aging. American Psychological Foundation Distinguished Teaching Award, 1975.

February 25, 1916 (1007)

Uriel G. Foa was born. Foa was instrumental in developing social exchange theory, based on evidence that social behavior is shaped by the exchange of tangible and intangible resources.

February 29, 1916 (1008)

Maria Montessori was awarded a U.S. patent for her "cut out geometrical figures for didactical purposes." The figures demonstrated the concept of division of wholes into smaller components.

March 4, 1916 (1009)

Hans Eysenck was born. Eysenck's factor-analytic theory of personality had as its main components the factors of Introversion/Extraversion and Stability/Instability. His noteworthy 1952 review of studies of the effectiveness of psychotherapy concluded that many studies were scientifically inadequate and that well-controlled studies revealed weak or no benefits of therapy.

March 22, 1916 (1010)

Nathan Kline was born. Kline was a psychiatrist who pioneered the use of drug therapy, especially the use of lithium carbonate in treating depression.

April 22, 1916 (1011)

Lee J. Cronbach was born. Cronbach's specialties were measurement, educational psychology, and the study of individual differences. In 1992, *Psychological Bulletin* published a list of its 10 most cited articles. Cronbach was first or only author of four of them. APA President, 1957; APA Distinguished Scientific Contributions Award, 1973.

April 25, 1916 (1012)

Conrad Kraft was born. Kraft's work in visual perception, engineering psychology, and human factors research, principally for the Boeing Company, has resulted in improvements in air travel safety. APA Distinguished Contribution for Applications in Psychology Award, 1973.

June 15, 1916 (1013)

Lewis M. Terman's book *The Measurement of Intelligence* was published.

June 15, 1916 (1014)

Herbert A. Simon was born. Simon is a leader in artificial intelligence, cognition, and decision making, and coauthor (with Allen Newell) of the first heuristic problem-solving computer program (1955). APA Distinguished Scientific Contribution Award, 1969; Nobel prize, 1978; National Medal of Science, 1986; American Psychological Foundation Gold Medal, 1988; APA Outstanding Lifetime Contribution Award, 1993.

June 22, 1916 (1015)

Leopold Bellak was born. Bellak's research has concentrated on the clinical use of the Thematic Apperception Test and on ego functions in patients with schizophrenia. He promoted the formation of the Schizophrenia Research Center at the National Institute of Mental Health. APA Award for Distinguished Professional Contributions, 1992.

July 1, 1916 (1016)

The Government Hospital for the Insane, the oldest U.S. federal mental hospital, was officially renamed St. Elizabeth's Hospital. The new name was derived from the tract of land on which the hospital is located and had been informally used since the Civil War to avoid the social stigma associated with the official name.

August 2, 1916 (1017)

Herman A. Witkin was born. Witkin's career began with studies in Gestalt psychology and perception. He later studied cognitive style using the Rod-and-Frame Test, the Embedded Figures Test, and cross-cultural and family processes methods to detect individual differences in field dependence–independence. His book *Psychological Differentiation* has been widely cited.

August 7, 1916   (1018)

Hans-Lukas Teuber was born. Teuber specialized in the study of brain mechanisms involved in visual perception, with special attention given to the effects of brain injury on vision. Karl S. Lashley Award, 1966; NASA Achievement Award, 1969.

August 21, 1916   (1019)

Milton Theaman was born. Theaman has promoted the autonomy of professional psychology through responsible standards of accountability and review procedures, by effective advocacy before health insurance organizations, and by inaugurating low-cost services at psychological service centers. APA Award for Distinguished Professional Contributions, 1982.

August 21, 1916   (1020)

Robert M. Gagné was born. Gagné has applied the experimental psychology of learning to the practical problem of effective instruction. His book *The Conditions of Learning* was a landmark volume that presented a comprehensive typology of learning. APA Distinguished Scientific Award for the Applications of Psychology, 1982.

August 30, 1916   (1021)

Virginia Staudt Sexton was born. Sexton's writing has illuminated the histories of special groups of psychologists, notably Roman Catholics, humanists, international psychologists, and women. Her organizational and academic work has broadened the scope of psychology and informed psychologists about their histories and relations with each other.

September 20, 1916   (1022)

The first meeting of the National Research Council was held.

October 22, 1916   (1023)

Julian B. Rotter was born. Rotter's social learning framework pioneered new behavioral approaches to personal and clinical psychology. He is best known for his description of internal versus external locus of control as a personality variable. APA Distinguished Scientific Contribution Award, 1988.

November 15, 1916   (1024)

The National Research Council created its Committee on Psychology for the purposes of war preparedness in 1916. Anthropology was added in 1919.

November 20, 1916   (1025)

Donald T. Campbell was born. Campbell's writing on research methods, measurement, and social psychology reflects broad interests in psychology, philosophy, and sociology. His *Experimental and Quasi-Experimental Designs for Research* (1963, with Julian Stanley) is a commonly cited source on research methods. APA Distinguished Scientific Contribution Award, 1970; APA President, 1975.

November 20, 1916 (1026)

Charles Osgood was born. Osgood's interest in psycholinguistics led to extensive study of the connotative meanings of words, as measured by his semantic differential technique. His work in the psychology of negotiation resulted in a strategy of graduated and reciprocated initiatives in tension-reduction (the GRIT strategy for reduction of intergroup tension). APA Distinguished Scientific Contribution Award, 1960; APA President, 1963.

December 6, 1916 (1027)

The New York Psychiatric Society appointed a committee on the activities of psychologists. The committee's later report urged disapproval of psychologists judging "the mental condition of sick, defective, or otherwise abnormal persons" and disapproval of "the application of psychology to responsible clinical work except . . . under the direct supervision of physicians."

January 23, 1917 (1028)

APA President Robert Yerkes wrote to President Wilson to offer his services in the event of war. The United States entered World War I on April 6, and by April 22 the APA Council had approved the association's involvement.

February 15, 1917 (1029)

Abraham A. Brill's English translation of Sigmund Freud's book *The History of the Psychoanalytic Movement* was published in the United States.

March 17, 1917 (1030)

Alphonse Chapanis was born. Chapanis was a prominent figure in the emergence of the field of human engineering from World War II studies of machine design and human operator variables. APA Distinguished Scientific Award for the Application of Psychology, 1978.

March 17, 1917 (1031)

The first issue of the *Journal of Applied Psychology* was published. G. Stanley Hall, John Wallace Baird, and Ludwig R. Geissler were editors of the journal.

April 18, 1917 (1032)

Edward L. Thorndike became the fifth psychologist elected to the National Academy of Sciences.

April 18, 1917 (1033)

Sigmund Koch was born. Koch produced studies of motivation and learning and is best known for his editorship of the comprehensive APA series of books, *Psychology: A Study of a Science* (1959–1963).

April 20, 1917 (1034)

Urie Bronfenbrenner was born. Bronfenbrenner, a developmental psychologist, emphasized the social context of child development, providing an impetus for Project Head Start. In the 1960s, his research on "mirror image" perceptions provided an understanding of Soviet–American relations. APA Award for Distinguished Contribution to Psychology in the Public Interest, 1987.

April 21, 1917 (1035)

The Iowa Child Welfare Research Station was created by the Iowa legislature. The research facility resulted from the efforts of Carl Seashore and activist parent Cora B. Hillis of Des Moines. The first director was Bird T. Baldwin. The facility was renamed the Institute of Child Behavior and Development in 1963.

April 22, 1917 (1036)

The APA Executive Council appointed 12 war service committees to direct psychological participation in World War I. Under the overall direction of APA President Robert Yerkes, the committees specialized in such matters as examination of recruits, aptitude testing, morale, training, motivation, emotional disorders, acoustics, vision, and aviation.

April 30, 1917 (1037)

John W. Thibaut was born. Thibaut was a specialist in conflict resolution, procedural justice, fairness, and, with H. H. Kelley, author of a comprehensive social exchange theory of interpersonal relations called *interdependence theory*. He founded the *Journal of Experimental Social Psychology* in 1965. APA Distinguished Scientific Contributions Award, 1983.

April 30, 1917 (1038)

George Ellery Hale, astronomer and chairman of the National Research Council (NRC), named APA President Robert Yerkes to be chairman of the NRC Psychology Committee. The committee, charged with coordinating psychology's response to World War I, held its first meeting at Columbia University on May 18, 1917, and its second meeting on June 28, 1917.

May 10, 1917 (1039)

Alvin M. Liberman was born. Liberman pioneered the study of acoustic and physiological bases of speech production and perception. APA Distinguished Scientific Contribution Award, 1980.

May 15, 1917 (1040)

Eleanor Emmons Maccoby was born. Maccoby's works include studies of child rearing, sex differences, public opinion, and the effects of television viewing. Her books *Patterns of Child Rearing* (1957, with Robert Sears and Harry Levin) and *The Psychology of Sex Differences* (1974, with Carol Jacklin) are frequently cited. APA Distinguished Scientific Contribution Award, 1988.

May 20, 1917 (1041)

David C. McClelland was born. McClelland is known for his work in motivation in general but best known for his work on achievement motivation and its measurement, causes, and correlates. His book *The Achieving Society* (1961) has been translated into several languages. APA Distinguished Scientific Contribution Award, 1987.

June 12, 1917 (1042)

John Garcia was born. Garcia is best known for his work on classical conditioning of taste aversions and studies of innate preparedness for learning. APA Distinguished Scientific Contribution Award, 1979.

June 14, 1917 (1043)

Julius Wagner von Jauregg first intentionally injected a syphilitic psychotic patient with malaria. He later found that the treatment reduced the patient's symptoms. Wagner von Jauregg won the 1927 Nobel prize for his work, which represented the first successful biological treatment for any psychiatric disorder.

August 26, 1917 (1044)

Olga E. de Cillis Engelhardt was born. Her varied interests included comparative, social, experimental, and industrial/organizational psychology. She worked for several corporations in training and evaluation. She was the first woman industrial/organizational psychologist to head a division of business and management.

September 16, 1917 (1045)

Jane D. Hildreth was born. Hildreth was a member of the first professional staff hired by the APA and served continuously from 1950 until her retirement in 1988, when her title was Director of Membership and Records. She was a legendary source of information about the evolution of the APA and its procedures, both formal and informal.

September 19, 1917 (1046)

The Stanford Revision and Extension of the Binet-Simon Scale for Measuring Intelligence, commonly known as the Stanford-Binet Intelligence Test, was published.

September 20, 1917 (1047)

Behaviorist John B. Watson was ordered from his professorship at Johns Hopkins University into active military service. Watson went to England to test aviators for the Signal Corps. He irreverently assessed American officers as "nincompoops" and military service as "a nightmare." Despite a near court-martial, Watson was honorably discharged as a major on November 30, 1919.

October 1, 1917 (1048)

James McKeen Cattell was dismissed from Columbia University for pacifist objections to World War I. Cattell, a founder of the American Association of University Professors, had a history of confronting the university administration over the faculty's role in governance. He sued Columbia over his dismissal, won $40,000, and founded the Psychological Corporation with the money.

October 18, 1917 (1049)

Mamie Phipps Clark was born. Clark's studies on the self-concepts and color preferences of African American children demonstrated the pervasive effects of racism and were cited in the U.S. Supreme Court decision on *Brown v. Board of Education*. Clark also founded the Northside Center for Child Development (1946) in the Harlem district of New York City.

October 28, 1917 (1050)

Patricia Cain Smith was born. Smith was the first woman to be granted tenure at Cornell University. Her interests were in industrial/organizational psychology, measurement, statistics, and job satisfaction. She developed the Job Descriptive Index, the Retirement Descriptive Index, and the Behaviorally Anchored Rating Scales.

December 24, 1917 (1051)

The U.S. War Department adopted the Army Alpha and Army Beta Tests of intellectual (Alpha) and physical (Beta) abilities, developed by Robert M. Yerkes. These were the first such tests administered to large numbers of individuals.

December 28, 1917 (1052)

The American Association of Clinical Psychologists (AACP) was founded at the Carnegie Institute of Technology. J. E. W. Wallin was the first chairman. The group promoted training and certification standards for the practice of clinical psychology. The AACP became the APA Section of Clinical Psychology, the APA's first special interest division, on December 31, 1919.

December 28, 1917 (1053)

At the 25th Annual Meeting of the APA, the equipment display included "Fifty Small Colored Pictures of Oriental Rugs for Esthetic Judgments," "A New Model Electro-Mechanical Stimulus Shuffler," and "a new form of the Self-Registering Tapping Board."

January 2, 1918 (1054)

Kenneth B. Little was born. Little's interests have been in clinical psychology and the history and systems of psychology. APA Executive Officer, 1969–1975.

January 8, 1918 (1055)

Sol L. Garfield was born. Garfield has concentrated on comprehensive surveys of psychotherapy research and the training of clinical psychologists. His *Handbook of Psychotherapy and Behavior Change* (1971), edited with Allen Bergin, has been the definitive summary of the field for more than 20 years. APA Award for Distinguished Professional Contributions, 1979.

February 6, 1918 (1056)

Jane Loevinger was born. Loevinger's interests have included women's attitudes, ego development, measurement, and test construction. She has been very active in the American Association of University Women.

March 5, 1918 (1057)

Robert Chin (Chen Yuli) was born. Chin's research focused on organizational theory and on social issues related to prejudice and racism. He was a cofounder of the Human Relations Center at Boston University and coauthor, with Warren Bennis and Kenneth Benne, of *The Planning of Change* (1961), an influential exposition of social psychology research applied to organizational settings.

April 4, 1918 (1058)

James Emmett Birren was born. Birren's years of experimental research on age-related characteristics of neurological, sensory, perceptual, and cognitive functions made him a leader in the field of behavior gerontology. APA Distinguished Scientific Contribution Award, 1968.

April 17, 1918 (1059)

Major Bird T. Baldwin became the first psychologist assigned to a military hospital, Walter Reed General Hospital in Washington, DC.

May 13, 1918 (1060)

Edwin Shneidman was born. Shneidman has been a pioneer in the scientific study of suicide and in the training of suicide prevention specialists. He was a cofounder of the Los Angeles Suicide Prevention Center (1952) and founder of the American Association of Suicidology (1968). APA Award for Distinguished Professional Contributions, 1987.

May 24, 1918 (1061)

Stephen B. Withey was born. Withey's work applied social psychological research methods to major social problems such as international relations, effects of television and other mass media, and public attitudes toward big business, science, and advanced technology.

May 26, 1918 (1062)

Irving L. Janis was born. Janis was a social psychologist best known for his contributions of classic works on communication and persuasion, military morale, psychological stress, fear-arousing persuasion, decision making, and the pattern of group decision processes he termed *groupthink*. APA Distinguished Scientific Contribution Award, 1981.

June 7, 1918 (1063)

Leo Postman was born. Postman primarily studied perception, learning, and memory. He participated in the beginnings of the "new look" school of perception that emphasized the role of cognitive factors such as emotional state and cognitive set in determining perceptions.

June 27, 1918 (1064)

The Vocational Rehabilitation Act (Public Law 65-178) was signed, providing the first federal rehabilitation programs.

July 15, 1918 (1065)

Brenda Langford Milner was born. Her studies of brain localization have shed light on the roles of the hippocampus and the temporal lobe in memory, the causes of epilepsy, and the nature of hemisphere dominance. APA Distinguished Scientific Contribution Award, 1973.

July 18, 1918 (1066)

In a telegram to the U.S. Army chief of staff, General John J. Pershing recommended mental testing of soldiers before overseas duty. Pershing wrote, "prevalence of mental disorders in replacement troops recently received suggests urgent importance of intensive effort in eliminating mentally unfit." The telegram was a turning point in military psychology.

July 22, 1918 (1067)

Max Siegel was born. Siegel's career in private practice as a clinical psychologist was accompanied by highly respected teaching and administration in clinical psychology and school psychology. His concern for professional standards of licensure and confidentiality led to political activism. APA President, 1983.

August 1, 1918 (1068)

Frances K. Graham was born. Her test for brain damage, the Graham-Kendall Memory for Designs Test, and her studies of the orienting reflex, heart rate change, and reflexive blinking in infants are well-known. APA Distinguished Scientific Contribution Award, 1990; American Psychological Society William James Fellow, 1990.

August 4, 1918 (1069)

Tracy Seedman Kendler was born. Kendler applied a behavioral approach to the study of learning and problem solving. Her many research articles focused on reversal shifts, mediating responses, and concept formation, with special attention given to these phenomena in young children.

August 8, 1918 (1070)

Margaret Kuenne Harlow was born. Her contributions were in the areas of clinical and comparative psychology. Harlow managed the primate laboratory at the University of Wisconsin for 20 years, established the Publication Office of the APA, and edited the *Journal of Comparative and Physiological Psychology* from 1951 to 1962.

September 15, 1918 (1071)

John V. Zuckerman was born. Zuckerman's career of teaching, scholarship, and administration focused on management psychology. He held positions in industry, government, and education, spending much of his career at the University of Houston's Department of Management.

October 2, 1918 (1072)

Richard L. Solomon was born. Solomon's research in how the nervous system relates the organism to its environment included fundamental studies of discrimination, word recognition thresholds, and conditioning. APA Distinguished Scientific Contribution Award, 1966; American Psychological Foundation Distinguished Teaching in Experimental Psychology Award, 1988.

November 1, 1918 (1073)

J. Wilbert Edgerton was born. Edgerton's research and advocacy efforts have improved rural mental health services, public mental health services, and community action organizations concerned with mental health. He was pivotal in securing passage of North Carolina's psychologist licensure law (1967). APA Award for Distinguished Professional Service, 1992.

November 7, 1918 (1074)

Douglas W. Bray was born. Bray influenced the early course of organization psychology by developing the first management assessment center and extending the assessment center concept to personnel selection, longitudinal studies of management, and professional accreditation. APA Award for Distinguished Professional Contributions, 1980.

December 27, 1918 (1075)

Milton Rokeach was born. Rokeach's studies in social psychology concentrated on the relation between the rigid, dogmatic personality style and attitudes, social ideology, prejudice, and problem solving. His book *The Open and Closed Mind* (1960) presented this research.

January 12, 1919 (1076)

Seymour B. Sarason was born. Sarason has focused on educational, school, and community psychology. He played a central role in founding the Yale University clinical program, was an early promoter of deinstitutionalization, defined test anxiety, and cofounded the Yale Psycho-Educational Clinic (1961). APA Award for Distinguished Contributions to Psychology in the Public Interest, 1984.

February 9, 1919 (1077)
Elizabeth Münsterberg Koppitz was born. Koppitz was an expert in learning disabilities and child assessment. She conducted normative studies of responses to the Bender-Gestalt Test and devised a scoring system for that instrument. She also created the Visual Aural Digit Span Test.

February 25, 1919 (1078)
Karl H. Pribram was born. Pribram's extensive work in physiological psychology has advanced a theory relating the structural and functional organizations of the brain. A recent proposal uses the hologram as a model for spatial representation in the brain.

March 24, 1919 (1079)
The Swiss Psychoanalytic Society was founded. Hermann Rorschach was the first vice president.

March 25, 1919 (1080)
Fred Attneave III was born. Attneave was a perceptual psychologist whose book *Applications of Information Theory to Psychology* (1959) strongly influenced modern cognitive psychology, scaling theory, and theories of pattern recognition.

May 1, 1919 (1081)
Floyd Ratliff was born. Ratliff's work has focused on the physiology of vision. He developed an apparatus to show that images stabilized on the retina will disappear. His work on inhibition and disinhibition in the retina and their effects on perception has served as a model for similar processes throughout the nervous system. APA Distinguished Scientific Contribution Award, 1984.

May 8, 1919 (1082)
Leon Festinger was born. Festinger's theories of cognitive dissonance and social comparison processes have had lasting influence on social, personality, and motivational psychology. APA Distinguished Scientific Contribution Award, 1959.

June 17, 1919 (1083)
William K. Estes was born. Estes's early work with B. F. Skinner led to increasingly precise mathematical descriptions of learning. Later work concentrated on cognitive organization of learned elements in memory and mathematical models of learning. APA Distinguished Scientific Contribution Award, 1962; American Psychological Society William James Fellow, 1990.

June 26, 1919 (1084)

Kenneth MacCorquodale was born. As a graduate student, MacCorquodale was influenced by B. F. Skinner. MacCorquodale's research interests were in learning theory, especially the analysis of verbal behavior. He was executive editor of the respected Century Psychology Series.

June 26, 1919 (1085)

M. Brewster Smith was born. Smith's interests were in social issues such as race relations, cross-cultural education, opinions about Russia, the avoidance of nuclear war, and personnel selection for the Peace Corps. He was president of Psychologists for Social Responsibility. APA President, 1978; APA Distinguished Contributions to Psychology in the Public Interest Award, 1988.

July 3, 1919 (1086)

Sigmund Freud's follower Victor Tausk committed suicide following rejection by Freud and potential failure in a romantic attachment. Freud's role in the development of Tausk's life has remained a subject of controversy.

July 22, 1919 (1087)

Beatrice Cates Lacey was born. Lacey's research, with John I. Lacey, has integrated neurophysiological and psychophysiological events and theories. The relation between cardiovascular activity, attention, and sensorimotor activity has been the proving ground of their theories. APA Distinguished Scientific Contribution Award, 1976; American Psychological Foundation Psychological Science Gold Medal, 1985.

October 20, 1919 (1088)

The National Research Council Division of Anthropology and Psychology was organized.

November 1, 1919 (1089)

Eliot Stellar was born. Stellar was a physiological psychologist with special interests in the roles of the brain in emotion and motivation. His *Physiological Psychology* (1950, with Clifford T. Morgan) was a standard text in the field. Stellar invented the drinkometer and the first rat stereotaxic apparatus. American Psychological Foundation Gold Medal, 1993.

November 22, 1919 (1090)

John B. Watson's book *Psychology, From the Standpoint of a Behaviorist* was published.

December 29, 1919 (1091)

The American Association of Clinical Psychologists (AACP), formed by discontented APA members in 1917, merged with the APA and became the Clinical Section, the first special interest division within the APA. Arnold Gesell of the AACP and Bird T. Baldwin of the APA chaired the committee that founded the new division.

III

1920–1939
BETWEEN THE WARS:
CONSOLIDATION AS AN
INDEPENDENT SCIENCE

The years between the world wars were marked by continued growth and division of psychological organizations, by an increased concern with professional standards of scientific and practicing psychologists, by the broadening of the testing movement, and by the births of many currently prominent psychologists.

The last event of the previous chapter was the reintegration of the American Association of Clinical Psychologists into the American Psychological Association (APA), but practicing psychologists continued to feel uneasy within the APA, which was still dominated by academicians and scientists. A second split with practitioners opened in 1937 with the formation of the American Association for Applied Psychology (AAAP; Entries 1447 and 1448), a successor to the New York-based Association of Consulting Psychologists (Entry 1422). Practitioners in testing and evaluation under the leadership of L. L. Thurstone formed the Psychometric Society (Entries 1408 and 1409), and psychologists with an active interest in political and public policy issues formed the Society for the Psychological Study of Social Issues (SPSSI; Entries 1426 and 1427). These special interest organizations became affiliates of the APA when they were founded. The AAAP later merged with the APA (Entry 1536), the SPSSI became APA Division 9 when the APA reorganized in 1945, and the Psychometric Society has maintained a separate identity, although the APA reserved a division number for it (Division 4) when the APA was reorganized in 1944–1945. Discussion of affiliated groups should also include mention of the founding of Psi Chi, the honor society in psychology, in 1929 (Entry 1312). It is interesting to note that Psi Chi is actually the third name that was proposed for this organization, adopted after the founders discovered that two earlier Greek letter names were already in use by other organizations.

Some new organizations continued to be formed along regional lines. The Western Psychological Association, for example, held its first meeting in 1921 (Entry 1122), the Rocky Mountain Psychological Association was founded in 1930, although an exact founding date has yet to be identified, and the Canadian Psychological Association was inspired (Entry 1464) and inaugurated (Entry 1501) shortly before World War II.

The communications role of the APA began between the wars with the purchase of the first APA journals, *Psychological Review, Journal of Experimental Psychology, Psychological Index, Psychological Monographs*, and *Psychological Bulletin* from Howard C. Warren (Entry 1191); the purchase of Morton Prince's *Journal of Abnormal and Social Psychology* (Entry 1123); and the publication of *Psychological Abstracts* (Entries 1217 and 1249). Editorial standards for journal articles were established during these years (Entries 1290 and 1532) and later became the *Publication Manual of the American Psychological Association*, a standard for style now in its 4th edition and adopted by many disciplines.

Although the communications enterprise of the APA served as a conduit for scholarly exchange, there were other signs that the APA was taking on a life of its own apart from the sponsorship of universities and academic psychologists. The time of the annual meeting was shifted from the academic Christmas holidays to the fall, and meeting sites "in the territory west of the Appalachian Mountains" were chosen. The APA was incorporated in 1925 (Entries 1192, 1193, and 1199), established committees to promote standards of conduct for animal experimentation (Entry 1195), clinical training (Entry 1406), and scientific and professional ethics (Entry 1473). These developments all served to separate the conduct of the APA from a basis in informal agreements among academic colleagues and made it possible to maintain the organization across generations of participants with little disruption.

Psychologists born during these years were educated in established university departments by members of a mature discipline and have become leaders of modern psychology. They include experimental psychologists Patrick Suppes (Entry 1135), Stanley Schachter (Entry 1138), Janet Taylor Spence (Entry 1170), Robert Zajonc (Entry 1172), Albert Bandura (Entry 1216), Paul Ekman (Entry 1386), George Miller (Entry 1093), Daniel Berlyne (Entry 1178), Ulrich Neisser (Entry 1292), Richard Atkinson (Entry 1298), Jerome Kagan (Entry 1297), Richard Thompson (Entry 1331), and George Sperling (Entry 1388).

Landmarks in experimental psychology during these years included the emergence of continental Gestalt psychology (Entry 1189) and the American behaviorism of Watson (Entries 1090, 1103, 1176, and 1209), Thorndike (Entry 1339 and 1373) and Tolman (Entry 1354). The Society of Experimental Psychologists awarded its first Warren Medal to Ernest Wever and Charles Brey for their work on auditory physiology (Entry 1416), and Ivan Pavlov visited the United States to address the IX International Congress of Psychology (Entries 1310 and 1311).

The interface between science and practice was marked by the emergence of barbiturates (Entries 1474 and 1479), the first of a flood of psychotherapeutic drugs. The first frontal lobotomies (Entry 1430) and electroconvulsive therapy sessions (Entry 1459) were reported, ushering in an era of widespread use of both of these techniques after World War II. The Hawthorne experiments were conducted in 1927, permanently altering the view of effective interventions in industrial settings and of the validity of any experiment in which human subjects are aware of their roles as participants.

Advances in applied psychology saw the first scientific methods used to select military airplane pilots (Entry 1486) and the founding of the first federal drug treatment facility (Entry 1294). Also noteworthy was the expansion of the intelligence and achievement testing movement (e.g., Entries 1232, 1234, 1236, 1301, and 1398), the publication of the Rorschach Test (Entry 1120), and the first *Mental Measurements Yearbook* to document the growing number of assessment instruments. Modern applied psychology and psychological practice have been shaped by the work of George Albee (Entry 1129), Robert Perloff (Entry 1113), William Bevan (Entry 1141), Fred Fiedler (Entry 1150), Donald Broadbent (Entry 1229), Nicholas Cummings (Entry 1183), Stanley Graham (Entry 1243), Rogers Wright (Entry 1250), Donald Peterson (Entry 1171), Frank Logan (Entry 1182), Joseph Matarazzo (Entry 1215), Martin Orne (Entry 1269), Martha

Mednick (Entry 1300), Edward Zigler (Entry 1320), Raymond Fowler (Entry 1335), and Florence Denmark (Entry 1355), all born before the death of Sigmund Freud, a refugee from the Nazi invasion of Austria, in London in 1939 (Entry 1488).

January 3, 1920 (1092)
Paul E. Meehl was born. His interests were in clinical psychology, especially clinical assessment, and in personality, learning, psychometrics, and the philosophy of science. APA Distinguished Scientific Contribution Award, 1958; APA President, 1962.

February 3, 1920 (1093)
George A. Miller was born. Miller's influential work in language and cognition, short-term memory, and literacy education has shaped the field of psycholinguistics and cognitive psychology. APA Distinguished Scientific Contribution Award, 1963; APA President, 1969; American Psychological Foundation Gold Medal Award for Lifetime Achievement in Psychological Science, 1990; National Medal of Science, 1991.

February 4, 1920 (1094)
Morton Deutsch was born. Deutsch has focused much of his work on significant social problems. He has produced advances in the understanding of racial prejudice, individual conformity, and social justice. APA Distinguished Scientific Contribution Award, 1987.

April 22, 1920 (1095)
Leonard D. Eron was born. Eron has produced exemplary applied research with empirical studies of the Thematic Apperception Test, studies of the effect of medical education on attitudes and personality, and landmark longitudinal studies of the effects of viewing televised violence on individual aggressiveness. APA Award for Distinguished Professional Contributions, 1980.

April 28, 1920 (1096)
James R. Angell was elected to the National Academy of Sciences, becoming the sixth psychologist elected to the Academy.

April 30, 1920 (1097)
A 3-day conference on relations between psychology and psychiatry began. The conference was sponsored by the National Research Council, and little progress was made toward establishing mutually respectful relations between the two professions.

May 27, 1920 (1098)

Hermann Rorschach signed a publishing contract with Bircher, of Bern, Switzerland, for 1,200 copies of *Psychodiagnostik*, the book explaining his inkblot interpretation technique. Bircher was the eighth publisher to consider the material and agreed to publish it only if the number of cards was reduced from Rorschach's 15 to the set of 10 now considered the standard set.

June 2, 1920 (1099)

The first federal legislation providing for rehabilitation of civilians disabled in industrial accidents was enacted by Congress (Public Law 66-219).

June 14, 1920 (1100)

Francis Cecil Sumner became the first African American to earn a PhD in psychology. Sumner earned the degree from Clark University, working under G. Stanley Hall. His dissertation, which he successfully defended on June 11, 1920, was titled "Psychoanalysis of Freud and Adler."

June 22, 1920 (1101)

Leta Stetter Hollingworth's book *Psychology of Subnormal Children* was published. The book was a standard text and reference source in the field for many years.

June 22, 1920 (1102)

Sigmund Freud's book *General Introduction to Psychoanalysis* was published in the United States.

August 23, 1920 (1103)

The Library of Congress received its copy of the issue of the *Journal of Experimental Psychology* that reported John B. Watson and Rosalie Rayner's "Little Albert" study.

September 16, 1920 (1104)

Carlos Albizu-Miranda was born. Albizu-Miranda received the American Psychological Foundation Award for the Development of Psychology Education in Puerto Rico in 1980. He helped found the Instituto Psicologico de Puerto Rico, later renamed the Caribbean Center for Advanced Studies. His interests were in clinical psychology, social class, and test performance.

October 17, 1920 (1105)

Norman Guttman was born. Guttman's work bridged Skinnerian behaviorism and physiological psychology. He studied stimulus control of operant behavior, stimulus generalization, perceptual processes in stimulus–response relations, and shapes of generalization gradients.

November 16, 1920 (1106)

Dorothea Jameson was born. Jameson, with Leo Hurvich, has been responsible for pioneering experiments on color vision and optics. Jameson was the third woman psychologist elected to the National Academy of Sciences (1975). Society of Experimental Psychologists Warren Medal, 1971; APA Distinguished Scientific Contribution Award, 1972.

November 27, 1920 (1107)

Gardner Lindzey was born. His interests were in personality, social psychology, and behavior genetics. Lindzey's books *Handbook of Social Psychology* (1954) and *Theories of Personality* (1957, with Calvin Hall) became standard texts. APA President, 1967.

December 1, 1920 (1108)

A. A. Brill's English translation of Sigmund Freud's book *Interpretation of Dreams* was published in the United States.

December 30, 1920 (1109)

At its annual meeting, the APA adopted a plan to devote six issues per year of *Psychological Bulletin* to abstracts of psychological literature. This was the first form of the present *Psychological Abstracts*, which began independent publication in 1927. The first abstracts issue of *Psychological Bulletin* was the January 1921 issue.

January 18, 1921 (1110)

Robert Glaser was born. Glaser's research in education developed from an early emphasis on individualized instruction and criterion-referenced testing to later explorations of cognitive models of classroom learning and "knowledge-dependent learning." APA Distinguished Scientific Award for the Applications of Psychology, 1987.

January 21, 1921 (1111)

Wendell Richard Garner was born. Garner is noted for applying experimental discipline and strict logic to the study of form and structure. Garner's contributions include work in psychophysics, discrimination, perception, and learning. APA Distinguished Scientific Contribution Award, 1964.

January 24, 1921 (1112)

Soviet premier V. I. Lenin issued a decree guaranteeing Ivan Pavlov extra food and maximum housing conveniences. Pavlov refused the privileges because they would not be extended to his laboratory animals and coworkers.

February 3, 1921 (1113)

Robert Perloff was born. Perloff's interests have been in industrial/organizational psychology, business administration, consumer behavior, and in the motivational aspects of self-interest versus altruism. He was the first president of the Association for Consumer Research and has held many offices in the APA throughout a lifetime of service to the profession. APA President, 1985.

February 16, 1921   (1114)
Harold H. Kelley was born. Kelley is a social psychologist who has focused on the processes of interpersonal perception and relationships in small groups. With John Thibaut, Kelley provided a comprehensive theory of social exchange. Kelley's theory of factors influencing causal inferences has stimulated much research. APA Distinguished Scientific Contribution Award, 1971.

February 25, 1921   (1115)
The first meeting of the American Vocational Guidance Association was held. The organization eventually became the American Association of Guidance and Development.

February 27, 1921   (1116)
John J. Conger was born. Conger is a clinical psychologist whose research in child, adolescent, and adult development reflected in his books *Adolescence and Youth: Psychological Development in a Changing World* and *Child Development and Personality* (with Paul H. Mussen). APA President, 1981; APA Award for Distinguished Contributions to Psychology in the Public Interest, 1986.

March 9, 1921   (1117)
Jane W. Kessler was born. Kessler developed an interdisciplinary and holistic approach to the treatment of children with mental retardation and emotional disorders. She was the first director of the Case Western Reserve Mental Development Center. APA Award for Distinguished Professional Contributions, 1981.

March 15, 1921   (1118)
The J. Walter Thompson advertising agency publicly announced hiring behaviorist John B. Watson. Watson's first job was to survey the market for rubber boots along the Mississippi River. His first account was Yuban coffee. Others included Odorono deodorant, Johnson and Johnson baby powder, Pond's cold cream, Camel cigarettes, Maxwell House coffee, and Scott toilet paper.

April 28, 1921   (1119)
The Psychological Corporation was incorporated. The incorporation papers were drawn up by Harlan F. Stone, later to become chief justice of the U.S. Supreme Court, and were signed by James McKeen Cattell, Edward L. Thorndike, and Robert S. Woodworth. In 1969, the Psychological Corporation was purchased by Harcourt Brace Jovanovich.

June 6, 1921   (1120)
Hermann Rorschach's book *Psychodiagnostik*, describing his inkblot method of personality assessment, was published in Switzerland by Bircher, the eighth publisher to review the manuscript and cards. Rorschach died 10 months afterward.

July 18, 1921   (1121)
Aaron T. Beck was born. Beck is known for his theory and research relating to
the assessment and treatment of the cognitive bases of depression and suicide. His
Beck Depression Inventory is an instrument commonly used to measure the strength
of depressive beliefs. APA Distinguished Scientific Award for the Applications of
Psychology, 1989.

August 4, 1921   (1122)
The first meeting of the Western Psychological Association (WPA) was held in
Berkeley, California. The first president of the WPA was Lewis Terman. The WPA
was originally an affiliate of the American Association for the Advancement of
Science.

August 7, 1921   (1123)
The Library of Congress received its copy of the first issue of the *Journal of Comparative Psychology*. Williams and Wilkins published the journal until 1947, when
the APA purchased it and named it the *Journal of Comparative and Physiological
Psychology* (JCPP). In 1983, the JCPP split into the *Journal of Comparative Psychology*
and *Behavioral Neuroscience*.

August 24, 1921   (1124)
Wilbert J. McKeachie was born. McKeachie is known for research, writing, and
training in psychology teaching methods and curriculum, and for his work in
personality and social behavior, motivation, and learning. APA President, 1976;
American Psychological Foundation Distinguished Teaching in Psychology Award,
1985; APA Award for Distinguished Career Contributions to Education and Training in Psychology, 1987.

August 25, 1921   (1125)
Hans H. Strupp was born. Strupp carried out some of the pioneering research
studies of the psychotherapeutic process. His writing has reported the critical
components of psychotherapy, relevant patient and therapist characteristics, the
measurement of outcomes, and the problem of negative effects. APA Award for
Distinguished Professional Contributions, 1987.

September 19, 1921   (1126)
Eric Lennenberg was born. Lennenberg's studies linked language acquisition and
functions to the physiology of the brain and vocal apparatus.

September 30, 1921   (1127)
Leon J. Yarrow was born. Yarrow's work focused on the important effects of early
experience on child development and resulted in many public program applications.
He studied transitioning infants from foster care to adoptive parents, maternal
deprivation, racially integrated summer camps, preschool experiences, and mastery
motivation in infancy.

December 14, 1921   (1128)

James Deese was born. Deese has specialized in psycholinguistics and the experimental psychology of learning. Deese's *Psychology of Learning* (1952) and *Psycholinguistics* (1970) are authoritative texts that reflect his expertise.

December 20, 1921   (1129)

George Albee was born. Albee's interests have been in community and clinical psychology. He has made major contributions to the establishment of the independent profession of psychology. Albee's early research was on the childhood intellectual development of adults with schizophrenia. APA President, 1970; APA Distinguished Professional Contribution Award, 1975; American Psychological Foundation Gold Medal, 1993.

December 28, 1921   (1130)

Joseph H. Grosslight was born. Grosslight and Leonard Bickman planned the pivotal National Conference on Graduate Education and Training in Psychology that met in Salt Lake City in 1987. APA Award for Distinguished Education and Training Contributions, 1988.

January 16, 1922   (1131)

Harry Levinson was born. Levinson has applied research in clinical psychology and health psychology to business management settings. His books *Emotional Health in the World of Work* (1964), *Executive Stress* (1970), and *CEO: Corporate Leadership in Action* (1984) represent this work. APA Award for Distinguished Professional Contributions, 1992.

January 24, 1922   (1132)

Ted Landsman was born. Landsman was a nondirective counseling and clinical psychologist active in training and professional affairs. His research focused on qualities of the healthy personality. He was the first licensed psychologist in Tennessee, an honor recognizing his advocacy for the adoption of the state's psychologist licensing law.

February 16, 1922   (1133)

Cecil Peck was born. After World War II, Peck earned one of the first doctoral degrees in clinical psychology in a Veterans Administration (VA) training program. In regional and national positions, he went on to guide and unify the psychological services of the VA through the 1950s and 1960s. APA Award for Distinguished Professional Contributions, 1984.

March 3, 1922   (1134)

Richard S. Lazarus was born. Lazarus is known for his research on psychological stress, coping and adaptation, and the relations between cognition, emotion, and motivation. APA Distinguished Scientific Contribution Award, 1989.

March 17, 1922 (1135)

Patrick Suppes was born. Suppes has worked in four major areas: measurement of subjective probability and utility, general learning theory, instructional computing, and semantics of natural language, especially children's language. APA Distinguished Scientific Contribution Award, 1972; National Medal of Science, 1990.

March 20, 1922 (1136)

Physiological psychologist Henri Piéron began a series of paranormal phenomenon experiments at the Sorbonne. The popular newspaper *L'Opinion* had urged that studies be done to see whether a spiritual medium, Eva Carrière, could produce ectoplasm under controlled conditions. Ectoplasm, said to be a vapor in the shape of a person, living or dead, was not observed during the studies.

March 28, 1922 (1137)

Joseph V. Brady was born. Brady's work in behavioral biology includes well-known studies of ulcers in "executive monkeys" and the selective effects of reserpine on anxiety responses. He later applied experimental methods to problems of space flight and the prevention of drug abuse. APA Distinguished Scientific Award for Applications of Psychology, 1991.

April 15, 1922 (1138)

Stanley Schachter was born. Schachter's prolific studies in social psychology have provided findings of major importance about the psychology of small-group processes, social and cognitive influences on emotion, obesity, affiliation, and economic decision making. APA Distinguished Scientific Contribution Award, 1969.

April 26, 1922 (1139)

Carl E. Seashore was elected to the National Academy of Sciences. Seashore was the seventh psychologist so honored.

April 28, 1922 (1140)

G. Stanley Hall's book *Senescence: The Last Half of Life* was published. Hall's work in developmental psychology was noteworthy for its time because he wrote about development beyond the childhood years.

May 16, 1922 (1141)

William Bevan was born. Bevan's research interests were in perception and cognition, vision, and human engineering. He pursued interests in psychology and public policy through his post at the John D. and Catherine T. Marshall Foundation. APA President, 1982; APA Distinguished Contributions to Psychology in the Public Interest Award, 1989.

May 30, 1922 (1142)

James Olds was born. Olds's studies of pleasure centers in the brain were the first in a distinguished career of investigations of the physiological bases of motivation.

American Association for the Advancement of Science Newcombe-Cleveland Award, 1956; Society of Experimental Psychologists Warren Medal, 1962; APA Distinguished Scientific Contribution Award, 1967.

June 2, 1922 (1143)

Carl Lange and William James's *The Emotions* was published. Lange and James proposed that the behavioral aspects of emotion precede the conscious experience of emotional arousal.

June 4, 1922 (1144)

Stanley F. Schneider was born. Schneider's 25 years of service at the National Institute of Mental Health was marked by the promotion of innovative education, training, and research efforts in psychology. APA Award for Distinguished Education and Training Contributions, 1988.

June 11, 1922 (1145)

Dalbir Bindra was born. Bindra's initial interests were in motivation and its relation to perception, learning, and cognition. His later work focused on the neural correlates of intelligent behavior. He played active roles in Canadian psychological organizations.

June 26, 1922 (1146)

Carolyn Wood Sherif was born. Sherif worked extensively in social psychology, developing a social judgment–involvement approach to the study of attitudes. Her work frequently focused on social problems such as gender issues and social power. American Psychological Foundation Distinguished Contribution to Education in Psychology Award, 1982.

July 1, 1922 (1147)

Lawrence J. O'Rourke became the director of Personnel Research for the U.S. Civil Service Commission. O'Rourke is thought to be the first psychologist regularly employed by the civilian government of the United States.

July 2, 1922 (1148)

Asher R. Pacht was born. Pacht's career has been devoted to improved treatment of clients in correctional settings by both psychological professionals and corrections officers and administrators. Special recognition has resulted from his work with sex offenders. APA Award for Distinguished Professional Contributions, 1982.

July 7, 1922 (1149)

Irvin Rock was born. Rock is noted for experiments in learning, sensation, and perception. Rock has concentrated on perceptual constancies and on interactions between sense modalities. His pivotal experiment demonstrating one-trial learning of paired-associates lists is often cited.

July 13, 1922   (1150)

Fred E. Fiedler was born. Fiedler's research has resulted in the contingency theory of leadership, describing effective leadership as a product of personal style and specific situational characteristics.

August 10, 1922   (1151)

The Council for Exceptional Children was founded.

August 11, 1922   (1152)

Ogden Lindsley was born. Lindsley was one of the founders of applied behavior analysis. With B. F. Skinner, he instituted a program at Boston State Hospital, where the behaviors of psychotic patients were modified through contingent reinforcement. Through the techniques of precision teaching, Lindsley later applied behavioral methods to special and regular education and industry.

September 12, 1922   (1153)

Mark R. Rosenzweig was born. Rosenzweig's studies of the effects of early environmental enrichment on brain weight and production of acetylcholine are well-known. More recent activity has focused on the biochemistry of memory and the international promotion of psychological science. APA Distinguished Scientific Contributions Award, 1982.

September 17, 1922   (1154)

Irving T. Diamond was born. Diamond's studies of the mammalian brain have contributed to the understanding of the topographical organization of sensory systems in a wide variety of species. APA Distinguished Scientific Contribution Award, 1988.

September 26, 1922   (1155)

In Berlin, Sigmund Freud read his last paper to an International Congress of Psychoanalysis. The title was "Some Remarks on the Unconscious." This was the last Congress that Freud attended.

October 25, 1922   (1156)

The first of a series of articles by journalist Walter Lippmann, attacking the Army Alpha Test of intellectual achievement, appeared in the *New Republic*. The articles, and replies by Lewis Terman and Edwin G. Boring, presented now-familiar controversies about intelligence testing to the American public.

November 1, 1922   (1157)

Charles B. Ferster was born. Ferster's work with B. F. Skinner on the key-pecking responses of pigeons led to the book *Schedules of Reinforcement* (1957). His interests in learning expanded to applied work with autistic children, institutional populations, and depressed and self-injurious individuals. He helped found the *Journal of the Experimental Analysis of Behavior* (1958).

November 1, 1922 (1158)

W. Grant Dahlstrom was born. Dahlstrom has specialized in applied research in empirical personality assessment, focusing on the Minnesota Multiphasic Personality Inventory (MMPI). His two-volume *An MMPI Handbook* (1972, 1975, with George S. Welsh and Leona Dahlstrom) is a standard reference work in the field. APA Award for Distinguished Professional Contributions, 1991.

December 14, 1922 (1159)

Roy Schafer was born. Schafer, a psychologist and psychoanalyst, has carried out influential work in diagnostic assessment with projective tests and in the revision of fundamental psychoanalytic concepts. He provided some of the first constructive critiques of the psychoanalytic psychology of women. APA Award for Distinguished Professional Contributions, 1982.

December 17, 1922 (1160)

Juanita H. Williams was born. Williams was a pioneer in the field of the psychology of women. She taught one of the first university courses on the topic in 1971 and wrote *Psychology of Women: Behavior in a Biosocial Context* (1977), an authoritative early text in the area.

December 31, 1922 (1161)

Wallace E. Lambert was born. Lambert's cross-national and psycholinguistic studies have focused on bilingualism: bilingual memory, neuropsychological correlates, and the roles of attention and motivation in second-language learning. Canadian Psychological Association President, 1969; APA Distinguished Scientific Award for Applications of Psychology, 1990.

January 3, 1923 (1162)

Wilbert E. Fordyce was born. Fordyce has implemented revolutionary treatments for pain-related suffering that are based on applied principles of operant conditioning. Suffering is viewed as a behavior that can be reduced by common principles of behavior. Pain clinics around the world employ Fordyce's techniques. APA Award for Distinguished Professional Contributions, 1986.

January 8, 1923 (1163)

George D. Goldman was born. Goldman has advanced the profession of psychology by being a cofounder and clinic director of the Adelphi University Postdoctoral Program in Psychotherapy and by legally defending the right of clinical psychologists to conduct private psychotherapy. APA Award for Distinguished Professional Contributions, 1988.

February 26, 1923 (1164)

The first annual meeting of the Council for Exceptional Children was held in Cleveland.

April 25, 1923 (1165)

Robert M. Yerkes was elected to the National Academy of Sciences, the eighth psychologist elected to the Academy.

May 28, 1923 (1166)

Henry P. David was born. David is noted for his international promotion of psychology and studies of reproductive behavior. He was the founder of the Transnational Family Research Institute (1972), an international organization for population studies. APA Award for Distinguished Contributions to the International Advancement of Psychology, 1992.

July 10, 1923 (1167)

Julian Hochberg was born. Hochberg's work has focused on the organization of perceptual elements and how this process is affected by information in the element, by perceiver expectations, and by selective attention. His work has extended to research with motion pictures. APA Distinguished Scientific Contribution Award, 1978.

July 17, 1923 (1168)

Jeanne Humphrey Block was born. Block is best known for her cross-cultural and longitudinal research on gender role socialization. Other noteworthy contributions have explored ego development, delay of gratification, characteristics of parents of schizophrenic children, student activism, and asthmatic children.

August 24, 1923 (1169)

Arthur Jensen was born. Jensen's research has been in individual differences and the relative contributions of genetic and environmental factors in intelligence. Jensen stirred a storm of controversy with a 1969 article contending that the extent to which environmental enrichment can influence IQ is limited by genetic factors and that these factors are related to race.

August 29, 1923 (1170)

Janet Taylor Spence was born. Spence was the first woman on the Northwestern University psychology faculty. Her research interests have included the measurement and effects of manifest anxiety, intrinsic motivation, achievement motivation, and gender-related issues. APA President, 1984; American Psychological Society President, 1988.

September 10, 1923 (1171)

Donald R. Peterson was born. He was the cofounder and first director of the first PsyD program of clinical psychology training in the United States at the University of Illinois (1968). The PsyD offered an alternative to research-oriented clinical training. APA Distinguished Professional Contributions Award, 1983; APA Distinguished Education and Training Contributions Award, 1989.

November 23, 1923 (1172)

Robert Zajonc was born. Zajonc's imaginative studies have explored the nature of social facilitation, the effects of mere exposure on liking, correlates of birth order, and the effects of muscular feedback on emotion. APA Distinguished Scientific Contribution Award, 1978.

December 31, 1923 (1173)

John W. Atkinson was born. Atkinson is best known for work in motivation, especially for the measurement of motives of achievement, affiliation, fear, sex, and aggression by means of responses to the Thematic Apperception Test. APA Distinguished Scientific Contribution Award, 1979.

January 23, 1924 (1174)

Floyd Allport's *Social Psychology* was published. This book was the first to present an experimental view of social psychology.

February 1, 1924 (1175)

Jum Clarence Nunnally was born. Nunnally's book *Psychometric Theory* (1967) is representative of his excellence as a psychometrician. His other interests were in data analysis, attitudes toward mental health, factor analysis, psycholinguistics, and psychotherapy.

February 5, 1924 (1176)

John B. Watson and William McDougall's "Battle of Behaviorism" debate, sponsored by the Psychological Club of Washington, DC, was held in the D.A.R. Memorial Constitutional Hall. McDougall was declared the winner of this debate that pitted his hereditarian position against Watson's environmental behaviorism.

March 20, 1924 (1177)

The Virginia Assembly passed a statute allowing sexual sterilization of institutionalized persons suffering from "hereditary forms of insanity that are recurrent, idiocy, imbecility, feeble-mindedness, or epilepsy." The law was one of several eugenic sterilization laws adopted by individual states.

April 25, 1924 (1178)

Daniel Berlyne was born. Berlyne is best known for his systematic studies of intrinsic motivation, curiosity, and exploratory behavior. He also contributed writing on aesthetics and the psychology of art. Canadian Psychological Association President, 1971–1972.

April 30, 1924 (1179)

Raymond Dodge became the ninth psychologist elected to the National Academy of Sciences.

May 5, 1924   (1180)

Harold A. Goolishian was born. Goolishian played a central role in the 1950s team that developed "multiple impact therapy," one of the first federally funded projects in family therapy. His interest in meanings communicated by language led to the "collaborative language systems approach" to psychotherapy.

June 17, 1924   (1181)

Robert M. Ogden of Cornell University wrote to German psychologist Kurt Koffka, inviting him to become a visiting lecturer. This was the first step in a process that brought Gestaltists Koffka, Köhler, Wertheimer, and Lewin to America, largely through Ogden's efforts.

July 22, 1924   (1182)

Frank A. Logan was born. Logan has done extensive work in learning, focusing on discrimination learning and the effects of variable amounts of reinforcement on response choice and strength.

July 25, 1924   (1183)

Nicholas Cummings was born. Cummings has been an advocate for the independent professional status of psychologists and has reshaped professional training in psychology. He was a founder of the California School of Professional Psychology (1968). APA President, 1979; President, American Psychological Foundation, 1984; APA Award for Distinguished Professional Contributions, 1984.

August 6, 1924   (1184)

Sophie Freud Loewenstein was born. Loewenstein, Sigmund Freud's granddaughter, specialized in social work, women's issues, and teaching. Her approach moved over time from a psychoanalytic orientation to a systems orientation.

October 27, 1924   (1185)

Sigmund Freud appeared on the cover of *Time* magazine for the first time.

November 18, 1924   (1186)

Dorothy Hansen Eichorn was born. Her interests were in developmental, experimental, and physiological psychology. She was the administrator of the Child Study Center at University of California, Berkeley, where she was involved in the Berkeley and Oakland growth studies.

November 25, 1924   (1187)

Jacqueline Jarrett Goodnow was born. Goodnow has been a pioneer in the study of cognitive development. Her studies of strategies of thinking and concept formation, cultural influences on thinking, perceptual activity, children's drawings, and social policy have combined progress in cognitive psychology with a focus on children.

December 5, 1924 (1188)

Jane Ross Mercer was born. Mercer developed the System of Multicultural Pluralistic Assessment, a culture-fair measure of adaptive abilities that reflects the contemporary broadening of the definition of intelligence.

December 17, 1924 (1189)

Max Wertheimer delivered a lecture defining Gestalt psychology to the Kant Society in Berlin. He said, "There are wholes, the behavior of which is not determined by their individual elements but where the part-processes are themselves determined by the intrinsic nature of the whole."

January 1, 1925 (1190)

Psychologist John B. Watson was named vice president at the J. Walter Thompson advertising agency.

January 1, 1925 (1191)

The APA made its first payment toward purchase of Howard C. Warren's Psychological Review Company. Warren's journals (*Psychological Review, Journal of Experimental Psychology, Psychological Index, Psychological Monographs,* and *Psychological Bulletin*) became the first to be published by the APA. The transfer was completed in 1929 by Warren's gift of his remaining 46% share.

January 2, 1925 (1192)

The American Psychological Association was incorporated.

January 9, 1925 (1193)

The APA certificate of incorporation was recorded in the Office of the Recorder of Deeds in the District of Columbia.

January 15, 1925 (1194)

Lewis M. Terman wrote the forward to his book *Genetic Studies of Genius.*

February 2, 1925 (1195)

APA president Madison Bentley appointed Robert M. Yerkes, Paul T. Young, and Edward C. Tolman to the Committee on Precautions in Animal Experimentation, the APA's first body concerned with the treatment of animals used in research. The current APA Committee on Animal Research and Ethics is a descendant of this committee.

February 11, 1925 (1196)

Virginia Eshelman Johnson was born. With William Masters, Johnson became famous for the thorough study of the human sexual response and for modern methods of therapy for sexual disfunctions. Johnson was also a country-western singer in the 1940s.

February 13, 1925 (1197)

Ravenna Helson was born. Helson's work has centered on the development of adult creativity. Her longitudinal studies have dealt with the nature of cultural patterns of personal and career expectations, personality stability, and the realization of creative potential in women.

February 17, 1925 (1198)

William J. McGuire was born. McGuire's social psychological research has focused on the nature of attitudes, attitude persistence, and attitude change. His studies of resistance to persuasion induced by "inoculation" procedures are widely cited. Later research has examined the content of spontaneous self-descriptions. APA Distinguished Scientific Contribution Award, 1988.

March 14, 1925 (1199)

The newly incorporated APA adopted its official seal and bylaws and assumed the property and membership of the unincorporated APA.

April 6, 1925 (1200)

Substitute teacher John Scopes was arrested for teaching evolution in his Dayton, Tennessee, high school biology class. The celebrated "monkey trial" followed. Scopes had agreed to the arrest to provide a court test of Tennessee's law banning the teaching of evolution in the public schools.

April 14, 1925 (1201)

Roger Brown was born. Brown is noted for his work in psycholinguistics and social psychology and for an important longitudinal study on language development in three children, Adam, Eve, and Sarah. APA Distinguished Scientific Contribution Award, 1971.

April 15, 1925 (1202)

The Amherst (Virginia) County Court ruled that Carrie Buck, institutionalized for "feeble-mindedness," should be sexually sterilized. The Carrie Buck case went to the U.S. Supreme Court, which upheld the Virginia decision in 1927. The case provided a test of eugenic sterilization laws found in some states.

May 13, 1925 (1203)

Carolyn Robertson Payton was born. Payton was a field assessment officer for trainees serving in the Peace Corps and eventually became the first woman director of the Peace Corps. Her interests were in minority issues, clinical psychology, and industrial/organizational psychology. APA Distinguished Professional Contributions Award, 1982.

May 16, 1925 (1204)

R. Duncan Luce was born. Luce helped to produce the first *Handbook of Mathematical Psychology* (1963). His specialties have been mathematical models, measurement theory, signal detection, and theories of decision and choice behavior. APA Distinguished Scientific Contribution Award, 1970.

May 30, 1925 (1205)

Stanley Moldawsky was born. Moldawsky has been a forceful advocate for professional psychology licensure standards, freedom of choice laws, and professional schools of psychology. He helped found the Graduate School of Applied and Professional Psychology at Rutgers University (1974). APA Distinguished Professional Contributions Award, 1988.

June 4, 1925 (1206)

In a letter to Wolfgang Köhler, Edwin G. Boring reported that the laboratory budget at Harvard University was $148, including $31 of Boring's own money.

July 7, 1925 (1207)

Herbert Dörken was born. Dörken has consistently promoted appropriate legislative and insurance industry recognition of the independent practice of professional psychologists. Numerous laws, insurance practices, and hospital accreditation procedures have been affected by his informed advocacy efforts. APA Award for Distinguished Professional Contributions, 1979.

July 10, 1925 (1208)

The Scopes "monkey trial" began. The trial was primarily a media event to promote Dayton, Tennessee, commercial interests. Lawyers Clarence Darrow and William Jennings Bryan debated the wisdom of teaching the theory of evolution, a major influence on modern psychology, in the public schools.

August 2, 1925 (1209)

The *New York Times* published a review of John B. Watson's book *Behaviorism*, saying that Watson turned psychology "inside out," transforming it "from an inward mental groping to an exact science of objective measurement and record." Watson's book included the famous "Give me a dozen healthy infants . . ." quote.

September 15, 1925 (1210)

The trustees of the University of Illinois approved the first sport psychology research laboratory in the United States. Coleman Roberts Griffith directed the lab until 1932, when it closed for lack of continued funding.

October 24, 1925 (1211)

Jack I. Bardon was born. Bardon was a pioneer in shaping the profession of school psychology through his teaching, supervision, and national committee work. In the 1980s, Bardon chaired the Task Force on the Structure of the APA, an attempt to reconcile differences between scientists and practitioners within the APA. APA Award for Distinguished Professional Contributions, 1981.

October 26, 1925   (1212)

David Premack was born. Premack is known for his work in learning and motivation. He has argued that reinforcement consists of the opportunity to engage in
a behavior. The "Premack principle" states that a low-probability behavior will be
performed if access to a high-probability behavior is contingent upon it. He has
also taught symbolic language to chimpanzees.

October 26, 1925   (1213)

James V. McConnell was born. McConnell is best remembered for excellence in
teaching and studies of chemical transmission of learning in flatworms. He founded
the irreverent *Worm Runner's Digest*, a journal combining humor and serious experimentation, in 1959. American Psychological Foundation Distinguished Contribution to Teaching in Psychology Award, 1976.

November 9, 1925   (1214)

In a letter to APA secretary John Anderson, Morton Prince offered to donate the
Journal of Abnormal and Social Psychology to the APA. The transfer was completed
on April 1, 1926.

November 12, 1925   (1215)

Joseph D. Matarazzo was born. Matarazzo's interests have been in clinical psychology and neuropsychology. An advocate for the advancement of professional
psychology, he headed the nation's first medical psychology program, at the Oregon
Health Sciences University School of Medicine. APA President, 1989; APA Award
for Distinguished Professional Contributions, 1991.

December 4, 1925   (1216)

Albert Bandura was born. Bandura is a major figure whose contributions have been
in moral development, observational learning, self-regulation, and self-referent
thought. He developed a comprehensive theory of social learning. APA President,
1974; APA Distinguished Scientific Contribution Award, 1980.

December 28, 1925   (1217)

The APA appointed a committee of three to "undertake to develop an adequate
abstracts journal covering the field of Psychology." The committee of Walter
Hunter, Samuel Fernberger, and Herbert Langfeld obtained $76,500 in develop-
ment funds from the Laura Spelman Rockefeller Memorial and the resulting journal,
Psychological Abstracts, appeared in January 1927.

January 1, 1926   (1218)

Jack G. Wiggins was born. Wiggins has conducted research on depression, selective
perception, and projective techniques. He helped found the National Register of
Health Service Providers in Psychology and the Council for the Advancement
of the Psychological Practices and Sciences and has advocated public funding of
psychological services. APA President, 1992.

January 5, 1926   (1219)

Jesse G. Harris, Jr., was born. Harris was a clinical psychologist whose research interests included premorbid competence and schizophrenia, clinical versus actuarial prediction, clinical diagnosis, and character structure and performance of Peace Corps volunteers.

January 27, 1926   (1220)

"Earl H.," the first infant in Clara M. Davis's diet self-selection study, was admitted to the study center. Davis found that, over time, infants who were allowed to choose from a wide range of foods selected a nutritionally balanced diet.

March 10, 1926   (1221)

The first "letter from Jenny," later the subject of articles and a book, *Letters From Jenny* (1965), by Gordon Allport, was written by Jenny Masterson. The letters provided a case study of abnormal personality.

March 20, 1926   (1222)

The first paper on the use of a teaching machine was published by Sidney Pressey in *School and Society*. Pressey's teaching machine had been demonstrated at the APA's annual meeting in Washington, DC, in 1924.

April 1, 1926   (1223)

The APA acquired the *Journal of Abnormal and Social Psychology* from Morton Prince. The journal was split into the *Journal of Personality and Social Psychology* and the *Journal of Abnormal Psychology* in 1965.

April 20, 1926   (1224)

Emory L. Cowen was born. Cowen's research, model programs, program evaluations, and workshops have been landmarks in the development of the field of community mental health. He pioneered methods of early detection and prevention of mental disorders. APA Award for Distinguished Contributions to Psychology in the Public Interest, 1989.

April 21, 1926   (1225)

William A. Scott was born. Scott's career in social psychology was divided between academic appointments in the United States and in Australia. His special interests were propaganda, cognitive complexity, social influences and values, and the adaptation of immigrants to a new culture.

April 24, 1926   (1226)

John T. Lanzetta was born. Lanzetta was an experimental social psychologist who studied group performance, imitation, postdecisional information seeking, and emotional expressivity at various times in his career.

April 24, 1926 (1227)

Charles W. Thomas II was born. Thomas was a cofounder of the Association of Black Psychologists (1968). His work focused on the importance of racial factors in human interactions, with special attention given to the positive aspects of the African American experience and the effects of racism in psychotherapy.

May 5, 1926 (1228)

The Behavior Research Fund was established at Chicago's Institute for Juvenile Research (IJR). The IJR was founded by psychiatrist William Healy and Mrs. W. F. Dummer in 1909, when it was called the Chicago Juvenile Psychopathic Institute. The Cook County Juvenile Court took over the institute in 1914. Healy, Grace Fernald, and Augusta Bronner pioneered delinquency research at the IJR.

May 6, 1926 (1229)

Donald E. Broadbent was born. Broadbent was an experimental and engineering psychologist whose research topics included short-term memory, choice reaction time, environmental stress, and vigilance. His filter model of selective attention was an early information-processing model of cognition. APA Distinguished Scientific Contribution Award, 1975.

June 3, 1926 (1230)

Carl N. Zimet was born. Zimet has promoted excellence in education and training in the professional practice of psychology. He directed the Chicago Conference on the Professional Preparation of Clinical Psychologists (1965) and first chaired the National Register of Health Service Providers in Psychology. APA Award for Distinguished Professional Contributions, 1987.

June 16, 1926 (1231)

Congress created the National Institute of Social Science.

June 23, 1926 (1232)

The College Entrance Examination Board's Scholastic Aptitude Test was first administered.

July 12, 1926 (1233)

Ivan P. Pavlov finished the forward to Gleb V. Anrep's English translation of his *Conditioned Reflexes*. Anrep chose to use the word *reinforce* in his translation, the first appearance of the word in its psychological context. For Anrep and Pavlov, it referred to the presentation of an unconditioned stimulus after observing a conditioned response.

July 23, 1926 (1234)

Florence Goodenough's Goodenough Intelligence Test for Kindergarten–Primary was published.

July 24, 1926 (1235)

Gerald R. Patterson was born. Patterson's research career has explored the dynamics of families with aggressive, antisocial, hyperactive children. Special attention has been paid to patterns of coercion in these families and effective strategies of treatment for children and parents. APA Distinguished Scientific Award for the Applications of Psychology, 1984.

July 29, 1926 (1236)

Florence L. Goodenough's *Measurement of Intelligence by Drawings* was published, describing Goodenough's Draw-A-Man Test.

August 11, 1926 (1237)

Edward E. Jones was born. Jones was responsible for the theory of correspondent inferences, one of the first systematic presentations of social psychological attribution theory. His other work included studies of ingratiation, social stigma, and interpersonal perception. APA Distinguished Scientific Contribution Award, 1977; American Psychological Society William James Fellow, 1990.

August 11, 1926 (1238)

Leonard Berkowitz was born. Berkowitz is known for his thorough research in the causes of aggression, including studies of the effect of the mere presence of weapons, of the imitation of media violence, and of the effects of cognitive priming and negative mood states. APA Distinguished Scientific Award for the Applications of Psychology, 1988.

August 14, 1926 (1239)

Paul A. Kolers was born. Kolers is known for his work in the perception of motion. He was also interested in symbols, semantics, remembering, and imagining. He developed a cognitive procedural theory, indicating that the mind can be understood through the study of the procedures necessary to complete complex mental acts.

August 22, 1926 (1240)

Gerald S. Lesser was born. In dual roles as professor of developmental psychology at Harvard University and chairman of the board of the Children's Television Workshop, Lesser combined excellent pedagogy and the medium of television in the award-winning *Sesame Street* and *The Electric Company*. APA Distinguished Contribution for Applications in Psychology Award, 1974.

September 7, 1926 (1241)

Arthur N. Wiens was born. Wiens has contributed to psychology as an educator, scholar, researcher, clinician, and administrator. His research has focused on the nature of the clinical interview. APA Distinguished Career Contributions to Education and Training in Psychology, 1991.

October 21, 1926 (1242)

Nadine Lambert was born. Lambert's research in educational settings has produced understanding of hyperkinesis in children, techniques for the early identification of emotional disabilities in children, and primary prevention procedures in school settings. APA Distinguished Professional Contributions Award, 1986.

November 26, 1926 (1243)

Stanley R. Graham was born. Graham is a private practitioner of psychotherapy active in promoting the independent status of psychologists in therapeutic settings. APA President, 1990; APA Distinguished Professional Contribution Award, 1991.

November 26, 1926 (1244)

Herbert Freudenberger was born. Freudenberger has integrated psychoanalytic and psychological principles in his work. He is best known for his description of the symptoms, etiology, and therapeutic response to burnout in mental health workers. APA Presidential Citation, 1990; APA Award for Distinguished Professional Contributions, 1992.

December 13, 1926 (1245)

Mortimer Mishkin was born. Mishkin was awarded the APA's Distinguished Scientific Contribution Award (1985) for his work on the functional organization of the primate brain, especially that of the frontal lobe and interotemporal cortex.

December 15, 1926 (1246)

Russell De Valois was born. De Valois undertook extensive research on primate color vision and pattern discrimination. APA Distinguished Scientific Contribution Award, 1977.

January 1, 1927 (1247)

The journal *Psychological Abstracts* began publishing abstracts of psychological literature, previously published in *Psychological Bulletin*.

January 11, 1927 (1248)

Leonard Goodstein was born. Goodstein's interests have been primarily in clinical and industrial/organizational psychology, organizational development, and consultation. APA Executive Vice President and Chief Executive Officer, 1985–1988.

January 12, 1927 (1249)

Marilyn K. Rigby was born. Rigby's research touched on a number of areas, but she was best known for excellence in teaching and for promoting the activities of Division 2 (Teaching of Psychology) of the APA.

January 24, 1927 (1250)

Rogers Hornsby Wright was born. Wright has been called the "father of professional psychology" for his assertive and productive advocacy of the views of independent practitioners. He has promoted insurance coverage of psychological services, independent peer review of services, licensure laws, and legislative lobbying. APA Distinguished Professional Contribution Award, 1985.

January 28, 1927 (1251)

Boris Fiodorovich Lomov was born. Lomov was the major organizer of postwar Soviet psychology. His research specialty was engineering psychology. Lomov's works were more frequently cited by Soviet authors from 1979 to 1989 than any other author's. He was director of the Institute of Psychology within the Academy of Sciences, USSR, from 1972 until his death in 1989.

January 29, 1927 (1252)

Theodore X. Barber was born. Barber is best known for his work on the nature of hypnosis and suggestibility. His contention is that the hypnotic state is not a separate kind of consciousness but a social event that permits exceptional compliance.

March 2, 1927 (1253)

Frank Restle was born. Restle was a major figure in the development of contemporary cognitive psychology and one of the first generation of mathematical psychologists. He applied a mathematical approach to the resolution of long-standing dilemmas of discrimination learning, paired-associates learning, and problem solving.

March 10, 1927 (1254)

Edwin A. Fleishman was born. Fleishman's work in applied psychology concentrated on studies of leadership, engineering psychology, and human performance. APA Distinguished Scientific Award for the Application of Psychology, 1980.

March 18, 1927 (1255)

Herbert C. Kelman was born. Kelman's career has been devoted to studies of social influence, conflict resolution, peace processes, civil rights issues, obedience, and international relations. He was a founder of the *Journal of Conflict Resolution* (1957). APA Award for Distinguished Contributions to Psychology in the Public Interest, 1981.

March 19, 1927 (1256)

Allen Newell was born. Newell made noteworthy contributions to understanding human cognition, problem solving, speech recognition, and organizational behavior. His work with Herbert Simon on artificial intelligence led to the first heuristic problem-solving computer program. APA Distinguished Scientific Contribution Award, 1985; National Medal of Science, 1992.

March 20, 1927   (1257)

Michael Wertheimer was born. Wertheimer has specialized in study and teaching of the history and systems of psychology. American Psychological Foundation Distinguished Teaching in Psychology Award, 1983; APA Award for Distinguished Career Contributions to Education and Training in Psychology, 1990.

March 26, 1927   (1258)

Barbara Snell Dohrenwend was born. Dohrenwend's interests were in community psychology, health psychology, and psychological epidemiology. Her research included studies of suffering, stress, locus of decision making, and interviewer behavior. She and Bruce Dohrenwend were frequent collaborators in this work.

March 28, 1927   (1259)

Charles D. Spielberger was born. Spielberger's research has focused on anxiety, curiosity, the expression and control of anger, and stress management. His State-Trait Anxiety Inventory has been widely used in treatment and research. APA President, 1991.

April 15, 1927   (1260)

In a letter to Shammai Feldman, Edward B. Titchener gave his advice on chairing a psychology department: "Give your decisions quickly and never give your reasons for them. Treat the youngsters kindly, but keep them busy. Have a seminary, if you like, and pool results. Pray without ceasing."

April 25, 1927   (1261)

The first data were gathered in the main "Hawthorne effect" experiment. The study was conducted by Elton Mayo in the relay assembly test room at the Hawthorne plant of the Western Electric Company in Chicago. The Hawthorne data were taken to demonstrate the important effects of human relations on productivity, although more recent analysis has moderated this interpretation.

April 26, 1927   (1262)

Percy W. Bridgman's book *The Logic of Modern Physics*, an exposition of the concept of operationism, was published.

May 2, 1927   (1263)

In the Carrie Buck case, the U.S. Supreme Court upheld a Virginia statute allowing sexual sterilization of institutionalized individuals suffering from "hereditary forms of insanity that are recurrent, idiocy, imbecility, feeble-mindedness, or epilepsy." Justice Oliver Wendell Holmes stated, "Three generations of imbeciles are enough."

May 26, 1927   (1264)

Endel Tulving was born. Tulving's research has focused on memory encoding and retrieval. Important early work described the organization of freely recalled words.

He has identified episodic, semantic, and procedural types of memory and corresponding autonoetic, noetic, and anoetic varieties of consciousness. APA Distinguished Scientific Contribution Award, 1983.

May 31, 1927 (1265)

Percy Tannenbaum was born. Tannenbaum's work with Charles Osgood and George Suci resulted in the development of the semantic differential technique for measuring the connotative meaning of words and of the congruity model of attitude consistency and change.

June 11, 1927 (1266)

Earl A. Alluisi was born. Alluisi's career in the U.S. Air Force and at several universities resulted in groundbreaking human engineering research. He founded performance research laboratories at the University of Louisville and Old Dominion University and pioneered in the development of the Multiple Task Performance Battery.

July 1, 1927 (1267)

The Institute for Child Guidance was founded in New York. The institute was part of the mental hygiene movement of the early 1900s. It supported research in the mental health of children, provided training facilities for child guidance professionals, and offered facilities for treating children with behavior disorders.

September 4, 1927 (1268)

John McCarthy was born. McCarthy is a mathematician whose work is of special importance to cognitive psychologists. He developed the computer language LISP, applied mathematical logic to computer programs that use commonsense knowledge and reasoning, and named and defined the field of artificial intelligence. National Medal of Science, 1990.

October 16, 1927 (1269)

Martin T. Orne was born. Orne is a psychological scientist and psychotherapist best known for his studies of hypnosis and demand characteristics in social psychology experiments. Orne has contended that the hypnotic state is not different from ordinary consciousness. APA Distinguished Scientific Award for the Applications of Psychology, 1986.

October 19, 1927 (1270)

Carrie Buck, a resident at a mental hospital, was sterilized in an operation by J. H. Bell at the State Colony for Epileptics and Feeble-minded in Lynchburg, Virginia. The legal protest over eugenic sterilization had been rejected by the U.S. Supreme Court.

December 1, 1927 (1271)
The *Journal of General Psychology* was first published. The journal was founded by Carl Murchison and Edward B. Titchener.

January 16, 1928 (1272)
Jack Brehm was born. Brehm's reactance theory describes human and animal responses to events that threaten or eliminate behavioral choices.

February 1, 1928 (1273)
B. F. Skinner published his first book on this date. It was a digest of anthracite coal mine arbitration in Pennsylvania.

February 1, 1928 (1274)
K. Warner Schaie was born. Schaie's interests in developmental psychology extend across all ages. Studies of the effectiveness of Head Start, longitudinal studies of intellectual development in adults, and training programs to reverse intellectual decline in aging persons represent his life span orientation. APA Distinguished Scientific Contributions Award, 1992.

March 3, 1928 (1275)
Theodore H. Blau was born. His interests have primarily been in clinical psychology and psychological assessment. A private practitioner specializing in child clinical psychology and neuropsychology, Blau has also been an expert consultant to police departments, child treatment facilities, alcoholism centers, and federal agencies. APA President, 1977.

April 10, 1928 (1276)
In a letter to Carl Murchison, Edwin G. Boring proposed the series of *History of Psychology in Autobiography* volumes. The first volume in the series was published on August 23, 1930.

April 25, 1928 (1277)
Lewis M. Terman became the 10th psychologist elected to the National Academy of Sciences.

May 11, 1928 (1278)
The first meeting of the Midwestern Psychological Association was held at Northwestern University. About 200 people attended. This was the third meeting of the group but the first to use its current name.

May 22, 1928 (1279)
A patent was awarded to Sidney Pressey for his "machine for intelligence tests," a multiple-choice device that evolved into the teaching machine. A second patent was awarded to Pressey for an improved version on March 4, 1930.

June 18, 1928 (1280)

David T. Lykken was born. Lykken is best known for extensive studies of factors affecting the validity of polygraph interrogation and for the development of the guilty knowledge technique, an improved alternative to conventional lie detector tests. APA Award for Distinguished Contribution to Psychology in the Public Interest, 1990.

June 19, 1928 (1281)

John A. Swets was born. Swets is best known for the development of signal detection theory. He applied the theory to understanding human sensation and perception, decision making, cognition, psychological measurement, and diagnostic processes. Society of Experimental Psychologists Warren Medal, 1985; APA Distinguished Scientific Contribution Award, 1990.

July 13, 1928 (1282)

Using psychic forces, novelist Upton Sinclair's brother-in-law in Pasadena, California, transmitted an image of a fork to Sinclair's wife in Long Beach. This and other such events are described in Sinclair's book *Mental Radio* (1930). The foreword to that book was written by psychologist William McDougall.

August 9, 1928 (1283)

John H. Flavell was born. Flavell is the major American interpreter of the work of Jean Piaget. Flavell's own studies of the cognitive development of the child have focused on memory strategies, role taking, knowledge about perception, and the distinction between appearances and reality. APA Distinguished Scientific Contribution Award, 1984.

September 12, 1928 (1284)

Robert P. Abelson was born. Abelson has contributed to the understanding of human behavior in its social and political context. His "script theory" is an attempt to characterize shared knowledge in forms accessible to computer simulation. APA Distinguished Scientific Contribution Award, 1986.

September 27, 1928 (1285)

Joachim Wohlwill was born. Wohlwill fled from the Nazis in Germany and Portugal, earning his PhD at the University of California, Berkeley, in 1957. He studied the relation between physical environment and behavior, especially the behavior of children.

September 28, 1928 (1286)

Joan Guilford was born. Guilford's specialties have been psychometrics, differential psychology, and industrial psychology.

October 9, 1928 (1287)

Philip Teitelbaum was born. Teitelbaum's thorough work has dealt with the role of the hypothalamus in hunger, thirst, learning, and motor coordination. APA Distinguished Scientific Contribution Award, 1978.

October 18, 1928 (1288)

Clara M. Davis's article "Self-Selection of Diet by Newly Weaned Infants" was published in the *American Journal of Diseases of Childhood*. Often cited in introductory texts, this classic study showed that infants will choose a well-balanced diet if given free choice of foods.

October 25, 1928 (1289)

Natalia Potanin Chapanis was born. Chapanis concentrated on physiological and clinical psychology, with special interests in neuropsychology, projective techniques, and transsexual behavior.

December 1, 1928 (1290)

The Conference of Editors and Business Managers of Anthropological and Psychological Journals adopted the first form of the APA publication manual. These "instructions in regard to preparation of manuscripts" appeared in the February issue of *Psychological Bulletin* in 1929. The authors wrote that "a badly prepared manuscript almost always suggests uncritical research and slovenly thinking."

December 7, 1928 (1291)

Noam Chomsky was born. Chomsky's transformational generative grammar represents a modern nativistic approach to thought and language. His views strongly countered theories of language that were based on elaborations of simple learning processes. APA Distinguished Scientific Contribution Award, 1984.

December 8, 1928 (1292)

Ulrich Neisser was born. Neisser has been a leader of modern cognitive psychology. His book *Cognitive Psychology* (1967) consolidated early findings in the field. His important papers have focused on pattern recognition, visual search, brief information processing, and memory. Neisser's psychology emphasizes active cognitive processes in the perceiving organism.

December 12, 1928 (1293)

Olivia M. Espin was born. Espin has expanded the domain of clinical and counseling psychology by promoting a dialogue between mainstream psychology and the worlds of immigrant and refugee women, Latina women, and lesbians. APA Award for Distinguished Professional Contributions, 1991.

January 19, 1929 (1294)

Congress founded the first federal drug treatment hospitals ("narcotics farms"), the U.S. Public Health Service Hospitals in Lexington, Kentucky, and Fort Worth,

Texas. The Lexington hospital, opened in May 1935, was probably the world's first facility of its kind, and it created the influential Addiction Research Center in 1948. The Fort Worth hospital opened in November 1938.

January 30, 1929   (1295)
Roger N. Shepard was born. Shepard pioneered work in cognitive structures, with special attention given to the invention of nonmetric multidimensional scaling. He also contributed to the understanding of cognitive process with his studies of mental rotation. APA Distinguished Scientific Contribution Award, 1976.

February 15, 1929   (1296)
Yale University announced the establishment of the Institute of Human Relations, involving "the cooperation of all of the departments of the University that are interested in the human being." The institute was formally dedicated on May 9, 1931.

February 25, 1929   (1297)
Jerome Kagan was born. Kagan's research in human development focused on studies of personality, self-concept, and cognitive organization. His books *Birth to Maturity* (1962, with Howard Moss), *Change and Continuity in Infancy* (1971), and *The Nature of the Child* (1984) report his findings. APA Distinguished Scientific Contribution Award, 1987.

March 19, 1929   (1298)
Richard C. Atkinson was born. Atkinson's research on memory, information processing, and decision making was recognized by the APA Distinguished Scientific Contribution Award in 1977. Atkinson served as director of the National Science Foundation from 1975 to 1980.

March 25, 1929   (1299)
Lois Wladis Hoffman was born. Hoffman's research on women's issues has included studies of the effects of maternal employment, fear of success, and role conflict in children. Her two-volume book *Review of Child Development Research* (1964, 1966, with Martin Hoffman) is her best known work.

March 31, 1929   (1300)
Martha T. Mednick was born. Mednick's interests have been in personality and social research, achievement motivation, and women's issues, especially African American women's issues. Her books *Research in Personality* (1963, with Sarnoff A. Mednick) and *Women and Achievement: Social and Motivational Analyses* (1975, with Sandra S. Tangri) reflect her expertise.

April 17, 1929   (1301)
The first Iowa Academic Meet contests were held in at least 223 Iowa high schools, with winners progressing to regional (April 26) and state (June 3–4) contests.

Under the direction of psychologist E. F. Lindquist after 1930, the program generated the Iowa Tests of Basic Skills, standard measures of academic achievement.

April 25, 1929 (1302)
The first meeting of what would become the Kansas Psychological Association was held in Manhattan, Kansas. At the time, the group was a section of the Kansas Academy of Science and sponsored its own program at the Academy's annual meeting. John C. Peterson was chairman of the group of psychologists.

May 2, 1929 (1303)
Rene A. Ruiz was born. Ruiz's interests were primarily minority issues such as minority mental heath services, care for elderly Hispanic clients, counseling and psychotherapy for Hispanics, and minority children. Ruiz helped form the National Hispanic Psychological Association.

May 10, 1929 (1304)
The constitution of Psi Chi, the national honor society in psychology, was presented at the third meeting of its organizing committee, held at the Midwestern Psychological Association meeting in Urbana, Illinois. The first two meetings were in May and December of 1928. Psi Chi was officially founded with the formal adoption of its constitution on September 4, 1929.

June 18, 1929 (1305)
B. F. Skinner's first journal article was received for publication. The title was "The Progressive Increase in the Geotropic Response of the Ant Aphaenogaster," published in the *Journal of General Psychology*. Skinner was junior author to T. Cunliffe Barnes.

July 17, 1929 (1306)
Manfred J. Meier was born. Meier has been the foremost figure in the development of professional clinical neuropsychology. His writing has focused on temporal lobe epilepsy, basal ganglia disease, and neuropsychological rehabilitation. He was the first president of the American Board of Neuropsychology. APA Award for Distinguished Professional Contributions, 1990.

August 25, 1929 (1307)
Edwin G. Boring wrote the foreword to his enduring text *History of Experimental Psychology*.

August 29, 1929 (1308)
Carl Murchison's book *Foundations of Experimental Psychology* was published.

August 29, 1929 (1309)
The first APA membership directory, the *Psychological Register*, was published by Carl Murchison.

September 1, 1929 (1310)

The first International Congress of Psychology meeting to be held in the United States began in New Haven, Connecticut. This was the Ninth International Congress and the third attempt to hold the meeting in the United States. The opening address was delivered by noted psychologist James R. Angell, president of Yale University.

September 2, 1929 (1311)

Ivan P. Pavlov addressed the Ninth International Congress of Psychology, meeting in the United States for the first time. His talk was delivered in Russian but with such enthusiasm that the audience applauded portions before the translation was given. On one occasion, the applause turned out to be for a description of laboratory apparatus.

September 4, 1929 (1312)

Psi Chi, the national honor society in psychology, was founded at the Ninth International Congress of Psychology by Edwin B. Newman, Frederick H. Lewis, and other students. Newman was elected president. Psi Chi was first named Sigma Pi, then Sigma Pi Sigma, until it was discovered that those were names of a social fraternity and a physics society. Psi Chi was chosen as the name in 1930.

September 7, 1929 (1313)

The APA accepted, "with deep appreciation," Howard C. Warren's gift of 60 shares of Psychological Review Company stock. The gift completed the transfer of Warren's journals (*Psychological Review, Psychological Bulletin, Journal of Experimental Psychology, Psychological Monographs,* and *Psychological Index*) to the APA.

October 11, 1929 (1314)

The Rutgers Psychological and Mental Hygiene Clinic was established by the trustees of Rutgers University. Henry E. Starr was the first director of this early clinic. The clinic specialized in evaluation, treatment, and research in learning and developmental disabilities.

October 16, 1929 (1315)

The Washington-Baltimore Branch of the APA, also known as the Psychological Group, first met at the Washington Child Research Center. Mandel Sherman was elected temporary chair and later became the first president of the group. This organization became the District of Columbia Psychological Association in 1946.

November 6, 1929 (1316)

Edwin G. Boring's classic book *A History of Experimental Psychology* was published. This was the first book in the distinguished Century Psychology Series, published by Appleton-Century-Crofts. The book was the primary text and reference work in the history and systems of psychology for decades.

January 9, 1930   (1317)

The *Journal of Social Psychology* was first published. The journal was founded by Carl Murchison and John Dewey. The original copyright holder was Clark University.

January 24, 1930   (1318)

Charles R. Schuster was born. Schuster's studies of behavioral pharmacology have changed the view of drug abuse from a disorder of the will to that of a behavior maintained and altered by basic mechanisms of operant and classical conditioning. Director, National Institute on Drug Abuse, 1986–1992; APA Distinguished Scientific Award for the Application of Psychology, 1992.

February 22, 1930   (1319)

Walter Mischel was born. Mischel contributed to personality theory and assessment through analysis of personality trait conceptions, studies of the perception and organization of personality constancies, and by making a case for cross-situational distinctiveness of behavior. APA Distinguished Scientific Contribution Award, 1982.

March 1, 1930   (1320)

Edward F. Zigler was born. Zigler's work has centered on learning and emotional development in children, with special attention given to mental retardation and education of disadvantaged children. APA Award for Distinguished Contribution to Psychology in the Public Interest, 1982; APA Distinguished Professional Contribution Award, 1986.

March 13, 1930   (1321)

Charles G. Matthews was born. Matthews has been the director of the prominent program in clinical neuropsychology at the University of Wisconsin–Madison. His service as an educator, journal editor, administrator, and policymaker were recognized by the APA Award for Distinguished Contribution to Education and Training in Psychology in 1992.

April 12, 1930   (1322)

The first meeting of the reorganized New York Branch of the APA was held. The Eastern Psychological Association is the successor to the New York Branch and numbers its annual meetings from this meeting. Robert S. Woodworth served as honorary president at this meeting, and Howard C. Warren was elected president for the following year.

May 5, 1930   (1323)

The First International Congress on Mental Hygiene was held in Washington, DC. William Alanson White presided over the meeting, and 41 countries were represented by those in attendance.

May 15, 1930 (1324)

The journal *Child Development* was first published by the Society for Research in Child Development. Buford J. Johnson was the first editor.

May 20, 1930 (1325)

Richard J. Herrnstein was born. Herrnstein's work has been in the history and systems of psychology and in the experimental analysis of behavior, with special attention given to the effect of reinforcement history on choice behavior. His book *IQ and the Meritocracy* (1973) presented a controversial view of the relation between remedial programs, hereditary intelligence, and social success.

May 22, 1930 (1326)

The *Journal of Experimental Psychology* received Ernest G. Wever and Charles W. Bray's manuscript, "The Nature of the Acoustic Response: The Relation Between Sound Frequency and Frequency of Impulses in the Auditory Nerve." Wever and Bray later received the first Society of Experimental Psychologists' Howard C. Warren Medal for this work.

June 20, 1930 (1327)

Carl Eisdorfer was born. Eisdorfer contributed significantly to the study of normal aging, the psychopathology of aging, and the health care of elderly individuals. He was instrumental in the early development of the National Institute on Aging. APA Award for Distinguished Professional Contributions, 1981.

July 16, 1930 (1328)

Sigmund Freud's book *Civilization and Its Discontents* was published in the United States.

July 23, 1930 (1329)

The first volume of Carl Murchison's *A History of Psychology in Autobiography* was published. Autobiographies of James M. Baldwin, Mary Whiton Calkins, Edouard Claparède, Raymond Dodge, Pierre Janet, Joseph Jastrow, Frederico Kiesow, William McDougall, Carl Seashore, Charles Spearman, Carl Stumpf, William Stern, Howard C. Warren, Theodor Ziehen, and Hendrick Zwaardemaker were included.

August 30, 1930 (1330)

Nancy Mayer Robinson was born. Robinson has specialized in research on behavior pathologies in children, mental retardation, giftedness, behavioral techniques of treatment and education, and the efficacy of daycare. Her book *The Mentally Retarded Child: A Psychological Approach* (1965; with Halbert B. Robinson) has been a definitive text.

September 6, 1930 (1331)

Richard F. Thompson was born. Thompson contributed to the scientific understanding of the neutral bases of behavior. His investigations of the neurophysiology of behavioral plasticity has shed light on the nature of learning and habituation. APA Distinguished Scientific Contribution Award, 1974.

November 7, 1930 (1332)

The *American Journal of Orthopsychiatry* was first published.

November 26, 1930 (1333)

Nathan Azrin was born. Azrin was one of the founders of applied behavior analysis. An early study used behavioral methods to eliminate towel hoarding in a psychotic woman. Later work applied behavioral principles to stuttering, toileting, enuresis, alcoholism, self-injurious behavior, and marital conflict. APA Distinguished Contribution for Applications in Psychology Award, 1975.

December 9, 1930 (1334)

Walter Cannon delivered an address to the Harvard Medical Society on heart rate and emotion. Cannon's research explored the physiology of emotional states.

December 22, 1930 (1335)

Raymond D. Fowler was born. Fowler's academic career was in clinical training and assessment. He headed court-ordered prison reform efforts in Alabama and has developed the first widely used computer-assisted interpretation system for the MMPI. APA President, 1988; APA Executive Vice President and Chief Executive Officer, 1989–present.

December 29, 1930 (1336)

The APA voted to poll its members on whether, in alternate years, first consideration for a site of the annual meeting be given to "institutions located in the territory west of the Appalachian Mountains." Members were also asked about changing the traditional December dates of the annual meeting to dates in the fall. The new fall schedule was adopted for the 1931 Toronto meeting.

December 30, 1930 (1337)

The University of Iowa dedicated its new psychology laboratory while the APA held its annual meeting on the Iowa campus. University of Iowa president Walter Jessup conducted the ceremonies. Addresses were given by Howard C. Warren, Walter Miles, Charles Judd, Edward A. Bott, and Robert S. Woodworth.

January 31, 1931 (1338)

The Psychograph, a device consisting of a helmet and movable rods designed so measurements could be made at 32 points on the skull, made its public debut at the Twin City Auto Show. The device was an excursion into automated phrenology.

February 2, 1931 (1339)

Edward L. Thorndike's book *Human Learning* was published.

February 21, 1931 (1340)

Ursula Bellugi was born. Bellugi and Edward S. Klima have studied extensively the neuropsychology of language, with special attention given to basic processes revealed by fluent users of American Sign Language. Their book *The Signs of Language* (1979) won the Outstanding Book Award from the Association of American Publishers. APA Distinguished Scientific Contributions Award, 1992.

April 13, 1931 (1341)

Martha E. Bernal was born. Bernal was the first Mexican American to receive a PhD in psychology. Her interests were in psychophysiology, behavior modification of disorderly children, parent training, and minority issues.

April 14, 1931 (1342)

Edward C. Tolman wrote the foreword to his book *Purposive Behavior in Animals and Men.*

April 19, 1931 (1343)

Stephen E. Goldston was born. Goldston has promoted primary prevention mental health programs throughout his long career at the National Institute of Mental Health. His book *Primary Prevention: An Idea Whose Time Has Come* (1977, with Donald Klein) called for greater support of preventive programs at that time. APA Award for Distinguished Professional Contributions, 1984.

April 29, 1931 (1344)

Margaret Floy Washburn was elected to the National Academy of Sciences. Washburn was the first woman psychologist elected to the Academy and only the second woman scientist of any kind honored in this way.

May 9, 1931 (1345)

The Institute of Human Relations was formally dedicated at Yale University. Speakers included Frank Angell, who was a prominent psychologist and president of Yale.

June 2, 1931 (1346)

Psychologist Leonard T. Troland patented a method of color photography that was part of the Technicolor process. Troland held many Technicolor patents: This one is apparently the earliest relating to the properties of the film and is based on research on the nature of color and color vision. Troland's work provides fine examples of applied visual research.

June 10, 1931 (1347)

Gordon Allport and Philip Vernon's personality scale *A Study of Values*, more commonly known as the Allport-Vernon Scale, was published.

June 15, 1931 (1348)

Carl Murchison's *A Handbook of Child Psychology* was first published.

June 26, 1931 (1349)

Winthrop and Luella Kellogg began their classic study comparing human and chimpanzee development. Their subjects were their infant son Donald and a newborn chimpanzee named Gua, both raised in their home under similar conditions.

September 13, 1931 (1350)

Clara Mayo was born. Mayo's goals were to understand and to help alleviate prejudice, sexism, and racism. As an applied social psychologist, she compared impression formation and nonverbal behavior of participants with different gender and ethnic backgrounds. Mayo spent a significant amount of time in courtrooms as an expert witness on the effects of prejudice.

October 17, 1931 (1351)

The first of a series of thirty 15-minute weekly radio lectures titled "Psychology Today" was broadcast over New York's WEAF and approximately 50 NBC-affiliated stations. The first lecture, an overview of scientific and applied psychology, was delivered by James R. Angell. The series was coordinated by Walter V. Bingham for the National Advisory Council of Radio in Education.

December 17, 1931 (1352)

James McGaugh was born. McGaugh's work in psychobiology has focused on factors that modulate and control learning, memory, mood, and motivation. APA Distinguished Scientific Contribution Award, 1981; American Psychological Society President, 1990.

January 9, 1932 (1353)

Elliot Aronson was born. Aronson's work in social psychology includes studies of cognitive dissonance, developing a method for reducing racial prejudice (*The Jigsaw Classroom*, 1978), writing an engaging textbook (*The Social Animal*, 1972), and coediting two editions of the *Handbook of Social Psychology* (1968, 1985). American Psychological Foundation Distinguished Teaching in Psychology Award, 1980.

January 9, 1932 (1354)

Edward C. Tolman's *Purposive Behavior in Animals and Men* was published. The book explained the theory and supportive research of Tolman's blend of cognitive and behavioral psychology.

January 28, 1932 (1355)

Florence L. Denmark was born. Denmark has been a leader in research and teaching of the psychology of women and was a founder of APA Division 35 (Psychology of Women). APA President, 1980; APA Award for Distinguished Contributions to Education and Training in Psychology, 1987; APA Award for Distinguished Contribution to Psychology in the Public Interest, 1992.

April 15, 1932 (1356)

The *Psychoanalytic Quarterly* was first published.

May 29, 1932 (1357)

Alfred M. Wellner was born. Wellner advanced the standards of professional psychology as chair of the APA Committee on Accreditation (1972–1977), chair of the APA Task Force on Standards for Providers (1970–1975), and executive officer of the National Register of Health Service Providers in Psychology. APA Award for Distinguished Professional Contributions, 1987.

May 30, 1932 (1358)

Walter Kintsch was born. Kintsch's studies of text comprehension and memory have led to the construction–integration model of discourse comprehension. The model describes the cognitive architecture of symbolic comprehension. APA Distinguished Scientific Contributions Award, 1992.

June 7, 1932 (1359)

David M. Green was born. Green was one of the founders of signal detection theory and promoted the application of information processing concepts to cognitive psychology. He has greatly clarified the mechanisms by which the ear processes the frequency, temporal, and spatial information in complex auditory signals. APA Distinguished Scientific Contribution Award, 1981.

August 6, 1932 (1360)

The first University of Iowa Child Welfare Pamphlet was published by the university's Child Welfare Research Station. The monograph was by Charles H. Cloy and was titled "Is My Child Underweight?" The series provided parents and teachers with brief guides to child development written in everyday language.

September 8, 1932 (1361)

The journal *Character and Personality* was first published by Duke University. The title was later changed to the *Journal of Personality*.

September 8, 1932 (1362)

The APA voted to apply for membership in the Inter-Society Color Council, a group concerned with color perception and industry standards. Clarence Ferree, A. T. Poffenberger, and Forrest Lee Dimmick were the first APA representatives on the Council. Their first informal report to the APA was made on September 8, 1933, and their first formal report was made on August 25, 1934.

September 10, 1932 (1363)

B. F. Skinner made his first paper presentation to an APA convention. The paper was titled "The Rate of Establishment of a Discrimination" and was read in Room C of Goldwin Smith Hall at Cornell University shortly after 3:00 p.m.

September 17, 1932 (1364)

Henry Tomes was born. Tomes has promoted increased ethnic diversity in professional psychology and increased sensitivity of all psychologists to aspects of minority group culture and experiences that affect psychological services. He was the first chair of the APA Board of Ethnic Minority Affairs. APA Award for Distinguished Professional Contributions, 1990.

September 21, 1932 (1365)

Melvin R. Novick was born. Novick was well-known as a consultant in measurement and statistics. He published numerous articles and books on psychological testing, in addition to a software data analysis package. He was also the chair of the committee that wrote the APA's *Standards for Educational and Psychological Testing* (1966).

October 27, 1932 (1366)

Sir Charles Sherrington and Edgar Adrian won the Nobel prize for their studies of the physiology of the neuron.

November 2, 1932 (1367)

The city of Zurich awarded Carl Jung a creative writing prize of 8,000 francs.

November 16, 1932 (1368)

Edwin G. Boring completed the foreword to his book *The Physical Dimensions of Consciousness*.

November 17, 1932 (1369)

As a 28-year-old graduate student, B. F. Skinner wrote his plan of career goals for ages 30–60: (a) Publish experimental descriptions of behavior, (b) promote behaviorism and operational definitions of psychological constructs, (c) develop a scientific theory of knowledge, and (d) develop a nonscientific theory of knowledge.

December 30, 1932 (1370)

Gordon Bower was born. Bower is a cognitive psychologist specializing in studies of human learning and memory, with particular attention given to the effects of imagery, organizational factors, and emotional states. APA Distinguished Scientific Contribution Award, 1979; American Psychological Society President, 1991.

January 16, 1933 (1371)

Judith Bardwick was born. Bardwick's specialties have been the psychology of women and organizational psychology. Her book *Psychology of Women* (1971) is a noteworthy treatment of the topic.

January 25, 1933 (1372)

Edwin G. Boring's book *Physical Dimensions of Consciousness* was published.

February 10, 1933 (1373)

In an article in *Science*, Edward L. Thorndike offered the evidence of spread of effect as proof of the law of effect.

March 23, 1933 (1374)

Philip G. Zimbardo was born. Zimbardo's work has centered on the psychology of social issues. He has studied deindividuation, institutionalized aggression and submission, obedience, shyness, anxiety and affiliation, and the consequences of time orientation. American Psychological Foundation Distinguished Contribution to Education in Psychology Award, 1975.

April 3, 1933 (1375)

Florence L. Geis was born. Geis's early work with Richard Christie, defining the Machiavellian personality style, received widespread attention. Most of her career, however, was devoted to excellence in research and instruction in gender bias. Geis was the first woman psychology faculty member at the University of Delaware.

April 28, 1933 (1376)

Wolfgang Köhler wrote, for the newspaper *Deutsche Allgemeine Zeitung*, the last anti-Nazi article to be published openly in Germany before World War II. The article defended Jewish professors recently dismissed from their university posts and pointed to the many contributions Jews had made to German culture.

May 10, 1933 (1377)

The Nazis burned thousands of books by Jewish authors, including Sigmund Freud, in the streets of Berlin.

June 19, 1933 (1378)

Time magazine reported Winthrop and Luella Kellogg's study of raising their son Donald and a baby chimpanzee, Gua, under the same conditions.

June 24, 1933 (1379)

The Society for Research in Child Development was organized.

July 13, 1933 (1380)

Beatrice Tugenhat Gardner was born. Gardner is a comparative psychologist who, with R. Allen Gardner, began Project Washoe, the first program to teach American Sign Language to a chimpanzee.

August 15, 1933 (1381)

Stanley Milgram was born. Milgram is well-known for his studies of obedience to authority, but he also wrote influential articles on the effects of urban environments on behavior and other topics in applied social psychology.

August 30, 1933 (1382)

Saul Sternberg was born. Sternberg's contributions to the field of information processing have included several experimental procedures, analytic techniques, and experimental models, including the Sternberg memory scanning paradigm and the serial exhaustive research model. APA Distinguished Scientific Contribution Award, 1987.

September 9, 1933 (1383)

Dalmas A. Taylor was born. Through his commitment to education and professional growth of minority students, Taylor has increased the ethnic diversity of psychology. He was the first director of the APA's Minority Fellowship Program. His research interests have focused on self-disclosure. APA Award for Distinguished Education and Training Contributions, 1991.

November 2, 1933 (1384)

The first operation to treat epilepsy by elevation of the skull cap was performed. The surgeon was Karl Ney of the New York Medical College and Flower Hospital. Drug treatments have replaced experimental surgical techniques such as this.

December 6, 1933 (1385)

Logan Wright was born. Wright is a clinical psychologist with a long record of advocacy for improvements in professional standards of education in psychology and legislation affecting professional psychology. APA President, 1986.

February 15, 1934 (1386)

Paul Ekman was born. Ekman's research has related emotional state to nonverbal behavior, with special emphasis on facial expression and nonverbal correlates of lying and deception. His cross-cultural studies have demonstrated universals of emotional expression. APA Distinguished Scientific Contribution Award, 1991.

March 5, 1934 (1387)

Daniel Kahneman was born. Kahneman studied the role of cognitive heuristics in judgments of uncertain events and thus created a new dimension in the understanding of cognitive processes. Kahneman worked with Amos Tversky to develop prospect theory. APA Distinguished Scientific Contribution Award, 1982.

March 28, 1934   (1388)
George Sperling was born. Sperling contributed to the fields of visual information processing and attention. He studied short-term visual persistence, the modeling of binocular vision, mechanisms and limitations of high-speed visual search, and the nature of attentional limits in visual perception. APA Distinguished Scientific Contribution Award, 1988.

August 4, 1934   (1389)
Allen E. Bergin was born. Bergin has concentrated on comprehensive surveys of psychotherapy research and writing on the place of religion and values in psychology. His *Handbook of Psychotherapy and Behavior Change* (1971), edited with Sol Garfield, has been the definitive summary of the field for more than 20 years. APA Award for Distinguished Professional Contributions, 1989.

August 14, 1934   (1390)
Charles A. Kiesler was born. Kiesler's interests have been in social psychology, attitudes and opinions, and mental health policy. APA Executive Officer, 1975–1979; APA Distinguished Contributions to Research in Public Policy, 1989; American Psychological Society President, 1989.

August 15, 1934   (1391)
The *Journal of Experimental Psychology* received John R. Stroop's manuscript, "Studies of Interference in Serial Verbal Reactions," the first report of the "Stroop effect."

August 26, 1934   (1392)
Wilhelm Reich was expelled from the International Psychoanalytic Society. Reich's dedication to a political theory that combined Marxism and psychoanalysis and his increasingly disorganized personality led to the split.

September 12, 1934   (1393)
Ivan Pavlov attacked Robert Yerkes and Wolfgang Köhler for their insight doctrines. The topic was the subject of three of Pavlov's "Wednesday meetings." Pavlov ridiculed Köhler for asserting that apes were intelligent on the basis of evidence that they sit for a period of time without doing anything before successfully performing difficult tasks.

September 12, 1934   (1394)
Carl Murchison's A *Handbook of General Experimental Psychology* was published.

October 20, 1934   (1395)
The organizing meeting of the American Board of Psychiatry and Neurology was held at the Hotel Commodore in New York. H. Douglas Singer was elected president.

December 5, 1934 (1396)

In one of "Pavlov's Wednesdays," Ivan Pavlov attacked Kurt Koffka and Kurt Lewin's objections to the concept of association.

December 20, 1934 (1397)

George Herbert Mead's book *Mind, Self, and Society: From the Standpoint of a Social Behaviorist* was published.

January 29, 1935 (1398)

The first general administration of the Iowa Tests of Basic Skills was held. Students in 217 Iowa school systems took the standardized achievement tests.

February 20, 1935 (1399)

In one of "Pavlov's Wednesdays," Ivan Pavlov attacked Pierre Janet as a psychologist but said that Janet fascinated him as a neurologist.

April 3, 1935 (1400)

The *Psychological Index* board of editors voted to discontinue publication of its bibliographic list of psychological literature with the June 1936 issue. The more comprehensive *Psychological Abstracts*, begun in 1927, had grown to become the principal guide to psychological literature.

April 3, 1935 (1401)

Emanuel Donchin was born. Donchin has played a major role in the emergence of cognitive psychophysiology with studies of event-related evoked brain potentials, such as the P-300 wave, which are related to meaningfulness, decision making, memory processes, and mental preparation. American Psychological Society William James Fellow, 1991.

May 2, 1935 (1402)

Carl Murchison's first A *Handbook of Social Psychology* was published.

June 26, 1935 (1403)

Leo Kanner's book *Child Psychiatry* was published. This was the first English-language text on the topic. Kanner later identified the syndrome called *infantile autism* and gave it its name (1944).

July 8, 1935 (1404)

Oscar K. Buros published *Educational, Psychological, and Personality Tests of 1933–34*. This was the first volume in the series that would become the *Mental Measurements Yearbooks*.

August 22, 1935 (1405)

Wolfgang Köhler resigned from the directorship of the Psychological Institute of the University of Berlin. Nazi anti-intellectual demands had made teaching and research secondary to ideological purity.

August 23, 1935 (1406)

The "Report of the Clinical Section of the APA" was published in *Psychological Clinic*. The report defined clinical psychology, described standards for training, and provided a guide to all of the psychological clinics in the United States. Andrew W. Brown chaired the reporting committee, and Robert A. Brotemarkle, Maud A. Merrill, and Clara H. Town served as members.

September 2, 1935 (1407)

Anne Treisman was born. Treisman's early research explored the phenomenon of selective attention and has broadened to explorations of how attention and object perception are integrated. Society of Experimental Psychologists Warren Medal, 1990; APA Distinguished Scientific Contribution Award, 1990.

September 4, 1935 (1408)

The Psychometric Society was founded in Ann Arbor, Michigan. Louis L. Thurstone was the first president of the organization. When the APA was reorganized in 1945, the Psychometric Society was invited to become Division 4 of the association. The Psychometric Society declined, and there is still no APA Division 4 today.

September 5, 1935 (1409)

The APA voted to approve a petition from the Psychometric Society for affiliation with the APA. Louis L. Thurstone, Paul Horst, and Myron W. Richardson submitted the petition.

November 8, 1935 (1410)

Norman R. F. Maier and Theodore C. Schneirla's *Principles of Animal Psychology* was published.

November 12, 1935 (1411)

The first modern surgery on the frontal lobes for treatment of mental disorders was performed by Egas Moniz at Santa Marta Hospital in Lisbon, Portugal. Moniz injected absolute alcohol into the frontal lobes of a mental patient through two holes drilled in the skull. Moniz later used a technique that severed neurons and led to the prefrontal lobotomy techniques of the 1940s.

November 27, 1935 (1412)

The editorial introducing the first issue of the *Journal of Psychology* was written. The first article was "A Tachistoscopic Device With Subhuman Primates," by Heinrich Klüver. Carl Murchison was the journal's first editor.

December 27, 1935 (1413)
The first modern psychiatric surgery to sever the neurons of the frontal lobe was performed. Portuguese surgeon Egas Moniz performed the operation at Santa Marta Hospital in Lisbon. Plugs, or "cores," of tissue were severed by rotating a wire loop inside the brain. Moniz won a Nobel prize for this work.

February 20, 1936 (1414)
The *Journal of Psychology* was first published. The original copyright holder was Dorothea Powell Murchison.

February 29, 1936 (1415)
Two days after the death of Ivan Pavlov, the Soviet government preserved his memory by ordering a monument to be erected in Leningrad (St. Petersburg), renaming the First Leningrad Medical Institute "The Pavlov Institute," maintaining his laboratory as a museum, preserving his brain, granting a pension to his widow, and publishing his collected works in four languages.

April 9, 1936 (1416)
The first Howard Crosby Warren Medal of the Society of Experimental Psychologists (SEP) was awarded to Ernest G. Wever and Charles W. Bray for their work on auditory physiology. The medal was established by Mrs. Catherine C. Warren as a memorial for her husband, one of the founders of the SEP and its first president after its 1929 reorganization.

April 11, 1936 (1417)
At its seventh annual meeting at Fordham University, the New York Branch of the APA changed its name to the Eastern Branch of the APA, a precursor of the Eastern Psychological Association.

April 26, 1936 (1418)
The German Institute for Psychological Research and Psychotherapy was organized. Psychiatrist Matthias Heinrich Göring, cousin of Reich Marshal Hermann Göring, assumed leadership of the new institute. The institute, commonly called the Göring Institute, promoted a non-Freudian, pro-Nazi, anti-Semitic view of psychotherapy.

May 11, 1936 (1419)
Ronald E. Fox was born. Fox's career as a psychotherapist, educator, and advocate for professional psychology included founding roles in the School of Professional Psychology at Wright State University (1977) and the Psychology Academy of the National Academies of Practice. APA Award for Distinguished Education and Training Contributions, 1992; APA President, 1994.

June 28, 1936 (1420)
Don Hake was born. Hake was a pioneer in the fields of experimental and applied behavior analysis. His studies of conditioned suppression, social facilitation, pun-

ishment, escape and avoidance conditioning, aggression, and cooperation found applications in clinical settings.

July 4, 1936 (1421)

The journal *Nature* published a short report by Hans Selye titled "A Syndrome Produced by Diverse Nocuous Agents." This was the first published description of Selye's "general adaptation syndrome" and described stressor-induced stages of alarm, adaptation, and exhaustion. The article, submitted on May 18, 1936, aroused considerable controversy and research.

July 15, 1936 (1422)

The Association of Consulting Psychologists (ACP) petitioned the APA for affiliate status. Gertrude Hildreth was president of the ACP at the time. The petition was tabled at the 1937 APA meeting and was not acted on at the 1938 meeting.

July 22, 1936 (1423)

B. F. Skinner met his future wife, Yvonne Blue, on this day.

August 8, 1936 (1424)

Sandra Wood Scarr was born. Scarr's studies of intelligence among adopted children have raised estimates of the contribution of environment to intelligence. Later work has focused on the quality of child care. She received the APA National Book Award for her *Mother Care/Other Care* (1985). APA Distinguished Contributions to Research in Public Policy Award, 1988.

August 27, 1936 (1425)

A committee on APA reorganization recommended inviting the Western Psychological Association, Midwestern Psychological Association, and Southern Society for Philosophy and Psychology to become affiliates of the APA.

September 1, 1936 (1426)

The Society for the Psychological Study of Social Issues (SPSSI) was founded in Room 104 of McNutt Hall, Dartmouth College. Ross Stanger was chair pro tem and Goodwin Watson was the first elected chair. SPSSI is now Division 9 of the APA.

September 3, 1936 (1427)

The Society for the Psychological Study of Social Issues (SPSSI) petitioned the APA to become an affiliate of the APA. Goodwin Watson was chair of SPSSI at the time and Isadore Krechevsky (David Krech) was secretary. The petition was approved by the APA on September 2, 1937. SPSSI is now Division 9 of the APA.

September 12, 1936 (1428)

Michael I. Posner was born. Posner is best known for his chronometric studies of the internal constituents of thought and his work in information processing and selective attention. His books *Chronometric Explorations of Mind* (1978) and *Cognition: An Introduction* (1974) exemplify his work. APA Distinguished Scientific Contribution Award, 1980.

September 14, 1936 (1429)

J. P. Guilford's book *Psychometric Methods* was published.

September 14, 1936 (1430)

The first frontal lobotomy performed in the United States was carried out by Walter Freeman and James Watts at the George Washington University Hospital. Freeman became a nationwide advocate for the procedure. By 1951, an estimated 18,608 lobotomies had been performed in the United States.

October 29, 1936 (1431)

The first Educational Testing Service Invitational Conference was held. At the time, it was called the Invitational Conference on Testing Problems and may be the oldest continuous conference on testing issues.

November 6, 1936 (1432)

George Stricker was born. Stricker has integrated clinical research, practice, training, and the promotion of professional psychology. He contributed to contemporary standards of peer review and served as the first editor of the APA's *Clinician's Research Digest*. APA Award for Distinguished Professional Contributions, 1990.

November 12, 1936 (1433)

The first verbal report of the use of insulin shock therapy for schizophrenia in the United States was made by Karl Bowman to the New York Society for Clinical Psychiatry. Bowman was director of the Bellevue Psychiatric Hospital in New York City at the time.

November 21, 1936 (1434)

An article in the *New York Times* reported the prefrontal lobotomies performed by Walter Freeman and James Watts, the first in the United States. The headline read "Find New Surgery Aids Mental Cases."

November 24, 1936 (1435)

Bonnie R. Strickland was born. Strickland may be best known for studies of locus of control of reinforcement, but her work has covered a range of social and personality variables. She helped develop the Nowicki-Strickland Children's Locus of Control Scale. She has served psychological organizations in many capacities. APA President, 1987.

December 5, 1936 (1436)

The irreverent Psychological Round Table first met. Many noteworthy psychologists have been members of the Round Table, but no members older than 40 years of age are allowed.

January 4, 1937 (1437)

Abraham A. Brill's English translation of Josef Breuer and Sigmund Freud's book *Studies in Hysteria* was published in the United States.

January 9, 1937 (1438)

The first published report of insulin shock therapy for schizophrenia in an American hospital appeared in the *Journal of the American Medical Association*. Julius Steinfeld was the author.

February 25, 1937 (1439)

The *Journal of Consulting Psychology* was first published by the Association of Consulting Psychologists (ACP), with Johnnie P. Symonds serving as editor. The APA acquired the journal in 1946 in a merger with the American Association for Applied Psychology, successor to the ACP. In 1968, the name of the journal became the *Journal of Consulting and Clinical Psychology*.

March 10, 1937 (1440)

B. F. Skinner became a member of Psi Chi, the national honor society in psychology, at the University of Minnesota. The chapter sent a letter to the national office, listing the new members. A special note was written to the side of Skinner's name, with a line drawn from his name to the note. It read, "A true friend of Psi Chi."

March 16, 1937 (1441)

Amos Tversky was born. Tversky's interests have included the analysis of psychological measurement and the nature of cognitive heuristics governing behavioral choice. Tversky worked with Daniel Kahneman to develop prospect theory. APA Distinguished Scientific Contribution Award, 1982.

April 22, 1937 (1442)

Patricia S. Goldman-Rakic was born. Goldman-Rakic carried out exhaustive studies of the neurological structures of the cortex underlying knowledge of the existence, character, and spatial location of objects. Later work has turned to the study of the neurophysiology of working, or short-term, memory. APA Distinguished Scientific Contribution Award, 1991.

May 1, 1937 (1443)

The Psychologists League, a group promoting employment of psychologists during the Depression, marched in the May Day parade in New York. May Day was an event in the Communist Party calendar, but the involvement of psychologists seems to have attracted little government attention.

May 7, 1937 (1444)

The Midwestern Psychological Association (MPA) voted to petition the APA for affiliated organization status. A May 12, 1937, letter from MPA Secretary–Treasurer Arthur G. Bills presented the petition. The action was approved by the APA on September 8, 1938.

May 31, 1937 (1445)

In a picture story titled "Rat Works Slot Machine for a Living," *Life* magazine described the performance of a rat named Pliny the Elder. Using the method of shaping, B. F. Skinner had trained Pliny to pull a chain to release a marble, pick up the marble, and drop it in a box for a food reinforcement.

August 26, 1937 (1446)

The Western Psychological Association (WPA) petitioned to become an affiliate organization of the APA. A letter from WPA Secretary Frank C. Davis presented the petition. The APA approved the petition on September 8, 1938.

August 30, 1937 (1447)

The first formal meeting of the American Association for Applied Psychology (AAAP) began in Minneapolis. Douglas Fryer was elected president by the 400 members. The AAAP succeeded the Association of Consulting Psychologists and focused on practice issues, in contrast to the academic orientation of the APA. The AAAP and APA reunited when the APA reorganized in 1944.

September 1, 1937 (1448)

The American Association for Applied Psychology (AAAP) petitioned to affiliate with the APA. A letter from AAAP Secretary Horace B. English presented the request, which the APA approved on September 8, 1938.

September 2, 1937 (1449)

Czech perception researcher Jan Purkinje was honored by appearing on a postage stamp issued by Czechoslovakia on this day.

October 1, 1937 (1450)

George W. Snedecor's text *Statistical Methods Applied to Experiments in Agriculture and Biology* was published. A second edition by Snedecor and William G. Cochran, titled only *Statistical Methods*, was widely used by psychologists.

October 4, 1937 (1451)

Joseph B. Rhine's book on parapsychology, *New Frontiers of the Mind: The Story of the Duke Experiments*, was published.

October 25, 1937 (1452)

David Pablo Boder received his charter from the State of Illinois for a psychological museum, perhaps the first such museum in the United States.

November 10, 1937 (1453)

The Indiana Psychological Association was incorporated.

December 2, 1937 (1454)

Ina Cepenas Uzgiris was born. Uzgiris has specialized in research on cognitive development in infants. She is best known for the development, with J. McVicker Hunt, of ordinal scales of acquisition of Piagetian stages.

January 19, 1938 (1455)

The *Journal of Parapsychology* was first published by Duke University.

February 15, 1938 (1456)

The *Journal of Neurophysiology* was first published by C. C. Thomas. Johannes Dusser de Barenne was the editor.

March 11, 1938 (1457)

The American Association on Mental Deficiency was incorporated in Pennsylvania.

March 15, 1938 (1458)

Freud's home in Vienna was overrun by Nazis, one day after the German occupation of Austria. The Nazis destroyed Freud's private library and publicly burned all of his books found in the Vienna public library.

March 15, 1938 (1459)

The first report of treatment of a mental patient by electroconvulsive shock was delivered by Italian psychiatrists Ugo Cerletti and Lucio Bini. The use of shock was based on Ladislas Meduna's theory that schizophrenia and epilepsy were antagonistic, although Meduna induced convulsions by chemical means in his therapies.

April 1, 1938 (1460)

The ninth annual meeting of the Eastern Psychological Association was held. This was the group's first meeting under its current name, having met as the Eastern Branch of the APA and the New York Branch of the APA in previous years. Karl S. Lashley was president of the organization at this time.

May 16, 1938 (1461)

Abraham A. Brill's *The Basic Writings of Sigmund Freud* was published.

June 4, 1938 (1462)

Sigmund Freud fled Austria, a victim of Nazi persecution. Before leaving, he was forced to sign a document testifying that he had received respectful treatment from the Nazis. Freud signed and added the sarcastic comment, "I can heartily recommend the Gestapo to anyone." Freud traveled to Paris and then to London, where he resided at 20 Maresfield Gardens in Hampstead.

June 6, 1938 (1463)

The Society for Personality Assessment was founded. The Society was originally named The Rorschach Institute and has maintained an emphasis on the Rorschach Test.

June 29, 1938 (1464)

The plan to organize the Canadian Psychological Association (CPA) originated at a dinner meeting of the Psychology Section of the American Association for the Advancement of Science (AAAS) during the annual meeting of the AAAS in Ottawa, Ontario. The dinner was held at 6:30 p.m. at the Chateau Laurier. The first official meeting of the CPA was held in 1940.

July 9, 1938 (1465)

The president of Indiana University wrote to entomologist Alfred Kinsey, authorizing him to offer a course in marriage. Kinsey's famous research on sexual behavior began with interviews of students in this course.

July 22, 1938 (1466)

Robert S. Woodworth wrote the foreword to the first edition of his classic text, *Experimental Psychology*.

August 11, 1938 (1467)

Edward L. Palmer was born. Palmer, an educational and developmental psychologist, has been director of research of the Children's Television Workshop, producers of the educational programs *Sesame Street* and *The Electric Company*. Palmer has supervised the educational and social content of the programs. APA Distinguished Contribution for Applications in Psychology Award, 1974.

August 13, 1938 (1468)

The Psychological Review Company was legally dissolved. This completed the transfer of five major journals from Howard C. Warren to the APA.

September 1, 1938 (1469)

Robert S. Woodworth's book *Experimental Psychology* was published. This edition and subsequent revisions with coauthor Harold Schlosberg became standard texts for decades.

September 2, 1938 (1470)

B. F. Skinner's book *The Behavior of Organisms* was published. There were 800 copies in the first printing, of which 548 had been sold by 1946.

September 7, 1938 (1471)

The Library of Congress received its copy of the first issue of *Psychological Record*.

September 8, 1938 (1472)

The APA voted to provide a subscription to *Psychological Bulletin* for each member. Seventy-five cents of each member's dues was allocated for this purpose. The action took effect on January 1, 1939.

September 8, 1938 (1473)

The APA Committee on Scientific and Professional Ethics was established. This was the APA's first group to deal with professional ethical issues, but it used unwritten, informal procedures to handle incidents that were brought to its attention. Robert S. Sessions chaired the committee.

October 13, 1938 (1474)

The drug Allonal (aprobarbitol; Hoffman-LaRoche) was approved for use by the U.S. Food and Drug Administration. Aprobarbitol is a barbiturate used as an antianxiety agent and as a sedative. The barbiturates are nonselective central nervous system depressants.

October 17, 1938 (1475)

Lauretta Bender's Visual Motor Gestalt Test, commonly called the Bender-Gestalt Test, was published.

October 30, 1938 (1476)

The Orson Welles radio broadcast of H. G. Wells's "War of the Worlds" was aired, on Halloween night. This realistic radio drama caused panic in many parts of the United States. The phenomenon was described in Hadley Cantril, Hazel Gaudet, and Herta Hertzog's book *The Invasion From Mars* (1940).

November 3, 1938 (1477)

Henry A. Murray's book *Explorations in Personality: A Clinical and Experimental Study of Fifty Men of College Age* was published. The staff of the Harvard Psychological Clinic assisted in writing the book.

December 21, 1938 (1478)

Members of the American Association for Applied Psychology met at Ohio State University to ratify the bylaws of the association and to approve affiliation with the APA and the American Association for the Advancement of Science.

December 23, 1938   (1479)

The drug phenobarbitol was first approved for use by the U.S. Food and Drug Administration. It was marketed as Dantol (Hoover). Luminal is also a trade name for phenobarbitol. Phenobarbitol is a barbiturate used as an antianxiety medication and as a sedative.

January 3, 1939   (1480)

J. Douglas Carroll was born. Carroll is known for his discovery and representation of structures underlying matrices of psychological data. He developed the individual-differences scaling model, which is used for the analysis of similarity data and has influenced perceptual and cognitive psychology. APA Distinguished Scientific Contribution Award, 1989.

February 28, 1939   (1481)

John Dollard, Leonard Doob, Neal E. Miller, O. Hobart Mowrer, and Robert Sears's book *Frustration and Aggression* was published.

May 3, 1939   (1482)

David Wechsler's book *The Measurement of Adult Intelligence* was published.

June 26, 1939   (1483)

Sigmund Freud appeared on the cover of *Time* magazine for the second time. *Time* reviewed Freud's book *Moses and Monotheism* in this issue, 3 months before Freud's death.

July 19, 1939   (1484)

Philip R. Laughlin was born. Through his service as chairperson of the Veterans Administration (VA) Psychology Representation Committee, Laughlin has been an articulate voice for excellence in psychological training and education within the VA. APA Distinguished Contribution to Education and Training in Psychology Award, 1989.

July 28, 1939   (1485)

Matina Souretis Horner was born. Horner is best known for her studies of achievement motivation in women and studies of the phenomenon of "fear of success" in talented women.

September 4, 1939   (1486)

One day after England declared war on Germany, Dean R. Brimhall, psychologist and administrator of the U.S. Civil Aeronautics Authority arrived at the APA convention in California to enlist the aid of psychologists in developing means of selecting the best candidates for the difficult task of airplane flight training. The resulting program involved about 30 different universities.

September 5, 1939 (1487)

The APA voted to "attempt to obtain a certificate from the United States Treasury Department indicating that contributions made to the Association may be deducted from the income tax of the donor."

September 21, 1939 (1488)

Sigmund Freud asked his physician Max Schur to administer morphine until Freud died. Until this time Freud had undergone many operations for cancer of the palate and jaw without the use of anesthetics or analgesics. Freud died on September 23, 1939.

IV

1940–1949
POSTWAR DIVERSITY
AND EXPANSION

The effects of World War II on modern psychology were not limited to the research, assessment, training, and clinical treatment activities of psychologists during the war itself (e.g., Entries 1496 and 1513), as important as those were. The organizational structure needed to coordinate the efforts of psychologists began with meetings of representatives of many organizations (Entries 1497, 1498, and 1517) but ended with proposals to restructure the American Psychological Association (APA) in a way that would maintain subdiscipline divisions and provide representative participation in organizational governance (Entries 1549 and 1563). An executive secretary, Dael Wolfle, was hired by the organization (Entries 1563 and 1570), and a small professional staff took over the affairs of the APA from professors and secretaries in academic departments. A new journal, the *American Psychologist*, disseminated news of the organization, research summaries, and articles about relevant legislation and public policy issues. The latent social mission of psychology had been awakened by the war. There was a provision for new divisions, and the first of these, a division for gerontologists, was admitted in 1945 (Entries 1569, 1572, and 1587).

The aftermath of the war made unprecedented demands on the nation's supply of clinical psychologists and psychotherapists and culminated in the active involvement of the APA in curriculum development and accreditation of graduate programs in clinical and counseling psychology. Responding to a request from the Veteran's Administration, an APA committee chaired by David Shakow compiled the desirable features of clinical training programs (Entries 1594 and 1616). The APA later (Entry 1627) published a list of graduate programs that met these criteria. This first list of APA-approved programs not only provided standards for clinical training but also signaled a more active role of the association in monitoring professional practice. The Boulder Conference of 1949 (Entry 1653) continued this momentum, establishing the enduring research–practitioner model of graduate education in clinical psychology.

Concern for quality control in psychological services extended to private and public practice in each state. The first state licensure law was passed in Connecticut soon after the war (Entry 1560), and the chair of the state's examining board, Walter Miles, had the honor of becoming the nation's first licensed psychologist (Entry 1562). The APA promoted certification and licensure legislation (Entry 1802), as did the newly formed Conference of State Psychological Societies (Entry 1617) and American Board of Examiners in Professional Psychology (Entries 1584 and 1604).

The growth of the number and diversity of mental measurement instruments continued through the war years. Many tests reflected advances in research in intelligence and personality, in statistical techniques such as factor analysis, and in empirical, rather than rational, bases for item selection. The Minnesota Multiphasic Personality Inventory was first published in 1942 (Entry 1525), the Thematic Apperception Test in 1943 (Entry 1539), and the Kuder Preference Record in 1945 (Entry 1557). The postwar years saw the introduction of Raymond Cattell's Sixteen Personality Factor Questionnaire (16PF; Entry 1659), the Wechsler Intelligence Scale for Children (Entry 1651), the Differential Aptitude Test (Entry 1615), and the Miller Analogies Test (Entry 1624).

Applied psychology also was affected by the emergence of the experiential study of group processes, typified by the "T-groups" of the National Training Laboratories (Entries 1582 and 1606). Originally designed as a tool for the analysis of interpersonal relationships in organizations, the technique spawned semitherapeutic sensitivity training groups in the 1960s and 1970s.

For experimental psychologists, the decade of the 1940s was marked by the emergence of comprehensive theories of learning, with lively debate and inventive critical experiments to test the adequacy of the competing viewpoints. Prominent books published during this era reflected this theme. Landmark volumes in learning were written by Skinner (Entry 1470), Hilgard and Marquis (Entry 1489), McGeoch (Entry 1521), Hull (Entry 1537), and Hilgard (Entry 1626).

Comprehensive books in other fields became the standard texts for the next generation of psychologists: Woodworth's *Experimental Psychology* (Entries 1466 and 1469), White's *The Abnormal Personality* (Entry 1636), Morgan's *Physiological Psychology* (Entry 1538), and Cronbach's *Essentials of Psychological Testing* (Entry 1655) are among these works. Two other works should be mentioned in this connection. One is Skinner's *Walden II* (Entry 1634). It provided intellectual fodder for popular articles on psychology, alarmed editorials in newspapers, arguments in college classrooms and dormitories, and at least two utopian communities still in existence. The other is Adorno, Frenkel-Brunswik, Levinson, and Sanford's early 1950 publication, *The Authoritarian Personality* (Entry 1661), a psychological response to revelations about Nazi atrocities during World War II that revealed the nature of authoritarian beliefs and individual differences in their strength. Research and commentary on authoritarianism was common in the academic journals and the popular press of the 1950s. World War II had pervasive effects on scientific, applied, and professional psychology.

February 28, 1940   (1489)
Ernest Hilgard and Donald Marquis's book *Conditioning and Learning* was published.

May 9, 1940   (1490)
Robert A. Rescorla was born. With Allen Wagner, Rescorla developed the Rescorla–Wagner theory of classical conditioning, a simple and elegant predictor of association strength in a variety of circumstances. He has emphasized the importance of probabilistic information in the learning history of the organism. APA Distinguished Scientific Contribution Award, 1986.

June 30, 1940   (1491)
Administration of the oldest U.S. federal mental hospital, St. Elizabeth's in Washington, DC, was transferred from the Department of the Interior to the Federal Security Agency, in the first of many moves. Others were to the Department of Health, Education, and Welfare (April 11, 1953), to the National Institute of

Mental Health (August 9, 1967), and to the District of Columbia (October 1, 1987).

July 23, 1940 (1492)

William G. Chase was born. Chase published a variety of articles on experimental cognitive psychology, focusing on sentence comprehension, memory span, and perception in the game of chess. He was interested in spatial knowledge and chunking strategies for memory.

August 10, 1940 (1493)

Representatives of the APA, American Association for the Advancement of Science, Society of Experimental Psychologists, Psychometric Society, American Association for Applied Psychology, and the Society for the Psychological Study of Social Issues met to discuss psychology's response to the war in Europe. The later Conference on Morale had its beginnings in this meeting.

August 13, 1940 (1494)

A book titled *The Psycho-Math Stud Poker System* was published, perhaps breaking new ground in applied psychology.

September 1, 1940 (1495)

The Hogg Foundation for Mental Health opened. The Hogg Foundation supports community mental health research and services. Grants in the 1980s averaged about $2.5 million per year.

September 16, 1940 (1496)

President Franklin Roosevelt signed the Selective Service Act. The Army General Classification Test (AGCT) had been devised by prestigious experts in testing and awaited the first draftees. Carl C. Brigham, Henry C. Garrett, Carrol L. Shartle, Louis L. Thurstone, and Walter Van Dyke Bingham (chair) were the civilian members of the AGCT committee, created in April 1940.

November 2, 1940 (1497)

The Conference on Morale, made up of delegates from the APA, American Association for the Advancement of Science, American Association for Applied Psychology, Society for the Psychological Study of Social Issues, Society of Experimental Psychologists, and Psychometric Society, held its first formal meeting to plan psychology's response to World War II.

November 3, 1940 (1498)

The National Research Council appointed the Emergency Committee in Psychology to mobilize psychological skills for service in World War II. The members were Gordon Allport, Robert Brotemarkle, Leonard Carmichael, Karl Dallenbach, Carl Guthe, Walter Hunter, Walter Miles, Carroll Pratt, Dael Wolfle, and Robert Yerkes.

November 7, 1940 (1499)

The U.S. Selective Service System issued its Medical Circular #1, a guide to minimum mental and personality inspection of draftees. Eight abnormal types were described: mental defect, psychopathic personality, mood disorder, syphilis of the central nervous system, psychoneurosis, grave mental and personality handicaps, chronic inebriety, and organic nervous system disease.

December 16, 1940 (1500)

Robert J. Resnick was born. Resnick's research in child clinical psychology has focused on attention deficit disorders and the adjustment of children to medical procedures. In the 1970s, his successful antitrust suit against Virginia Blue Cross and Blue Shield established the right of professional psychologists to receive direct payment for their services. APA President, 1995.

December 30, 1940 (1501)

The first official annual meeting of the Canadian Psychological Association was held at McGill University in Montreal. President Edward A. Bott presided over the 26 psychologists in attendance. Presenters included Magda Arnold, Donald O. Hebb, C. Roger Myers, L. S. Penrose, and Mary D. Salter. The annual dues were set at $2.

February 11, 1941 (1502)

The journal *Educational and Psychological Measurement* was first published.

April 12, 1941 (1503)

Alan Kent Malyon was born. Malyon was a clinical psychologist interested in gay and lesbian issues. He spearheaded the successful drive to remove homosexuality as a pathological condition in the *Diagnostic and Statistical Manual of Mental Disorders* of the American Psychiatric Association.

May 2, 1941 (1504)

The drug chloral hydrate, manufactured by Kremers-Urban, was approved for use by the U.S. Food and Drug Administration. Chloral hydrate is a nonbarbiturate sedative used in the treatment of anxiety. Noctec is a contemporary trade name for chloral hydrate.

June 1, 1941 (1505)

Richard E. Nisbett was born. Nisbett's studies have described the bases of attributions and inferences about one's own behavior and the behavior of others, with special attention given to misattributions and predictable biases in inference. APA Distinguished Scientific Contribution Award, 1991.

June 16, 1941 (1506)

The Education Ministry of the German Third Reich announced training and examination standards for certification as a psychologist. Candidates were examined in the conscious and unconscious life of individual and community, developmental psychology, characterology, hereditary psychology, the psychology of expression, biomedical science, and philosophy and ideology.

July 1, 1941 (1507)

Neal Miller and John Dollard wrote the foreword to their book *Social Learning and Imitation*.

July 11, 1941 (1508)

Leonard Bickman was born. Bickman and Joseph H. Grosslight planned the pivotal National Conference on Graduate Education and Training in Psychology that met in Salt Lake City in 1987. APA Award for Distinguished Education and Training Contributions, 1988.

August 28, 1941 (1509)

Erich Fromm's *Escape from Freedom* was published. The book applied psychoanalytic methods to the problems of culture and society.

October 4, 1941 (1510)

The Institute of Psychology was formed at the University of Ottawa. This was an important step in establishing independent departments of psychology in Canadian universities. Twelve students initially enrolled in Ottawa's Institute of Psychology.

November 1, 1941 (1511)

The newsletter of the Educational Psychology Division of the American Association for Applied Psychology was first published. This later became the APA Division 15's *Educational Psychologist*. William Clark Trow established the newsletter.

November 11, 1941 (1512)

Thirteen women psychologists met at the Manhattan apartment of Alice Bryan to plan a national organization to promote the employment of women psychologists in government during wartime. The all-male Emergency Committee in Psychology, formed in 1940, had excluded women from its plans. The National Council of Women Psychologists grew from this meeting.

December 8, 1941 (1513)

The first data were gathered for the World War II studies later published under the title *American Soldier*, edited by Samuel S. Stouffer. The attack on Pearl Harbor had occurred on the previous day. The official name of the series of "American Soldier" studies was Studies in Social Psychology in World War II.

December 8, 1941 (1514)

The organizing meeting of the National Council of Women Psychologists was called. Seven days later, approximately 50 women met and the organization was officially founded.

December 15, 1941 (1515)

The National Council of Women Psychologists (NCWP) was founded. The group was formed to promote the government services of women psychologists during World War II. Gladys C. Schwesinger was the first executive secretary of the group. After the war, the NCWP changed its name to the International Council of Psychologists.

January 10, 1942 (1516)

The first version of E. F. Lindquist's Iowa Every-Pupil Tests of Basic Skills was published. The test is now known more simply as the Iowa Tests of Basic Skills.

June 14, 1942 (1517)

The first meeting of the National Research Council Emergency Committee was held in Vineland, New Jersey, to determine psychological participation in World War II. Robert Yerkes chaired the group. The coordination required of the participating groups helped to forge the modern, reorganized APA.

June 19, 1942 (1518)

The 50th annual meeting of the APA was canceled, in compliance with World War II travel restrictions.

July 1, 1942 (1519)

The Statistical Research Group was formed at Columbia University. The group applied scientific methods to wartime manufacturing and quality control, an early development in modern industrial psychology.

July 1, 1942 (1520)

The Yale Laboratories of Primate Biology were renamed the Yerkes Laboratories of Primate Biology, as Karl Lashley replaced Robert M. Yerkes as director and Harvard University began to share support of the facility with Yale University.

August 12, 1942 (1521)

John A. McGeoch's book *The Psychology of Human Learning* was published.

August 12, 1942 (1522)

Martin E. P. Seligman was born. Seligman is well-known for his studies of learned helplessness and the relation between helplessness and depressive mood disorder. His research on preparedness emphasizes genetic constraints on learning. APA Distinguished Scientific Award for Early Career Contribution to Psychology, 1976; American Psychological Society William James Fellow, 1991.

September 15, 1942 (1523)

Michael S. Pallak was born. Pallak's interests have been in the social psychology of attitudes and behavior. APA Executive Officer, 1979–1985.

October 3, 1942 (1524)

Lenore Walker was born. Walker's studies of domestic violence as a public health hazard brought attention to the battered woman syndrome and the development of a scientific literature about its characteristics. She has promoted local and national intervention to respond to the problem of domestic violence. APA Award for Distinguished Professional Contributions, 1987.

October 30, 1942 (1525)

Starke R. Hathaway and J. Charnley McKinley's Minnesota Multiphasic Personality Inventory was first published. The University of Minnesota held the original copyright to the test.

November 9, 1942 (1526)

Ignacio Martín-Baró was born. Martín-Baró was a social psychologist who promoted a culturally relevant science applied to the problems of Latin America. He founded the journal *Revista de Psicologia de El Salvador*. Martín-Baró was killed in 1989 by men in military uniforms during a raid on a Jesuit residence on a university campus in El Salvador.

November 24, 1942 (1527)

The James McKeen Cattell Fund was begun. The Cattell Fund, established with a gift of 600 shares of Psychological Corporation stock, is currently used to supplement the sabbatical stipends of five or six recipients each year. Paul Achilles was the first managing trustee of the fund.

November 30, 1942 (1528)

Time magazine featured a story on the prefrontal lobotomy operations by Walter Freeman and James Watts, of the George Washington University Hospital. *Time* said, "some 300 people in the U.S. have had their psychoses surgically removed."

December 28, 1942 (1529)

At 2:30 p.m., Clark Hull mailed the final corrected galley proofs of his *Principles of Behavior* to his publisher, Appleton-Century-Crofts.

January 6, 1943 (1530)

Patrick H. DeLeon was born. DeLeon, a clinical and forensic psychologist and executive assistant to U.S. Senator Daniel K. Inouye, has provided an informed influence on the congressional treatment of psychological services in public health policy. APA Award for Distinguished Service in the Public Interest, 1984; APA Distinguished Professional Contribution Award, 1986 and 1989.

March 22, 1943 (1531)

The Education Ministry of the German Third Reich clarified its psychologist certification law by listing four possible areas of certification: educational, vocational, industrial, and business psychology. Certification in psychotherapy was deliberately excluded. Psychiatrists had complained that an earlier law appeared to equate their credentials with those of psychologists.

April 11, 1943 (1532)

The APA Board of Editors authorized the second guide to APA editorial style. John Anderson and Willard Valentine wrote the guide, which was published as an article in *Psychological Bulletin* in 1944.

April 16, 1943 (1533)

Albert Hofmann, a research chemist, left work due to "a remarkable restlessness" and "dizziness." Later, he experienced a "stream of fantastic pictures, extraordinary shapes" and "intense . . . colors." Dermal absorption of LSD-25, a substance he was working with, was suspected. Although unintentional, this was the first LSD-induced psychedelic experience.

April 19, 1943 (1534)

Albert Hofmann took the first intentional LSD "trip" to confirm his suspicions resulting from accidental absorption of the chemical 3 days earlier. His experience was a hellish nightmare of threatening images.

May 29, 1943 (1535)

The Intersociety Constitutional Convention (ICC), composed of 26 delegates from nine psychological societies in the United States, met at the Hotel Pennsylvania in New York City. The ICC was formed to coordinate the participation of psychologists in World War II. The beginnings of the modern structure and administration of the APA were proposed at this meeting.

May 31, 1943 (1536)

The American Association for Applied Psychology merged with the APA. The event occurred in New York at a meeting of psychologists planning the role of psychology in World War II. Edwin G. Boring chaired the meeting. Ernest R. Hilgard was chairman of the committee that later wrote the bylaws for the new, reconstituted APA.

August 17, 1943 (1537)

Clark Hull's book *Principles of Behavior* was published. Hull explained his hypothetico–deductive theory of behavior and provided supportive evidence in that book.

September 14, 1943 (1538)

Clifford T. Morgan's book *Physiological Psychology* was published. This edition and its revisions became standard college texts.

November 8, 1943 (1539)

The standard form of Henry A. Murray's Thematic Apperception Test (TAT) was published. An earlier form of the TAT appeared in a 1935 article in the *Archives of Neurology and Psychiatry*, written by Christiana D. Morgan and Murray.

December 4, 1943 (1540)

Allied bombing in World War II destroyed Wilhelm Wundt's original Leipzig psychology laboratory.

December 16, 1943 (1541)

Gary R. VandenBos was born. His interests have been in professional psychology and psychotherapy. VandenBos has actively promoted the independent status of psychological providers and has presided over the growth of the APA's book publications in psychology. APA Acting Chief Executive Officer, 1988–1989.

December 31, 1943 (1542)

The drug Desoxyn (methamphetamine; Abbott Laboratories) was approved for use by the U.S. Food and Drug Administration. Methamphetamine is a central nervous system stimulant and is used in the treatment of attention deficit hyperactivity disorder in children.

February 13, 1944 (1543)

Stanley Sue was born. Sue's specialties have been research and training in community psychology. He has explored social issues that affect Asian Americans and the delivery of psychological services to that population. Sue was a founder of the Asian American Psychology Association (1972). APA Award for Distinguished Contribution to Psychology in the Public Interest, 1986.

June 22, 1944 (1544)

Sandra Lipsitz Bem was born. Bem is noted for her work in the independent nature of masculine and feminine gender roles and the measurement and behavioral correlates of androgyny. She has also investigated gender bias in public media and gender schema in self-perception and interpersonal perception. APA Distinguished Scientific Award for Early Career Contribution to Psychology, 1976.

July 1, 1944 (1545)

Congress created the modern U.S. Public Health Service from several prior agencies by enacting the Public Health Service Act, Public Law 78-410. The National Institutes of Health were created by the same act.

July 30, 1944 (1546)

James S. Jackson was born. Jackson has worked toward a psychology responsive to national mental health issues and to the special problems of minorities, urban youth, and elderly individuals. He was a founder of the Black Students Psychological Association (1969). In 1983, Jackson won the first APA Distinguished Award for an Early Career Contribution to Psychology in the Public Interest.

September 9, 1944 (1547)

Judith Rodin was born. Rodin is known for innovative studies of the factors influencing excessive behavior, with special attention given to obesity. On December 16, 1993, Rodin was elected president of the University of Pennsylvania, the first woman president of an Ivy League school. APA Distinguished Scientific Award for Early Career Contribution to Psychology, 1977.

September 11, 1944 (1548)

Edward L. Thorndike and Irving Lorge's *Teacher's Word Book of 30,000 Words* was published. The monumental word-counting project was funded by the Roosevelt administration's Works Progress Administration as a productive way of employing academics during the Depression.

September 12, 1944 (1549)

The reorganized APA was approved, establishing the current Council of Representatives and the first 19 divisions. Robert Yerkes, John Anderson, Leonard Carmichael, and Edwin G. Boring devised the plan. The dues were raised to $15 and included subscriptions to the membership register, the *American Psychologist*, *Psychological Bulletin*, and *Psychological Abstracts*.

September 28, 1944 (1550)

Leo Kanner's article "Early Childhood Autism" was published in the *Journal of Pediatrics*. It was the first article on the topic. Kanner coined the term *autism*.

October 7, 1944 (1551)

The Connecticut State Psychological Society, a forerunner of the present Connecticut Psychological Association, was founded.

December 22, 1944 (1552)

Gail E. Wyatt was born. Wyatt has studied the effects of abortion, childhood sexual abuse, sexual assault, and sexual practices among women, especially African-American women. She was the first ethnic minority group member to receive the NIMH Research Scientist Award (1992). APA Award for Distinguished Contribution to Research in Public Policy, 1992.

February 16, 1945 (1553)

The APA Journal Committee recommended publishing the *American Psychologist*. The new journal was to take over publication of association activities, previously reported in *Psychological Bulletin*.

March 30, 1945 (1554)

Stephen F. Morin was born. Morin has been a leader in focusing psychological science and practice on gay and lesbian issues and problems associated with AIDS. He was the first chair of the Association of Lesbian and Gay Psychologists and the first president of APA Division 44 (Lesbian and Gay Issues). APA Award for Distinguished Professional Contributions, 1988.

May 3, 1945 (1555)

The *Journal of Clinical Psychology* was first published. Frederick C. Thorne was the journal's editor.

May 6, 1945 (1556)

Abraham Maslow began his "good human being" notebook, recording the characteristics of exceptionally well-adjusted college students. His hierarchial theory of self-actualization developed from these observations.

May 7, 1945 (1557)

G. Frederick Kuder's Personal Reaction Survey, the first version of the Kuder Preference Record, was published. The Kuder Preference Record has remained a standard occupational interest survey.

May 28, 1945 (1558)

The Quebec Psychological Association became an affiliate of the Canadian Psychological Association.

June 2, 1945 (1559)

B. F. Skinner began writing his manuscript for *The Sun is But a Morning Star*. Before publication in 1948, the title of this work was changed to *Walden Two*.

July 19, 1945 (1560)

The first U.S. state law for certification or licensure of psychologists was signed by Governor Raymond Baldwin of Connecticut. Walter R. Miles of the Yale University School of Medicine chaired the first board of examiners and was the first certified psychologist. Fifty other psychologists were certified in Connecticut the first year.

July 19, 1945 (1561)

Science: The Endless Frontier was published. This work was a report from physicist Vannevar Bush to President Truman, urging the formation of a single agency for federal support of scientific research. The National Science Foundation, created in 1950, was the result.

August 30, 1945 (1562)

The first certificate to practice psychology was granted by a U.S. state board of examiners in psychology. The Connecticut board granted the certificate to its chair, Walter R. Miles, on the occasion of the first meeting of the board. The Connecticut certification law, the nation's first, had been enacted on July 19, 1945.

September 6, 1945   (1563)
The modern, reorganized APA was officially inaugurated. Within a few months, Dael Wolfle was installed as the first executive secretary.

September 7, 1945   (1564)
The APA Board of Directors voted to publish the *American Psychologist*. The first issue appeared in January 1946.

September 28, 1945   (1565)
The *Ladies Home Journal* published an article about the baby-tender built by B. F. Skinner to serve as an environmentally controlled crib for his daughter Debbie. The article, titled "Baby in a Box," created widespread misunderstanding, occasional angry reactions, and persistent false rumors of child abuse and maladjustment.

December 10, 1945   (1566)
Otto Fenichel's book *The Psychoanalytic Theory of Neurosis* was published.

December 19, 1945   (1567)
Max Wertheimer's book *Productive Thinking* was published. The book describes a Gestalt psychology approach to problem solving and creativity.

December 26, 1945   (1568)
Ludy T. Benjamin, Jr., was born. Benjamin's work has included influential research and writing on the history of psychology and the teaching of psychology. American Psychological Foundation Distinguished Teaching in Psychology Award, 1986.

December 27, 1945   (1569)
APA Division 20 (Adult Development and Aging), the first APA division created by petition from the APA membership, was admitted by the APA Council of Representatives. The division had two earlier titles—Old Age and Maturity and Adulthood and Old Age—before adopting its present name.

January 7, 1946   (1570)
The APA's flagship journal, the *American Psychologist*, was first published. Dael Wolfle, then executive director of the APA, was the first editor.

January 12, 1946   (1571)
Johann Pestalozzi, a pioneer in child study and educational psychology, appeared on a postage stamp issued by Switzerland, his native land, on the occasion of the 200th anniversary of his birth.

February 19, 1946 (1572)

The petition to form the APA's Division 20, Adult Development and Aging, was submitted by Sidney Pressey, the division's first chair. The Council of Representatives had already admitted the division late in 1945. This was the first division added after the 19 created by the modern reorganization of the APA. The division was first named the Division of Old Age and Maturity.

February 28, 1946 (1573)

The Connecticut State Psychological Society was incorporated. The organization's name was changed to the Connecticut Psychological Association on November 10, 1964.

March 4, 1946 (1574)

The drug Benadryl (diphenhydramine; Parke-Davis) was approved for use by the U.S. Food and Drug Administration. Diphenhydramine is primarily prescribed as an antihistamine but is used in mental health settings as an antianxiety treatment and to combat drug-induced Parkinsonism created by other antipsychotic and antianxiety medication.

March 26, 1946 (1575)

The Commonwealth of Virginia passed its licensure law for the practice of psychology. This was the nation's first *licensing* law and the second state to regulate professional psychology, preceded by Connecticut's *certification* law in 1945. Dorota Rymarkiewiczowa chaired the committee that promoted the legislation.

March 29, 1946 (1576)

The first meeting of the Pennsylvania Psychological Association was held.

April 19, 1946 (1577)

The *Manual of Child Psychology*, edited by Leonard Carmichael, was published. In 1970, Paul H. Mussen assumed the editorship of the book, which was then titled *Carmichael's Manual of Child Psychology* in recognition of Carmichael's comprehensive summary of the field.

April 21, 1946 (1578)

Baruch Fischhoff was born. Fischhoff's focuses have been both the basic and applied aspects of mathematical decision theory. He has applied decision theory to problems of environmental resource decisions, the evaluation of expert judgment, and perceived risk of sexual assault. APA Award for Distinguished Contributions to Psychology in the Public Interest, 1990.

May 16, 1946 (1579)

The British Columbia Psychological Association became an affiliate of the Canadian Psychological Association.

May 21, 1946 (1580)
The Washington–Baltimore Branch of the APA and the Clinical Psychologists Group of the District of Columbia held a joint meeting to discuss merging the two organizations. A joint resolution to form one organization, the District of Columbia Psychological Association, was subsequently approved by the two memberships.

May 22, 1946 (1581)
Benjamin Spock's *The Commonsense Book of Baby and Child Care* was published. Spock's book influenced child rearing in America for several decades. Its child-centered orientation contrasted sharply with the adult-centered training approaches of its immediate predecessors.

June 24, 1946 (1582)
The Connecticut Workshop in Intergroup Relations began. The workshop was conducted by Kurt Lewin's Research Center for Group Dynamics at MIT and was held at the State Teacher's College of Connecticut at New Britain. The "T-group" method of experiential learning about interpersonal relations and the National Training Laboratory had their beginnings here.

July 3, 1946 (1583)
The National Mental Health Act (Public Law 79-487) was signed by President Truman, authorizing the surgeon general to improve public mental health through programs of research and treatment. Psychiatrist Robert H. Felix was instrumental in promoting this legislation and in the subsequent founding of the National Institute of Mental Health.

August 4, 1946 (1584)
The American Board of Examiners in Professional Psychology was founded in Pittsburgh. The name of the body was later changed to the American Board of Professional Psychology.

September 3, 1946 (1585)
Reginald Ruggles Gates's book *Human Genetics* was published. In addition to coverage of physiological characteristics, Gates's influential text reviewed many studies of inheritance of psychological traits, such as intelligence and personality. In other writing, Gates promoted the practice of eugenics.

September 5, 1946 (1586)
A convocation at the University of Pennsylvania, held in conjunction with the annual meeting of the APA, commemorated the 50th anniversary of the founding of the first psychological clinic. The clinic had been founded in 1896 by Lightner Witmer.

September 6, 1946 (1587)
The first meeting of the APA's Maturity and Old Age Interest Group was held. The group had been admitted as Division 20 of the APA, the first division estab-

lished by petition in the modern APA. Sidney Pressey led the petition drive for the new division.

October 8, 1946 (1588)

The Department of Psychology was founded at the University of Saskatchewan. T. W. Cook was the only psychology professor when classes began in 1947.

October 29, 1946 (1589)

Samuel Renshaw was awarded a patent for what appears to be the first tachistoscopic projector. The device had an adjustable opening in a wheel that rotated in front of a projector lens at a known speed. The duration of the projected image was controlled by varying the number of degrees of arc in the opening.

November 1, 1946 (1590)

John T. Monahan was born. Monahan is a forensic psychologist with a special interest in violent behavior and the legal treatment of people with mental illness. He coordinated the drive for acceptance of the American Psychology-Law Society as APA Division 41 and was the first president of the new division. APA Award for Distinguished Contributions to Research in Public Policy, 1990.

November 23, 1946 (1591)

The first meeting of the Georgia Psychological Association was held at Emory University. Herman Martin was elected first president of the organization.

December 4, 1946 (1592)

The District of Columbia Psychological Association (DCPA) held its first annual meeting at George Washington University; 81 people attended. Thelma Hunt was temporary chair of the new organization. The DCPA serves both as a state psychological association and as a regional association because many of its members live in Maryland and Virginia.

December 6, 1946 (1593)

The Oklahoma Psychological Association was founded. John Rohrer was the acting president at the founding meeting.

January 26, 1947 (1594)

The first list of APA-evaluated graduate programs in clinical psychology was chosen. Forty graduate schools completed self-report surveys and a list of characteristics was assembled by a committee chaired by Robert R. Sears. The impetus for the effort was a request from the Veterans Administration for advice about postwar hiring and professional training standards.

January 27, 1947 (1595)

The *American Journal of Psychotherapy* was first published by the American Association for the Advancement of Psychotherapy.

February 15, 1947 (1596)

The Ontario Psychological Association was founded in Toronto. C. Roger Myers was elected its first president.

March 3, 1947 (1597)

Life magazine carried an uncritically optimistic article about the effects of prefrontal lobotomy surgery. The article was titled "Psychosurgery: Operation to Cure Sick Minds Turns Surgeon's Blade Into an Instrument of Mental Therapy." The article was accompanied by a cartoon showing a tyrannical frontal lobe subdued by the operation.

March 8, 1947 (1598)

Michael J. Saks was born. Saks has successfully brought the logic of psychological research methods, principles of statistical analysis, and studies of psychosocial assumptions to bear on a wide range of legal and public policy concerns. APA Award for Distinguished Contributions to Psychology in the Public Interest, 1987.

March 13, 1947 (1599)

Gerald P. Koocher was born. Koocher is recognized for his service activities in children's legal rights, services to families of severely ill children, and the education and protection of consumers of mental health services. APA Award for Distinguished Professional Contributions, 1992.

March 17, 1947 (1600)

Shari Seidman Diamond was born. Diamond's studies of factors affecting decision making by juries, criminal sentencing decisions, and deceptive advertising exemplify her successful application of psychological methods to legal questions. APA Award for Distinguished Contributions to Research in Public Policy, 1991.

March 25, 1947 (1601)

Ellen Langer was born. Langer's mindfulness theory, which describes the effect of information processing on social responses, has been applied to problems as varied as arthritis, burnout, and acceptance of deviance. She was the first woman tenured in the Harvard University Department of Psychology (1981). APA Distinguished Contributions to Psychology in the Public Interest Award, 1988.

April 8, 1947 (1602)

The Institute for Sex Research, popularly known as the Kinsey Institute, was incorporated in Indiana.

April 12, 1947 (1603)

The first recommendations for certification of Canadian psychologists was presented by the Certification Committee of the Canadian Psychological Association at the association's annual meeting in Ottawa.

April 23, 1947 (1604)

The American Board of Examiners in Professional Psychology (ABEPP) was incorporated. Dael Wolfle, ABEPP chairman, signed the articles of incorporation. The organization is now named the American Board of Professional Psychology.

June 12, 1947 (1605)

Leonard Saxe was born. Saxe's analyses of social issues research, performed for the Congressional Office of Technology Assessment, have affected federal legislation. His topics have included the effectiveness of psychotherapy, alcohol abuse treatments, polygraph testing, and children's mental health. APA Distinguished Contribution to Psychology in the Public Interest Award, 1989.

June 16, 1947 (1606)

The first National Training Laboratory for Group Dynamics began at the Gould Academy in Bethel, Maine. This 3-week summer session was the birthplace of the T-group, an experiential method of learning about interpersonal relations for enhanced group effectiveness. The early versions were called basic skills training (BST) groups, later shortened to training (T) groups.

June 30, 1947 (1607)

Walter Van Dyke Bingham retired from his post as chief psychologist of the U.S. War Department during World War II. During his term of service, Bingham developed and administered the Army General Classification Test, a landmark instrument in personnel psychology.

July 2, 1947 (1608)

The first half of Alfred Kinsey's manuscript of *Sexual Behavior in the Human Male* was mailed to its publisher, W. W. Norton.

August 1, 1947 (1609)

The APA Division 16 (School Psychology) newsletter was first published.

August 1, 1947 (1610)

Austin H. Riesen's article "Development of Visual Perception in Man and Chimpanzee" was published in *Science*.

August 5, 1947 (1611)

The first Scandinavian Meeting of Psychologists was held in Oslo. About 400 psychologists from Finland, Iceland, Denmark, Sweden, and Norway attended. Presiding officer Harald Schjelderup addressed the gathering on the importance of psychology in winning the war and consolidating the peace.

August 15, 1947 (1612)

José Szapocznik was born. Szapocznik has distinguished himself with research and practice in mental health issues of Hispanic populations. He has paid special

attention to family therapy techniques and problems of drug abuse. APA Award
for Distinguished Professional Contributions, 1991.

August 27, 1947 (1613)
The Georgia Psychological Association was incorporated.

August 29, 1947 (1614)
The first meeting of German psychologists after World War II was held in Bonn.
The *Berufsverban Deutscher Psychologen* (Professional Association of German Psychologists) was founded by a Dr. Jakobsen and Max Simoneit, one of the group
that plotted the July 20, 1944, attempt on Hitler's life.

September 8, 1947 (1615)
The manual for George K. Bennett, Harold G. Seashore, and Alexander G.
Wesman's Differential Aptitude Test was published.

September 10, 1947 (1616)
The first APA standards for training clinical psychologists were accepted by the
APA Council of Representatives. The standards, called the Shakow Report, were
written by the APA Committee on Training in Clinical Psychology, chaired by
David Shakow and formed in response to a request by the Public Health Service
and the Veterans Administration for professional criteria.

September 11, 1947 (1617)
The first meeting of the Conference of State Psychological Societies was held in
Detroit.

September 16, 1947 (1618)
The first forms of Wilfred S. Miller's Miller Analogies Test, Graduate Level were
published. This measure of academic achievement continues to be used to evaluate
applicants to graduate programs.

October 29, 1947 (1619)
The Educational Testing Service was founded to take over the college entrance
testing functions of several other organizations: the College Entrance Examination
Board, the American Council on Education, the Carnegie Foundation for the
Advancement of Teaching, and the Carnegie Corporation of New York.

December 1, 1947 (1620)
B. F. Skinner was elected professor of psychology at Harvard University. The
appointment became effective July 1, 1948.

December 5, 1947 (1621)
Alfred A. Strauss and Laura Lehntinen's book *Psychopathology and Education of the
Brain Injured Child* was published, a landmark in special education.

December 19, 1947 (1622)

The Educational Testing Service was chartered by the New York State Board of Regents. Henry Chauncey was the first president of the Educational Testing Service.

January 4, 1948 (1623)

Alfred Kinsey's book *Sexual Behavior in the Human Male* was published. Kinsey's extensive surveys of sexual behavior in men attracted great popular interest and was commonly known as "The Kinsey Report."

January 5, 1948 (1624)

The manual for the Miller Analogies Test was published.

January 13, 1948 (1625)

The Library of Congress received its copy of the first issue of the journal *Human Relations*. The journal was edited by a joint committee of the Tavistock Institute of Human Relations and the Research Center for Group Dynamics.

January 23, 1948 (1626)

Ernest R. Hilgard's book *Theories of Learning* was published. Hilgard's comprehensive text became required reading for generations of graduate students.

March 8, 1948 (1627)

The first list of APA-approved programs in clinical psychology, based on site visits and published criteria, was selected by a committee meeting in Chicago and headed by David Shakow. Thirty-six graduate schools were on this first list.

March 25, 1948 (1628)

Governor Earle Clements of Kentucky signed his state's licensure law for psychologists. Kentucky was the third state to adopt legislation regulating the practice of psychology.

March 29, 1948 (1629)

Lithium was first used in a trial treatment of manic behavior. Australian John F. J. Cade gave lithium citrate to "a little wizened man of 51 who had been in a chronic state of excitement for five years. He was amiably restless, dirty, destructive, and interfering." The treatment was surprisingly effective and the patient was discharged on July 9, 1948.

May 6, 1948 (1630)

The journal *Personnel Psychology* was first published. G. Frederick Kuder was the editor of the journal.

May 8, 1948 (1631)

The North Carolina Psychological Association was created at the business meeting of the Psychology Section of the North Carolina Academy of Sciences. William McGee was elected the association's first president.

May 28, 1948 (1632)

The Canadian Board of Examiners in Professional Psychology was founded.

May 28, 1948 (1633)

A preliminary version of the Kuder Preference Record Examiner's Manual was published.

June 8, 1948 (1634)

B. F. Skinner's *Walden Two* was published. The publisher, Macmillan, agreed to publish the book only on the condition that Skinner also write an introductory text for them.

June 18, 1948 (1635)

The first meeting of the California State Psychological Association, now named the California Psychological Association, was held in San Francisco. The meeting was organized by Neil Warren in response to an article in the *Los Angeles Examiner* on quackery in psychotherapy.

June 25, 1948 (1636)

Robert W. White's *The Abnormal Personality*, a classic text in the area, was first published.

July 1, 1948 (1637)

The Iowa Psychological Association was founded.

July 12, 1948 (1638)

Alfred C. Kinsey set an attendance record for the Harmon Gymnasium at the University of California, Berkeley, with a lecture on his research on human sexual behavior.

August 3, 1948 (1639)

Claude E. Shannon's article "A Mathematical Theory of Information," the first complete information theory, appeared in the *Bell System Technical Journal.* This pivotal contribution to cognitive psychology was introduced to psychologists by George Miller and Frederick Frick in their *Psychological Review* article, "Statistical Behavioristics and Sequences of Responses" (1949).

October 9, 1948 (1640)

The Maritime Psychological Association was founded at Acadia University, Nova Scotia. The first president was William Henry Dalton Vernon.

October 23, 1948 (1641)

The first regular meeting of the North Carolina Psychological Association was held. Annual dues were $1.50.

December 11, 1948 (1642)

The first meeting of the Intercollegiate Psychological Association was held at Teachers College, Columbia University. Seventeen member colleges were represented.

January 12, 1949 (1643)

The organizational meeting of the Hawaii Psychological Association was held at the University of Hawaii. Theodore Forbes was elected president.

January 17, 1949 (1644)

Quinn McNemar's *Psychological Statistics* was published. The book served as a standard text for many years.

March 9, 1949 (1645)

APA Division 6 (Physiological–Comparative) and Division 3 (Theoretical–Experimental) voted 243 to 25 to combine to form the Division of Experimental Psychology (Division 3). The union lasted until 1962, when Division 6 was reestablished, retaining its original emphasis.

March 20, 1949 (1646)

In a letter to President Harry S Truman, the APA Board of Directors protested the vigorous application of Truman's Executive Order 9855, requiring loyalty oaths of federal employees and empowering local "loyalty boards" to investigate individuals suspected of disloyalty to the United States. The APA did not, however, protest the executive order's abridgement of civil rights.

March 23, 1949 (1647)

The first volume of *American Soldier* was published. These comprehensive studies of behavior during wartime were landmarks in military, organizational, and social psychology. The first volume focused on adjustment to army life. A second volume (April 22, 1949) dealt with combat and its aftermath. Samuel A. Stouffer supervised this research effort.

April 1, 1949 (1648)

The National Institute of Mental Health (NIMH) was founded, as provided by Public Law 79-487. The NIMH replaced the U.S. Public Health Service (USPHS) Division of Mental Hygiene, which was itself a 1930 reconstruction of the USPHS Narcotics Division.

April 26, 1949   (1649)
The Ohio Psychological Association was incorporated. George A. Kelly, Ruth
Ortleb, and Ronald R. Greene signed the articles of incorporation.

May 15, 1949   (1650)
John A. Glover was born. Glover's research centered on two areas: the development
of problem-solving and creative abilities, and factors affecting information processing and recall of text materials.

July 19, 1949   (1651)
The Wechsler Intelligence Scale for Children was first published.

August 19, 1949   (1652)
An anonymous prize of $100 for the best psychology article of 1948 was awarded
to Louis L. Thurstone's "Psychological Implications of Factor Analysis," published
in the *American Psychologist*.

August 20, 1949   (1653)
The Colorado Conference on Graduate Education in Clinical Psychology began.
The conference produced the well-known Boulder scientist–practitioner model of
clinical education. The scientist–practitioner model has continued to be the stan-
dard referent for models of clinical preparation in the years following the Boulder
Conference.

September 7, 1949   (1654)
Frank Beach delivered his APA Division 3 presidential address, "The Snark was
a Boojum." This frequently reprinted talk documented and decried reliance on the
Norway rat as an experimental subject.

September 21, 1949   (1655)
Lee J. Cronbach's book *Essentials of Psychological Testing* was published.

September 24, 1949   (1656)
The organizing committee of the Arizona Psychological Association first met.

October 27, 1949   (1657)
Walter R. Hess won the Nobel prize for his research on the functions of the
midbrain.

November 15, 1949   (1658)
Donald O. Hebb's book *The Organization of Behavior: A Neuropsychological Theory*
was published.

December 1, 1949 (1659)

The Sixteen Personality Factor Questionnaire (16PF) was published by Raymond B. Cattell and his Institute for Personality and Ability Testing at the University of Illinois. The personality trait test was based on Cattell's factor analysis of self-report statements.

December 15, 1949 (1660)

S. S. Stevens was appointed chair of the National Research Council Division of Anthropology and Psychology.

V

1950–1969
PSYCHOLOGY COMES OF AGE

The postwar expansion of the science, application, and practice of psychology continued through the decades of the 1950s and 1960s and was joined by a new interest in public policy issues. The science of behavior was focused on social issues such as racial and gender discrimination, advocacy for the rights of people confined in institutional settings, and equal educational opportunity. The publication of *The Authoritarian Personality* in 1950 (Entry 1661) was followed by Gordon Allport's *The Nature of Prejudice* (Entry 1755) and the U.S. Supreme Court *Brown v. Board of Education* decision (Entry 1765) in 1954. Experimental evidence about the effects of racism (Entry 1693) affected the outcome of *Brown v. Board of Education*, and studies of the effects of early environment on later learning inspired the first Head Start schools (Entries 2053 and 2079), still a successful implementation of applied research.

Some public policy activities centered on one or another demographic group, for example, the Association of Black Psychologists (Entry 2201) was founded in 1968 and African American students brought their demands to the attention of the American Psychological Association (APA) membership by presenting them from the podium reserved for the presidential address in 1969 (Entry 2241). The site of the 1969 convention was itself the product of a public policy decision (Entry 2240). It had been moved from Chicago to Washington, DC, on short notice to protest the treatment of anti-Vietnam War demonstrators in Chicago at the Democratic National Convention in 1968.

Because the courts and legislatures are vehicles of social change, psychologists have found themselves presenting their research in those venues as well as in traditional scholarly media. The 1950s and 1960s saw the first submission of a "friend of the court," or *amicus curiae* brief by the APA and increased activity at the federal level as enactment of social and scientific program legislation called on psychological expertise for implementation. The National Science Foundation was established in 1950 (Entry 1666) and bolstered in 1958 (Entry 1871) after the Soviet Union launched *Sputnik*, the first artificial satellite. The Educational Research Act (Entry 1769), the Community Mental Health Centers Act (Entry 2040), and the founding of the National Institute of Child Health and Human Development (Entries 1999 and 2007) are examples of legislation that called for the participation of psychologists.

Traditional psychological science, practice, and applications all expanded during these two decades. Psychologist licensing legislation proceeded until all 50 states had enacted licensure or certification procedures by 1977. Traditional graduate schools of clinical psychology were hard-pressed to meet the demand for practitioners, and independent schools of professional psychology were created to meet the need. The first completely independent graduate school of professional practice, the California School of Professional Psychology, was founded in 1968 (Entries 2183, 2226, 2275, and 2335).

Of particular interest to experimental and practicing psychologists and to the general public was the appearance of psychotherapeutic drugs. Many well-known agents, including Seconal (Entry 1669), Thorazine (Entries 1683 and 1760), Dilantin (Entry 1723), Ritalin (Entry 1803), Valium (Entry 2042), lithium carbonate (Entries 1629 and 2259), and Haldol (Entry 2152) were approved for use in these years. The histories of these drugs reveal that virtually none of them were synthesized with the intention of producing a drug useful in psychotherapy, a testimony to the value of basic research and creative observation. The world of more traditional psychotherapy was being stretched by the tensions between Carl Rogers's client-centered therapy (Entry 1684) and behavior modification therapy based on the principles of operant conditioning (e.g., Entries 1686, 1864, 1876, and

2238). B. F. Skinner and Rogers debated their positions (Entries 1826 and 1987) on occasion, with little evidence of rapprochement.

As the giants of humanistic and behavioral psychology debated, the founding events of contemporary cognitive psychology occurred reasonably close to each other in time. In April 1956, George A. Miller's article "The Magical Number Seven, Plus or Minus Two: Some Limits on Our Capacity for Processing Information" was published in *Psychological Review* (Entry 1808). In August 1956, Bruner, Goodnow, and Austin's book *A Study of Thinking* (Entry 1820) was published, and 3 days later Herbert Simon and Allen Newell completed the first computer run successfully simulating human problem solving (Entry 1821). In September 1956, a meeting at the Massachusetts Institute of Technology (Entry 1829) brought together Simon, Newell, Miller, Noam Chomsky, John Swets, David Green, and others who promoted an information-processing model of thought and memory. The meeting is sometimes cited as the starting point of the "cognitive revolution" in psychology, but it is clear that work in this direction had been underway for some time.

Many seminal works in applied and scientific psychology were published during these 20 years. Clark Hull's *A Behavior System* (Entry 1717) presented a comprehensive model of behavior, and S. S. Stevens's *Handbook of Experimental Psychology* (Entry 1691), B. F. Skinner's *Science and Human Behavior* (Entry 1686), Lee Cronbach's *Educational Psychology* (Entry 1754), Anne Anastasi's *Psychological Testing* (Entry 1763), and N. L. Gage's *Handbook of Research on Teaching* (Entry 2010) all served as major statements of their fields. Progress in industrial and organizational applications of psychology was announced by the appearance of Ernest J. McCormick's *Human Engineering* (Entry 1865), Rensis Likert's *New Patterns of Management* (Entry 1961), and Victor H. Vroom's *Work and Motivation* (Entry 2049), all of which have become classics. Although all of these works were exceptionally influential, one not yet mentioned was cited far more often than any other. In an 8-year period from 1969 to 1977, B. J. Winer's *Statistical Principles in Experimental Design* (Entry 1986) received four times as many citations than any other book in the behavioral sciences.

The growth of the APA kept pace with the growth of the discipline. The APA purchased its first headquarters building in 1952 (Entries 1674, 1708–1709, and 1711) but had outgrown these quarters only 9 years later and constructed a new building at 1200 17th Street, NW, in Washington, DC (Entries 1972, 2005, and 2100) beginning in 1961. The association's role in monitoring professional standards in testing (Entry 1676) and ethics (Entry 1730) continued, and its role in establishing standards and approved programs in clinical psychology expanded to graduate programs in counseling psychology (Entries 1699 and 1734) and clinical internships (Entries 1675 and 1835). A series of hour-long television programs titled "Focus on Behavior" was prepared by the APA and broadcast on National Educational Television, forerunner of the Public Broadcasting System (Entry 2034). As psychology moved energetically into the postwar world, a milestone of another sort was passed as Lightner Witmer, founder of the first psychological clinic and last surviving founding member of the APA, died in 1956 (Entry 1819).

March 15, 1950 (1661)

Theodor W. Adorno, Else Frenkel-Brunswik, Daniel J. Levinson, and R. Nevitt Sanford's *The Authoritarian Personality* was published. The book introduced the California F Scale, an instrument that made authoritarianism a dominant theme of social psychology in the 1950s.

April 20, 1950 (1662)

Anna Freud spoke at Clark University's 60th anniversary celebration on "The Contribution of Psychoanalysis to Genetic Psychology." Her father had delivered a noteworthy lecture series in 1909 at Clark's 20th anniversary celebration, the occasion of his only trip to America. Each Freud received an honorary Doctor of Laws degree from Clark.

April 22, 1950 (1663)

The first official meeting of the Arizona Psychological Association was held. H. Clay Skinner was the first president.

May 5, 1950 (1664)

The West Virginia Psychological Association was founded at Bethany College in Bethany, West Virginia. The first president was Quin F. Curtis, who also chaired the psychology department at West Virginia University from 1948 to 1968.

May 9, 1950 (1665)

Lafayette R. (L. Ron) Hubbard published *Dianetics*, a popular psychology book that eventually spawned the Church of Scientology, a cult and business centered around the promotion of Hubbard's theory and techniques.

May 10, 1950 (1666)

The National Science Foundation was created by Public Law 81-507, the National Science Foundation Act of 1950. President Truman signed the bill into law shortly before 6:00 a.m. in a train car in Pocatello, Idaho.

May 17, 1950 (1667)

The Porteus Maze Test was published in the United States. It was originally designed by Stanley Porteus to be a nonverbal intelligence test for mentally retarded children in Melbourne, Australia.

July 10, 1950 (1668)

Hermann von Helmholtz, the great physiologist of the 19th century, appeared on a postage stamp of the German Democratic Republic (the former East Germany).

July 19, 1950 (1669)

The drug Seconal (secobarbital sodium; Eli Lilly) was approved for use by the U.S. Food and Drug Administration. Secobarbital is a barbiturate and depresses activity in the central nervous system. It is used as an antianxiety agent and as a sedative.

July 20, 1950 (1670)

The first *Annual Review of Psychology* was published. Calvin P. Stone was the editor of the volume and the first article was "Growth, Development, and Decline," by Harold E. Jones and Nancy Bayley.

August 13, 1950 (1671)

The first White House Conference on Aging began. This first conference was called the National Conference on Aging, and the present name was adopted in 1961 for the second conference. Federal Security Administrator Oscar R. Ewing presided over 800 delegates to the 3-day meeting.

August 15, 1950 (1672)

The National Institute on Neurological Disease and Blindness was authorized by Public Law 81-692. This agency is now called the National Institute on Neurological Disorders and Stroke.

August 20, 1950 (1673)

James J. Gibson's book *The Perception of the Visual World* was published.

September 6, 1950 (1674)

The APA appointed a committee to find a building suitable for its first headquarters. At the time, the APA was housed in the American Association for the Advancement of Science building at 1515 Massachusetts Avenue, Washington, DC, now the Tunisian Embassy. The committee was chaired by Jerry Carter and included Dael Wolfle and Fillmore H. Sanford.

September 6, 1950 (1675)

The APA Council of Representatives approved publication of the first standards for APA-approved predoctoral internships in clinical psychology. The standards were published in the November 1950 issue of the *American Psychologist*.

September 6, 1950 (1676)

The APA appointed the Committee on Test Standards, the first committee on this subject since the 1909–1919 Committee on Measurements. Lee J. Cronbach chaired the committee, which was charged with preparing a "statement on technical standards for evaluating tests and the contents of test manuals."

September 7, 1950 (1677)

The APA notified Governor Earl Warren of California and University of California president Robert Sproul that it was recommending that APA members not accept positions at the University of California until "tenure conditions improve." The university had discharged professors who had refused to sign a loyalty oath as part of their contract. The oath was later declared illegal.

September 13, 1950 (1678)

The National Mental Health Association was created by a merger of the National Committee for Mental Hygiene, the National Mental Health Foundation, and the Psychiatric Foundation.

October 13, 1950 (1679)

Linda A. Teplin was born. Teplin's studies of how police interact with individuals perceived as having mental disorders, her work on the prevalence of mental disorders in jail populations, and her development of an assessment scale to aid in referral of inmates for psychological evaluation were recognized by the APA Award for Distinguished Contribution to Research in Public Policy in 1992.

October 19, 1950 (1680)

Erik H. Erikson's *Childhood and Society* was published.

October 28, 1950 (1681)

The first forms of the Graduate Record Examination were published.

November 22, 1950 (1682)

The National Institute on Neurological Disease and Blindness began operation. This agency is now called the National Institute on Neurological Disorders and Stroke.

December 11, 1950 (1683)

Chlorpromazine (Thorazine) was first synthesized at the Laboratoires Rhone-Poulenc/Specia. A commonly used antipsychotic drug, chlorpromazine was first developed as an antihistamine. Henri Laborit found it useful in reducing surgical shock. One reason it was tried on patients with schizophrenia was because, like cold-water bath treatments, it lowered body temperature.

January 2, 1951 (1684)

Carl Rogers's book *Client-Centered Therapy* was published. The book described the philosophy and practice of nondirective psychotherapy.

January 29, 1951 (1685)

S. S. Stevens dated the foreword to his classic book *Handbook of Experimental Psychology*.

February 6, 1951 (1686)

B. F. Skinner's *Science and Human Behavior* was first published in a mimeographed version by Skinner himself. The Macmillan Company's publication of the book appeared on January 20, 1953.

February 15, 1951 (1687)

The Kuder Preference Record, a standard measure of occupational interests, was published.

February 21, 1951 (1688)

The state of Georgia passed its law providing for the licensing of psychologists. Governor Herman Talmadge appointed Austin S. Edwards, Herman Martin, and Larry Ross to the first board of psychological examiners on March 27, 1952.

March 29, 1951 (1689)

The drug Phenergan (promethazine; Wyeth) was approved for use by the U.S. Food and Drug Administration. Promethazine is a phenothiazine derivative and is used in clinical settings as an antianxiety agent and as a sedative. It also is prescribed as an antihistamine and motion sickness medication.

April 23, 1951 (1690)

Governor Luther W. Youngdahl of Minnesota signed his state's psychologist certification legislation. Minnesota was the fifth state to adopt regulatory legislation for the practice of psychology. Because there was little charlatanism in the state at the time, the Minnesota Psychological Association promoted the law as a preventive and public education measure.

May 2, 1951 (1691)

S. S. Stevens's classic *Handbook of Experimental Psychology* was published.

May 14, 1951 (1692)

Solomon Asch's book chapter "Effects of Group Pressure Upon the Modification and Distortion of Judgments" appeared in Harold Guetzkow's *Groups, Leadership, and Men*. Asch here presented his studies of the effects of conformity on line length judgments. The studies had been sponsored by the Human Relations and Morale Branch of the Office of Naval Research.

May 23, 1951 (1693)

Psychologist Kenneth Clark left New York's Penn Station with lawyers Thurgood Marshall and Robert Carter to testify to the damaging effects of segregation on self-esteem in African American children in the case of *Briggs v. Elliott*. The case, heard in Charleston, South Carolina, was the NAACP's first attack on school segregation, culminating in *Brown v. Board of Education*.

June 27, 1951 (1694)

The first National Conference on the Undergraduate Curriculum in Psychology began. Dael Wolfle chaired the conference, held at Cornell University.

June 27, 1951 (1695)

The first conference on improving instruction in undergraduate psychology in the United States began at Cornell University. Dael Wolfle served as chair. Other participants were Claude E. Buxton, Charles N. Cofer, John W. Gustad, Robert B. MacLeod, and Wilbert J. McKeachie. The group recommended course objectives and a sample curriculum for psychology departments.

July 15, 1951 (1696)

The International Union of Psychological Science was founded at the International Congress of Psychology in Stockholm. The organization's original name was the International Union of Scientific Psychology.

July 19, 1951 (1697)

The first Assembly of the International Union of Psychological Science was held in Stockholm. At the time the organization was named the International Union of Scientific Psychology.

July 27, 1951 (1698)

The Human Resources Research Office (HumRRO) was founded by an agreement between the U.S. Army and George Washington University. HumRRO investigates psychological warfare, leadership, morale, and training. Army Chief Psychologist Harry Harlow conceived the idea of HumRRO and Meredith Crawford was its first director. HumRRO's name is now the Human Resources Research Organization.

August 30, 1951 (1699)

Responding to a request from the Veterans Administration, a conference of members of APA Division 17 (Counseling Psychology) produced the first APA Standards for Training Counseling Psychologists. Edward Boudin, Frances Robinson, C. Gilbert Wrenn, and Donald Super led the effort. After site visits, 17 doctoral programs were granted APA approval.

November 14, 1951 (1700)
Fritz Redl and David Wineman's book *Children Who Hate* was published.

November 23, 1951 (1701)
This was the date of the 1951 Dartmouth versus Princeton football game. Conflicting perceptions among spectators at the game were the basis of Albert Hastorf and Hadley Cantril's article titled "They Saw a Game: A Case Study," published in the *Journal of Abnormal and Social Psychology*.

December 20, 1951 (1702)
The Interamerican Society of Psychology (ISP) was founded during the Fourth International Congress on Mental Health in Mexico City. Eduardo Krapf of Argentina was the first president of the organization. Werner Wolff of Bard College was instrumental in forming the ISP. The official founding followed a constitutional assembly held on December 17, 1951.

January 15, 1952 (1703)
Lee J. Cronbach's text *Educational Psychology* was published for classroom trials.

January 19, 1952 (1704)
The first human test of the antipsychotic drug chlorpromazine, now marketed as Thorazine, was conducted on a manic patient at the Val de Grace military hospital in Paris by Joseph Hamon, with Jean Paraire and Jean Velluz. Chlorpromazine was first developed as an antihistamine, was later used to prevent surgical shock, and was finally widely adopted as an antipsychotic drug.

March 21, 1952 (1705)
The first forms of the Edwards Personal Preference Survey (EPPS) were published. The EPPS is designed to measure a set of personality variables drawn from Henry Murray's theory of needs. The needs for achievement, affiliation, dominance, and aggression, for example, have been the focus of much research.

April 14, 1952 (1706)
Romania issued a postage stamp honoring Ivan Pavlov.

May 2, 1952 (1707)
Fritz Redl and David Wineman's *Controls From Within* was published.

May 15, 1952 (1708)
The APA was granted a permit by the Washington, DC, zoning board to purchase its first office building, at 1333 16th Street, NW.

May 16, 1952 (1709)
The APA bought its first headquarters building, nicknamed "the fortress," at 1333 16th Street, NW, Washington, DC. The purchase price was $90,000, and $140,000

of renovations were anticipated. The building was described as having five stories, 30 rooms, 10 baths, and a wine cellar.

June 4, 1952 (1710)

Gary B. Melton was born. Melton's research has focused on the concerns of children and adolescents, addressing such topics as children's understanding of their own rights, child abuse, the impact of school prayer, children in rural settings, and legal applications of developmental research. APA Distinguished Contribution to Psychology in the Public Interest Award, 1985.

June 18, 1952 (1711)

The APA was granted a District of Columbia building permit to begin remodeling its newly purchased but decrepit headquarters building at 1333 16th Street, NW. The staff occupied the building on December 30, 1952.

July 8, 1952 (1712)

Neuroanatomist Santiago Ramón y Cajal appeared on a Spanish postal stamp.

July 28, 1952 (1713)

George Mandler and Seymour Sarason's article "A Study of Anxiety and Learning" was published in the *Journal of Abnormal and Social Psychology*. The article introduced the phenomenon of test anxiety.

August 1, 1952 (1714)

The final draft of the APA's *Ethical Standards of Psychologists* was submitted to the APA Council of Representatives, who formally adopted it as policy the next day.

August 19, 1952 (1715)

Susan T. Fiske was born. Fiske's program of social psychological research has probed the nature of causal attributions, social schema, perceived nuclear threat, gender stereotyping, and responses to adversity. Her findings have been cited in recent gender discrimination lawsuits. APA Award for Distinguished Contribution to Psychology in the Public Interest, 1991.

November 12, 1952 (1716)

Hans J. Eysenck's article "The Effects of Psychotherapy: An Evaluation" was published in the *Journal of Consulting Psychology*. Eysenck's review of controlled studies of traditional psychotherapy showed nonsignificant differences between treated and untreated individuals.

November 19, 1952 (1717)

Clark Hull's book *A Behavior System* was published, explaining Hull's hypothetico–deductive theory of behavior.

November 20, 1952 (1718)

The District of Columbia Psychological Association was incorporated. Thelma Hunt was chair of the committee on incorporation.

December 5, 1952 (1719)

The Iowa Board of Education approved the construction of an electronic machine to score the Iowa Tests of Basic Skills (ITBS). The machine, invented by psychologists Everet F. Lindquist and Phillip J. Rulon, was the first scanning machine to sense pencil marks on a standard response form. The first formal use of the machine was on March 16, 1955, to score the 1955 ITBS.

December 24, 1952 (1720)

The Soviet Union issued a Vladimir Bekhterev postage stamp to honor his work in the neurology of classical conditioning.

December 24, 1952 (1721)

Jean Piaget's book *Origins of Intelligence in Children* was published in the United States (Cook translation).

January 5, 1953 (1722)

The *Journal of the American Psychoanalytic Association* was first published.

January 6, 1953 (1723)

The antiepileptic drug Dilantin (phenytoin; Parke-Davis) was approved for use by the U.S. Food and Drug Administration. Phenytoin appears to control seizures by promoting sodium efflux from neurons, increasing the threshold of stimulation for neural firing.

January 12, 1953 (1724)

The *International Journal of Clinical and Experimental Hypnosis* was first published by the Society for Clinical and Experimental Hypnosis. Martin T. Orne was the journal's editor.

January 15, 1953 (1725)

The first Nebraska Symposium on Motivation was held. This first meeting was officially named Current Theory and Research in Motivation: A Symposium. Judson Brown, Harry Harlow, and Leo Postman were featured speakers. The Nebraska Symposium on Motivation was adopted as the name for the second and subsequent annual meetings.

February 1, 1953 (1726)

The Human Resources Research Office (HumRRO) published its first technical report, "A Psychological Study of Troop Reactions to an Atomic Explosion."

February 21, 1953 (1727)
Biochemist James Watson built the first accurate model of the DNA molecule, the carrier of information determining inherited characteristics. Watson and Francis Crick's model was published in the April 25, 1953, issue of *Nature*. They won the Nobel prize for this work in 1962.

March 9, 1953 (1728)
Suzanne Langer's book *Feeling and Form*, a landmark in aesthetic psychology, was published.

March 19, 1953 (1729)
The Walter Van Dyke Bingham Lecture Series was endowed with funds from the estate of that prominent industrial psychologist. The series supported addresses by talented young psychologists. The first address was delivered in 1954 by Lewis M. Terman.

April 10, 1953 (1730)
The APA's *Ethical Standards of Psychologists* was first published. Nicholas Hobbs chaired the committee that produced these first published standards of ethical professional behavior.

April 10, 1953 (1731)
Tennessee Governor Frank Clement signed the state's original legislation providing for the licensing of psychologists. The board of examiners was appointed on July 21, 1953. Ted Landsman chaired the committee that developed the legislation and guided its progress through the legislature.

April 13, 1953 (1732)
The National Mental Health Bell was cast, using metal from chains and shackles formerly used to restrain mental patients. The bell, cast by the McShane Foundry of Baltimore, became the symbol of the National Mental Health Association.

April 30, 1953 (1733)
Janet Taylor's article "A Personality Scale of Manifest Anxiety" was published in the *Journal of Abnormal and Social Psychology*.

April 30, 1953 (1734)
The APA Education and Training Board approved the first evaluations of doctoral programs in counseling psychology. Seventeen programs were selected for this first list of APA-approved programs.

June 3, 1953 (1735)
The Measurement Research Center, of Iowa City, was incorporated. This company offered the first electronic scoring of test response forms, using equipment invented by psychologists Everet F. Lindquist and Phillip Rulon.

June 8, 1953 (1736)

The American Psychological Foundation (APF) was incorporated. The APF was created to receive donations and to financially support worthy projects in psychology. J. McVicker Hunt was elected president of the first board of directors.

July 13, 1953 (1737)

1.74 inches (4.42 cm) of rain fell on Ellsworth, Maine. Wilhelm Reich claimed credit for producing the rain, attributing it to his orgone-powered "Cloudbuster" rainmaker.

July 24, 1953 (1738)

A letter from the Southwestern Psychological Association Organizing Committee, composed of Wayne H. Holzman, Harry Helson, and Saul Sells, invited members of the APA living in the southwestern United States to form a new regional association. The first meeting of the Southwestern Psychological Association was held on December 3–5, 1953, in San Antonio.

July 26, 1953 (1739)

An APA committee recommended compiling the first *Directory of Psychological Service Centers*.

August 24, 1953 (1740)

Sexual behavior researcher Alfred Kinsey appeared on the cover of *Time* magazine.

September 4, 1953 (1741)

Eugene Aserinsky and Nathanial Kleitman first reported rapid eye movement (REM) sleep in an article titled "Regularly Occurring Periods of Eye Motility and Concomitant Phenomena During Sleep," published in *Science*. The article inspired the expansion of modern sleep research.

September 14, 1953 (1742)

Alfred C. Kinsey's book *Sexual Behavior in the Human Female* was published, creating popular discussion equal to the 1948 publication of Kinsey's book on male sexual behavior.

September 23, 1953 (1743)

The proceedings of the first Nebraska Symposium on Motivation were published. The name of the first meeting was Current Theory and Research on Motivation: A Symposium. The name was changed to the current one in 1954.

September 25, 1953 (1744)

Edgar Doll's *The Measurement of Social Competence: A Manual for the Vineland Social Maturity Test* was published.

October 8, 1953 (1745)

Volume 1 of Ernest Jones's *The Life and Work of Sigmund Freud* was published. Jones's series comprises the standard biography of Freud.

October 13, 1953 (1746)

In a presentation to the annual meeting of the American Personnel and Guidance Association, Eric Berne formulated "The Transactional System of Group Therapy," later to become a dominant popular psychology of the 1960s. Transactional analysis was popularized by Tom and Amy Harris's book *I'm OK—You're OK*.

October 29, 1953 (1747)

The antipsychotic drug Serpasil (reserpine; CIBA Pharmaceutical) was approved for use by the U.S. Food and Drug Administration. Reserpine was the first major tranquilizer used in the treatment of mental patients. A *rauwolfia* derivative, reserpine acts to deplete the neurotransmitters norepinephrine, dopamine, and serotonin in the brain.

November 13, 1953 (1748)

The journal *Science* published the first description of S. S. Stevens's power law of psychophysics. The brief announcement described a paper titled "On the Brightness of Lights and the Loudness of Sounds," delivered by Stevens to the National Academy of Sciences at its annual meeting at the Massachusetts Institute of Technology.

November 18, 1953 (1749)

Carl Hovland, Irving Janis, and Harold Kelley's book *Communication and Persuasion* was published.

November 27, 1953 (1750)

David C. McClelland, John W. Atkinson, Russell A. Clark, and Edgar L. Lowell's book *The Achievement Motive* was published.

December 3, 1953 (1751)

The first meeting of the Southwestern Psychological Association (SWPA) began at the Gunter Hotel in San Antonio, in conjunction with the Texas Psychological Association meeting. Wayne H. Holtzman was chair of the SWPA organizing committee. The first independent meeting of the SWPA began on December 16, 1954 in Oklahoma City. Gardner Murphy was president at that time.

December 10, 1953 (1752)

The first Interamerican Congress of Psychology began in Ciudad Trujillo (now Santo Domingo), Dominican Republic. The congress was opened by Pedro Troncoso Sanchez, the Secretary of Education for the Dominican Republic. Psychologist Andrés Avelino of the Dominican Republic was elected president.

December 12, 1953 (1753)

Lee J. Cronbach and Goldine C. Gleser's article "Assessing Similarity Between Profiles" was published in *Psychological Bulletin.*

January 4, 1954 (1754)

Lee J. Cronbach's book *Educational Psychology* was published.

January 29, 1954 (1755)

Gordon Allport's book *The Nature of Prejudice* was published.

February 8, 1954 (1756)

The Tennessee Psychological Association was chartered.

February 15, 1954 (1757)

The *Journal of Counseling Psychology* was first published. C. Gilbert Wrenn was editor of the journal.

March 1, 1954 (1758)

Robert Woodworth and Harold Schlosberg finished writing the foreword to their classic text, *Experimental Psychology.*

March 25, 1954 (1759)

Lewis M. Terman delivered the first Walter Van Dyke Bingham Lecture, "The Discovery and Encouragement of Exceptional Talent." The series was funded by an endowment from Bingham's estate.

March 26, 1954 (1760)

The antipsychotic drug Thorazine (chlorpromazine hydrochloride; Smith, Kline, and French) was approved by the U.S. Food and Drug Administration. It was the first of the phenothiazines put into general use and works primarily by blocking the neural transmitter dopamine. Thorazine became widely, even abusively, used in institutional settings.

April 7, 1954 (1761)

The first meeting of the Christian Association for Psychological Studies was held in Grand Rapids, Michigan. The group's original name was the American Calvinistic Conference on Christianity, Psychology, and Psychiatry. The banquet fee for the first meeting was $1.75.

April 21, 1954 (1762)

The West Virginia Psychological Association was incorporated. Robert P. Fischer and Herman G. Canady were signers of the original incorporation document.

April 23, 1954 (1763)

Anne Anastasi's book *Psychological Testing* was published. This text became required reading in university courses through several editions.

May 4, 1954 (1764)

The Alabama Psychological Association was incorporated. Thomas F. Staton, Alonzo J. Davis, and D. A. R. Perryman were the incorporators.

May 17, 1954 (1765)

The U.S. Supreme Court unanimously ruled that racially segregated education was inherently illegal in *Brown v. Board of Education*. The ruling resulted in many studies of the psychology of social issues dealing with interracial relations and racial integration.

May 26, 1954 (1766)

Robert Woodworth and Harold Schlosberg's classic text *Experimental Psychology* was published.

June 2, 1954 (1767)

Rudolf Arnheim's *Art and Visual Perception* was published.

July 1, 1954 (1768)

In *Durham v. U.S.*, the U.S. Court of Appeals formulated the "product rule," or "Durham rule," for insanity pleas: If the crime could be shown to be the product of mental disease or mental defect, the defendant could not be criminally responsible. *Durham* was later overturned by the federal court in *U.S. v. Brawner* (June 23, 1972).

July 26, 1954 (1769)

By signing the Educational Research Act (Public Law 83-531), President Eisenhower established the first extensive federal program of educational research.

July 26, 1954 (1770)

Enabling legislation to establish the White House Conference on Education (Public Law 83-530) was passed.

August 22, 1954 (1771)

The Thayer Conference on functions, qualifications, and training of school psychologists began at the Hotel Thayer in West Point, New York. Norma Cutts's report of the conference, titled *School Psychologists at Mid-Century*, became the first hardcover book related to education and training to be published by the APA.

August 25, 1954 (1772)

Abraham Maslow's book *Motivation and Personality* was published. The book explained Maslow's hierarchical theory of human motivation toward the self-actualized state.

August 25, 1954 (1773)

Volume 1 of Gardner Lindzey's *Handbook of Social Psychology* was published. Volume 2 followed on October 7, 1954.

August 26, 1954 (1774)

The Missouri Psychological Association was founded and legally incorporated.

September 6, 1954 (1775)

The Southeastern Psychological Association (SEPA) was founded at the annual meeting of the APA in New York. John B. Wolfe, of the University of Mississippi, organized the meeting and was elected temporary president. The region represented by the SEPA is the same as that of the Southern Society for Philosophy and Psychology, but only the SEPA is an affiliate of the APA.

September 27, 1954 (1776)

David Riesman appeared on the cover of *Time* magazine. Riesman's work relating culture to behavior was popularized by his book *The Lonely Crowd*.

November 9, 1954 (1777)

The drug Doriden (glutethimide; Rorer) was approved for use by the U.S. Food and Drug Administration. Glutethimide is a nonbarbiturate hypnotic that suppresses the activity of the neurotransmitter acetylcholine. It is prescribed as an antianxiety medication.

December 6, 1954 (1778)

The drug Amytal (amobarbital sodium; Lilly) was approved for use by the U.S. Food and Drug Administration (FDA). Amobarbital is a barbiturate and is used as an antianxiety agent and as a sedative. Amytal is a trade name frequently prescribed, but amobarbital sodium was first approved by the FDA on April 18, 1939, when it was marketed by Parke-Davis as Thioethamyl.

December 16, 1954 (1779)

The manual for the Edwards Personal Preference Survey (EPPS) was published. The EPPS has been a widely used personality test, designed to measure a number of motivating needs, such as the needs for achievement, affiliation, and aggression.

December 16, 1954 (1780)

The Southwestern Psychological Association (SWPA) became an affiliate organization of the APA. The SWPA was holding its second annual meeting in Oklahoma City at the time and received the news in a telegram from APA executive secretary Fillmore H. Sanford.

December 21, 1954 (1781)

The doomsday group studied by Leon Festinger, Henry Riecken, and Stanley Schachter predicted that the world would end on this day. The behavior of the group was reported in the book *When Prophesy Fails* (1956), a case study in cognitive dissonance. This group's prophesy was not fulfilled.

January 18, 1955   (1782)
The drug Noludar (methyprylon; Hoffman-LaRoche) was approved for use by the U.S. Food and Drug Administration. Methyprylon is a nonbarbiturate hypnotic that increases the threshold of arousal in the brain stem. It is prescribed as an antianxiety medication.

January 28, 1955   (1783)
Charles Osgood and Percy Tannenbaum's article "The Principle of Congruity in the Prediction of Attitude Change" was published in *Psychological Review*. The article described a social psychological theory of attitude balance and change.

February 14, 1955   (1784)
Carl Jung appeared on the cover of *Time* magazine.

February 23, 1955   (1785)
Johann Karl Friedrich Gauss, one of the first to describe the ubiquity of the normal distribution, was featured on a West German postage stamp.

February 23, 1955   (1786)
The Wechsler Adult Intelligence Scale was published.

March 2, 1955   (1787)
Arkansas governor Orval Faubus signed his state's legislation providing for licensure of psychologists. John P. Anderson, Jean Gardiner, Oddist Murphree, Jerome Schiffer (Chair), and Joseph V. West were members of the first board of examiners.

March 21, 1955   (1788)
With the signature of Governor Albert D. Rosellini, Washington became the ninth state to adopt legislation regulating the professional practice of psychology. Ruth Levy was the chair of the state psychological association's legislation committee.

April 1, 1955   (1789)
The South Carolina Psychological Association was founded and legally incorporated.

April 15, 1955   (1790)
George A. Kelly's book *The Psychology of Personal Constructs* was published.

April 28, 1955   (1791)
The drug Miltown (meprobamate; Wallace Laboratories) was approved for use by the U.S. Food and Drug Administration (FDA). Meprobamate is a propanediol

that affects the thalamus and the limbic system and causes muscle relaxation. It is prescribed as an antianxiety medication. Equanil (Wyeth) is another trade name for meprobamate and was approved by the FDA on August 26, 1955.

April 29, 1955   (1792)
The Kansas Psychological Association was incorporated.

May 6, 1955   (1793)
The Karen Horney Clinic, a center for research, training, and low-cost treatment, was opened in New York City. The clinic was a memorial to the neo-Freudian psychoanalyst.

May 22, 1955   (1794)
The first annual meeting of the Southeastern Psychological Association (SEPA) was held at the Biltmore Hotel in Atlanta, with 268 members in attendance. John B. Wolfe was elected president. The founding meeting of the SEPA was held in New York in 1954.

May 23, 1955   (1795)
Lee J. Cronbach's article "Processes Affecting Scores on 'Understanding of Others' and 'Assumed Similarity' " was published in *Psychological Bulletin*.

June 17, 1955   (1796)
The journal *Psychological Reports* published its first issue. Robert B. Ammons and Carol H. Ammons were the journal's editors.

June 20, 1955   (1797)
Solomon Asch's *Scientific American* article "Opinions and Social Pressure," reviewing his conformity research, was published.

July 8, 1955   (1798)
Donald O. Hebb's article "Drives and the CNS (Conceptual Nervous System)" was published in *Psychological Review*.

July 28, 1955   (1799)
The Mental Health Study Act (Public Law 84-182) was signed into law. The act authorized the National Institute of Mental Health to oversee a nationwide study and evaluation of mental illness.

July 30, 1955   (1800)
Lee J. Cronbach and Paul E. Meehl's article "Construct Validity in Psychological Tests" was published in *Psychological Bulletin*.

August 1, 1955 (1801)

The drug Placidyl (ethchlorvynol; Abbott Laboratories) was approved for use by the U.S. Food and Drug Administration (FDA). Ethchlorvynol is used as an antianxiety agent and as a sedative. Placidyl is a commonly used trade name, but ethchlorvynol first won FDA approval under the trade name Arvynol (Pfizer) on January 12, 1955.

September 2, 1955 (1802)

The APA Council of Representatives approved the APA's first model legislation for state licensure of professional psychologists. Later revisions appeared in 1967, 1979, and 1987.

December 5, 1955 (1803)

The drug Ritalin (methylphenidate; CIBA Pharmaceutical) was approved for use by the U.S. Food and Drug Administration. Methylphenidate is a mild stimulant of the central nervous system, increasing supplies of the neurotransmitter dopamine. Its paradoxic effect in children has led to its use as a treatment for attention deficit hyperactivity disorder.

December 15, 1955 (1804)

The first computer program to simulate human problem solving, written by Herbert Simon and Allen Newell, completed its first hand simulation run. The program simulated heuristic problem solving of the proof of Theorem 2.15 in the *Principia Mathematica* of Whitehead and Russell.

January 15, 1956 (1805)

The journal *Social Work* was first published.

February 2, 1956 (1806)

The APA journal *Contemporary Psychology* was first published, with Edwin G. Boring as editor.

February 13, 1956 (1807)

The journal *Behavioral Science* was first published by the Mental Health Research Institute of the University of Michigan.

April 6, 1956 (1808)

George A. Miller's article "The Magical Number Seven, Plus or Minus Two: Some Limits on Our Capacity for Processing Information" was published in *Psychological Review*. The article is often cited as a pioneering study in modern cognitive psychology.

April 7, 1956 (1809)

Jean Henri Fabre, a pioneer in ethology, was pictured on a postage stamp issued by France on this day.

April 12, 1956 (1810)
The drug Atarax (hydroxyzine hydrochloride; Roerig) was approved for use by the U.S. Food and Drug Administration. Hydroxyzine is a diphenylamine and is prescribed as an antianxiety medication. Its action may be due to suppression of subcortical brain activity.

April 18, 1956 (1811)
Governor Averell Harriman of New York signed that state's original psychologist certification legislation. New York psychologists had proposed legislation for more than 10 years before successfully overcoming objections and winning passage of this law.

April 23, 1956 (1812)
Sigmund Freud appeared on cover of *Time* magazine for third time.

April 27, 1956 (1813)
The organizing meeting of the Mississippi Psychological Association was held. Herdis L. Deabler of Gulfport chaired the organizing committee.

May 2, 1956 (1814)
In a paper titled "Current Developments in Complex Information Processing," Allen Newell announced the invention of the first computer program to simulate human problem solving to a meeting on computers and automation in Washington, DC. The computer program was written by Newell and Herbert A. Simon.

May 11, 1956 (1815)
The Virginia Psychological Association was founded.

May 12, 1956 (1816)
The organizational meeting of the South Dakota Psychological Association was held in Aberdeen for the purpose of drafting a constitution, electing officers, and appointing committees.

June 8, 1956 (1817)
Joseph V. Brady's article "Assessment of Drug Effects on Emotional Behavior" was published in *Science*. The article reported the selective effects of reserpine on anxiety responses and was followed by the establishment of behavioral pharmacology laboratories at virtually every major U.S. pharmaceutical company.

June 15, 1956 (1818)
Ivan Sechenov's likeness appeared on a stamp issued by the Soviet Union on this day.

July 19, 1956 (1819)
Lightner Witmer died. Witmer was the last surviving founding member of the APA and the originator of modern clinical psychology.

August 6, 1956 (1820)

Jerome S. Bruner, Jacqueline J. Goodnow, and George A. Austin's book *A Study of Thinking* was published. The book was a product of the Harvard Cognition Project, founded by Bruner and conducted in Harvard University's Laboratory of Social Relations. Bruner has cited the book as a beginning point of contemporary cognitive psychology.

August 9, 1956 (1821)

The first computer run successfully simulating human problem solving was completed. Herbert A. Simon and Allen Newell were the principal investigators on this project. The program used heuristic problem-solving methods to prove Theorem 2.01 of Whitehead and Russell's *Principia Mathematica*.

August 28, 1956 (1822)

The Legislative Assembly of Quebec granted a charter to the Corporation of Psychologists of the Province of Quebec, the professional psychology organization of the province.

September 2, 1956 (1823)

Physiologist Hans Selye delivered the invited address to the APA's convention in Chicago. Selye's topic was "The Psychosomatic Implications of the General Adaptation Syndrome."

September 2, 1956 (1824)

Robert S. Woodworth was presented with the first American Psychological Foundation Gold Medal at the APA annual meeting in Chicago. Woodworth was honored for his contributions to experimental psychology.

September 2, 1956 (1825)

The first APA Awards for Distinguished Scientific Contributions were presented. Carl Rogers, Wolfgang Köhler, and Kenneth Spence won the awards. The Awards for Distinguished Scientific Contribution are the oldest of the major achievement awards granted by the APA.

September 4, 1956 (1826)

Behaviorist B. F. Skinner and humanist Carl Rogers debated the topic of control of human behavior at the 1956 APA meeting.

September 4, 1956 (1827)

Division 21 of the APA (Applied Experimental and Engineering Psychology) was admitted by the APA Council of Representatives. The division was originally named the Division of Engineering Psychology. An organizing committee of Karl Kryter, Harry Older, and Franklin Taylor was appointed to inaugurate the division's activities.

September 4, 1956   (1828)
The first general business meeting of the Corporation of Psychologists of the Province of Quebec was held. J. S. A. Bois was honorary president of the organization and Gerald M. Mahoney was elected president.

September 11, 1956   (1829)
The Special Group on Information Theory of the Institute of Electrical and Electronics Engineers met at the Massachusetts Institute of Technology. This meeting has been cited as the beginning of the cognitive revolution in psychology. George A. Miller, Herbert Simon, Allen Newell, Noam Chomsky, David Green, and John Swets were among those in attendance.

September 20, 1956   (1830)
Indoklon, a synthetic convulsant taken by inhalation, was first used in the treatment of schizophrenia. The trials were done at Spring Grove Hospital, Maryland, by John C. Krantz, Jr. Because naturally occurring convulsions sometimes accompany improvement in people with schizophrenia, chemically and electrically induced convulsions have been explored as therapeutic methods.

October 2, 1956   (1831)
The Iowa Psychological Association was incorporated.

October 9, 1956   (1832)
Harrison Gough's California Personality Inventory was published.

November 29, 1956   (1833)
An informal meeting was held at the University of New Mexico to organize the New Mexico Psychological Association. James J. Calvert, Robert F. Utter, Roger J. Weldon, and John Salazar called this first meeting. The first formal business meeting was held on March 15, 1957, at the Veterans Hospital in Albuquerque.

December 14, 1956   (1834)
A constituent assembly met to organize the Psychological Society of the Russian Soviet Federal Socialist Republic Academy of Pedagogical Sciences. The Society was officially founded on December 24, 1957.

December 31, 1956   (1835)
The first list of APA-approved clinical internship programs was published in the *American Psychologist*. Twenty-seven institutions qualified for approval.

January 4, 1957   (1836)
Calvin Hall and Gardner Lindzey's book *Theories of Personality* was published. This review of historical and contemporary theories became a standard text in the area.

January 9, 1957 (1837)

Louisiana Psychologists, Inc., was incorporated, with Bernard Bass as president. Louisiana Psychologists, like similar organizations in other states, operated in the absence of state certification or licensing laws to regulate the professional practice of psychology. Nonstatutory certification was superseded in each state as regulatory laws were passed.

January 15, 1957 (1838)

Corbett Thigpen and Herrey Cleckley's book *Three Faces of Eve* was published. This story of multiple personality is frequently cited in introductory texts and was made into a motion picture with the same name.

February 27, 1957 (1839)

The antipsychotic drug Trilafon (perphenazine; Schering) was approved for use by the U.S. Food and Drug Administration. Perphenazine is one of the phenothiazines, possibly acting by blocking dopamine receptors in the brain.

March 1, 1957 (1840)

James Bryant Conant met with a group of educators, Carnegie Corporation staff, and Educational Testing Service staff to plan a comprehensive survey of American high schools. The resulting book, *The American High School Today*, influenced the nature of school psychology and school counseling.

March 19, 1957 (1841)

The U.S. Food and Drug Administration enjoined Wilhelm Reich from further distribution and sales of "orgone accumulators," Reich's multilayered, boxlike "collectors of universal psychic force." Reich disobeyed the order and was sentenced to prison for 2 years for contempt of court. He died in prison on November 3, 1957.

March 28, 1957 (1842)

The constitution of the Christian Association for Psychological Studies was adopted at the group's first business meeting in Holland, Michigan.

April 6, 1957 (1843)

The antidepressant effects of monamine oxidase (MAO) inhibitors were first announced by Harry Loomer at a meeting in Syracuse, New York. The drug was iproniazid, marketed as Marsilid, and was already in use to treat tuberculosis. It was used to treat 400,000 cases of depression in the first year. Marsilid is no longer sold, but its successor, Marplan, is widely prescribed.

April 8, 1957 (1844)

The antipsychotic drug Compazine (prochlorperazine; Smith, Kline, and French) was approved for use by the U.S. Food and Drug Administration. Prochlorperazine is also prescribed for severe nausea and vomiting.

April 15, 1957 (1845)

The state of Maryland approved its psychology licensure law. The law became effective on July 1, 1957.

April 24, 1957 (1846)

Robert Sears, Eleanor Maccoby, and Kurt Lewin's book *Patterns of Child Rearing* was published.

May 16, 1957 (1847)

The state of New Hampshire passed its psychology certification law. The law became effective on July 1, 1957.

May 20, 1957 (1848)

Pioneer physiologist William Harvey appeared on a postage stamp issued by the Soviet Union.

June 14, 1957 (1849)

S. S. Stevens's article "On the Psychophysical Law" was published in *Psychological Review*. The article was the first thorough exposition of the power law of psychophysics.

June 17, 1957 (1850)

The first Air Force Interdisciplinary Behavioral Sciences Conference began at the University of New Mexico. The conference organizers were Paul Walter, Jr., and Ralph D. Norman.

June 19, 1957 (1851)

The Parapsychological Association, a society for researchers in that field, was founded.

July 16, 1957 (1852)

Governor Goodwin Knight signed California's original psychologist certification law into effect.

July 26, 1957 (1853)

Lowell Randall first reported the sedative effect in humans of the benzodiazepine chlordiazepoxide. The drug was synthesized by Leo Sternbach and left on a shelf for 18 months. Almost thrown out in a lab cleanup, it was tested on animals because the chemical analysis had already been done. The drug was eventually marketed for anxiety reduction as Librium (Hoffman-LaRoche).

August 27, 1957 (1854)

Leon Festinger's book A *Theory of Cognitive Dissonance* was published. Research in cognitive dissonance dominated experimental social psychology in the 1960s.

September 2, 1957 (1855)
APA President Lee J. Cronbach delivered his APA presidential address in New York on the two disciplines of scientific psychology, experimental and correlational. The address was frequently reprinted in books of readings on psychology.

September 2, 1957 (1856)
Charles Osgood, George Suci, and Percy Tannenbaum's book *The Measurement of Meaning* was published. The book described the semantic differential technique of measuring connotative meanings of words.

September 2, 1957 (1857)
The first American Psychological Foundation Distinguished Scientific Writing Award was presented to Ernest Havemann for his *Life* magazine articles on psychology appearing on January 7 and February 4, 1957. In 1969 psychological presentations in the nonprint media became eligible for this award and its name was changed to the National Media Award.

September 2, 1957 (1858)
Behaviorist John Watson, near the end of his life, was honored at the annual meeting of the APA. At the last moment, overcome with emotion at the prospect of appearing before an organization he had been separated from for 40 years, Watson sent his son to the ceremony in his place.

September 6, 1957 (1859)
The antidepressant effects of the tricyclic imipramine were first publicly announced at the Second International Congress of Psychiatry in Zurich. The drug was synthesized during research on antihistamines. Tofranil is one common trade name for imipramine.

September 14, 1957 (1860)
Social philosopher Auguste Comte appeared on a French postage stamp issued on this day.

September 16, 1957 (1861)
The antipsychotic drug Vesprin (triflupromazine, Squibb) was approved for use by the U.S. Food and Drug Administration. Triflupromazine is one of the phenothiazines and may work by blocking dopamine receptors in the brain.

September 18, 1957 (1862)
The film *The Three Faces of Eve*, based on Corbett Thigpen and Herrey Cleckley's case report of multiple personality, was copyrighted by Twentieth Century-Fox.

September 25, 1957 (1863)
The Human Factors Society was officially established at its first national meeting and constitutional convention in Tulsa, Oklahoma. Laurence E. Morehouse was

interim president of the organization until Renato Contini was elected president. In 1993 the organization's name was changed to the Human Factors and Ergonomics Society.

October 22, 1957 (1864)
Charles B. Ferster and B. F. Skinner's *Schedules of Reinforcement* was published.

October 23, 1957 (1865)
Ernest J. McCormick's landmark book *Human Engineering* was published. In later revisions the book was titled *Human Factors in Engineering and Design*.

November 25, 1957 (1866)
The APA assumed publication of the *Journal of Educational Psychology*. William Clark Trow, James B. Stroud, and Stephen M. Corey continued as editors under APA ownership. The journal was first published by Warwick and York in 1910 under the editorship of W. C. Bagley, J. Carleton Bell, Carl E. Seashore, and Guy Montrose Whipple.

December 12, 1957 (1867)
The first certificate to practice professional psychology in the state of New York was awarded to Frank S. Freeman, chair of the State Board of Examiners in Psychology. James E. Allen, State Commissioner of Education, made the presentation. New York's certification law had been passed on April 18, 1956.

December 24, 1957 (1868)
The Russian Soviet Federal Socialist Republic (RSFSR) Psychological Society, a branch of the RSFSR Academy of Pedagogical Sciences, was founded by Order 495 of RSFSR Minister of Education E. Afanasenko. The Society had been authorized by the Academy's Presidium on January 16, 1957.

January 7, 1958 (1869)
John W. Atkinson's article "Motivational Determinants of Risk-Taking Behavior" was published in *Psychological Review*.

January 25, 1958 (1870)
Philippe Pinel appeared on a French postage stamp issued on this day.

January 27, 1958 (1871)
In a special message to Congress, President Eisenhower called for a fivefold increase in the budget of the National Science Foundation. One result was Title V of the National Defense Education Act, providing improvements in school testing, counseling, and guidance services. The president's message came 4 months after the Soviet launch of *Sputnik I* (October 4, 1957).

February 7, 1958   (1872)
Abram Amsel's article "The Role of Frustrative Nonreward in Noncontinuous Reward Situations" was published in *Psychological Bulletin*.

April 9, 1958   (1873)
APA Division 12 (Clinical Psychology) conducted the first NIMH-sponsored conference, "Research in Psychotherapy," held in Washington, DC. The conference addressed the issues of goals, assessment, and research problems in psychotherapy. The published report of the meeting, *Research in Psychotherapy, Volume 1*, was the APA's first book on the substantive content of psychology.

April 10, 1958   (1874)
The *Journal of the Experimental Analysis of Behavior* was first published by the Society for the Experimental Analysis of Behavior. Charles B. Ferster was the journal's editor.

April 12, 1958   (1875)
The Wyoming Psychological Association was founded. Alvin Howard was the first president.

April 17, 1958   (1876)
Joseph Wolpe's book *Psychotherapy by Reciprocal Inhibition* was published, describing the method of systematic desensitization.

April 21, 1958   (1877)
Horace English and Ava English's *Dictionary of Psychological and Psychoanalytical Terms*, a standard reference work for many years, was published.

May 2, 1958   (1878)
The petition to create APA Division 22 (Rehabilitation Psychology) was submitted to the APA Council of Representatives.

May 28, 1958   (1879)
The drug Vistaril (hydroxyzine pamoate; Pfizer) was approved for use by the U.S. Food and Drug Administration. Hydroxyzine is a diphenylamine and is prescribed as an antianxiety medication. Its action may be due to suppression of activity in subcortical regions of the brain.

June 5, 1958   (1880)
Fritz Heider's book *The Psychology of Interpersonal Relations* was published.

August 1, 1958   (1881)
Allen Newell, Marvin E. Shaw, and Herbert A. Simon's article "Elements of a Theory of Human Problem Solving" was published in *Psychological Bulletin*. The

article was the first exposition of the information-processing approach in psychology.

August 29, 1958 (1882)
Psi Chi, the national honor society in psychology, was accepted as an APA-affiliated organization. Psi Chi was founded in 1929.

September 2, 1958 (1883)
The National Council on Psychological Aspects of Disability became Division 22 of the APA. The division is now titled Rehabilitation Psychology.

September 6, 1958 (1884)
Federal support for university training in special education was established by Public Law 85-926.

September 19, 1958 (1885)
The journal *Human Factors* was first published by the Human Factors Society. Stanley Lippert edited the journal.

September 25, 1958 (1886)
The first meeting of APA Division 22 (Rehabilitation Psychology) was held. Frederick Whitehouse was the division's first president.

September 29, 1958 (1887)
Joseph V. Brady's article "Ulcers in Executive Monkeys" was published on this day in *Scientific American*.

October 13, 1958 (1888)
The North Dakota Psychological Association was incorporated.

October 13, 1958 (1889)
The antipsychotic drug Stelazine (trifluoperazine; Smith, Kline, and French) was approved for use by the U.S. Food and Drug Administration. Trifluoperazine is a phenothiazine derivative, probably acting to block dopamine receptors in the brain.

October 21, 1958 (1890)
James G. March and Herbert A. Simon's book *Organizations* was published.

October 25, 1958 (1891)
The first annual meeting of the Wyoming Psychological Association was held.

November 10, 1958 (1892)
The drug chlorprothixene was first administered to a human in field trials conducted in Denmark. One of the general class of thioxanthenes, it is used as an antipsychotic

drug. It was marketed in Europe on March 28, 1959, and approved by the U.S. Food and Drug Administration on March 23, 1962, as Taractan (Hoffman-LaRoche).

November 21, 1958   (1893)
The drug Trancopal (chlormezanone; Winthrop Breon) was approved for use by the U.S. Food and Drug Administration. Chlormezanone is used as an antianxiety medication.

January 1, 1959   (1894)
The first comprehensive prepaid psychotherapy benefit in an insurance plan was implemented by Nicholas Cummings at the Kaiser-Permanente Health Plan on the West Coast.

January 5, 1959   (1895)
Harry Harlow's article "The Nature of Love" was published by the *American Psychologist*.

January 12, 1959   (1896)
Volume 1 of Sigmund Koch's *Psychology: A Study of a Science* was published. The volume covered sensory, perceptual, and physiological psychology. Six volumes in this series were eventually published between 1959 and 1963.

March 11, 1959   (1897)
Donald T. Campbell and Donald W. Fiske's article "Convergent and Discriminant Validation by the Multitrait-Multimethod Matrix" was published in *Psychological Bulletin*. When a citation count was done in 1992, this article was found to be the most often cited article published in *Psychological Bulletin* in the past 40 years. It had been cited over 2,000 times.

March 17, 1959   (1898)
The California Psychological Association was incorporated. The organization began in 1948 and was called the California State Psychological Association until July 27, 1990.

March 18, 1959   (1899)
Leon Festinger and J. Merrill Carlsmith's article "Cognitive Consequences of Forced Compliance" was published in the *Journal of Abnormal and Social Psychology*. This was the cognitive dissonance study in which participants were paid either $1 or $20 to lie about their enjoyment of a boring task.

March 20, 1959   (1900)
Utah's Governor Clyde signed that state's original psychologist certification legislation. Utah was the 14th state to pass regulatory legislation for the professional practice of psychology.

April 9, 1959 (1901)

The Virginia Psychological Association was incorporated.

April 16, 1959 (1902)

The antidepressant drug Tofranil (imipramine; Rorer and Geigy) was approved for use by the U.S. Food and Drug Administration (FDA). Imipramine was the first tricyclic antidepressant. It probably enhances neurotransmission by blocking reuptake of the neurotransmitter norepinephrine. Janimine (Abbott Laboratories) is also imipramine and was approved by the FDA on April 8, 1977.

April 23, 1959 (1903)

Stanley Schachter's book *The Psychology of Affiliation* was published.

April 28, 1959 (1904)

Louis L. Thurstone's *The Measurement of Values*, a classic book on attitude scaling, was published.

May 28, 1959 (1905)

The antipsychotic drug Mellaril (thioridazine; Sandoz) was approved for use by the U.S. Food and Drug Administration. Thioridazine is one of the phenothiazines and may work by blocking dopamine receptors in the brain.

June 13, 1959 (1906)

Eighteenth-century histologist Marie François Xavier Bichat appeared on a French postage stamp issued on this day.

June 24, 1959 (1907)

The first All-Union Congress of the Russian Soviet Federal Socialist Republic Psychological Society began in Moscow and continued until July 4, 1959. A. A. Smirnov was elected chairman.

June 29, 1959 (1908)

The antidepressant drug Nardil (phenelzine; Parke-Davis) was approved for use by the U.S. Food and Drug Administration. Phenelzine is a monamine oxidase inhibitor that increases the supply of the neurotransmitters norepinephrine and serotonin by interfering with their metabolic breakdown.

July 1, 1959 (1909)

The antidepressant drug Marplan (isocarboxazid; Hoffman-LaRoche) was approved for use by the U.S. Food and Drug Administration. Isocarboxazid is a monamine oxidase inhibitor that operates by interfering with the breakdown of the neurotransmitters norepinephrine and serotonin.

July 17, 1959 (1910)

The *Archives of General Psychiatry* was first published by the American Medical Association.

July 18, 1959 (1911)
The newsletter of the Christian Association for Psychological Studies was first published.

August 8, 1959 (1912)
Argentina issued a postage stamp honoring Ivan Pavlov.

August 19, 1959 (1913)
John W. Thibaut and Harold H. Kelley's book *The Social Psychology of Groups* was published.

August 21, 1959 (1914)
The state of Michigan enacted its original psychologist certification law, Act 257 of the Public Acts of 1959.

August 28, 1959 (1915)
J. P. Guilford's article "The Three Faces of Intellect" was published in the *American Psychologist*. The article summarized Guilford's theory of operations, products, and contents of intelligence.

September 3, 1959 (1916)
The first organized child-care service facility at an APA convention opened in Cincinnati. Only a few children were served, and the effort was not repeated until 1971, when the Task Force on Women in Psychology and the APA Council of Representatives sponsored a service that cared for 355 children. A child-care service has been available in most subsequent years.

September 9, 1959 (1917)
The antipsychotic drug Permitil (fluphenazine; Schering) was approved for use by the U.S. Food and Drug Administration (FDA). Fluphenazine is one of the phenothiazine antipsychotics, probably acting by blocking dopamine receptors in the brain. Prolixin (Squibb) is another trade name for fluphenazine and was approved by the FDA on September 15, 1959.

September 17, 1959 (1918)
Lloyd R. Peterson and Margaret J. Peterson's article "Short-Term Retention of Individual Verbal Items" was published in the *Journal of Experimental Psychology*.

September 23, 1959 (1919)
Elliot Aronson and Judson Mills's article "Effect of Severity of Initiation on Liking for a Group" was published in the *Journal of Abnormal and Social Psychology*.

October 9, 1959 (1920)
Robert W. White's article "Motivation Reconsidered: The Concept of Competence" was published in *Psychological Review*.

November 7, 1959 (1921)

The first American College Test (ACT) was administered to about 7,500 students. The ACT was a product of the Iowa program of academic achievement testing, directed by Everet F. Lindquist.

November 19, 1959 (1922)

Representatives of 16 state psychology boards meeting in Chicago agreed that a national organization was needed to establish uniform licensing examination procedures. A constitutional committee, chaired by Joseph R. Sanders, was appointed and undertook steps eventually leading to the formation of the American Association of State Psychology Boards.

December 4, 1959 (1923)

The first American behavioral experiment in space was carried out on the rhesus monkey SAM, who performed a shock-avoidance task during a suborbital flight launched at the NASA Flight Center at Wallops Island, Virginia. SAM was trained by W. Lynn Brown. Frederick H. Rowles, Jr., directed the project for the U.S. Air Force. A second such flight was made on January 21, 1960.

December 15, 1959 (1924)

Lloyd M. Dunn and Leota M. Dunn's Peabody Picture Vocabulary Test was published.

December 31, 1959 (1925)

The organizing meeting of the Psychonomic Society was held at the 1959 meeting of the American Association for the Advancement of Science. Clifford T. Morgan chaired the meeting.

February 24, 1960 (1926)

The U.S. Food and Drug Administration approved the distribution of the benzodiazepine chlordiazepoxide. Hoffman-LaRoche marketed the drug under the trade name Librium. The drug's inventor, Leo Sternbach, filed its U.S. patent application on May 15, 1958. A second benzodiazepine, diazepam (Valium), followed in 1963.

February 29, 1960 (1927)

The *Time* magazine issue for this date reported "headway on long-neglected mental health programs." Data showed a decline in the U.S. rate of institutionalized mental patients from 335.7 to 319.3 per 100,000 from 1956 to 1958.

March 1, 1960 (1928)

The Gerbrands cumulative recorder mechanism was patented. Ralph Gerbrands invented a clutch and reset mechanism that gave his recorder a competitive advantage over similar equipment and contributed to the success of the Gerbrands Corporation.

March 12, 1960 (1929)

The first published announcement of the effects of chlordiazepoxide (Librium) appeared in the *Journal of the American Medical Association*. The author was Titus H. Harris.

March 14, 1960 (1930)

Ernst Hans Gombrich's book *Art and Illusion: A Study in the Psychology of Pictorial Representation* was published.

March 16, 1960 (1931)

George A. Miller, Eugene Galanter, and Karl H. Pribram's *Plans and the Structure of Behavior* was published.

March 21, 1960 (1932)

Eleanor J. Gibson and Richard Walk's article "The Visual Cliff" was published in *Scientific American*. The article reported studies of depth perception in infants to a broad audience.

March 31, 1960 (1933)

Milton Rokeach's book *The Open and Closed Mind: Investigations Into the Nature of Belief Systems and Personality Systems* was published. Twenty-two coauthors assisted in producing the book.

April 1, 1960 (1934)

Thomas Szasz's article "The Myth of Mental Illness" was published in the *American Psychologist*.

May 6, 1960 (1935)

The Research Foundation of the National Mental Health Association was founded.

May 10, 1960 (1936)

In a letter to Anthony Sutich, Abraham Maslow suggested the name for the *Journal of Humanistic Psychology*. The proposed title up to this time had been the *Journal of Self Psychology*.

May 20, 1960 (1937)

The APA Board of Directors accepted a $15,000 grant from the Society for Investigation of Human Ecology for senior psychologists to visit the Soviet Union. In 1977 it was disclosed that the Central Intelligence Agency (CIA) secretly funded the grant, hoping to learn more about Soviet behavioral research. The project was code named MKULTRA by the CIA.

June 8, 1960 (1938)

The Psychology Society was founded in New York. The society promotes the interests of psychological practitioners.

June 10, 1960   (1939)
William Dement's article "The Effect of Dream Deprivation" was published in
Science.

June 11, 1960   (1940)
Jean-Martin Charcot, pioneer neurologist and investigator of hypnotism, appeared
on a postage stamp issued by France.

June 23, 1960   (1941)
Daniel Berlyne's book *Conflict, Arousal and Curiosity* was published.

August 31, 1960   (1942)
The organizing meeting of the American Association of State Psychology Boards
(AASPB) was held in Chicago. Joseph R. Sanders presided over delegates from
23 state boards as they adopted a provisional constitution and an executive committee. The AASPB was formally founded a year later. The group's name changed
to the Association of State and Provincial Psychology Boards in 1991.

September 3, 1960   (1943)
The first meeting of the APA's History of Psychology Group was held. The meeting
was attended by 26 participants, including leaders Robert I. Watson, David Bakan,
and John C. Burnham. The group later became APA Division 26.

September 6, 1960   (1944)
The APA Council of Representatives admitted Division 23 (Consumer Psychology). Dik Twedt was the division's first president.

September 7, 1960   (1945)
Douglas P. Crowne and David Marlowe's article "A New Scale of Social Desirabil-
ity Independent of Psychopathology" was published in the *Journal of Consulting
Psychology*.

September 8, 1960   (1946)
The Pennsylvania Psychological Association was incorporated.

September 21, 1960   (1947)
E. James Archer's monograph "Reevaluation of the Meaningfulness of All Possible
CVC Trigrams" was published by *Psychological Monographs*.

September 21, 1960   (1948)
George Sperling's monograph "The Information Available in Brief Visual Presentations" was published by *Psychological Monographs*.

October 29, 1960   (1949)
The steering committee that planned the founding meeting of the New England
Psychological Association met in Cambridge, Massachusetts. M. Curtis Langhorne

was the primary promoter of a New England association separate from the Eastern Psychological Association. The first annual meeting of the organization was held on October 20, 1961.

January 3, 1961 (1950)

George Homans's book *Social Behavior: Its Elementary Forms* was published.

January 31, 1961 (1951)

A chimpanzee named HAM performed a series of operant avoidance tasks during a space flight that was part of Project Mercury, the first American manned space flight program. HAM, trained by Charles B. Ferster, Jack Findley, and Joseph V. Brady, contended with two schedules of bar-pressing for shock avoidance. In an 18-minute suborbital flight, HAM made only two errors.

February 21, 1961 (1952)

George S. Reynolds's article "Behavioral Contrast" was published in the *Journal of the Experimental Analysis of Behavior.*

February 21, 1961 (1953)

The antidepressant drug Parmate (tranylcypromine; Smith, Kline, and French) was approved for use by the U.S. Food and Drug Administration. Tranylcypromine is a monamine oxidase inhibitor that increases the supply of the neurotransmitters norepinephrine and serotonin by interfering with their metabolic breakdown.

March 18, 1961 (1954)

The constitution of the American Association of State Psychology Boards was approved and its 21 charter state board affiliates were approved at a meeting of the provisional executive committee in the APA headquarters building. Chester C. Bennett presided over the meeting. The organization is now named the Association of State and Provincial Psychology Boards.

April 7, 1961 (1955)

The antidepressant drug Elavil (amitriptyline; Merck, Sharp, and Dohme) was approved for use by the U.S. Food and Drug Administration (FDA). Amitriptyline is a tricyclic antidepressant, affecting neurotransmission by inhibiting reuptake of norepinephrine and serotonin. Endep (Hoffman-LaRoche) is also amitriptyline and was approved by the FDA on May 12, 1975.

April 18, 1961 (1956)

The psychologist certification law of the state of Colorado was enacted. The law became effective on July 1, 1961. Colorado was the 17th state or province to enact regulatory legislation.

April 20, 1961 (1957)

The *Journal of Humanistic Psychology* was first published. The journal was edited by Anthony Sutich.

June 6, 1961 (1958)
The first Human Factors Research Symposium was held at Los Angeles State College, now California State University, Los Angeles.

June 20, 1961 (1959)
The experimental edition of the Illinois Test of Psycholinguistic Abilities (ITPA), by Samuel A. Kirk and James J. McCarthy, was published. The ITPA is used in diagnosing learning disabilities.

June 22, 1961 (1960)
The psychologist certification law of the state of Florida was signed by the governor. This statute was actually the second passed by the legislature. The first had been declared unconstitutional by the state's supreme court on May 6, 1961.

August 8, 1961 (1961)
Rensis Likert's book *New Patterns of Management*, a landmark in organizational psychology, was published.

August 18, 1961 (1962)
Arnold Buss's book *The Psychology of Aggression* was published.

August 30, 1961 (1963)
The American Association of State Psychological Boards held its first formal annual meeting at New York's Hotel Commodore during the APA convention. Chester C. Bennett was the first president. The new organization comprised 29 state boards. Its name was changed to the Association of State and Provincial Psychology Boards in 1991.

September 5, 1961 (1964)
The organizing meeting of the APA's reconstituted Division 6 (Physiological and Comparative Psychology) was held. The original Division 6 had merged with Division 3 (Theoretical-Experimental Psychology) in 1949 but reconstituted itself as a separate division in 1962. Sidney Weinstein led the petition drive for the reborn division.

September 5, 1961 (1965)
The first annual meeting of the Society for Psychophysiological Research was held in New York. Chester W. Darrow was president of the organization.

September 15, 1961 (1966)
Donald E. Broadbent's *Behavior* was published.

September 28, 1961 (1967)
David C. McClelland's book *The Achieving Society* was published.

October 9, 1961 (1968)
The Montana Psychological Association was incorporated.

October 19, 1961 (1969)
Georg von Békésy won the Nobel prize for his studies of the physiology of hearing. He provided evidence for the traveling wave theory of pitch perception.

October 20, 1961 (1970)
The first annual meeting of the New England Psychological Association began at Brandeis University in Waltham, Massachusetts. M. Curtis Langhorne, who promoted the formation of a New England association separate from the Eastern Psychological Association, was elected temporary chairman. The first president, Edwin G. Boring, was elected in January 1962.

October 24, 1961 (1971)
Donn Byrne's article "Interpersonal Attraction and Attitude Similarity" was published in the *Journal of Abnormal and Social Psychology*.

December 12, 1961 (1972)
The APA bought property for a new headquarters building located at 1200 17th Street, NW, Washington, DC, for $1.1 million. Building costs were estimated at $2.39 million.

January 10, 1962 (1973)
The petition to create APA Division 24 (Theoretical and Philosophical Psychology) was submitted. Joseph Lyons and Joe Shoben promoted the formation of the division.

January 20, 1962 (1974)
Eric Berne's *Transactional Analysis Journal* was first published.

January 23, 1962 (1975)
Keller Breland and Marian Breland's article "The Misbehavior of Organisms" was published in the *American Psychologist*.

January 29, 1962 (1976)
Howard Kendler and Tracy Kendler's article "Vertical and Horizontal Processes in Problem Solving" was published in *Psychological Review*. The article was later cited as a "citation classic" by *Current Contents*.

February 7, 1962 (1977)
The APA filed its first amicus curiae brief in a legal case, *Jenkins v. U.S.*, heard in the U.S. Court of Appeals for the District of Columbia Circuit. The original trial judge had ruled that psychologists were not competent to testify about the

defendant's sanity. The Court of Appeals on June 7, 1962, found expert testimony by psychologists acceptable and ordered a new trial.

March 1, 1962 (1978)
Herman A. Witkin, Ruth B. Dyk, Hanna F. Faterson, Donald R. Goodenough, and Stephen A. Karp's book *Psychological Differentiation: Studies of Development* was published.

March 14, 1962 (1979)
The petition to re-create APA Division 6 (Physiological and Comparative Psychology) was submitted. An earlier Division 6 had merged with Division 3 (Experimental Psychology) in 1949. The re-created Division 6 reestablished separate subfield representation. Sidney Weinstein promoted the creation of the division.

March 21, 1962 (1980)
The Oregon Psychological Association was incorporated.

March 21, 1962 (1981)
The province of Quebec adopted its psychologist certification law.

April 2, 1962 (1982)
The Hawaii Psychological Association was incorporated.

April 14, 1962 (1983)
The Saskatchewan Psychological Association was incorporated.

April 27, 1962 (1984)
The Spencer Foundation was incorporated. The Spencer Foundation supports behavioral science research related to education. The foundation was begun by a bequest from Lyle M. Spencer, the founder of Science Research Associates, Inc.

May 15, 1962 (1985)
The term "learning disabilities" first appeared in print in the first edition of Samuel A. Kirk's book, *Educating Exceptional Children.*

June 4, 1962 (1986)
B. J. Winer's authoritative book *Statistical Principles in Experimental Design* was published. From 1969 to 1977 this book was cited in 5,279 articles, four times more citations than any other social science book.

June 11, 1962 (1987)
This was the first of 2 days of debate between B. F. Skinner and Carl Rogers on the topic of "Education and the Control of Human Behavior" at the University of Minnesota at Duluth.

June 11, 1962 (1988)

The state of Delaware adopted its original licensure legislation regulating the practice of psychology.

June 13, 1962 (1989)

John E. Overall and Donald R. Gorham's article "The Brief Psychiatric Rating Scale" was published in *Psychological Reports*.

July 12, 1962 (1990)

The *Journal of Verbal Learning and Verbal Behavior* was first published by Academic Press. Leo Postman was the journal's editor.

August 21, 1962 (1991)

Endel Tulving's article "Subjective Organization in Free Recall of 'Unrelated' Words" was published in *Psychological Review*.

September 1, 1962 (1992)

This was the effective date of the founding of the Department of Psychology at Colorado State University, following approval by the Colorado State Board of Agriculture.

September 4, 1962 (1993)

Donald W. MacKinnon's article "The Nature and Nurture of Creative Talent" was published in the *American Psychologist*.

September 4, 1962 (1994)

The APA Council of Representatives admitted Division 24 (Theoretical and Philosophical Psychology).

September 4, 1962 (1995)

The APA Council of Representatives admitted the recreated Division 6 (Physiological and Comparative Psychology).

October 3, 1962 (1996)

Stanley Schachter and Jerome Singer's article "Cognitive, Social, and Physiological Determinants of Emotional State" was published in *Psychological Review*.

October 15, 1962 (1997)

Norman Sundberg and Leona Tyler's *Clinical Psychology*, a standard text, was published.

October 16, 1962 (1998)

Thomas Kuhn's *The Structure of Scientific Revolutions* was published. Kuhn described revolutionary change in science as a social process of "paradigm shifts," not a product of the discovery of new facts.

October 17, 1962   (1999)

The National Institute of Child Health and Human Development was authorized by Public Law 87-838.

October 25, 1962   (2000)

Fuller and Company won the contract to build the APA headquarters building at 1200 17th Street, Washington, DC. The bid was submitted on October 18, 1962.

October 27, 1962   (2001)

The Psychological Association of Alberta and the Psychologists Association of Alberta merged to become the Psychologists Association of Alberta. A. J. B. Hough was the president of the combined organization.

November 30, 1962   (2002)

John Paul Scott's article "Critical Periods in Behavioral Development" was published in *Science*.

December 4, 1962   (2003)

Martin T. Orne's article "On the Social Psychology of the Psychology Experiment: With Particular Reference to Demand Characteristics and Their Implications" was published in the *American Psychologist*.

December 6, 1962   (2004)

The first Joseph P. Kennedy, Jr., Foundation Awards for work in mental retardation were announced. Winners were the National Association for Retarded Children, Samuel Kirk, Ivar Folling, Murray Barr, Joe Hin Tijo, and Jerome Lejeune.

December 17, 1962   (2005)

The Morgan Guaranty Trust Co. offered the APA a loan for the construction of the 1200 17th Street, NW, headquarters building. The APA borrowed $2,750,000 at 5½% interest.

January 22, 1963   (2006)

Albert Bandura, Dorothea Ross, and Sheila Ross's article "Imitation of Film-Mediated Aggressive Models" was published in the *Journal of Abnormal Psychology*. This was the well-known "Bobo Doll" study of imitated aggression.

January 30, 1963   (2007)

The National Institute of Child Health and Human Development began operation.

February 5, 1963   (2008)

In a message to Congress, President Kennedy called for a national program of community mental health centers and a national program for prevention, service, and research in mental retardation. The Maternal and Child Health and Mental

Retardation Amendment and the Community Mental Health Centers Act were passed later in the year.

February 23, 1963 (2009)

Psychologists Interested in the Advancement of Psychotherapy (PIAP), an organization founded in 1960, became a section of APA Division 12 (Clinical Psychology). Eugene Gendlin was the president of PIAP at the time. In 1967 this interest group again became independent as Division 29 (Psychotherapy) of the APA.

March 1, 1963 (2010)

Nathaniel L. Gage's *Handbook of Research on Teaching* was published.

March 13, 1963 (2011)

Tolman Hall, the psychology building on the campus of the University of California, Berkeley, was formally dedicated. Berkeley President Clark Kerr, University of California Chancellor Edward W. Strong, and Berkeley Provost Ernest R. Hilgard spoke at the occasion.

March 25, 1963 (2012)

The state of Nevada adopted its psychology licensure law. The state's board of psychological examiners was created shortly afterward, on July 1, 1963.

April 3, 1963 (2013)

John H. Flavell's book *The Developmental Psychology of Jean Piaget* was published.

April 11, 1963 (2014)

George Sperling's article "A Model for Visual Memory Tasks" was published in *Human Factors*.

April 15, 1963 (2015)

Richard M. Cyert and James G. March's book *A Behavioral Theory of the Firm* was published.

May 3, 1963 (2016)

The first volume of the *Handbook of Mathematical Psychology*, edited by R. Duncan Luce, Robert Bush, and Eugene Galanter, was published.

May 24, 1963 (2017)

Groundbreaking ceremonies were held for the APA's newest headquarters building at 1200 17th Street, NW, Washington, DC. Charles Osgood, president of the APA, conducted the ceremonies.

May 27, 1963 (2018)

The Association of Psychologists of Nova Scotia held its first annual meeting. D. N. W. Doig was elected president. F. H. Page and W. H. Coons had served as presidents of the association before this first annual meeting was held.

May 29, 1963   (2019)
The state of Oregon adopted its first law regulating the practice of psychology. The law took effect on July 1, 1963. This certification law was superseded by a licensure law in 1973.

May 29, 1963   (2020)
The District of Columbia Psychological Association approved a proposal to develop nonstatutory certification procedures. The first certificates were issued to Eugene Stammeyer, Charles R. Wilson, and Andrea Doman. Certification of this kind by state associations preceded licensure legislation in many states. Statutory licensure began in the District of Columbia in 1971.

June 15, 1963   (2021)
Excavation began on the APA's newest headquarters building at 1200 17th Street, NW, Washington, DC. The architect for the building was Vlastmil Koubek and the contractor was Fuller and Company.

June 28, 1963   (2022)
The Republic of Nigeria offered to buy the old APA headquarters building at 1333 16th Street, NW, Washington, DC, for $350,000. The building cost the APA $90,000 in 1952.

July 1, 1963   (2023)
The state of Idaho enacted its licensure law for the practice of psychology.

July 1, 1963   (2024)
The state of New Mexico enacted its professional psychologist certification law. The first board of examiners included Ralph D. Norman, Harold E. Paine, Robert S. Utter, Manuel N. Brown, and Joe E. Green. New Mexico later enacted a comprehensive licensure procedure on June 16, 1989.

August 14, 1963   (2025)
A Central Intelligence Agency document outlined a program of behavioral research on hypnosis, amnesia, and pain. Funds were channeled through the "Human Ecology Fund" to institutions that did not know their true source. Carl Rogers, Edgar Schein, Martin Orne, Charles Osgood, and Wilse Webb were among the unwitting participants in this project.

August 15, 1963   (2026)
The state of Illinois adopted its psychology licensure law.

August 22, 1963   (2027)
The journal *Psychotherapy: Theory, Research, and Practice* was first published by Psychologists Interested in the Advancement of Psychotherapy (PIAP). PIAP later

(1967) became Division 29 (Psychotherapy) of the APA. Eugene T. Gendlin was the editor. In 1984, the name of the journal became *Psychotherapy* and Donald K. Freedheim assumed the editorship from Arthur Kovacs.

August 26, 1963   (2028)
Albert Bandura and Richard Walters's book *Social Learning and Personality Development* was published.

August 26, 1963   (2029)
William L. Hays's text *Statistics for Psychologists* was published.

August 28, 1963   (2030)
The first meeting of the Association for Humanistic Psychology was held in Philadelphia. Abraham Maslow and Anthony Sutich organized the meeting. The organization was originally called the American Association for Humanistic Psychology.

September 1, 1963   (2031)
At a meeting with Robert I. Watson, the Psychology Press agreed to financially sponsor the *Journal of the History of the Behavioral Sciences*. The first issue was published in 1965.

September 2, 1963   (2032)
A group that later formed the Council of Chairmen of Graduate Departments of Psychology (CCGDOP) held an informal meeting at the APA convention in Philadelphia. The meeting was sponsored by the APA Education and Training Board. CCGDOP was founded in 1964, held its first formal meeting in 1965, and became the Council of Graduate Departments of Psychology in 1979.

September 16, 1963   (2033)
The state of Alabama approved its psychology licensure law. The law became effective on October 1, 1963.

September 29, 1963   (2034)
The APA's *Focus on Behavior* series began on National Educational Television. The series was narrated by APA Executive Officer John Darley, and the first show was "The Conscience of a Child."

October 1, 1963   (2035)
The Max Planck Institute for Human Development and Education was founded in Berlin. Friedrich Edding (economics), Dietrich Goldschmidt (sociology), and Saul B. Robinson (educational sciences) were the first directors of the institute.

October 15, 1963 (2036)

Stanley Milgram's article "Behavioral Study of Obedience" was published in the *Journal of Abnormal and Social Psychology*. Milgram's demonstration of situational control over destructive obedience has been of interest for over three decades.

October 15, 1963 (2037)

Richard Held and Alan Hein's article "Movement-Produced Stimulation in the Development of Visually Guided Behavior" was published in the *Journal of Comparative and Physiological Psychology*.

October 23, 1963 (2038)

The New England Psychological Association was incorporated. Herbert J. Hoffmann was president of the board of directors.

October 24, 1963 (2039)

The Maternal and Child Health and Mental Retardation Amendment (Public Law 88-156) was signed by President Kennedy. It provided for research on the links between maternal health and mental retardation in children.

October 31, 1963 (2040)

The Community Mental Health Centers Act (Public Law 88-164) was signed by President Kennedy. This was the first federal legislation to support mental health facilities outside the model provided by large mental hospitals. The act provided funds for construction and operation of community facilities across the nation. Within 4 years, there were almost 300 such centers.

November 14, 1963 (2041)

The Mississippi Psychological Association received its state corporate charter.

November 15, 1963 (2042)

The drug Valium (diazepam; Hoffman-LaRoche) was approved for use by the U.S. Food and Drug Administration. Diazepam is a benzodiazepine and is used as an antianxiety agent and as a sedative. At one time, Valium was the most frequently prescribed medication in the United States. Undesirable side effects and the potential for abuse have moderated its use.

January 3, 1964 (2043)

Milton Rokeach's book *The Three Christs of Ypsilanti* was published. The book presents classic case studies of abnormal personality.

January 15, 1964 (2044)

Jerome Bruner's article "The Course of Cognitive Growth" was published in the *American Psychologist*.

January 27, 1964 (2045)

The journal *Psychonomic Science* was first published by the Psychonomic Society. Clifford T. Morgan was the editor.

March 13, 1964 (2046)

New York tavern manager Kitty Genovese was murdered as she returned to her apartment in the early morning. None of the more than 30 witnesses intervened to help her. The murder stimulated decades of social psychological studies of bystander intervention.

March 20, 1964 (2047)

The petition to create APA Division 25 (Experimental Analysis of Behavior) was submitted. B. F. Skinner promoted the formation of the division.

April 14, 1964 (2048)

Charles Cofer and Mortimer Appley's widely used textbook *Motivation* was published.

June 5, 1964 (2049)

Victor H. Vroom's book *Work and Motivation* was published.

June 10, 1964 (2050)

The *American Psychologist* published a brief but influential article by Diana Baumrind titled "Some Thoughts on Ethics of Research: After Reading Milgram's 'Behavioral Study of Obedience.'" Baumrind's criticisms of the treatment of human participants in Milgram's studies stimulated a thorough revision of the ethical standards of psychological research.

June 19, 1964 (2051)

The U.S. Senate passed the Civil Rights Act of 1964, desegregating public accommodations and schools and eliminating racial discrimination in employment and voting. Psychological studies affected the legislation and resulted from its passage, and many psychologists have been influential in implementing its provisions.

July 16, 1964 (2052)

The state of Louisiana approved its psychology licensure law. The law became effective on July 29 of the same year.

August 20, 1964 (2053)

The Economic Opportunities Act of 1964 (Public Law 88-452) was passed. Project Head Start, an application of psychological studies of the effects of early intervention, was funded by Title II (Community Action Programs) of the act.

September 2, 1964 (2054)

Fred N. Kerlinger's book *Foundations of Behavioral Research: Educational and Psychological Inquiry* was published. Kerlinger's book became a standard text in the field.

September 7, 1964 (2055)

The Council of Chairmen of Graduate Departments of Psychology was founded at an informal meeting of department chairs at the annual meeting of the APA in Los Angeles. Lloyd Humphreys of the University of Illinois chaired this meeting and was elected first chairman of the organization. The group later changed its name to the Council of Graduate Departments of Psychology.

September 8, 1964 (2056)

The APA Council of Representatives admitted Division 25 (Experimental Analysis of Behavior). Joseph V. Brady was the first president of the division.

September 16, 1964 (2057)

The Gerbrands Corporation, manufacturer of experimental psychology laboratory equipment, was incorporated.

November 6, 1964 (2058)

The antidepressant drug Aventyl (nortriptyline; Eli Lilly) was approved for use by the U.S. Food and Drug Administration (FDA). Nortriptyline is a tricyclic antidepressant, affecting reuptake of the neurotransmitters norepinephrine and serotonin. Pamelor (Sandoz), another trade name for nortriptyline, was approved by the FDA on November 6, 1977.

November 18, 1964 (2059)

The term *debriefing*, borrowed from British military jargon, was first used in its psychological context in an article by Stanley Milgram published in the *American Psychologist*. Milgram used the term to describe the postexperimental measures taken in his studies of obedience.

November 20, 1964 (2060)

The antidepressant drug Norpramin (desipramine; Merrell Dow) was approved for use by the U.S. Food and Drug Administration (FDA). Desipramine is a tricyclic antidepressant, acting to increase the neurotransmitters norepinephrine and, to a lesser extent, serotonin by interfering with their reuptake. Pertofrane (Rorer) is also desipramine and was approved by the FDA on December 18, 1964.

November 27, 1964 (2061)

Neal E. Miller was awarded the National Medal of Science by President Lyndon Johnson for his work on learning and motivation.

November 28, 1964 (2062)

The Old Saybrook Conference, a milestone in the humanistic psychology movement, was held in Old Saybrook, Connecticut.

December 10, 1964 (2063)

Sweden honored Ivan Pavlov by issuing a postage stamp with his portrait on this day.

December 18, 1964 (2064)

The Texas Psychological Association was incorporated.

January 13, 1965 (2065)

Unable to sleep in the early morning, Fred Keller planned the teaching technique later called the personalized system of instruction. The first classroom trials began on February 10, 1965.

January 19, 1965 (2066)

The APA's *Journal of Personality and Social Psychology* was first published, with Daniel Katz as its editor. This journal assumed publication of the social psychology portion of the *Journal of Abnormal and Social Psychology*, which began publication in 1921, itself a successor to the *Journal of Abnormal Psychology*, first published by Morton Prince in 1906.

February 2, 1965 (2067)

The *Journal of Experimental Social Psychology* was first published. The journal was edited by John W. Thibaut.

February 2, 1965 (2068)

The *Journal of the History of the Behavioral Sciences* was first published, with Robert I. Watson as the editor. Watson and psychiatrist Eric T. Carlson promoted the founding of the journal.

February 10, 1965 (2069)

The first classroom trials of Fred Keller's personalized system of instruction began at Arizona State University.

February 19, 1965 (2070)

The state of Wyoming approved its psychology licensure law.

March 4, 1965 (2071)

The *Journal of Applied Behavioral Science* was first published, with Goodwin Watson as the editor. The journal was published by the National Training Laboratory.

March 13, 1965 (2072)

The first Conference on Professional and Social Issues in Psychology began at the Drake Hotel in Chicago. The meeting was called by the Los Angeles Society of

Clinical Psychologists because of perceived neglect of professional and social issues by the APA. The group eventually became Division 31 (State Psychological Association Affairs) of the APA.

March 31, 1965 (2073)
Nancy C. Waugh and Donald A. Norman's article "Primary Memory" was published in *Psychological Review*.

April 5, 1965 (2074)
Roger Brown's classic text *Social Psychology* was published.

April 21, 1965 (2075)
The state of Arizona passed its law regulating the licensure of psychologists. The law took effect on July 20, 1965.

April 30, 1965 (2076)
The American Association for Accreditation of Laboratory Animal Care held its organizational meeting in Des Plaines, Illinois. The member organizations of the association, including the APA, promote humane animal care in research laboratories through accreditation of laboratories conforming to its standards.

May 3, 1965 (2077)
Queen Elizabeth II granted a royal charter to the British Psychological Society. The society had been founded in London in 1901.

May 4, 1965 (2078)
The Education of Psychologists for Community Mental Health Conference was held at Swampscott, Massachusetts. The conference, sponsored by Boston University and the South Shore Mental Health Center, has been cited as a founding event in the history of community psychology. Chester C. Bennett chaired the conference committee.

May 18, 1965 (2079)
The founding of the first Head Start programs was announced by President Lyndon Johnson.

May 19, 1965 (2080)
Noam Chomsky's book *Aspects of the Theory of Syntax* was published. The book promoted a nativistic view of thought and language.

June 4, 1965 (2081)
The drug Serax (oxazepam; Wyeth) was approved for use by the U.S. Food and Drug Administration. Oxazepam is a benzodiazepine and is used as an antianxiety agent and as a sedative.

June 7, 1965 (2082)

A U.S. Senate subcommittee on constitutional rights convened hearings on non-voluntary psychological testing by employers. Use of the MMPI and projective tests as employment screening instruments provoked questioning by legislators and ridicule by newspaper humor columnists. Senator Sam Ervin was chairman of the subcommittee.

June 8, 1965 (2083)

APA Executive Director Arthur Brayfield testified before a U.S. Senate subcommittee on the constitutionality of nonvoluntary psychological testing by public and private employers. The subcommittee was chaired by Senator Sam Ervin.

June 10, 1965 (2084)

George K. Bennett, president of the Psychological Corporation, testified about the validity of the MMPI before a U.S. Senate committee on the constitutionality of nonvoluntary psychological testing by employers.

June 11, 1965 (2085)

Morton E. Bitterman's article "Phyletic Differences in Learning" was published in the *American Psychologist*.

June 28, 1965 (2086)

The state of Oklahoma enacted its licensure law for psychologists.

June 29, 1965 (2087)

Philip J. Siegmann, executive editor of *Psychological Abstracts*, recommended to the APA Publications Board the first use of computers in compiling *Psychological Abstracts*. The "Photon process" was adopted. The January 1966 issue was the first to be published using the new process instead of linotype and index cards.

July 7, 1965 (2088)

The petition to create APA Division 26 (History of Psychology) was submitted. Ronald Mayer represented the petitioning group.

July 16, 1965 (2089)

Robert Zajonc's article "Social Facilitation" was published in *Science*.

August 10, 1965 (2090)

The *Handbook of Clinical Psychology*, edited by Benjamin Wolman, was first published.

August 23, 1965 (2091)

The psychiatric drug Triavil (Merck, Sharp, and Dohme) was approved for use by the U.S. Food and Drug Administration (FDA). Triavil is a combination of the antipsychotic perphenazine (Trilafon), which is a phenothiazine derivative, and the tricyclic antidepressant amitriptyline (Elavil). Etrafon (Schering) is also perphenazine and amitriptyline and was approved by the FDA on December 30, 1965.

August 27, 1965 (2092)
The Chicago Conference on Professional Preparation of Clinical Psychologists was held. The conference proposed greater emphasis on professional preparation than on scientific training.

August 30, 1965 (2093)
Michael Argyle and Janet Dean's article "Eye-Contact, Distance, and Affiliation" was published in *Sociometry*.

August 30, 1965 (2094)
Michael Wallach and Nathan Kogan's book *Modes of Thinking in Young Children* was published.

September 2, 1965 (2095)
The Society of Experimental Social Psychology was founded in Chicago.

September 5, 1965 (2096)
Fred Keller first presented his personalized system of instruction to a professional audience. His address was delivered to the 73rd Annual Meeting of the APA.

September 5, 1965 (2097)
The first formal meeting of the Council of Chairmen of Graduate Departments of Psychology began at 1:00 p.m. during the annual meeting of the APA in Chicago. Lloyd Humphreys of the University of Illinois was chairman of the organization. In 1979, the group adopted its present name, the Council of Graduate Departments of Psychology.

September 6, 1965 (2098)
Community psychologists attending an open meeting at the APA annual meeting in Chicago voted to seek APA division status. The group became APA Division 27 (Community Psychology).

September 7, 1965 (2099)
APA Division 26 (History of Psychology) was granted official status by the APA Council of Representatives. Robert I. Watson was instrumental in the formation of the new division.

October 16, 1965 (2100)
The dedication ceremony of the APA headquarters building at 1200 17th Street, NW, Washington, DC, was held. The speaker was Donald F. Hornig, Special

Assistant to President Johnson for Science and Technology. The central office staff began to move into portions of the building on October 1, 1964.

November 1, 1965 (2101)

Joseph J. Schildkraut's article "The Catecholamine Hypothesis of Affective Disorders: A Review of Supporting Evidence" was published in the *American Journal of Psychiatry*.

November 5, 1965 (2102)

The film *Behavior Theory in Practice*, by Ellen Reese, was copyrighted.

November 15, 1965 (2103)

The Archives of the History of American Psychology was founded at the University of Akron. The university's board of directors endorsed and funded the archives and appointed John A. Popplestone the director of the collection.

November 23, 1965 (2104)

The antianxiety drug Quaalude (methaqualone; Lemmon) was approved by the U.S. Food and Drug Administration (FDA). It was discovered in a World War II search for artificial antimalarial drugs when the Japanese cut off supplies of cinchona bark. Its effects made methaqualone a popular illicit drug. Methaqualone was first approved by the FDA as Dimethacol (Pennwalt) on April 25, 1960.

December 7, 1965 (2105)

The journal *Perception and Psychophysics*, edited by Clifford T. Morgan, was first published by the Psychonomic Society.

December 31, 1965 (2106)

Israel Goldiamond's article "Self Control Procedures in Personal Behavior Problems" was published in *Psychological Reports*. The article reported the successful use of behavior analytic techniques in the treatment of troublesome personal behavior.

January 17, 1966 (2107)

Daniel Katz and Robert L. Kahn's book *The Social Psychology of Organizations* was published.

January 21, 1966 (2108)

Wendell R. Garner's article "To Perceive Is to Know" was published in the *American Psychologist*.

January 28, 1966 (2109)

Richard F. Thompson and William A. Spencer's article "Habituation: A Model Phenomenon for the Study of Neuronal Substrates of Behavior" was published in *Psychological Review*.

January 28, 1966 (2110)

The petition to create APA Division 27 (Community Psychology) was submitted. Robert Reiff promoted the formation of the division.

January 31, 1966 (2111)

The journal *Multivariate Behavioral Research* was first published by the Society of Multivariate Experimental Psychology. Desmond S. Cartwright was the journal's editor.

February 9, 1966 (2112)

The APA's *Standards for Educational and Psychological Tests and Manuals* was first published. John W. French and William B. Michael chaired the committee that wrote this set of standards. Later revisions were titled *Standards for Educational and Psychological Testing.*

February 15, 1966 (2113)

Julian Rotter's monograph "Generalized Expectancies for Internal Versus External Control of Reinforcement" was published.

February 25, 1966 (2114)

Edward T. Hall's book *The Hidden Dimension* was published. The book described the effects of personal space on interpersonal behavior.

April 11, 1966 (2115)

William Masters and Virginia Johnson's book *Human Sexual Response* was published. Masters and Johnson's research attracted widespread popular attention and had important effects on the practice of psychological counseling.

April 20, 1966 (2116)

Mark R. Rosenzweig's article "Environmental Complexity, Cerebral Change, and Behavior" was published in the *American Psychologist.*

April 27, 1966 (2117)

Herbert M. Lefcourt's article "Internal Versus External Control of Reinforcement: A Review" was published in *Psychological Bulletin.*

May 9, 1966 (2118)

The state of Mississippi approved its licensure law for psychology.

May 19, 1966 (2119)

Frances K. Graham and Rachel K. Clifton's article "Heart-Rate Change as a Component of the Orienting Response" was published in *Psychological Bulletin.* The article was later featured as a "citation classic" by *Current Contents.*

May 23, 1966   (2120)

The petition to create APA Division 28 (Psychopharmacology and Substance Abuse) was submitted. Harley Hanson represented the petitioning group.

June 21, 1966   (2121)

The chimpanzee named Washoe began her training in American Sign Language at the University of Nevada at Reno. Reno is the county seat of Washoe County. R. Allen Gardner and Beatrice Gardner conducted this research.

July 1, 1966   (2122)

Daniel Berlyne's article "Curiosity and Exploration" was published in *Science*.

August 5, 1966   (2123)

Saul Sternberg's article "High Speed Scanning in Human Memory" was published in *Science*. This article reported that the time taken to detect an item in short-term memory is proportional to the number of items in memory. It is frequently cited in introductory psychology texts.

August 18, 1966   (2124)

James J. Gibson's book *The Senses Considered as Perceptual Systems* was published.

August 22, 1966   (2125)

Jerome S. Bruner's book *Studies in Cognitive Growth* was published. Eleven coauthors collaborated on this publication project of Harvard University's Center for Cognitive Studies.

August 24, 1966   (2126)

The Federal Republic of Germany (West Germany) issued a Gottfried Leibniz postage stamp.

August 24, 1966   (2127)

The first federal legislation to protect animal research subjects was enacted. The Animal Welfare Act charged the Secretary of Agriculture with developing humane standards of handling, care, treatment, and transportation of dogs, cats, nonhuman primates, guinea pigs, hamsters, and rabbits used in research.

September 4, 1966   (2128)

The petition to create APA Division 29 (Psychotherapy) was submitted. The petitioning group was Psychologists Interested in the Advancement of Psychotherapy, a section of APA Division 12 (Clinical). Hans Strupp and Reuben Fine promoted the creation of the division.

September 4, 1966   (2129)

The first meeting of APA Division 27 (Community Psychology) was held.

September 6, 1966 (2130)

David M. Green and John A. Swets's *Signal Detection Theory and Psychophysics* was published.

September 6, 1966 (2131)

The APA Council of Representatives admitted Division 27 (Community Psychology). Robert Reiff was the division's first president.

September 6, 1966 (2132)

The APA Council of Representatives admitted Division 28 (Psychopharmacology and Substance Abuse). Murray Jarvik was the division's first president. The division's original title was Behavioral Pharmacology.

September 12, 1966 (2133)

Murray Glanzer and Anita Cunitz's article "Two Storage Mechanisms in Free Recall" was published in the *Journal of Verbal Learning and Verbal Behavior*.

September 12, 1966 (2134)

Endel Tulving and Zena Pearlstone's article "Availability Versus Accessibility of Information in Memory for Words" was published in the *Journal of Verbal Learning and Verbal Behavior*.

September 20, 1966 (2135)

New Jersey enacted its psychology licensure law, the Practicing Psychologists Licensing Act. The law became effective immediately.

September 28, 1966 (2136)

Entered in B. F. Skinner's notebook: "The economic forces behind the designers of cars are fantastically powerful. When will the design of a better way of life be as strongly supported?"

October 12, 1966 (2137)

Robert Rosenthal's *Experimenter Effects in Behavioral Research* was published.

October 16, 1966 (2138)

The California legislature made possession of LSD-25 illegal. The federal government soon followed suit in banning this psychoactive drug. In San Francisco and in New York City, the occasion was marked by a protest "be-in." Space does not permit a satisfactory description of a be-in.

November 11, 1966 (2139)

The Artificial Intelligence Special Interest Committee of the Association for Computing Machinery (ACM) was formed. The group became an official special interest group of the ACM on May 3, 1968.

December 6, 1966 (2140)

Lafayette R. (L. Ron) Hubbard patented a "device for measuring and indicating changes in resistance of a living body" that is used supposedly to measure personal psychological adjustment in Hubbard's pseudotherapeutic system called *dianetics*.

December 8, 1966 (2141)

Eleanor Maccoby's book *The Development of Sex Differences* was published.

December 16, 1966 (2142)

Aldridge Bousfield and Weston Bousfield's article "Measurements of Clustering and of Sequential Constancies in Repeated Free Recall" was published in *Psychological Reports*.

February 1, 1967 (2143)

Robert Rescorla's article "Pavlovian Conditioning and its Proper Control Procedures" was published in *Psychological Review*.

February 17, 1967 (2144)

Arthur Jensen delivered a pivotal address on "Social Class, Race, and Genetics: Implications for Education" to the American Educational Research Association's annual meeting. The address helped to reignite the controversy over racial differences in intelligence.

March 8, 1967 (2145)

James D. Thompson's book *Organizations in Action: Social Science Bases of Administrative Theory* was published.

March 8, 1967 (2146)

The first meeting of the North American Society for the Psychology of Sport and Physical Activity (NASPSPA) was held at the Stardust Hotel in Las Vegas. Arthur T. Slater-Hammel was the first president of NASPSPA. Early meetings of the organization were held in conjunction with those of the American Association of Health, Physical Education, and Recreation.

March 10, 1967 (2147)

The Vermont Psychological Association was incorporated.

March 13, 1967 (2148)

The North American Society for the Psychology of Sport and Physical Education was incorporated, shortly following association's first annual meeting.

March 13, 1967 (2149)

The state of North Dakota adopted its licensure law for psychologists.

March 31, 1967   (2150)
Charles Truax and Robert Carkhuff's book *Toward Effective Counseling and Psychotherapy* was published.

April 3, 1967   (2151)
Entered this day in B. F. Skinner's notebook: "Strange to say, I am an Emersonian, a Thoreauvian. I want what they wanted. But I want it as part of a successful conception of human behavior. Maybe *Walden Two* was an apter title than I knew."

April 12, 1967   (2152)
The antipsychotic drug Haldol (haloperidol; McNeil Pharmaceutical) was approved for use by the U.S. Food and Drug Administration. Haloperidol was the first of the butyrophenone series of major tranquilizers and came to be widely used in institutional settings.

April 15, 1967   (2153)
Governor Docking of Kansas signed that state's psychologist certification law. The law took effect on July 1, 1967, and the first meeting of the board of examiners was held in Topeka on August 27. James Hartman of Wichita was chosen first chairman of the board.

April 24, 1967   (2154)
The state of Alaska approved its psychology licensure law. The law became effective on July 1, 1967. In 1980, the state audit of the board of psychology examiners resulted in criticism of the board and the licensure law. In response to "sunset" legislation, the law was granted only a 2-year renewal. Eventual improvements led to long-term reinstatement of the licensure law.

May 2, 1967   (2155)
The Nebraska legislature passed the state's original psychologist licensing act. D. Craig Affleck was the chairman of the first board of examiners.

May 9, 1967   (2156)
Martin Seligman and Steven Maier's article "Failure to Escape Traumatic Shock" was published in the *Journal of Experimental Psychology*. The article described the "learned helplessness" paradigm.

May 16, 1967   (2157)
J. P. Guilford's book *The Nature of Human Intelligence* was published. Guilford's three-factor theory of intelligence was presented in the book.

May 24, 1967   (2158)
Richard F. Thompson's *Foundations of Physiological Psychology* was published. The book was a popular adoption in college courses.

May 29, 1967 (2159)
Daryl Bem's article "Self-Perception: An Alternative Interpretation of Cognitive Dissonance Phenomena" was published in *Psychological Review*.

June 8, 1967 (2160)
The state of Hawaii enacted its licensure law regulating the practice of psychology.

June 23, 1967 (2161)
The state of North Carolina ratified its licensure law for psychologists. The law became effective on July 1 of the same year. J. Wilbert Edgerton was instrumental in promoting passage of this legislation.

June 28, 1967 (2162)
Robert J. Douglas's article "The Hippocampus and Behavior" was published in *Psychological Bulletin*.

June 30, 1967 (2163)
The APA first contracted to sell machine-readable entries from *Psychological Abstracts* to an external agency, the National Clearinghouse for Mental Health Information at the National Institute of Mental Health. The contracted price was $22 per abstract.

July 24, 1967 (2164)
The drug Navane (thiotixene; Roerig) was approved for distribution by the U.S. Food and Drug Administration. One of the general class of thioxanthenes, it is used as an antipsychotic agent.

August 30, 1967 (2165)
The first edition of Sol L. Garfield and Allen E. Bergin's *Handbook of Psychotherapy and Behavior Change: An Empirical Analysis* was published.

September 1, 1967 (2166)
Martin Luther King, Jr., addressed an audience of about 5,000 at the APA annual meeting. His topic was "The Role of the Behavioral Scientist in the Civil Rights Movement."

September 3, 1967 (2167)
The first J. P. Guilford Awards for outstanding student research were presented by Psi Chi, the national honor society in psychology. The winners were Roy Dreistadt, of the New School for Social Research, and Darryl B. Neill, of Florida Presbyterian College.

September 5, 1967 (2168)
The APA Council of Representatives admitted Division 29 (Psychotherapy). The new group was originally Psychologists Interested in the Advancement of Psycho-

therapy, a section of APA Division 12 (Clinical Psychology). Fred E. Spaner was the first president of the new division.

September 12, 1967   (2169)
Ulrich Neisser's book *Cognitive Psychology* was published.

September 12, 1967   (2170)
The First Congress of the International Association for the Scientific Study of Mental Deficiency began in Montpellier, France.

September 27, 1967   (2171)
The antidepressant drug Vivactil (protriptyline; Merck Sharp and Dohme) was approved for use by the U.S. Food and Drug Administration. Protriptyline is a tricyclic antidepressant. It probably enhances neurotransmission by blocking reuptake of the neurotransmitters norepinephrine and serotonin.

October 7, 1967   (2172)
The psychology licensure law for the state of Maine became effective and the board of examiners in psychology was created.

October 18, 1967   (2173)
Haldan Hartline, George Wald, and Ragnar Granit won the Nobel prize for their studies of the chemistry and physiology of vision.

October 26, 1967   (2174)
The first report of the sign language performance of the chimpanzee named Washoe was delivered by R. Allen Gardner and Beatrice Gardner at the annual meeting of the Psychonomic Society.

November 24, 1967   (2175)
Alvin M. Liberman, Franklin Cooper, Donald Shankweiler and Michael Studdert-Kennedy's article "Perception of the Speech Code" was published in *Psychological Review*.

December 15, 1967   (2176)
The first version of the Wide Range Achievement Test was published by Joseph Jastak, Sidney Bijou, and Sarah Jastak.

January 2, 1968   (2177)
Thomas H. Holmes and Richard H. Rahe published the Schedule of Recent Experience, a noteworthy scale for assessing the stressful impact of readjusting to recent life events. An earlier version of the scale had appeared in the *Journal of Psychosomatic Medicine*.

January 17, 1968   (2178)
Allan Paivio and Stephen Madigan's article "Imagery and Association Value in Paired-Associate Learning" was published in the *Journal of Experimental Psychology*.

January 26, 1968   (2179)
Paul Brown and Herbert Jenkins's article "Auto-Shaping of the Pigeon's Key-Peck" was published in the *Journal of the Experimental Analysis of Behavior*.

February 1, 1968   (2180)
The petition to create APA Division 30 (Psychological Hypnosis) was submitted. Adel Mahran organized the petition drive.

February 13, 1968   (2181)
The National Medal of Science was presented by President Johnson to Harry Harlow. The date of announcement of the award was December 31, 1967.

February 26, 1968   (2182)
Walter Mischel's book *Personality and Assessment* was published.

March 11, 1968   (2183)
The first meeting of the founding board of the California School of Professional Psychology, the nation's first independent professional school of psychology, was convened by Nicholas Cummings.

March 11, 1968   (2184)
The antiepileptic drug Tegratol (carbamazepine; Geigy Pharmaceutical) was approved for use by the U.S. Food and Drug Administration. The physiological action of carbamazepine remains unknown.

March 21, 1968   (2185)
A national invitational meeting of school psychologists in Columbus, Ohio, resulted in the formation of the National Association of School Psychologists. The Ohio School Psychology Association organized the meeting.

March 21, 1968   (2186)
Governor Robert McNair signed South Carolina's original psychologist licensure act into law. The law took effect immediately.

April 2, 1968   (2187)
Robert Rosenthal and Lenore Jacobson's book *Pygmalion in the Classroom* was published. The book reported the effects of teacher expectancies on teacher and student behavior.

April 12, 1968   (2188)
The *Journal of Applied Behavior Analysis* was first published. Montrose Wolf was the editor of the journal.

April 12, 1968 (2189)

Donald Baer, Montrose Wolf, and Todd Risley's article "Some Current Dimensions of Applied Behavior Analysis" was published in the *Journal of Applied Behavior Analysis*.

April 12, 1968 (2190)

Fred Keller's article "Goodbye, Teacher . . ." was published in the *Journal of Applied Behavior Analysis*. The article described the application of behavioral principles to instruction.

April 25, 1968 (2191)

John G. Darley and Bibb Latané's article "Bystander Intervention in Emergencies: Diffusion of Responsibility" was published in the *Journal of Personality and Social Psychology*.

May 10, 1968 (2192)

The petition to create APA Division 31 (State Psychological Association Affairs) was submitted. Allen Williams was instrumental in forming the division.

July 31, 1968 (2193)

Norman Anderson's article "Likableness Ratings of 555 Personality-Trait Words" was published in the *Journal of Personality and Social Psychology*.

August 28, 1968 (2194)

Roger Kirk's widely used text *Experimental Design: Procedures for the Behavioral Sciences* was published.

August 28, 1968 (2195)

The Committee on Health Insurance, chaired by Nicholas Cummings, held its first meeting of state psychological association insurance chairs. They launched a campaign for "freedom of choice" laws, allowing insurance coverage of psychological services without medical supervision or referral. New Jersey and California passed such laws in 1969, but Governor Reagan vetoed California's law.

August 31, 1968 (2196)

The second organizing meeting of APA Division 31 (State Psychological Association Affairs) was held. The meeting was sponsored by the Conference on Professional and Social Issues of Psychology. This attempt at APA affiliation was successful, but an earlier organizing meeting of August 31, 1966 submitted a petition for division status that was deferred by the APA.

August 31, 1968 (2197)

The first meeting of the Council of Undergraduate Psychology Departments was held in San Francisco. Robert Harper of Knox College was the first president of the group. In 1986 the organization changed its name to the Council of Teachers of Undergraduate Psychology.

August 31, 1968   (2198)
Eric Hoffer, longshoreman and social philosopher, delivered an invited address to the APA annual meeting in San Francisco.

September 1, 1968   (2199)
The organizing meeting of the American Psychology-Law Society was held in the Mark Hopkins Hotel in San Francisco during the APA convention. Jay Ziskin and Eric Dreikurs were instrumental in establishing the new organization. The society merged with Division 41 of the APA in 1984.

September 2, 1968   (2200)
The organizational meeting for APA Division 30 (Psychological Hypnosis) was held in San Francisco in the Hunt Room of the Fairmont Hotel. Adel Mahran chaired the planning committee.

September 2, 1968   (2201)
The Association of Black Psychologists was formed. Charles W. Thomas, formerly of the University of Southern California, and Robert L. Green, of Michigan State University, were elected cochairs of the organization. Ernestine Thomas served as the association's national secretary.

September 26, 1968   (2202)
Nelson Goodman's book *Languages of Art* was published.

September 30, 1968   (2203)
The journal *Behavior Research Methods and Instrumentation* was first published by the Psychonomic Society. Joseph B. Sidowski was the editor of the new journal. The name of the journal was later changed to *Behavior Research Methods, Instruments, and Computers*.

September 30, 1968   (2204)
The Federal Aviation Administration was directed to expand its human factors research activities. Psychologist Clay Fushee was subsequently named chief scientific officer for human factors research.

October 5, 1968   (2205)
The organizational meeting of Cheiron, the International Society for the History of the Behavioral and Social Sciences, was held in New York, at New York University. The word *Cheiron* was not part of the original name, but was added within the first year.

October 6, 1968 (2206)

The APA Council of Representatives admitted Division 30 (Psychological Hypnosis). Ernest R. Hilgard was the first president of the division.

October 6, 1968 (2207)

The APA Council of Representatives admitted Division 31 (State Psychological Association Affairs).

October 9, 1968 (2208)

Roger Sperry's article "Hemisphere Deconnection and Unity in Conscious Awareness" was published in the *American Psychologist*.

October 15, 1968 (2209)

The Soviet Union authorized doctoral-level degrees in psychology. Previously, degrees were awarded in "pedagogical sciences" with a specialty in psychology.

October 24, 1968 (2210)

Public Law 90-636 created the National Institute on Neurological Disorders and Stroke by renaming the National Institute of Neurological Diseases.

November 23, 1968 (2211)

The first board meeting of APA Division 31 (State Psychological Association Affairs) was held. Rogers Wright was the founding president of Division 31.

December 2, 1968 (2212)

Daniel P. Kimble's article "Hippocampus and Internal Inhibition" was published in *Psychological Bulletin*.

December 13, 1968 (2213)

Garrett Hardin's article "The Tragedy of the Commons" was published in *Science*. The article used decision theory to explain why jointly held resources are over-exploited by individual users.

December 17, 1968 (2214)

The Louisiana Psychological Association was incorporated.

December 30, 1968 (2215)

The first meeting of the International Society for Developmental Psychobiology was held in Dallas.

January 17, 1969 (2216)

The National Medal of Science was presented to B. F. Skinner by President Lyndon Johnson. The date of the announcement of the award was January 2, 1969.

January 20, 1969 (2217)

The APA journal *Developmental Psychology* was first published. Boyd R. McCandless was the journal's editor.

January 22, 1969 (2218)

Entered in B. F. Skinner's notebook: "Utopias are easy to enjoy but not to produce . . . . One can picture a good life by analyzing one's feelings, but one can achieve it only by arranging environmental contingencies."

January 31, 1969 (2219)

Neal E. Miller's article "Learning of Visceral and Glandular Responses," describing instrumental conditioning of autonomic responses, was published in *Science*.

February 3, 1969 (2220)

The antipsychotic drug Quide (piperacetazine; Dow) was approved for use by the U.S. Food and Drug Administration.

February 13, 1969 (2221)

Jacob Cohen's article "Multiple Regression as a General Data-Analytic System" was published in *Psychological Bulletin*.

February 21, 1969 (2222)

The *Harvard Educational Review* published Arthur Jensen's article "How Much Can We Boost IQ and Scholastic Achievement?" The article provoked widespread research and debate over the roles of heredity, race, and environment in determining intelligence.

March 14, 1969 (2223)

The founding and first annual meeting of the National Association of School Psychologists was held in St. Louis.

March 15, 1969 (2224)

Indiana's psychologist certification law was passed on this date.

March 20, 1969 (2225)

The APA Publications Board and APA Council of Editors approved the use of metric measurements in APA journals, beginning in 1970.

March 23, 1969 (2226)

The California School of Professional Psychology was incorporated with two campuses: San Francisco and Los Angeles. A campus in San Diego was added in 1971, and a campus in Fresno was added in 1972.

April 1, 1969 (2227)

The journal the *Counseling Psychologist* was first published by Division 17 of the APA. John M. Whitely was the first editor of the journal.

April 23, 1969 (2228)

Donald T. Campbell's article "Reforms as Experiments" was published in the *American Psychologist*.

April 30, 1969 (2229)

The first West Virginia University Conference on Life-Span Developmental Psychology was held in Morgantown, West Virginia. Don C. Charles was the first of 19 speakers addressing the research and theory theme of the conference.

May 1, 1969 (2230)

The *National Association of School Psychologists Newsletter* was first published.

May 3, 1969 (2231)

Niccolò Machiavelli was featured on an Italian postage stamp. Machiavelli gave his name to a personality scale designed by Richard Christie and Florence Geis (1970) to measure the manipulative personality style.

May 8, 1969 (2232)

John Bowlby's book *Attachment and Loss* was published.

May 16, 1969 (2233)

The state of Rhode Island passed its psychology certification law.

May 22, 1969 (2234)

Allan Paivio's article "Mental Imagery in Associative Learning and Memory" was published in *Psychological Review*.

June 1, 1969 (2235)

The constitution of the American Psychology-Law Society was ratified. In September, 1969, the first official meeting was held, and Jay Ziskin was elected president. The society merged with APA Division 41 in 1984.

June 14, 1969 (2236)

Texas Governor Preston Smith signed Senate Bill 667, establishing certification and licensure of psychologists in the state.

August 2, 1969 (2237)

The first issue of the *APA Experimental Publication System* was published. The publication was a catalog of unreviewed and unedited manuscripts available for a fee. The system was eventually terminated because of the unreliable quality of documents.

August 11, 1969 (2238)

Albert Bandura's book *Principles of Behavior Modification* was published.

August 14, 1969 (2239)

Joseph Wolpe's book *Practice of Behavior Therapy* was published.

August 29, 1969 (2240)

The APA convention did *not* begin in Chicago, as originally scheduled. Because of Chicago police brutality in dealing with Vietnam War protesters at the Democratic National Convention in 1968, the APA moved its convention to Washington, DC, in 1969. The convention began on August 31.

September 1, 1969 (2241)

Members of the Black Students Psychological Association (BSPA) took the stage before George Miller's APA presidential address. BSPA president Gary Simpkins presented a request to address the Council of Representatives the next day with a list of demands. APA support of the activities of the BSPA followed.

September 1, 1969 (2242)

George A. Miller delivered his often-quoted "giving psychology away" APA presidential address in Washington, DC. The formal title of the address was "Psychology as a Means of Promoting Human Welfare."

September 3, 1969 (2243)

The first American Psychological Foundation National Media Award was presented to John Sharnik and Harry Morgan of CBS News for telecasts titled "LSD: The Spring Grove Experiment" and "The Farthest Frontier." The National Media Award replaced and broadened scope of the Distinguished Scientific Writing Award, begun in 1957 for representations of psychology in the print media.

September 10, 1969 (2244)

Robert R. Carkhuff's *Helping and Human Relations: A Primer for Lay and Professional Helpers* was published.

September 23, 1969 (2245)

The antidepressant drug Sinequan (doxepin; Pfizer) was approved for use by the U.S. Food and Drug Administration. Doxepin is a tricyclic antidepressant, possibly operating by inhibiting reuptake of the transmitter substances norepinephrine, dopamine, and serotonin. Adapin (Pennwalt) is another trade name for doxepin and was approved on January 31, 1972.

September 26, 1969 (2246)

The Soviet Union issued a postage stamp honoring Ivan Pavlov.

October 27, 1969 (2247)

University of California, Berkeley, student Prosenjit Poddar killed his former girlfriend Tatiana Tarasoff. Because Poddar had told his psychotherapist of his intentions, the California Supreme Court eventually decided that the therapist had an obligation to warn Tarasoff. The case had far-reaching implications for client–therapist relations.

November 10, 1969   (2248)
The first television broadcast of the children's educational show *Sesame Street* was made. *Sesame Street* intentionally employed principles of learning and developmental psychology in its presentation of academic and social skills. Edward L. Palmer led the *Sesame Street* research and evaluation team.

November 21, 1969   (2249)
The APA journal *Professional Psychology* was first published. The journal began as a joint project of the APA and APA Division 12 (Clinical Psychology), with Donald K. Freedheim as the editor. The title of the journal became *Professional Psychology: Research and Practice* in 1983. Norman Abeles was the new editor at that time.

December 10, 1969   (2250)
The state of Wisconsin approved its psychology licensure law. The law became effective on April 16, 1970.

December 15, 1969   (2251)
The Arkansas Psychological Association was incorporated.

VI

1970–1985
A PARTNERSHIP OF SCIENCE
AND PRACTICE

When considering events of the most recent decades, the line between history and current events becomes less distinct and the lasting significance of events becomes more difficult to judge. Some events of the recent past relate to legal and legislative issues, such as testing standards, experimenter ethics, and patients' rights, that have been of continuous concern to psychologists. Other issues, such as drug abuse, media violence, insurance coverage of independently provided services, and ethnic minority issues, might have been unfamiliar to the founders of the American Psychological Association (APA) or might have seemed to them improper concerns for a psychological scientist. Indeed, the current membership and the profession at large is divided on whether a professional organization should be actively involved in matters of legal advocacy and public policy. It is useful to separate these advocacy activities into two groups, the application of psychological knowledge to social issues and legal cases affecting the status and conduct of psychological practitioners.

The first hints of a more active involvement of psychologists in social issues appeared after World War II and continued to grow in the atmosphere of political idealism of the Kennedy administration and Vietnam War era. Associations, journals, and conferences were founded to represent the interests of Hispanic (Entries 2247 and 2509), Asian American (Entries 2345 and 2645), African American (Entries 2201, 2290, 2394, and 2446), gay and lesbian (Entries 2368, 2540, and 2567), and women psychologists (Entries 2278, 2292, and 2407). These groups brought attention not only to the need for equal opportunities within a profession historically dominated by White men, but they also pointed out that research and clinical practice tended to view heterosexual White men as the "normal" subjects or clients, producing research findings and clinical procedures that may not generalize well to other groups. These concerns were strong enough to stimulate formation of APA divisions representing the interests of women (Entries 2343, 2357, and 2367), gays and lesbians (Entries 2567, 2624, and 2630), and ethnic minorities (Entries 2664 and 2617) by the mid-1980s.

The impact of social issues advocacy on APA structure and procedures has been pervasive. APA journals did not have a policy of anonymous review of manuscripts before 1972, when women psychologists brought the issue of gender bias to the attention of journal editors (Entry 2333). Non-sexist language guidelines were adopted (Entries 2437 and 2470), and a policy of canceling the APA convention in states that had not ratified the Equal Rights Amendment (Entry 2474) followed soon afterward. The APA inaugurated minority fellowships for graduate study in psychology in 1975 (Entry 2417) and an Office of Ethnic and Cultural Affairs in 1979 (Entry 2504). Gay and lesbian practitioners, supported by the APA, were instrumental in removing homosexuality from the disorders listed in the *Diagnostic and Statistical Manual of Mental Disorders* of the American Psychiatric Association. A reading of any recent issue of the *APA Monitor* will show that social issues advocacy continues to engage the attention of the APA.

The second kind of advocacy, that which has asserted the right of psychologists to independent practice, has been both a reaction to court decisions affecting psychologists and a proactive effort by practitioners to achieve equality with other health care providers. In courts and legislatures, psychological practitioners fought to change the requirement of physician referral as a prerequisite of insurance payment of services and hospital staff privileges (e.g., Entries 2266, 2364, 2393, 2398, 2448, 2489, and 2548). Practitioners were alarmed when licensure laws were repealed in Florida and South Dakota and put on probation in Alaska (Entry 2523) because of "sunset" procedures. Renewed efforts restored licensure in those states.

Federal legislation such as the Education Amendments Act, creating the National Institute of Education (Entry 2330), the Education for All Handicapped Children Act (Public Law 94-142; Entry 2439), and the Children With Specific Learning Disabilities Act (Entry 2261) provided new support for applied research and services. Two legal advocacy organizations—the Council for the Advancement of the Psychological Professions and Sciences (Entry 2299) and the Association for the Advancement of Psychology (Entry 2375)—were formed in 1971 and 1974, respectively, and merged in 1975 (Entries 2345 and 2413). Today it is commonplace for psychologists and APA officers to testify before Congress, hold informative briefings for congressional staff personnel, and advocate letter writing campaigns to influence legislation.

The APA filed its first lawsuit during these years (Entry 2577), and its legal advocacy efforts have grown since then. Pivotal court cases during this period include the *Tarasoff* decision, compelling practitioners to take steps to protect people whom they believe may be harmed by a client (Entries 2247 and 2450); the *Pennsylvania Association for Retarded Children* decision, mandating minimally restrictive care of institutional clients (Entry 2326); and the *Larry P. v. Riles* case, banning the use of standardized instruments to identify children for placement in remedial classes (Entry 2414). All of these cases were decided by state courts, but the U.S. Supreme Court has affected psychological practice by, for example, banning indefinite confinement of those judged incompetent to be tried for their crimes (Entry 2329), striking the inappropriate use of intelligence tests in occupational screening (Entry 2426), affirming the right of institutionalized individuals to treatment (Entry 2427), and deciding that state insurance laws requiring mental health coverage were not preempted by the federal Employee Retirement Income Security Act, which did not have the requirement (Entry 2642).

Apart from the emergence of public policy advocacy, these 15 years saw such scientific developments as the first comprehensive computer statistics packages, BMD (Entry 2274) and SPSS (Entry 2276), the discovery of endorphins (Entry 2421), the division of the *Journal of Experimental Psychology* into three journals, and the approval for use of the antianxiety drug Halcion (Entry 2599).

In the world of psychological practice, the California School of Professional Psychology admitted and graduated its first students (Entries 2275 and 2335), the National Council of Professional Schools of Psychology was founded (Entry 2453), and the APA first extended its clinical program accreditation to a professional school of psychology. Behavior modification programs, especially those treating institutionalized clients, came under attack and were exonerated by investigative panels (Entries 2318, 2377, 2390, and 2429).

Finally, no discussion of these years would be complete without mention of the APA's purchase of the popular magazine, *Psychology Today* (Entries 2603 and 2605). This attempt to bring a high-quality presentation of psychological science and practice to the general public led the APA into a financial crisis in the mid-1980s.

January 23, 1970 (2252)
The journal *Cognitive Psychology* was first published by Academic Press. Walter Reitman was the editor of the journal.

February 3, 1970 (2253)
Delos D. Wickens's article "Encoding Categories of Words: An Empirical Approach to Meaning" was published in *Psychological Review*.

February 3, 1970 (2254)
Robert C. Bolles's article "Species-Specific Defense Reactions and Avoidance Learning" was published in *Psychological Review*. The article was later commended as a "citation classic" by *Current Contents*.

February 17, 1970 (2255)
Inge Broverman, Donald Broverman, Frank Clarkson, Paul Rosencrantz, and Susan Vogel's article "Sex-Role Stereotypes and Clinical Judgments of Mental Health" was published in the *Journal of Consulting and Clinical Psychology*.

February 17, 1970 (2256)
West Virginia passed its original bill regulating the licensing of psychologists. West Virginia was the 42nd state with a licensing or certification law.

February 27, 1970 (2257)
The antipsychotic drug Serentil (mesoridazine; Sandoz) was approved for use by the U.S. Food and Drug Administration. Mesoridazine is a phenothiazine, acting to reduce neuronal inputs to the reticular formation and depress the activity of the hypothalamus.

April 6, 1970 (2258)
The National Commission on Accreditation (NCA) recognized the APA as an accrediting body in general professional psychology. The action resolved problems

with the NCA over programs in school psychology. The University of Texas was the first APA-approved program in school psychology (1970).

April 6, 1970 (2259)
Lithium carbonate, an effective treatment for bipolar mood disorders, was first approved for use by the U.S. Food and Drug Administration under the trade names Eskalith (Smith, Kline, and French), Lithonate (Reid-Rowell), and Lithane (Roerig and Miles). The physiological action of lithium remains unknown, but it may affect several neurotransmitter systems.

April 7, 1970 (2260)
The drug Dalmane (flurazepam; Hoffman-LaRoche) was approved for use by the U.S. Food and Drug Administration. Flurazepam is a benzodiazepine used as an antianxiety agent and as a sedative.

April 13, 1970 (2261)
The Children With Specific Learning Disabilities Act, providing funds for research, professional training, and services, was passed by Congress. It appeared as Title VI(G) of the Elementary and Secondary Education Act of 1970 (Public Law 91-230).

April 17, 1970 (2262)
The journal *Behavior Genetics* was first published. The journal was begun by Steven Vandenberg and John DeFries and was adopted in 1973 by the Behavior Genetics Association as its official journal.

April 22, 1970 (2263)
The journal *Behavior Therapy* was first published by the Association for the Advancement of Behavior Therapy. Cyril M. Franks was the editor of the journal.

May 1, 1970 (2264)
The U.S. Office of Education recognized the APA as a nationally recognized accrediting agency. The APA had been evaluating programs in clinical and counseling psychology since the early 1950s.

May 25, 1970 (2265)
Sex behavior researchers William Masters and Virginia Johnson appeared on the cover of *Time* magazine.

June 23, 1970 (2266)
The Civilian Health and Medical Program of the Uniformed Services (CHAMPUS) was directed to recognize the independent practice of qualified psychologists, free of medical referral, in all of the states. This administrative policy of the Department of Defense was not written into federal legislation until 1976.

July 1, 1970 (2267)

The Black Students Psychological Association (BSPA) office opened at the APA headquarters building. Ernestine Thomas was the first BSPA administrator.

July 14, 1970 (2268)

Lee J. Cronbach and Lita Furby's article "How Should We Measure Change—Or Should We?" was published in *Psychological Bulletin*.

August 27, 1970 (2269)

The first annual meeting of the Association for Consumer Research was held at the Murray D. Lincoln Campus Center at the University of Massachusetts at Amherst. Robert Perloff, later president of the APA (1985), was elected president of the new organization.

August 31, 1970 (2270)

The portrait of developmental and educational psychologist Maria Montessori appeared on an Italian postage stamp.

September 4, 1970 (2271)

The first APA Division 16 (School Psychology) Distinguished Service Award was awarded posthumously to Edward L. French for "innovative practice in administration of psychological services, policy determination, research, and training."

September 4, 1970 (2272)

The first "open forum" meeting was held at an APA convention. The traditional reading of the reports of the treasurer and executive officer was replaced by an opportunity to address officers in a town meeting format. Women's issues such as APA office space, representation on policy-making boards, and child care at conventions dominated the first open forum.

September 5, 1970 (2273)

The first American Psychological Foundation Distinguished Contributions to Education in Psychology Awards were presented to Fred S. Keller and Freda Gould Rebelsky at the APA convention in Miami Beach.

September 16, 1970 (2274)

Wilfrid J. Dixon's *BMD Manual* (2nd ed.) was published. BMD was one of the first comprehensive statistical packages for the computer.

September 21, 1970 (2275)

Classes began at the California School of Professional Psychology's (CSPP) initial campuses in San Francisco and Los Angeles. The CSPP was the nation's first independent professional school of psychology.

September 25, 1970 (2276)

Norman H. Nie, Dale H. Bent, and C. Hadlai Hull's first Statistical Package for the Social Sciences (SPSS) manual was published. Revisions of this computer statistical package continue to be widely used by behavioral scientists.

September 28, 1970 (2277)

A steering committee to promote the formation of APA Division 33 (Mental Retardation and Developmental Disabilities) was appointed during the American Association on Mental Deficiency Region 10 meeting.

October 3, 1970 (2278)

Although they were not on the agenda, women psychologists presented the APA Council of Representatives with a set of proposals to recognize and expand the role of women in psychology and the APA. The Council formed a Task Force on the Status of Women in Psychology. Helen S. Astin chaired the task force. An assertive women's presence in the APA began with this event.

October 13, 1970 (2279)

Senator John McClelland led the U.S. Senate in adopting a resolution to reject the report of the President's Commission on Obscenity and Pornography. Basing its findings on extensive psychological and sociological research, the commission had found no evidence for a causal connection between pornography and criminal behavior or deviant sexual behavior.

October 15, 1970 (2280)

Julius Axelrod, Sir Bernard Katz, and Ulf von Euler won the Nobel prize for their studies of the chemistry of nervous transmission. These studies contributed to the understanding of the biology of behavior.

October 30, 1970 (2281)

The Services and Facilities for the Mentally Retarded and Persons With Other Developmental Disabilities Act (Public Law 91-517) provided federal support for new facilities and a national advisory council.

October 31, 1970 (2282)

The first Educational Testing Service Award for Distinguished Service for Measurement was given to psychologist Everet F. Lindquist.

December 15, 1970 (2283)

The organizing meeting of the Jean Piaget Society was held. The idea for the society was first advanced by Lois Macomber of Temple University. Macomber was also the first president of the association.

January 8, 1971   (2284)
The Practice of Psychology Act for the District of Columbia (Public Law 91-657) was signed by President Nixon. This licensing legislation had been introduced in Congress by Senator Alan Bible (D–NV). Licensure legislation introduced in 1966 and 1967 had not been approved by Congress.

January 18, 1971   (2285)
The Jean Piaget Society was incorporated in Pennsylvania, marking the official founding of the organization.

February 27, 1971   (2286)
The state of Montana passed its licensing law for psychologists. The law became effective on January 1, 1972.

March 8, 1971   (2287)
In *Griggs v. Duke Power Co.*, the U.S. Supreme Court ruled that the irrelevant use of intelligence tests as employment screening instruments constituted racial discrimination and was unconstitutional.

March 27, 1971   (2288)
The journal of the National Association of School Psychologists, now named *School Psychology Review*, was first published. Its first title was *School Psychology Digest*.

April 27, 1971   (2289)
Eleanor Jack Gibson was elected to the National Academy of Sciences. Gibson was the second woman psychologist elected to the Academy. The first was Margaret Floy Washburn in 1931.

May 5, 1971   (2290)
The first national meeting of the Black Students Psychological Association was held in Atlanta. Ernestine Thomas was the first national administrator of the organization.

May 7, 1971   (2291)
The APA *Monitor* announced that the membership had approved the revised Albee system of voting for members of the APA Council of Representatives. The system calls for members to allocate 10 votes among division and state representatives.

May 7, 1971   (2292)
The APA *Monitor* reported the first meeting of the Association for Women in Psychology in early 1971. No traditional officers were elected, but Joan Berman, chair of the External Communications Committee, provided the report.

May 8, 1971 (2293)
Grenada issued a postage stamp honoring American functionalist psychologist and educational philosopher John Dewey.

May 17, 1971 (2294)
Washington became the first state to pass legislation banning discrimination on the basis of gender. Gender discrimination became a focus of the public policy interests of psychologists during this period.

May 26, 1971 (2295)
The first annual symposium of the Jean Piaget Society was held at Temple University. The 700 charter members of the organization were addressed by Piaget and Barbel Inhelder at the first plenary session. Lois Macomber was the first president of the society.

June 17, 1971 (2296)
The petition to create APA Division 32 (Humanistic Psychology) was submitted. Don Gibbons was instrumental in forming the division.

July 4, 1971 (2297)
The first Symposium of the International Society for the Study of Behavioral Development was held in Nijmegen, The Netherlands.

July 19, 1971 (2298)
The APA Monitor announced a trial run of the Current Research Summaries project, designed to compensate for publication lag. Readers of journal articles could request summaries of last-minute findings submitted by authors. The Journal of Counseling Psychology, Journal of Experimental Psychology, and Journal of Educational Psychology participated.

July 19, 1971 (2299)
The APA Monitor reported the organizational meeting of the Council for the Advancement of the Psychological Professions and Sciences, a political advocacy organization, in Washington, DC. Rogers Wright was elected president.

August 11, 1971 (2300)
Allan Paivio's book Imagery and Verbal Processes was published.

August 14, 1971 (2301)
Philip Zimbardo's Stanford prison experiment began with the mock arrests of college student volunteers who had been assigned the roles of prisoners in the simulation study. The roles so strongly controlled the behavior of the mock guards and prisoners that the experiment was terminated on August 20, less than halfway through the two weeks planned for the study.

September 3, 1971 (2302)

U.S. Senator Fred Harris (D–OK) received the American Psychological Foundation Distinguished Achievement Award, the first nonpsychologist so honored. Harris was a strong supporter of social science research.

September 4, 1971 (2303)

APA President Kenneth E. Clark announced to the APA Publications and Communications Caucus the online availability of *Psychological Abstracts* tapes for the years 1967–1970. The service was called Psychological Abstracts Direct Access Terminal.

September 4, 1971 (2304)

Senator Fred Harris (D–OK) received the American Board of Professional Psychology Award for Contributions to Psychology. Harris was a consistent supporter of social and behavioral science legislation.

September 5, 1971 (2305)

The APA Council of Representatives admitted Division 32 (Humanistic Psychology). The organizing meeting of the new division was held on the same day at the Sheraton Park Hotel in Washington, DC.

September 5, 1971 (2306)

Leona Tyler was awarded the Edward K. Strong Memorial Gold Medal for her theoretical and practical work in vocational interest testing.

September 20, 1971 (2307)

B. F. Skinner appeared on the cover of *Time* magazine.

September 24, 1971 (2308)

Albert Bandura's book *Social Learning Theory* was published.

October 3, 1971 (2309)

Entered in B. F. Skinner's notebook: "Systems will always need change but not necessarily in the style of rebellion. Rebels are defined by their aversive techniques, not by the fact that they try to change things."

October 27, 1971 (2310)

The first meeting of the Society for Neuroscience was held in Washington, DC. Psychologist Neal Miller was president at this first meeting.

November 9, 1971 (2311)

The state of Massachusetts approved its psychology licensure law.

November 10, 1971 (2312)

The first meeting of the Society for Computers in Psychology (SCP) was held at St. Louis University under the sponsorship of the National Science Foundation.

The first president was Donald I. Tepas. The SCP has traditionally met on the day preceding the meeting of the Psychonomic Society.

November 12, 1971 (2313)

The *APA Monitor* announced that three new information services were available: PASAR (Psychological Abstracts Search and Retrieval) provided literature searches by mail, PADAT (Psychological Abstracts Direct Access Terminal) allowed direct on-line access to the *Psychological Abstracts* database, and PATELL (Psychological Abstracts Tape Edition Lease or Licensing) leased database tapes to subscriber institutions. Syracuse University was the first PATELL customer.

November 15, 1971 (2314)

Daniel Berlyne's book *Aesthetics and Psychobiology* was published.

November 23, 1971 (2315)

The APA's first Journal Supplement Abstract Service *Catalog of Selected Documents in Psychology* was published. The publication listed sources of well-designed replications, technical reports, reviews of controversial issues, annotated bibliographies, and other material of interest that was ineligible for conventional journal publication.

November 29, 1971 (2316)

An early form of the System of Multicultural Pluralistic Assessment was published by Jane Mercer and June Lewis. The instrument, at that time, was titled the Adaptive Behavior Inventory for Children.

December 12, 1971 (2317)

The *Journal of Clinical Child Psychology* was first published by Division 12 (Clinical Psychology) of the APA. Gertrude J. Williams was the journal's editor.

December 15, 1971 (2318)

U.S. Representative Cornelius Gallagher took the floor of the House to attack federal grant support of B. F. Skinner while Skinner wrote *Beyond Freedom and Dignity*. Gallagher evoked an image of a society whose citizens are conditioned by "an elite, composed of mirror-images of Dr. Skinner, who will make this choice so absolutely essential to our future."

December 16, 1971 (2319)

The Institute of Psychology of the USSR Academy of Sciences was founded by Resolution #1076 of the Academy of Sciences Presidium. The USSR Council of Ministers had authorized the institute on December 6, 1971, with Decree 2602. Boris Fiodorovitch Lomov was appointed the first director of the institute.

December 31, 1971 (2320)
The report *Television and Growing Up: The Effects of Televised Violence* was presented to the U.S. surgeon general. Psychologists Irving L. Janis and Alberta E. Siegel served on the committee that wrote the report. The report both summarized and generated much research in social psychology.

January 3, 1972 (2321)
Allen Newell and Herbert Simon's book *Human Problem Solving* was published.

March 23, 1972 (2322)
The state of Pennsylvania adopted its licensure law for psychologists, the Professional Psychologists Practice Act.

April 6, 1972 (2323)
The petition to create APA Division 33 (Mental Retardation and Developmental Disabilities) was submitted. Thomas McCullough and Allen Barclay were instrumental in creating the division.

April 18, 1972 (2324)
The *APA Monitor* reported an emergency ruling by Federal District Court Judge Frank M. Johnson, Jr., in *Wyatt v. Stickney*. The case was brought on behalf of people with mental retardation in two Alabama institutions when staff cuts resulted in intolerable conditions. The judge ordered improvements while the case was being heard, and Raymond D. Fowler supervised the improvements.

April 18, 1972 (2325)
The *APA Monitor* reported that APA Division 12 (Clinical Psychology) dropped its division membership requirement of completion of an APA-approved clinical internship.

May 5, 1972 (2326)
In *Pennsylvania Association for Retarded Children v. Commonwealth of Pennsylvania*, the state court assured educational access to retarded children. Commonly called the "PARC decision," this action fundamentally altered school procedures and the roles of special educators in the schools.

May 5, 1972 (2327)
Peter Lindsay and Donald Norman's book *Human Information Processing: An Introduction to Psychology* was published.

May 18, 1972 (2328)
The Menninger Conference on Postdoctoral Education in Clinical Psychology began in Topeka, Kansas. The conference was attended by 42 representatives of postdoctoral training programs, university departments of psychology, the APA, and the National Institute of Mental Health.

June 7, 1972 (2329)

In its ruling on *Jackson v. Indiana*, the U.S. Supreme Court declared it unconstitutional to indefinitely confine persons accused of crimes but judged mentally incompetent to stand trial.

June 23, 1972 (2330)

The National Institute of Education, created to conduct and support research in education, was established by Title XIV of Public Law 92-318, the Education Amendments Act of 1972.

June 23, 1972 (2331)

Ohio passed a licensure law for psychologists, the 46th state to do so.

June 23, 1972 (2332)

The drug Tranxene (clorazepate; Abbott Laboratories) was approved for use by the U.S. Food and Drug Administration. Clorazepate is a benzodiazepine and is used as an antianxiety agent and as a sedative.

July 1, 1972 (2333)

The APA's *Journal of Counseling Psychology* and *Psychological Bulletin* became the second and third APA journals to adopt anonymous reviewing practices. The first was the *American Psychologist*, edited by Charles Gersoni, in January 1972. This practice, now common, was first instigated as a result of claims of gender discrimination.

August 19, 1972 (2334)

The first of two articles on psychologist Neal E. Miller was published by the *New Yorker* magazine. The articles, written by Gerald Jonas, won the first APA National Media Grand Prix Award in 1973. The award gave special recognition to one of the five winners of APA National Media awards for psychology-related presentations in periodicals, films, television, radio, and books.

August 28, 1972 (2335)

The first doctorates were awarded by the California School of Professional Psychology (CSPP), the nation's first independent professional school of psychology. These graduates had entered CSPP six trimesters earlier with master's degrees, advanced training, and state licensure.

September 2, 1972 (2336)

The first APA Board of Professional Affairs Award for Distinguished Professional Contributions was made at the APA annual meeting in Honolulu. The recipient was Carl Rogers. His award address, delivered August 28, 1973, was titled "The Emerging Person: A New Revolution."

September 3, 1972 (2337)
Georg von Békésy, physiologist and winner of the Nobel prize, gave the invited address to the APA annual meeting in Honolulu. His topic was "Edge Phenomena in Different Sense Organs."

September 4, 1972 (2338)
The first student travel scholarships to the annual meeting of the APA sponsored by an APA division were presented by APA Division 29 (Psychotherapy). Four students were honored with the awards at the APA convention in Honolulu.

September 5, 1972 (2339)
The APA Council of Representatives admitted Division 33 (Mental Retardation and Developmental Disabilities).

October 23, 1972 (2340)
The Pennsylvania Board of Examiners in Psychology began operation.

October 25, 1972 (2341)
The publication of an operations memo marked the beginnings of Operation START (Special Treatment and Rehabilitation Training). Operation START was a trial application of behavior modification techniques at the Federal Medical Center for Prisoners in Springfield, Missouri. The program was canceled in February 1974 amid protests over the abusive behavior of guards.

October 30, 1972 (2342)
Title XI of the Social Security Amendments Act of 1972 created Professional Standards Review Organizations. In 1974, the APA created its Committee on Professional Standards Review to coordinate with mental health delivery review organizations.

November 22, 1972 (2343)
The organizational meeting of the group that would become APA Division 35 (Psychology of Women) was held. The first president was Elizabeth Douvan.

December 5, 1972 (2344)
The APA granted its first accreditation for doctoral programs in clinical psychology to a professional school of psychology, the Fuller Theological Seminary Graduate School of Psychology in Pasadena, California.

December 14, 1972 (2345)
The Asian American Psychological Association was founded. Stanley Sue organized the founding meeting, and Derald Sue was elected the first president.

December 26, 1972 (2346)
Fergus I. M. Craik and Robert S. Lockhart's article "Levels of Processing: A Framework for Memory Research" was published in the *Journal of Verbal Learning and Verbal Behavior*.

January 5, 1973 (2347)
The petition to create APA Division 34 (Population and Environmental Psychology) was submitted. Sidney Newman headed the petitioning group.

January 17, 1973 (2348)
The journal *Memory and Cognition*, edited by George E. Briggs, was first published by the Psychonomic Society.

January 19, 1973 (2349)
David Rosenhan's article "On Being Sane in Insane Places" was published in *Science*. Rosenhan and seven others gained admission to mental hospitals by imitating schizophrenic behavior. Once admitted, they resumed normal behavior but found that the staff members could not detect their normalcy. The article is often cited in introductory texts.

January 31, 1973 (2350)
The *Bulletin of the Psychonomic Society* was first published, with Clifford T. Morgan as its editor.

February 8, 1973 (2351)
After a presentation by Charles Silverstein, the Nomenclature Committee of the American Psychiatric Association agreed to review the status of homosexuality as a psychiatric disorder. This was an important step in the eventual deletion of homosexuality as a pathological condition in the *Diagnostic and Statistical Manual of Mental Disorders*.

February 26, 1973 (2352)
The journal *Animal Learning and Behavior* was first published by the Psychonomic Society. Abram Amsel was the first editor of the journal.

March 9, 1973 (2353)
In an article in *Science,* Candace Pert and Solomon Snyder of the Johns Hopkins Medical School announced the first biochemical identification of opiate receptors in the brain. Eric Simon (New York University) and Lars Terenius (Uppsala University) are credited with concurrent discovery. Discovery of the brain's natural opioides, or endorphins, followed in 1975.

March 22, 1973 (2354)
Albert Bandura's book *Aggression: A Social Learning Analysis* was published.

April 1, 1973 (2355)
This was the last day of an APA Council of Representatives meeting later described as a "watershed" meeting. In an *APA Monitor* article, George Albee cited bloc voting domination of newer divisions (Divisions 16–32) and the new requirement

of presidential candidate position papers as signs of a shift from "an educational-scientific society to a kind of professional guild à la AMA [American Medical Association]."

April 6, 1973 (2356)

The E. F. Lindquist Center for Measurement was dedicated at the University of Iowa. Lindquist was a noteworthy psychometrician and statistician. He developed the Iowa Tests of Basic Skills and the American College Test. With Phillip Rulon, Lindquist invented the first electronic test scoring machine (1955).

May 9, 1973 (2357)

The petition to create APA Division 35 (Psychology of Women) was submitted. Nancy Anderson headed the petitioning group.

May 14, 1973 (2358)

The Seventh Annual Meeting of the North American Society for the Psychology of Sport and Physical Activity (NASPSPA) began in Monticello, Illinois. This was the first NASPSPA meeting held independently of the annual meeting of the American Association of Health, Physical Education, and Recreation. Ranier Martens of the University of Illinois organized the meeting.

June 15, 1973 (2359)

National Autistic Children's Week was declared.

July 10, 1973 (2360)

The Wayne County (Michigan) Circuit Court rendered a landmark verdict in *Kaimowitz v. Michigan Department of Mental Health.* The court ruled that a sexual psychopath prisoner was incapable of freely consenting to participation in a study comparing drug therapy with amygdalectomy in the control of his condition. The study was ruled unconstitutional.

July 22, 1973 (2361)

Oregon's Governor Tom McCall signed into law Senate Bill 275, instituting the state's current licensure form of psychologist regulation. The law replaced regulation by credential, which protected the use of the title *psychologist* but did not regulate the practice itself.

July 25, 1973 (2362)

The APA Conference on Patterns and Levels of Professional Training began in Vail, Colorado. The Vail Conference was the first to strongly endorse the professional model of graduate training and the PsyD degree.

July 27, 1973 (2363)

Daniel Kahneman's book *Attention and Effort* was published.

August 17, 1973   (2364)

The Council for the Advancement of the Psychological Professions and Sciences filed a class action suit against Blue Cross/Blue Shield. The "Blues" would not cover psychological services for federal employees without a physician's referral. The suit was eventually dismissed when federal legislation (Public Law 93-363) removed the referral requirement.

August 26, 1973   (2365)

The Psychologists Interested in Religious Issues board voted to seek APA divisional status. This was followed by a vote of the members on February 15, 1974. The group eventually became APA Division 36 (Psychology of Religion).

August 30, 1973   (2366)

The APA Council of Representatives admitted Division 34 (Population and Environmental Psychology). Vaida Thompson was the first divisional president.

August 30, 1973   (2367)

The APA Council of Representatives admitted Division 35 (Psychology of Women).

August 30, 1973   (2368)

The Association of Gay Psychologists' Caucus held its first meeting at the APA convention in Montreal. This was the first advocacy effort on behalf of gay and lesbian psychologists and led to an APA task force on lesbian and gay concerns.

August 31, 1973   (2369)

The first APA Distinguished Contribution for Applications of Psychology Award was presented at the APA convention in Montreal to Conrad Kraft of the Boeing Company for his work on perceptual characteristics of night landing approaches.

September 17, 1973   (2370)

The island nation of Grenada issued postage stamps honoring Sigmund Freud and Carl Jung. Freud was featured on a 3¢ stamp, Jung on a 35¢ stamp.

October 8, 1973   (2371)

The first World Mental Health Conference was held in Sydney, Australia.

December 10, 1973   (2372)

Nobel prizes were awarded to Konrad Lorenz, Karl von Frisch, and Nikolaas Tinbergen for their ethological studies of animal behavior.

December 15, 1973   (2373)

The American Psychiatric Association removed homosexuality from the *Diagnostic and Statistical Manual of Mental Disorders'* list of psychiatric disorders. The nomenclature was revised to "sexual orientation disturbance," which "by itself, does not necessarily constitute a psychiatric disorder."

January 18, 1974 (2374)

The antipsychotic drug Moban (molindone; DuPont) was approved for use by the U.S. Food and Drug Administration. Molindone is a major tranquilizer that reduces activity in the reticular activating system.

January 19, 1974 (2375)

The APA Council of Representatives established a legal advocacy organization, the Association of American Psychologists, later named the Association for the Advancement of Psychology (AAP). The council had earlier declined endorsement of an existing advocacy group, the Council for the Advancement of the Psychological Professions and Sciences.

January 21, 1974 (2376)

The National Institute of Mental Health released a report on psychosurgery, concluding that current techniques should be considered experimental and that psychosurgery should not be used on prisoners or individuals incapable of freely giving their informed consent.

February 14, 1974 (2377)

The U.S. Law Enforcement Assistance Administration announced the termination of behavior modification programs in federal prisons. On the next day, the APA called for the "evaluation of the use and misuse of behavior modification procedures in the criminal justice system." Sidney Bijou headed the APA panel.

February 15, 1974 (2378)

The New Jersey Higher Education Board authorized the New Jersey School of Applied and Professional Psychology at Rutgers University. It was the first graduate school of psychology, independent but coordinated with a university, offering the PsyD degree. Samuel B. Kutash was instrumental in founding the Rutgers program.

March 6, 1974 (2379)

The *APA Monitor* announced the APA's receipt of the National Science Foundation Human Behavior Curriculum for the Secondary Schools grant. John Bare of Carleton College headed the project, which was abruptly terminated in March 1976, possibly because of congressional criticism of another social science curriculum project titled "Man: A Course of Study."

March 6, 1974 (2380)

The bylaws of the newly created Association of American Psychologists, later named the Association for the Advancement of Psychology (AAP), appeared in the *APA Monitor*. The AAP is a legal advocacy group that represents the interests of psychologists.

April 17, 1974 (2381)

Immanuel Kant appeared on a West German postage stamp.

April 22, 1974 (2382)

The Sudden Infant Death Syndrome Act (Public Law 93-270) was signed. The act provided counseling services for parents and provided for research on the links between maternal health and mental retardation in children.

May 1, 1974 (2383)

The Midwestern Association for Behavior Analysis (MABA) was founded. Israel Goldiamond was the first president of the organization. MABA later became the Association for Behavior Analysis International.

May 14, 1974 (2384)

Public Law 93-282 was passed, creating the Alcohol, Drug Abuse, and Mental Health Administration (ADHMA) and two new institutes: the National Institute on Alcohol Abuse and Alcoholism and the National Institute on Drug Abuse. The National Institute of Mental Health was the third, and biggest, institute in the ADHMA.

May 28, 1974 (2385)

The state of Iowa approved its psychology licensure law. The law became effective on July 1, 1975.

May 30, 1974 (2386)

The U.S. Department of Health, Education, and Welfare published the final form of its strengthened standards for the protection of human participants in the *Federal Register*. Special provisions were made for participants with limited ability to give informed consent: children, prisoners, and mental patients.

May 30, 1974 (2387)

The first meeting of the Council of the National Register of Health Service Providers in Psychology was held. The first national register was published on July 15, 1975.

June 1, 1974 (2388)

The National Register of Health Service Providers in Psychology was founded.

June 5, 1974 (2389)

The petition to create APA Division 36 (Psychologists Interested in Religious Issues; now called Psychology of Religion) was submitted. Virginia Staudt Sexton headed the petitioning group.

July 12, 1974   (2390)

The APA Commission on Behavior Modification, chaired by Sidney Bijou, first met to examine the ethical use of behavior modification in prisons. It found that some unethical methods were wrongly labeled *behavior modification*, that some protests were raised because the procedure actually controlled behavior, and that following existing ethical standards would resolve most problems.

July 12, 1974   (2391)

President Nixon signed Public Law 93-348, providing protection for human participants in biomedical and behavioral research. Senator Edward Kennedy was primary sponsor of the bill. Two psychologists, Joseph Brady and Eliot Stellar, were named to the first National Commission for the Protection of Human Subjects of Biomedical and Behavioral Research.

July 25, 1974   (2392)

The first edition of the APA's book *Thesaurus of Psychological Index Terms* was published. Robert G. Kinkade edited this reference work.

July 30, 1974   (2393)

Federal "freedom of choice" legislation (Public Law 93-363) was signed by President Nixon. The law removed the requirement for physician referral or supervision of psychological services paid for by the Federal Employees Health Benefit Act. Clinical psychologists achieved parity with other providers of health services for 8.5 million federal employees nationwide.

August 25, 1974   (2394)

The *Journal of Black Psychology* was first published by the Association of Black Psychologists. William David Smith was editor of the journal.

August 30, 1974   (2395)

The first APA Master Lecture was presented by Kurt Schlesinger on "Behavior Genetics: Current Status and Perspective" at the 82nd Annual Convention in New Orleans.

August 31, 1974   (2396)

The first APA Distinguished Scientific Awards for Early Career Contributions were presented at the APA convention in New Orleans to Norman T. Adler, John M. Neale, and Michael Turvey. The Early Career Award is presented for significant contributions by psychologists not more than 6 years beyond their doctoral degree.

September 4, 1974   (2397)

The APA Council of Representatives approved the APA's *Standards for Providers of Psychological Services.* Alfred M. Wellner (1970–1971) and Durrand F. Jacobs (1972–1974) chaired the standards committee. The title was changed to *General Guidelines for Providers of Psychological Services* with the 1987 revision.

September 7, 1974 (2398)

The Federal Employee Work Injury Compensation program was expanded by Public Law 93-416 to include coverage of psychological services.

September 19, 1974 (2399)

The first APA Tennis Tournament began in Santa Fe, New Mexico. The tournament appears not to have endured as an annual event.

October 8, 1974 (2400)

The first National Conference on Experiential Education was held at Estes Park, Colorado.

October 9, 1974 (2401)

The first Interamerican Congress of Clinical Psychology began in Porto Alegre, Brazil.

October 21, 1974 (2402)

The APA's Division 2 (Teaching of Psychology) first published its journal, *Teaching of Psychology*. Robert S. Daniel was the journal's editor.

November 9, 1974 (2403)

James J. Jenkins's article "Remember That Old Theory of Memory? Well, Forget It!" was published in the *American Psychologist*.

November 22, 1974 (2404)

Daryl Bem and Andrea Allen's article "On Predicting Some of the People Some of the Time: The Search for Cross-Situational Consistencies in Behavior" was published in *Psychological Review*.

December 5, 1974 (2405)

The television documentary "Primate" appeared on Public Broadcasting System stations. The show depicted callous treatment of primate subjects at the Yerkes Primate Research Center. In the ensuing public outcry, researchers charged the producer, Frederick Wiseman, with bias and misrepresentation.

December 14, 1974 (2406)

Statistician Adolphe Quételet appeared on a postage stamp issued by Belgium.

December 26, 1974 (2407)

Eleanor E. Maccoby and Carol N. Jacklin's book *Psychology of Sex Differences* was published.

December 31, 1974 (2408)

The "Buckley Amendment" to the Elementary and Secondary Education Act of 1965 was signed by President Ford. The amendment made school records available to parents and college students and altered school counseling practices. The regulations had been published in the *Federal Register* of June 17, 1976, with an effective date of November 19, 1973.

January 8, 1975 (2409)

The drug Nembutol (pentobarbital sodium; Abbott Laboratories) was approved for use by the U.S. Food and Drug Administration. The first approval of pentobarbitol sodium was awarded on August 31, 1939, to Premo Pharmaceuticals. Pentobarbitol is a barbiturate used as an antianxiety agent and as a sedative.

January 9, 1975 (2410)

The *Journal of Experimental Psychology: Animal Behavior Processes* was first published by the APA. Allen R. Wagner served as editor. The new journal was created by division of the content of the earlier *Journal of Experimental Psychology*.

January 20, 1975 (2411)

The *Journal of Experimental Psychology: Human Perception and Performance* was first published by the APA. Michael I. Posner was the journal's editor. The journal was one of four created by dividing the content of the *Journal of Experimental Psychology*.

January 20, 1975 (2412)

The *Journal of Experimental Psychology: Human Learning and Memory* was first published by the APA, with Lyle E. Bourne as editor. Its content had previously been part of the *Journal of Experimental Psychology*. The title of the journal was changed to *Journal of Experimental Psychology: Learning, Memory, and Cognition* in 1982.

January 26, 1975 (2413)

The APA Council of Representatives urged two competing political action bodies, the Council for the Advancement of the Psychological Professions and Sciences and the Association for the Advancement of Psychology, to merge and form "a single advocacy organization for the good of American psychology." The merger occurred on September 2, 1975.

February 5, 1975 (2414)

The California Board of Education declared a moratorium on the use of intelligence tests for placement of students into programs for the educable mentally retarded. The action followed the California Supreme Court's decision in *Larry P. v. Wilson Riles* that racial bias resulted from the practice. The same case was made for Hispanic students in *Diana v. State Board of Education*.

February 25, 1975 (2415)

The antipsychotic drug Loxitane (loxapine; Lederle Laboratories) was approved for use by the U.S. Food and Drug Administration. Loxitane was the first of the dibenzoxazepine class of antipsychotic drugs.

March 21, 1975   (2416)
The first Annual Research Conference on the Profoundly Mentally Retarded was held at the Monterey Peninsula, California.

March 28, 1975   (2417)
The *APA Monitor* announced the APA Minority Fellowship Program, funded with a $1 million grant from the National Institute for Mental Health Center for Minority Group Mental Health Programs, headed by psychologist Dalmas Taylor. The first awards were given to 24 students.

April 15, 1975   (2418)
Richard F. Thompson's text *Introduction to Physiological Psychology* was published.

April 24, 1975   (2419)
U.S. Representative John Conlan (R–AZ) attacked "Man, A Course of Study" (MACOS), a federally funded fifth-grade social science curriculum developed by Jerome Bruner and John Bare that included coverage of non-Western cultures. Representative Conlan charged that MACOS "brainwashes children with a dishonest view of man," and the MACOS grant was eventually canceled.

April 26, 1975   (2420)
Sensory psychologist Dorothea Jameson was elected to the National Academy of Sciences. Jameson was the third woman psychologist elected to the Academy.

May 2, 1975   (2421)
Biochemist John Hughes, working at the University of Aberdeen, Scotland, announced the discovery of the first endogenous opiate (endorphin), which he called "enkephalin." Endogenous opiates are naturally occurring pain reducers whose action is mimicked by morphine.

May 31, 1975   (2422)
The New Directions for Research on Women conference began in Madison, Wisconsin. The conference was organized by Julia Sherman and Florence Denmark of the APA's Committee on Women and chaired by Martha Mednick. The National Institute of Mental Health and the Ford Foundation sponsored the conference.

June 4, 1975   (2423)
The antiepileptic drug Klonopin (clonazepam; Hoffman-LaRoche) was approved for use by the U.S. Food and Drug Administration. Clonazepam is a benzodiazepine used primarily for absence, or petit mal, seizures.

June 6, 1975   (2424)
The first National Conference on Rational–Emotive Therapy and Cognitive Behavior Modification began in Chicago.

June 25, 1975　　　　　　　　　　　　　　　　　　　　　　　　(2425)

The first Vermont Conference on Primary Prevention of Psychopathology opened in Burlington, Vermont.

June 25, 1975　　　　　　　　　　　　　　　　　　　　　　　　(2426)

The U.S. Supreme Court ruled, in *Moody v. Albemarle Paper Company*, that inappropriate psychological testing had been used for the purpose of racial discrimination. The practice was declared unconstitutional and back pay was awarded to the plaintiffs.

June 26, 1975　　　　　　　　　　　　　　　　　　　　　　　　(2427)

In *O'Connor v. Donaldson*, the U.S. Supreme Court ruled that a nondangerous mentally ill person capable of living outside of an institution cannot be institutionalized without being provided treatment. In this case, O'Connor had been held for almost 15 years for "care, maintenance, and treatment" in a Florida state hospital.

June 29, 1975　　　　　　　　　　　　　　　　　　　　　　　　(2428)

The APA Board of Directors voted to join the American Association for the Advancement of Science (AAAS) in sponsoring a Congressional Science Fellow, representing the interests of psychology during a legislative internship. AAAS Congressional Science Fellow Pamela Ebert, a University of Georgia specialist in visual perception, helped to persuade the board.

July 9, 1975　　　　　　　　　　　　　　　　　　　　　　　　(2429)

The National Institute of Mental Health released "Behavior Modification: Perspective on a Current Issue," the government's first study on behavior modification. The report indicated success in treating phobias, compulsive behavior, and sexual dysfunction and cautioned against abuses of the legal rights of treated individuals.

July 15, 1975　　　　　　　　　　　　　　　　　　　　　　　　(2430)

The first edition of the *National Register of Health Services Providers in Psychology* was published, with 6,877 registrants included. The register was edited by Alfred Wellner.

July 21, 1975　　　　　　　　　　　　　　　　　　　　　　　　(2431)

The *Wall Street Journal* published an article critical of the comparative cultures component of the fifth-grade curriculum called "Man, A Course Of Study" (MACOS), devised by Jerome Bruner and funded by the National Science Foundation. The article was inserted in the *Congressional Record* by Senators Buckley and Beall and Representative Symms. The MACOS grant was eventually terminated.

August 15, 1975　　　　　　　　　　　　　　　　　　　　　　　(2432)

Charles A. Kiesler became the executive officer of the APA, succeeding Kenneth B. Little and preceding Michael S. Pallak.

August 29, 1975   (2433)
The APA Council of Representatives endorsed the proposed Equal Rights Amendment to the U.S. Constitution.

September 2, 1975   (2434)
The APA Council of Representatives admitted Division 36 (Psychology of Religion). The division was originally named Psychologists Interested in Religious Issues.

September 2, 1975   (2435)
The independent Council for the Advancement of the Psychological Professions and Sciences and the APA's Association for the Advancement of Psychology (AAP) merged into a single advocacy organization, the AAP, at a meeting in Chicago.

September 9, 1975   (2436)
The Oklahoma Psychological Association was incorporated. Ellen Oakes, Melvyn Price, and Kenneth Sanvold were the original incorporating officers.

October 24, 1975   (2437)
The report of the Association for Women in Psychology's Ad Hoc Committee on Sexist Language was published in the *APA Monitor*. The report condemned sexist language in psychology, listed common practices, recommended changes, and rebutted common objections to change.

November 12, 1975   (2438)
The Utah Psychological Association was incorporated.

November 29, 1975   (2439)
Public Law 94-142, the Education for All Handicapped Children Act, was signed by President Ford. The law mandated assessment and programs for children with mental and physical disabilities, including those with learning disabilities. Entire college special education courses are taught on the implications of this act.

January 13, 1976   (2440)
The U.S. District Court ruled in *Wyatt v. Stickney* that conditions in Alabama prisons were unconstitutionally cruel. The state was ordered to contract with the University of Alabama to implement an improvement plan. Psychologist Raymond D. Fowler headed the team that submitted its plan on June 25, 1976. Court supervision of these prisons ended on September 22, 1987.

January 24, 1976   (2441)
After reports from its consultant, the Arthur D. Little Company, the APA decided not to move its Central Office operations out of Washington, DC. Austin, Texas,

Charlottesville, North Carolina, and Raleigh-Durham, North Carolina, were the possible alternative sites.

February 2, 1976 (2442)
Marvin Dunnette's *Handbook of Industrial and Organizational Psychology* was published.

February 21, 1976 (2443)
The first Annual Symposium on Behavioral and Learning Disorders was held at the Devereux Schools in Santa Barbara, California.

February 26, 1976 (2444)
The state of South Dakota adopted its psychology licensure law.

April 24, 1976 (2445)
Entered this day in B. F. Skinner's notebook: "We know about our behavior but not about its causes. Hence we believe that we cause it. But we do not always seem to be causing it and hence the belief in the unconscious: We behave because of causes which we do not know about."

April 29, 1976 (2446)
The first Annual Symposium on the Delivery of Mental Health Services to the Black Consumer was held.

May 15, 1976 (2447)
The first Symposium on Chicano Psychology began, sponsored by the Ford Foundation and the University of California, Irvine. The keynote speaker was Alfredo Castaneda of Stanford University.

May 18, 1976 (2448)
The Health Insurance Association of America adopted a Model Psychologist Direct Recognition Bill, formally endorsing "freedom of choice" legislation in every state. This type of legislation provides payment for services provided by clinical psychologists without physician supervision or referral.

June 16, 1976 (2449)
The first National Conference on Education and Credentialing was held, sponsored jointly by the APA, the American Association of State Psychology Boards, and the National Register of Health Service Providers in Psychology.

July 1, 1976 (2450)
The California Supreme Court, ruling in *Tarasoff v. Regents of the University of California*, decided that when a psychotherapist knows of a client's threat of harm to another person, "he incurs an obligation to use reasonable care to protect the

intended victim against such danger." This court decision altered the nature of the therapist–client relationship.

July 1, 1976 (2451)

The state of Vermont adopted its psychologist licensure law.

July 29, 1976 (2452)

The first National Asian American Psychology Training Conference was held in Long Beach, California. The conference addressed the special needs for psychological research and service related to Asian American populations.

August 11, 1976 (2453)

The first meeting of the National Council of Schools of Professional Psychology was convened by founder and president pro tem Nicholas Cummings. Gordon Derner was unanimously elected the first president.

August 26, 1976 (2454)

CBS broadcast a dramatic special titled "The Tenth Level," dramatizing Stanley Milgram's obedience research. The show starred William Shatner in the role of Professor Stephen Turner. Milgram said his most significant act as a technical advisor was to recommend which journals should be on the professor's desk. "I recommended the whole glorious APA list," he said.

September 3, 1976 (2455)

Consumer advocate Ralph Nader delivered an invited address titled "Bringing Psychology into the Consumer Movement" to the APA annual convention in Washington, DC. Nader criticized the influence of educational and psychological testing, with special attention given to the practices of the Educational Testing Service.

October 7, 1976 (2456)

The petition to create APA Division 37 (Child and Youth Services) was submitted. Milton Shore headed the petitioning group.

October 11, 1976 (2457)

Sandra Wood Scarr and Richard A. Weinberg's article "IQ Test Performance of Black Children Adopted by White Families" was published in the *American Psychologist*. IQ score gains were a strong argument for an environmentalist view of intelligence.

October 24, 1976 (2458)

The London *Sunday Times* published a letter from Oliver Gillie accusing Sir Cyril Burt of altering his data on kinship and intelligence. The charge was repeated in a *Times* article of October 25 by Tim Devlin.

December 14, 1976   (2459)

The drug Centrax (prazepam; Parke-Davis) was approved for use by the U.S. Food and Drug Administration. Prazepam is a benzodiazepine used as an antianxiety agent and as a sedative.

December 20, 1976   (2460)

Theodore Millon's Millon Clinical Multiaxial Inventory was published. An earlier form of the instrument was called the Millon-Illinois Self Report Inventory.

December 27, 1976   (2461)

The Nebraska Psychological Association was incorporated.

January 29, 1977   (2462)

The APA Council of Representatives admitted Division 37 (Child and Youth Services). The division's name was later changed to Child, Youth, and Family Services.

February 23, 1977   (2463)

The Rosemead Graduate School of Psychology, of Rosemead, California, became the first independent professional school of psychology to be accredited by a regional accrediting association, the Western Association of Schools and Colleges. The school specializes in pastoral counseling.

March 29, 1977   (2464)

The first informal meeting of the President's Commission on Mental Health was held. President Jimmy Carter created the commission, carrying out a campaign promise of his wife, Rosalynn. Psychologists John Conger and Beverly Long served on the commission.

April 18, 1977   (2465)

The APA published a trial issue of *Psychology* magazine. The magazine was designed to appeal to "the educated lay public," but the APA Council of Representatives decided later in 1977 not to go ahead with production of the magazine.

April 19, 1977   (2466)

In *Ingraham v. Wright*, the U.S. Supreme Court concluded that corporal punishment in the schools is not unconstitutional. An earlier similar case denied hearing by the Court (*Baker v. Owen*, October 20, 1975) prompted the APA Council of Representatives to oppose corporal punishment in a resolution passed January 24, 1975.

May 14, 1977   (2467)

The first Georgetown University Conference on Biofeedback was held.

May 24, 1977 (2468)

The first public hearings of President Carter's President's Commission on Mental Health were held in Philadelphia. Rosalynn Carter was present and continued to support strongly the work of the commission.

June 1, 1977 (2469)

In a White House ceremony, psychologist Richard C. Atkinson was sworn in as director of the National Science Foundation.

June 9, 1977 (2470)

The APA published new "Guidelines for Nonsexist Language in APA Journals" in the *American Psychologist*.

July 28, 1977 (2471)

With the signature of Governor Teasdale, the state of Missouri passed its law regulating the licensure of psychologists. Missouri was the last of the 50 states to adopt a licensure law.

August 7, 1977 (2472)

The *Washington Post* carried a feature article describing the U.S. government's interest in psychic research. The article contended that the Central Intelligence Agency, the U.S. Navy, the National Aeronautics and Space Administration, and other federal agencies have supported and uncritically accepted the findings of studies in parapsychology.

August 25, 1977 (2473)

The American Association of State Psychology Boards adopted its guidelines for licensure applicants.

August 28, 1977 (2474)

The APA Council of Representatives voted to cancel annual conventions in states that had not ratified the proposed Equal Rights Amendment to the U.S. Constitution. Contracts with Atlanta (1979), New Orleans (1980), and Las Vegas (1981) were canceled, despite the advice of the APA Board of Directors and legal staff to apply the resolution only to uncontracted future convention sites.

September 13, 1977 (2475)

Robert A. Baron's book *Human Aggression* was published.

September 30, 1977 (2476)

The drug Ativan (lorazepam; Wyeth) was approved for use by the U.S. Food and Drug Administration. Lorazepam is a benzodiazepine used as an antianxiety agent and as a sedative.

October 5, 1977 (2477)

The APA purchased a 46,000 sq ft (4,300 sq m) office building at 1400 North Uhle Street, Arlington, Virginia, for slightly more than $2 million to house its publications, communications, and business affairs staff.

November 17, 1977 (2478)

The Parent Interview Kit for the System of Multicultural Pluralistic Assessment (SOMPA) was published. Jane Mercer was the author of the SOMPA.

November 30, 1977 (2479)

J. Allen Hobson and Robert W. McCarley's article "The Brain as a Dream State Generator: An Activation-Synthesis Hypothesis of the Dream Process" was published in the *American Journal of Psychiatry*. The article was cited widely in introductory texts.

December 10, 1977 (2480)

The current Alaska Psychological Association was founded at the Hotel Captain Cook, with Ron Ohlson as president. An earlier association began in the late 1960s but dissolved after licensing legislation was approved. A second, short-lived, association was created on April 4, 1971, with Harry H. Post, Jr., as president.

December 23, 1977 (2481)

In *Halderman v. Pennhurst State School and Hospital*, a U.S. District Court found restrictive conditions at the institution for people with mental retardation violated the ban on "separate but equal" schools. The decision strengthened the use of the "least restrictive treatment" principle, even though the U.S. Supreme Court later reversed the decision on technical grounds. The case was eventually settled in 1984.

December 23, 1977 (2482)

The antidepressant drug Limbitrol (Hoffman-LaRoche) was approved for use by the U.S. Food and Drug Administration. Limbitrol is a combination of the tricyclic antidepressant amitriptyline (Elavil) and the benzodiazepine antianxiety drug chlordiazepoxide (Librium).

April 17, 1978 (2483)

Raymond D. Fowler, chair of the University of Alabama psychology department and future chief executive officer of the APA, ran in the Boston Marathon. He said, "the Boston Marathon is a religious experience, like seeking the Holy Grail." Fowler's time was 3 hours, 20 minutes.

April 24, 1978 (2484)

The South Dakota Psychological Association was incorporated.

April 26, 1978 (2485)

The Ohio legislature passed a law requiring insurance carriers to provide mental health outpatient services in all contracts covering inpatient services.

April 27, 1978 (2486)

The first annual Virginia Tech Symposium of Applied Behavioral Science began in Blacksburg, Virginia.

April 27, 1978 (2487)

The final report of the President's Commission on Mental Health was submitted to President Jimmy Carter by the commission's honorary president, Rosalynn Carter. Mental health program improvements had high priority in the Carter administration.

May 1, 1978 (2488)

The *Behavior Analyst*, the journal of the Association for Behavior Analysis International, was founded. Scott W. Wood was the journal's editor.

May 3, 1978 (2489)

California became the first state to grant hospital staff privileges to psychologists. State Senator Paul Carpenter, a psychologist, wrote the legislation, which was signed by Governor Jerry Brown.

May 11, 1978 (2490)

The APA's Committee on Research Support first met. Its members were Frances D. Horowitz, David A. Jenness, Robert L. Kahn, Joseph B. Morgan, James L. McGaugh, and Sally E. Sperling.

May 14, 1978 (2491)

The APA's Dulles Conference was held. The conference resulted in the formation of the APA's Office of Cultural and Ethnic Affairs, later called the Ethnic Minority Affairs Office and now part of the Public Interest Directorate.

June 23, 1978 (2492)

The first four graduates in a pilot program at the University of California, Berkeley, were awarded their Doctor of Mental Health degrees. The 5-year program included 2 years in health, psychology, and medicine and a 3-year internship.

August 27, 1978 (2493)

The APA Council of Representatives voted to approve the petition to establish Division 38 (Health Psychology), doubling the number of divisions from the original 19 created in the 1946 reorganization of the APA.

August 27, 1978 (2494)

The APA Council of Representatives adopted Guidelines for the Specialty Training and Certification of High School Teachers of Psychology. The APA has conducted an active high school teacher information program.

August 28, 1978 (2495)

Gloria Steinem, prominent author and speaker on women's issues, delivered the invited address to the annual meeting of the APA in Toronto.

August 29, 1978 (2496)

The charter meeting of APA Division 38 (Health Psychology) was held in Toronto. Joseph Matarazzo and Stephen Weiss were instrumental in founding Division 38.

August 29, 1978 (2497)

The first APA Award for Distinguished Contributions to Psychology in the Public Interest was presented to Kenneth B. Clark at the APA convention in Toronto.

October 5, 1978 (2498)

The first annual meeting of the National Hospice Organization was held in Washington, DC. The organization promotes home care services, including psychological counseling, to terminally ill persons and their families.

November 9, 1978 (2499)

The first Institute on Teaching Psychology to Undergraduates was held at the University of Illinois at Champaign-Urbana.

November 19, 1978 (2500)

The Society of Behavioral Medicine was founded in Chicago.

November 24, 1978 (2501)

The *APA Monitor* published APA Division 17's (Counseling Psychology) "Principles Concerning the Counseling and Therapy of Women."

December 15, 1978 (2502)

The first meeting of the APA Ad Hoc Committee on Minority Affairs was held. The resulting APA Office of Ethnic and Cultural Affairs opened in January 1979, with Esteban Olmedo as its first director.

December 18, 1978 (2503)

A search warrant was issued to Hawaiian authorities to inspect the Medicare records of psychotherapist Virgil Willis for evidence of fraud. There was no reason to suspect fraud and Willis brought suit, challenging the search. His complaint was upheld in 1983. The action confirmed the confidentiality of client records.

January 1, 1979 (2504)

The APA Office of Ethnic and Cultural Affairs first opened. Esteban Olmedo, former associate director of the UCLA (University of California, Los Angeles) Spanish-Speaking Mental Health Research Center, was the first director.

January 1, 1979 (2505)

The *APA Monitor* announced that the *American Psychologist* and the *APA Monitor* would be available in tape-recorded editions, primarily for use by blind persons.

February 2, 1979 (2506)

The organizational meeting of APA Division 40 (Clinical Neuropsychology) was held in New York. Louis Costa was instrumental in winning APA division status.

February 21, 1979 (2507)

The *Journal of the Asian American Psychological Association* was first published.

March 5, 1979 (2508)

In its decision on *Detroit Edison v. National Labor Relations Board*, the U.S. Supreme Court upheld the confidentiality of employee test scores. The National Labor Relations Board had ordered Detroit Edison to release employee aptitude test scores to its employee union.

March 15, 1979 (2509)

The *Hispanic Journal of Behavioral Sciences* was first published. The editor was Amado Padilla.

March 17, 1979 (2510)

The first meeting to organize the Cognitive Science Society was held at the Dallas–Fort Worth Airport. The formation of the society had been instigated by Allan Collins and Roger Schank, and Schank arranged this preliminary meeting of 12 cognitive scientists.

March 28, 1979 (2511)

At about 4:00 p.m., a temporary clog developed in a feed water line at the Three Mile Island nuclear power plant near Harrisburg, Pennsylvania. An analysis of the human responses and mechanical design characteristics of the Three Mile Island crisis became a classic in the fields of human factors and engineering psychology.

April 1, 1979 (2512)

The APA's *Journal of Personality and Social Psychology* changed its editorial policy, creating three sections of the journal: Attitudes and Social Cognition, Interpersonal Relations and Social Interaction, and Personality Processes and Individual Differences.

April 5, 1979 (2513)

The John B. Watson Symposium was held in Greenville, North Carolina, in commemoration of Watson's birth in 1878. Conference participants included B. F. Skinner, Fred Keller, and James V. McConnell.

April 13, 1979 (2514)

The North Carolina Psychological Association was incorporated.

April 25, 1979 (2515)

The first Conference on Prevention was held in Hartford, Connecticut.

April 27, 1979 (2516)

The first annual Clinical Social Work Conference on Family Therapy was held in Portsmouth, Virginia.

April 28, 1979 (2517)

The APA *Monitor* published new criteria for accreditation of doctoral programs in professional psychology. The standards incorporated greater emphasis on practitioner training, as recommended by the Vail Conference on Graduate Training.

April 30, 1979 (2518)

In *Addington v. Texas*, the U.S. Supreme Court ruled that a person may not be civilly committed to a mental institution unless the state presents "clear and convincing" evidence they require hospitalization. This standard of evidence is greater than the "preponderance of evidence" rule for civil cases but not as strong as the "beyond reasonable doubt" rule for criminal cases.

June 12, 1979 (2519)

The antidepressant drug Surmontil (trimipramine; Wyeth) was approved for use by the U.S. Food and Drug Administration. Trimipramine is a tricyclic antidepressant. It may work by enhancing neurotransmission in the brain through blocking reuptake of the neurotransmitters norepinephrine and serotonin.

June 20, 1979 (2520)

The U.S. Supreme Court, in its decision of *Parham v. J. R.*, held that parents may not commit minor children to mental institutions without a finding by a neutral fact finder that institutionalization is appropriate. The case was brought on behalf of children who might have been committed because of chronic misbehavior instead of serious mental illness.

June 23, 1979 (2521)

The American Association for the Study of Mental Imagery held its first Annual Imagery Conference in Los Angeles.

June 26, 1979   (2522)

The Supreme Court ruled that U.S. Senator William Proxmire was not immune from prosecution in a defamation suit brought by psychologist Ronald Hutchinson. On April 18, 1975, Hutchinson received one of Proxmire's "Golden Fleece" awards for studying causes of aggression in monkeys. Proxmire's speech mocked and defamed Hutchinson, who sued Proxmire on April 16, 1976.

July 1, 1979   (2523)

Because of "sunset" legislation, Florida and South Dakota allowed their psychology licensure laws to expire. In Florida, hundreds of new applications for psychologist business licenses were received by county occupational licensing offices, many from people with no credentials. These two states and Alaska were the only states to lose licensure procedures to sunset laws.

July 1, 1979   (2524)

The American Mental Health Counselors Association, a division of the American Personnel and Guidance Association, began to accept candidates for certification by its newly established National Academy of Certified Clinical Mental Health Counselors.

July 25, 1979   (2525)

The APA received its first peer review case from the Civilian Health and Medical Program of the Uniformed Services (CHAMPUS), beginning a 6-month trial period. In all, 45 cases were reviewed during this period. William Claiborn was the original director of the APA/CHAMPUS project.

August 13, 1979   (2526)

The first public meeting of the Cognitive Science Society was held in La Jolla, California, in conjunction with a separately organized Conference on Cognitive Science arranged by Donald Norman. Allan Collins was the first chairman of the Cognitive Science Society.

August 20, 1979   (2527)

The first Annual Conference on Wilderness and Psychology was held in Great Falls, Montana.

September 2, 1979   (2528)

The APA's annual convention introduced a trial format called "Dine with Distinguished Colleagues." For a fee, conventioneers could choose breakfast with Nicholas Cummings, Nicholas Hobbs, or Sandra Scarr or lunch with Kenneth Clark, Albert Ellis, or Harold Kelly. The experiment appears not to have become a tradition.

September 2, 1979 (2529)

U.S. Representative Bella Abzug delivered the invited address to the APA convention in New York City. Her topic was "Social and Political Issues Related to Women."

September 3, 1979 (2530)

The APA Council of Representatives approved admission of Division 39 (Psychoanalysis). Reuben Fine headed the petitioning group.

September 3, 1979 (2531)

The APA Council of Representatives approved creation of Division 40 (Clinical Neuropsychology).

September 4, 1979 (2532)

The first Edwin B. Newman Psi Chi/APA Research Awards were presented. The winners, Michael S. Fanselow of the University of Washington and Natalie P. Porter of the University of Delaware, were recognized for excellence in a graduate research project. Florence Denmark and Nicholas Cummings presented the awards.

September 14, 1979 (2533)

Ohio's first school of professional psychology opened at Wright State University in Dayton. APA president Nicholas Cummings, Senator Daniel Inouye, and Allen Barclay, associate dean of the new school, presided at opening ceremonies.

September 14, 1979 (2534)

In *Rennie v. Klein*, the U.S. District Court for New Jersey ruled that all mental patients must give written consent prior to the administration of psychotropic agents.

October 16, 1979 (2535)

In its ruling on *Larry P. v. Wilson Riles*, the U.S. District Court ruled that California's use of standardized intelligence testing in the schools was discriminatory and therefore illegal. The plaintiffs pointed out that testing resulted in a disproportionate number of African-American students being identified for classes for the educable mentally retarded.

October 17, 1979 (2536)

President Carter signed Public Law 96-88, creating the U.S. Department of Education. Section 209 of the law created the Office of Educational Research and Improvement.

October 30, 1979 (2537)

The petition to form APA Division 41 (Psychology and Law) was submitted. John Monahan submitted the petition. The APA Council of Representatives approved division status on September 3, 1980. Monahan was elected the first president of the new division.

December 13, 1979 (2538)
The first convention of the Society of Behavioral Medicine began in San Francisco. W. Stewart Agras was president at this first meeting.

January 1, 1980 (2539)
The clinical classification system of the third edition of the American Psychiatric Association's *Diagnostic and Statistical Manual of Mental Disorders* (*DSM–III*) officially replaced the second edition (*DSM–II*) system.

January 18, 1980 (2540)
The APA Council of Representatives formed a continuing Committee on Gay Concerns. On May 23, 1985, the committee voted to change its name to the Committee on Lesbian and Gay Concerns, a change subsequently approved by the APA.

February 5, 1980 (2541)
The Association for Behavior Analysis International was formed from the Midwestern Association for Behavior Analysis.

February 5, 1980 (2542)
Psi Beta, the national honor society in psychology for community and junior colleges, admitted its first chapter, Northampton County Area Community College in Bethlehem, Pennsylvania.

March 16, 1980 (2543)
The first grants were made from the APA's Psychology Defense Fund. The grants assisted psychologists in *Hutchinson v. Proxmire*, *Virginia Academy of Clinical Psychologists v. Virginia Blue Cross-Blue Shield*, and in the state of Alaska, where "sunset" legislation had terminated the state board of psychological examiners.

March 21, 1980 (2544)
The APA's Arthur W. Melton Library was dedicated.

March 24, 1980 (2545)
Senator William Proxmire paid $10,000 in an out-of-court settlement of a defamation suit brought by psychologist Ronald Hutchinson (*Hutchinson v. Proxmire*). Proxmire had ridiculed Hutchinson's aggression research in one of his "Golden Fleece Award" speeches on misallocation of federal funds. The settlement came only after the U.S. Supreme Court ruled that Proxmire was not immune to prosecution.

March 28, 1980   (2546)

The Max Planck Institute for Psycholinguistics opened in Nijmegen, The Netherlands. Dutch psychologist Willem Levelt was the first director of the institute. The institute expanded in size and moved to new quarters on April 18, 1986.

June 9, 1980   (2547)

The petition to create APA Division 42 (Psychologists in Independent Practice) was filed. Richard Samuels was the chair of the petitioning group. The Council of Representatives approved the division on January 23, 1981.

June 16, 1980   (2548)

The Fourth District Court of Appeals ruled that two Blue Shield groups in Virginia were liable for antitrust violations for policies that denied psychologists direct payment for services. Robert Resnick and the Virginia Academy of Clinical Psychologists were the successful plaintiffs. The U.S. Supreme Court (February 23, 1981) declined to review the decision and "The Blues" paid $405,651.

July 1, 1980   (2549)

After a 6-month trial period, the APA received its first regular peer review case from the Civilian Health and Medical Program of the Uniformed Services (CHAMPUS). The APA had contracted with CHAMPUS to evaluate outpatient services.

September 1, 1980   (2550)

The first lecture in the APA's G. Stanley Hall Lecture Series was delivered at the APA convention in Montreal. The topic was "Current Challenges in Personality," by Walter Mischel.

September 1, 1980   (2551)

The Max Planck Institute's Center for Psychology and Human Development was founded in Berlin. Psychologist Paul B. Baltes was appointed as its director.

September 3, 1980   (2552)

The APA Council of Representatives approved creation of Division 41 (Psychology and Law). The division merged with the American Psychology–Law Society in 1984, and the division adopted the name of the American Psychology–Law Society at that time.

September 3, 1980   (2553)

The first APA Division 2 Teaching Awards were presented to Keith Jacobs of Loyola University in New Orleans, Susan Warner, a graduate teaching assistant at the University of Florida, and James Eison of Roane State (Tennessee) Community College. The awards were inaugurated and presented by Division 2 President David Cole, of Occidental College.

September 22, 1980 (2554)

The antidepressant drug Asendin (amoxapine; Lederle Laboratories) was approved for use by the U.S. Food and Drug Administration. Amoxapine is a dibenzoxazepine antidepressant. It may operate by reducing reuptake of norepinephrine and serotonin and blocking dopamine receptors in the brain.

October 7, 1980 (2555)

President Jimmy Carter signed the Mental Health Systems Act of 1980. The legislation was designed to distribute to the states responsibility for treatment established in 1963 with the Community Mental Health Centers Act. Improvements in services to young, elderly, minority, women, rural, and poor clients were specifically targeted.

October 13, 1980 (2556)

Under relaxed international relations, an APA delegation departed for the People's Republic of China to present lectures and establish reciprocal scholarly exchanges. Florence Denmark, Neal Miller, Herbert Simon, Raymond Fowler, and Harold Stevenson were members of this group.

November 10, 1980 (2557)

Peter M. Bentler and Douglas G. Bonett's article "Significance Tests and Goodness of Fit in the Analysis of Covariance Structures" was published in *Psychological Bulletin*.

December 1, 1980 (2558)

The antidepressant drug Ludiomil (maprotiline; CIBA Pharmaceutical) was approved for use by the U.S. Food and Drug Administration. Maprotiline is a tetracyclic antidepressant that may operate by selectively inhibiting reuptake of the neurotransmitter norepinephrine.

December 7, 1980 (2559)

The Federation of Behavioral, Psychological, and Cognitive Sciences was founded. Eight scientific societies were charter members. George Mandler was elected president and Emanuel Donchin vice president. The Federation educates policymakers, serves as an advocate for psychology, and informs member organizations about funding and policy issues.

January 10, 1981 (2560)

Vytautas Bieliauskas's House-Tree-Person Test was published.

January 23, 1981 (2561)

The APA Council of Representatives approved creation of Division 42 (Psychologists in Independent Practice).

February 27, 1981 (2562)

The drug Restoril (temazepam; Sandoz Pharmaceuticals) was approved for use by the U.S. Food and Drug Administration. Temazepam is a benzodiazepine and is used as an antianxiety agent and as a sedative.

March 2, 1981 (2563)

Gordon Bower's article "Mood and Memory" was published in the *American Psychologist*.

April 23, 1981 (2564)

Judith Rodin's article "Current Status of the Internal–External Hypothesis for Obesity: What Went Wrong?" was published in the *American Psychologist*.

June 1, 1981 (2565)

The Minnesota Psychological Association was incorporated.

June 5, 1981 (2566)

The first report of a case of acquired immunodeficiency syndrome (AIDS) in the United States was made by the Centers for Disease Control in Atlanta. Psychologists have actively studied behavioral, physiological, and attitudinal factors involved in AIDS transmission and personal and social responses to AIDS.

July 24, 1981 (2567)

A task force for the psychological study of lesbian and gay issues first met in Anaheim, California. The group later formed APA Division 44.

August 13, 1981 (2568)

With the passage of the Omnibus Budget Reconciliation Act of 1981, Congress ended the formal federal support of community mental health centers that began in 1963. Previously dedicated funds were reduced and made part of a mental health block grant program.

August 26, 1981 (2569)

U.S. Senator Daniel K. Inouye of Hawaii delivered the invited address to the APA annual meeting in Los Angeles. His topic was "Health and Science Policy: Impact of the Reagan Administration."

September 24, 1981 (2570)

The drug Paxipam (halazepam; Schering) was approved for use by the U.S. Food and Drug Administration. Halazepam is a benzodiazepine and is used as an antianxiety agent and as a sedative.

October 9, 1981 (2571)

David Hubel and Torsten Wiesel won Nobel prizes for their work in visual development. They performed pioneering single-cell recordings of the visual cortex, demonstrating the presence of simple, complex, and hypercomplex feature detector cells.

October 9, 1981 (2572)
Roger Sperry was awarded the Nobel prize for his split brain research that demonstrated the functional independence and differentiation of abilities of the two cerebral hemispheres.

October 16, 1981 (2573)
The drug Xanax (alprazolam; Upjohn) was approved for use by the U.S. Food and Drug Administration. Alprazolam is a benzodiazepine and is used as an antianxiety agent and as a sedative.

November 5, 1981 (2574)
Psi Beta, the national honor society in psychology for community and junior colleges, was incorporated in Tennessee and officially founded. Carol Tracy was the founding officer.

November 17, 1981 (2575)
Howard Gardner became the first psychologist to win a MacArthur Prize Fellows award. The awards are made to secretly nominated individuals of exceptional talent and carry no reporting or productivity requirements. Gardner was a Boston University developmental psychologist and neurologist whose Project Zero studied the nature of creativity and its development.

November 23, 1981 (2576)
The trial of physiological psychologist Edward Taub ended. Taub was found guilty of cruel treatment of research animals at the Institute for Behavioral Research. Testimony and photos were submitted by lab assistant Alex Pacheco, an animal rights activist. Taub claimed that the photos had been staged and that his procedures were humane. On appeal, five of six counts were reversed.

December 2, 1981 (2577)
The APA filed its first lawsuit. The action was brought on behalf of three U.S. government workers receiving mental health care threatened by cuts in the federal budget. The plaintiffs contended that mental health services were cut more than other health care services and that their well-being was jeopardized. The case was dismissed on April 30, 1982.

December 22, 1981 (2578)
The Cambridge Center for Behavioral Studies was incorporated. The first director was Robert Epstein. The purpose of the center is to direct behavioral research toward solving social problems.

December 24, 1981 (2579)

The antidepressant drug Desryl (trazodone; Mead Johnson) was approved for use by the U.S. Food and Drug Administration. Trazodone is a triazolopyridine, chemically unrelated to other antidepressants. It may operate by selectively inhibiting reuptake of the neurotransmitter serotonin.

January 14, 1982 (2580)

The *Journal of Experimental Psychology: Human Learning and Memory* began publication under a new name, the *Journal of Experimental Psychology: Learning, Memory, and Cognition*. Richard M. Shiffrin was editor of the journal at the time.

January 27, 1982 (2581)

The APA Presidential Citation was presented to Rosalynn Carter in recognition of her public leadership and service for improved mental health services. Carter was instrumental in convening the Presidential Commission on Mental Health during Jimmy Carter's presidency. The presentation was made by outgoing APA president John J. Conger, a member of the commission.

February 5, 1982 (2582)

The Association for Media Psychology, now APA Division 46, was founded in San Diego.

March 19, 1982 (2583)

Purdue University dedicated its new psychology building. Neal Miller was guest speaker at the occasion and F. Robert Brush was department chair at the time.

June 4, 1982 (2584)

Social Scientists Against Nuclear War was founded at an organizational meeting at the City University of New York. Robert Rieber and Howard Gruber were organizers of this first meeting.

June 12, 1982 (2585)

Several hundred members of Psychologists for Social Responsibility marched in a New York City mass demonstration supporting nuclear disarmament.

June 18, 1982 (2586)

In a unanimous decision in *Mills v. Rogers*, the U.S. Supreme Court concluded that the Constitution protects the right of involuntarily committed mental patients to refuse treatment with antipsychotic drugs.

June 18, 1982 (2587)

The U.S. Supreme Court decided the case of *Youngberg v. Romeo*. Nicholas Romeo, a profoundly retarded 33-year-old, was confined to his bed to avoid self-inflicted and other injuries at the Pennhurst State School and Hospital. The Court decided he had rights to safety, effective treatment, freedom of movement, and freedom from restraint.

June 21, 1982   (2588)
In deciding *Blue Shield of Virginia v. McCready*, The U.S. Supreme Court granted Carol McCready legal standing to sue Blue Shield of Virginia for treble damages for antitrust violations under the provisions of the Clayton Act. Blue Shield had denied McCready reimbursement for mental health services because she was a clinical psychologist, not a psychiatrist.

August 23, 1982   (2589)
U.S. Representative Barbara Mikulski (D–MD) addressed the annual convention of the APA, meeting in Washington, DC. Her topic was "Social Policy and Women in the 1980s."

August 23, 1982   (2590)
The organizational meeting of the APA Student Affiliate Organization was held at the APA convention in Washington, DC. Bruce Crow of Nova University called the meeting.

August 24, 1982   (2591)
U.S. Surgeon General C. Everett Koop addressed the annual convention of the APA in Washington, DC. His talk was titled "Perspective on Future Health Care." Koop was known for taking stands on issues such as smoking, AIDS, abortion, and birth control that followed research and medical evidence regardless of political sensitivities.

September 2, 1982   (2592)
The Colorado Psychological Association was incorporated.

September 13, 1982   (2593)
The International Union of Psychological Science (IUPsyS) was admitted to the prestigious International Council of Scientific Unions (ICSU), ending 30 years of denied petitions for membership. The action was taken at the ICSU's General Assembly in Cambridge, England. The IUPsyS was represented by vice president Mark R. Rosenzweig.

September 27, 1982   (2594)
The APA *Monitor* announced completion of the APA's first television public service messages. Copies were sent to 400 television stations in the United States and were first broadcast in Little Rock, Chicago, and Orlando.

September 30, 1982   (2595)
The Human Resources Research Office (HumRRO) won a 7-year, $23 million U.S. Army grant to revise personnel selection. It was the largest single behavioral science research and development grant ever awarded.

November 2, 1982   (2596)

Electroconvulsive shock therapy was banned in Berkeley, California, by a voter-approved ballot initiative measure. The ban was later overturned by the courts because it abridged the patient's right to treatment prescribed by his or her doctor.

November 4, 1982   (2597)

The petition to create the APA's Division 43 (Family Psychology) was submitted. Richard Mikesell headed the petitioning group. Because of an APA moratorium on new divisions, Division 43 was not approved until August 26, 1984.

November 15, 1982   (2598)

Ellen Winner's book *The Experimental Psychology of Beauty* was published.

November 15, 1982   (2599)

The drug Halcion (triazolam; Upjohn) was approved for use by the U.S. Food and Drug Administration. Triazolam is a benzodiazepine used as an antianxiety agent and as a sedative.

November 17, 1982   (2600)

Howard Gardner's book *Art, Mind, and Brain* was published.

January 14, 1983   (2601)

The Nicholas Hobbs Laboratory of Human Development was dedicated at Vanderbilt University. Hobbs, an APA president (1966), founded the nation's first mental retardation training program, contributed research that stimulated Project Head Start, and founded programs for emotionally disturbed children in homelike residential centers.

January 19, 1983   (2602)

The APA Division 16 journal, *Professional School Psychology*, was authorized by the division's executive council. The journal began publication in 1986 and changed its title to the *School Psychology Quarterly* in 1990.

January 22, 1983   (2603)

The APA Council of Representatives approved the purchase of *Psychology Today* magazine. The actual purchase was carried out in February 1983.

February 11, 1983   (2604)

The first issue of the APA journal *Behavioral Neuroscience* was published. The journal continued portions of the discontinued *Journal of Comparative and Physiological Psychology* (JCPP) and JCPP editor Richard F. Thompson continued as editor of the new journal.

February 18, 1983   (2605)

The APA agreed to buy *Psychology Today* magazine from the Ziff-Davis Publishing Company for $3.8 million. The APA also took out a loan for up to $2.5 million to cover transition costs.

March 9, 1983   (2606)

The APA's *Journal of Comparative Psychology* was first published. Jerry Hirsch was the journal's editor. This journal and *Behavioral Neuroscience* were created by a division of the former *Journal of Comparative and Physiological Psychology* (JCPP). Interestingly, the JCPP was first published in 1921 under the title of the *Journal of Comparative Psychology*.

April 26, 1983   (2607)

Public Law 98-24 mandated a peer review process for programs administered by the National Institute of Mental Health, the National Institute on Alcohol Abuse and Alcoholism, and the National Institute on Drug Abuse.

May 4, 1983   (2608)

The Society for Behavioral Pediatrics held its first scientific meeting in Washington, DC, in conjunction with the meeting of the Ambulatory Pediatric Association. At the meeting, Michael M. Cohen, of the Montefiore Hospital, New York, received the first W. T. Grant Foundation Lectureship Award in Behavioral and Developmental Pediatrics.

May 23, 1983   (2609)

The National Working Conference on Education and Training in Health Psychology began in Harriman, New York. The conference recognized the growing body of knowledge in health psychology and recommended procedures for the orderly development of professional practice in the field. Stephen Weiss chaired the conference.

May 31, 1983   (2610)

The Society for Behavioral Pediatrics was incorporated in Maryland. Sanford B. Freidman was the first president of the society. At the time, the organization was named the Society for Developmental and Behavioral Pediatrics.

June 29, 1983   (2611)

In its decision of *Jones v. U.S.*, the U.S. Supreme Court ruled that a criminal who has successfully used the insanity plea can be confined for treatment for an indeterminate length of time. In this case, Jones had been confined for 8 years after successfully pleading not guilty by reason of insanity to charges of shoplifting.

July 5, 1983   (2612)

In its decision of *People v. Kirk L. Hughes*, the New York Court of Appeals held that testimony obtained through hypnosis was not valid.

July 6, 1983 (2613)

In *Barefoot v. Estelle*, a convicted murderer claimed that psychiatrists as a class were incompetent to judge his future dangerousness. On this day the U.S. Supreme Court delivered a decision denying this claim.

July 14, 1983 (2614)

The first issue of *Psychological Documents*, a continuation of the *Catalog of Selected Documents in Psychology*, was published by the APA.

September 16, 1983 (2615)

Paul Ekman, Robert Levenson, and Wallace Friesen's article "Autonomic Nervous System Activity Distinguishes Among Emotions" was published in *Science*. The article was widely cited in psychology texts.

October 4, 1983 (2616)

The District of Columbia passed a city ordinance requiring extension of hospital staff privileges to licensed clinical psychologists. Although some states had laws allowing hospitals to give (or deny) privileges to psychologists, this strongly worded law mandated hospital privileges.

October 13, 1983 (2617)

The first Conference on Urban Mental Health was held at Queens Village, New York.

November 8, 1983 (2618)

The first genetic test for Huntington's disease was announced by molecular biologist James Gusella and other researchers at Massachusetts General Hospital. They had roughly located the genetic marker for the disorder on the fourth chromosome. Huntington's disease is a progressive nervous disorder named for Long Island physician George Huntington, who first described it in 1872.

December 10, 1983 (2619)

The Joint Commission for the Accreditation of Hospitals approved new guidelines permitting licensed individual psychology practitioners to become members of the medical staffs of hospitals without restriction.

February 24, 1984 (2620)

Industrial psychologist Lillian M. Gilbreth appeared on a 40¢ U.S. postage stamp, part of the Great Americans series of 1980–1984. The stamp was issued on this day in Montclair, New Jersey. Gilbreth is the only psychologist ever to appear on a U.S. postage stamp.

February 24, 1984 (2621)

The APA Division 29 journal, *Psychotherapy: Theory, Research, and Practice*, shortened its name to *Psychotherapy*. Donald K. Freedheim became the editor at the same time, replacing Arthur Kovacs.

April 30, 1984 (2622)
Edward N. Pugh won the first National Academy of Sciences Leonard Troland Award. The award is given annually to a psychologist who advances research on the relation between the physical world and conscious experience. Pugh's award cited his work on the eye's mechanisms of color adaptation, receptor transduction, and sensitivity control.

May 22, 1984 (2623)
The first World Conference on Behavioral Economics was convened at Princeton, New Jersey. Benny Gilad of Rutgers University was the conference organizer.

June 5, 1984 (2624)
The petition to form APA Division 44 (Society for the Psychological Study of Lesbian and Gay Issues) was filed. Stephen F. Morin was instrumental in creating Division 44.

June 25, 1984 (2625)
The Virginia Psychological Foundation was created. This was the first state psychological foundation.

July 31, 1984 (2626)
The antipsychotic drug Orap (pimozide; Gate) was approved for use by the U.S. Food and Drug Administration. Pimozide acts to block dopamine receptors in the brain.

August 9, 1984 (2627)
The New Hampshire Psychological Organization was incorporated.

August 24, 1984 (2628)
Pediatrician Benjamin Spock delivered an invited address to the APA's annual convention. Spock's paper was titled "Can Our Society Be Saved?"

August 26, 1984 (2629)
The APA Council of Representatives approved the creation of APA Division 43 (Family Psychology).

August 26, 1984 (2630)
The APA Council of Representatives approved the creation of APA Division 44 (The Society for the Psychological Study of Lesbian and Gay Issues).

October 12, 1984 (2631)
The first Mid-America Conference for Teachers of Psychology began on the campus of Indiana State University in Evansville. This conference has provided the dominant model for other regional conferences on teaching undergraduate psychology. Joseph Palladino was instrumental in organizing the conference.

October 19, 1984 (2632)

Congress established the U.S. Institute of Peace. Ironically, the legislation was made a part of the Department of Defense Authorization Act to prevent a veto by President Reagan. The institute was a longtime interest of Senator Jennings Randolph (D–WV) and promotes study of negotiation, conflict resolution, and relations between persons and nations.

November 30, 1984 (2633)

The final report of the APA Task Force on Victims of Crime and Violence was submitted. Morton Bard chaired this committee, which summarized research on the responses of victims to their circumstances, psychological help for victims, and legal and public policy issues.

November 30, 1984 (2634)

The APA Presidential Citation was awarded to U.S. Assistant Attorney General Lois Haight Harrington for bringing public attention to the mental health needs of crime victims.

January 17, 1985 (2635)

The APA and the National Register of Health Service Providers in Psychology were found by a federal court in Virginia to be not guilty of antitrust law violations in a suit brought by four psychologists.

February 1, 1985 (2636)

The APA Council of Representatives approved the "Criteria for Designation of Doctoral Programs in Psychology" developed by the APA, the American Association of State Psychology Boards, and the National Register of Health Service Providers in Psychology.

February 12, 1985 (2637)

The Florida Psychological Association was incorporated. Alan Gessner, Myron Bilak, Karen Steingarten, Judith Steward, Parke Fitzhugh, and Suzanne Bennett Johnson were the incorporating officers and directors.

February 26, 1985 (2638)

In *Ake v. Oklahoma*, the U.S. Supreme Court ruled that, in cases in which a defendant's sanity may become an issue, he or she has a right to obtain psychiatric help in preparing an insanity defense. If necessary, the service must be provided at public expense. In this case, Glen B. Ake was accused of two murders and could not obtain a psychiatric evaluation.

March 9, 1985 (2639)

The first annual meeting of the Society of Psychologists in Management was held in Tampa, Florida.

March 12, 1985 (2640)

The best-selling novel *When the Bough Breaks*, written by psychologist Jonathan Kellerman, was published. Kellerman's story involved psychologist hero Alex Delaware in a case of murder and child sexual abuse.

March 27, 1985 (2641)

The APA *Monitor* announced the production of two series of 30- and 60-second public service messages for radio. One series was on stress and one was on psychological research. The tapes were made available to state psychological associations for local distribution.

June 3, 1985 (2642)

In *Metropolitan Life Insurance Company v. Massachusetts*, the U.S. Supreme Court unanimously ruled that state insurance laws requiring mental health coverage are not preempted by the federal Employee Retirement Income Security Act (ERISA), which lacks this requirement. The ERISA decision strengthened mental health coverage and freedom-of-choice legislation.

July 2, 1985 (2643)

American Biodyne, the first national comprehensive health plan completely managed by psychologists, was incorporated by Nicholas Cummings.

August 21, 1985 (2644)

The APA Board of Directors signed a contract with the Eldan Company of Toluca Lake, California, to develop and produce a series of hour-long television shows based on the magazine *Psychology Today*, owned at that time by the APA.

August 22, 1985 (2645)

The first national convention of the Asian American Psychological Association was held in Los Angeles. At the meeting, Robert Chin was awarded the association's first Distinguished Contribution Award.

August 23, 1985 (2646)

Norman Cousins, former publisher of the *Saturday Review* and author of *The Healing Heart*, delivered an invited address to the APA annual convention in Los Angeles. Cousins's address was titled "New Dimensions in Healing" and described the effects of positive attitude and humor on recovery from illness.

August 24, 1985 (2647)

The first APA Committee on Women in Psychology Leadership Awards were given to Florence Denmark, Carolyn Payton, and Laurie Eyde.

September 7, 1985 (2648)

Leonard Goodstein assumed the post of APA Executive Officer, replacing Michael Pallak, who served from 1979 to 1985. Goodstein served until 1988 and was then replaced by Gary VandenBos on an interim basis.

October 26, 1985 (2649)

The *APA Monitor* announced the availability of PsycLIT, the CD-ROM-based search and retrieval database of abstracts of psychological literature. The annual subscription cost was initially set at $5,000.

December 23, 1985 (2650)

In an amendment to the Animal Welfare Act, Congress required primate researchers to provide a "physical environment adequate to promote the psychological well-being of primates." The law promoted research on behavioral correlates of laboratory environments and altered experimental practices.

VII

1986–PRESENT
THE SECOND CENTURY

The perspective afforded by only a few years is too narrow to confidently describe lasting trends in psychology since 1985. The American Psychological Association (APA), burdened by the financial strain of supporting *Psychology Today*, sold the magazine in 1988 (Entry 2716). The APA rebounded from the crisis with new vigor, aided by an active publication and communications program. A growing number of professional books, the availability of psychological abstracts and literature searching software on CD-ROM disks (Entry 2674), electronic transmission of the Science Directorate Funding Bulletin (Entry 2730), and the Scientific Psychology Action Network newsletter (Entry 2768) are examples of the expansion of the APA's information exchange program beyond conventional journal publication.

In 1988, the APA, in partnership with the Trammell Crow Company, purchased land for a new building at 750 First Street, NE in Washington, DC (Entries 2728, 2746, and 2748) and was ready to occupy the building in time for the APA's centennial in 1992 (Entries 2787 and 2800). Just as the financial crisis was being resolved, a crisis that divided the membership of the APA was developing.

In the early days of the APA, psychologists in applied practice felt themselves a minority in an organization dominated by academic and scientific psychologists. The practitioners formed splinter organizations to promote their interests. In recent years, some scientific and academic psychologists thought that the inequality had shifted in the opposite direction. A plan to restructure the APA in response to the concerns of scientist members was rejected by the Board of Directors (Entry 2679) and the membership (Entry 2718). In the end, the American Psychological Society (APS) was formed by the core of scientific and applied psychologists who promoted the reorganization plan (Entries 2719 and 2735). The APS conducts active journal, convention, student affiliate, legislator education, and awards programs. The emotion that accompanied the split has cooled, but the long-term relationship between the APA and APS has yet to be played out.

A review of recent events makes it difficult to ignore the increased national recognition paid to prominent psychologists. Psychological organizations have always honored leaders in the field, but only recently have psychologists frequently received the National Medal of Science, the nation's highest award for scientific achievement. The first psychologist to receive the National Medal of Science was Neal Miller, in 1964 (Entry 2061). After Harry Harlow in 1968 (Entry 2181) and B. F. Skinner in 1969 (Entry 2216), there was a space of 17 years in which no psychologists were honored. Beginning in 1986, however, there has been at least one psychologist recipient nearly every year. They include Herbert Simon (Entry 2654), Anne Anastasi (Entry 2685), Roger Sperry (Entry 2747), Patrick Suppes (Entry 2769), John McCarthy (Entry 2770), George Miller (Entry 2792), Allen Newell (Entry 2808), and Eleanor Gibson (Entry 2809).

New techniques for studying the biology of behavior have produced findings in recent years that have affected both psychological science and practice. Among these have been the development of new psychotherapeutic drugs, such as BuSpar (Entry 2675), Prozac (Entry 2704), and Clozaril (Entry 2745), holding the potential for fewer undesirable side effects than older preparations. Insight into the causes and treatment of Parkinson's disease has been gained from the use of fetal tissue transplants to stimulate the brain's production of dopamine (Entry 2707), and the genetic code for Huntington's disease has been discovered (Entry 2824).

The effects of courts and legislatures on psychological practice have continued into recent years. The most influential recent court decisions might have been the *CAPP v. Rank* decision in California (Entry 2597) and the *Virginia Academy of Clinical Psychologists v. Virginia Blue Cross/Blue Shield* (Entry 2548) decision in Virginia. These decisions affirmed the right of psychologists to independently admit, diagnose, treat, and discharge mental inpatients, free from psychiatric supervision. Other decisions have prohibited the forced administration of drugs to involuntarily admitted mental patients (Entry 2663), let stand the military's exclusion of gays and lesbians (Entry 2754), overturned the murder conviction of a defendant forced to take antipsychotic drugs while he was on trial (Entry 2806), and ruled that "death qualification" requirements do not violate one's right to an impartial jury (Entry 2659).

Legislature education efforts by state and national organizations have resulted in the passage of influential laws. Of these, the California "duty to protect" law, limiting the liability of therapists whose clients harm others (Entry 2651), may have the greatest effect. Other new laws have provided for state systems of advocacy for people with mental illness (Entry 2660), established a National Center on Child Abuse and Neglect (Entry 2715), prohibited employers from using polygraph evidence in making hiring decisions (Entry 2717), and provided penalties for the destruction of laboratory animal care facilities (Entry 2817).

After commenting on these related clusters of events, one is left with other events that do not fit easily into a coherent story. What will be the eventual importance of the recent formation of the Social, Behavioral, and Economic Sciences Directorate of the National Science Foundation (Entry 2793) or the National Institute of Mental Health Division of Basic Brain and Behavioral Sciences (Entry 2752)? How will psychology be affected by the establishment of an Internet electronic bulletin board providing contact with Russian psychologists (Entry 2791) or the Federal Trade Commission order prohibiting the APA from enforcing portions of the Ethical Principles of Psychologists that restrict certain kinds of advertising (Entries 2708 and 2822)? As scientific psychology moves into its second century it has taken on a form in many ways alien to the interests of its pioneers. It seems safe to predict that the next century's psychology being built by today's events will be equally different from contemporary psychology.

January 1, 1986   (2651)

The California legislature enacted the nation's first "duty to protect" law, limiting the liability of psychotherapists whose clients harm other people when the therapist may have prior knowledge of the client's intent to harm. The law was a response to the *Tarasoff* case, in which a psychotherapist was found liable for damages when his client murdered an ex-girlfriend.

January 30, 1986 (2652)
APA President Robert Perloff presented the APA Presidential Citation to Nancy Reagan for her efforts in combating drug abuse. Reagan promoted the "Just Say No" campaign against drug abuse.

January 31, 1986 (2653)
The APA Council of Representatives voted to raise the dues of licensed professional psychologist members by $50 to support the costs of professional advocacy.

March 12, 1986 (2654)
Herbert A. Simon was awarded the National Medal of Science for his work on artificial intelligence, cognition, decision making, and rational behavior. Simon and Allen Newell wrote the first heuristic problem-solving computer program in 1955.

March 12, 1986 (2655)
The APA journal *Psychology and Aging* was first published. M. Powell Lawton was the journal's first editor.

March 21, 1986 (2656)
The first biennial conference of the Society for Research on Adolescence began in Madison, Wisconsin.

March 27, 1986 (2657)
The Idaho Psychological Association was incorporated.

April 11, 1986 (2658)
The first Annual Conference on Applied Social Psychology was held in Santa Cruz, California.

May 5, 1986 (2659)
In *Lockhart v. McCree*, the U.S. Supreme Court ruled that "death qualified" juries do not violate the Sixth Amendment's provision for an impartial jury. In an amicus curiae brief, the APA had submitted research evidence showing that juries selected because they are willing to impose the death penalty are also more likely to convict a defendant.

May 23, 1986 (2660)
Congress passed Public Law 99-319, the Protection and Advocacy for Mentally Ill Individuals Act of 1986. The act provided for state agencies to advocate for client rights and to investigate and report abuse of people with mental illness.

June 2, 1986 (2661)
The petition to create APA Division 46 (Media Psychology) was submitted. Edith Levin was instrumental in creating Division 46.

June 2, 1986 (2662)
In *Bowen v. City of New York*, the U.S. Supreme Court permitted thousands of people with mental illness to seek retroactive disability benefits cut off by the Social Security Administration. The Social Security Administration had set up an unpublicized list of serious mental disorders judged deserving of aid and had excluded the "undeserving" whose condition did not appear on the list.

June 10, 1986 (2663)
In *Rivers v. Katz*, the New York State Court of Appeals ruled that patients involuntarily committed to a state mental hospital cannot be forced to take antipsychotic drugs without a court order.

June 25, 1986 (2664)
The petition to create APA Division 45 (Ethnic Minority Issues) was submitted. Maxine Rawlins was instrumental in creating this division.

June 26, 1986 (2665)
In *Ford v. Wainwright*, the U.S. Supreme Court ruled that convicts who become insane while awaiting execution for a capital crime cannot be executed because it would violate the Eighth Amendment prohibition against cruel and unusual punishment.

June 28, 1986 (2666)
The last clinical diagnostic category referring to homosexuality, "ego-dystonic homosexuality," was removed from the *Diagnostic and Statistical Manual of Mental Disorders* by the American Psychiatric Association.

July 14, 1986 (2667)
The Kentucky Psychological Association was incorporated.

August 18, 1986 (2668)
The petition to create APA Division 47 (Exercise and Sport Psychology) was submitted. William Morgan was head of the petitioning group.

August 22, 1986 (2669)
Journalist Carl Rowan gave the invited address to the APA convention in Washington, DC. Rowan's address was titled "Empowerment, Minorities, Politics."

August 24, 1986 (2670)
The APA Council of Representatives admitted APA Division 45 (Ethnic Minority Issues).

August 24, 1986 (2671)
The APA Council of Representatives admitted APA Division 46 (Media Psychology).

August 24, 1986 (2672)
The APA Council of Representatives admitted APA Division 47 (Exercise and Sport Psychology).

August 25, 1986 (2673)
APA's Division 1 (General Psychology) presented its first William James Book Award for an integrative publication in psychology to George Mandler for his book *Mind and Body* (1984).

September 17, 1986 (2674)
The APA signed the first licensing agreement for PsycLIT with Indiana University at Bloomington.

September 29, 1986 (2675)
The drug BuSpar (buspirone; Bristol Myers) was approved for use by the U.S. Food and Drug Administration. Buspirone is a nonbarbiturate, nonbenzodiazepine antianxiety medication. Its mechanism is unknown, but it has affinity for serotonin and dopamine receptors in the brain. It appears to be less sedating and less addictive than benzodiazepines and barbiturates.

October 8, 1986 (2676)
Congress passed Public Law 99-457, amending the Education for All Handicapped Children Act (Public Law 94-142) by providing for state programs of early intervention for infants and toddlers with disabilities. Programs were to include individualized family service plans for the cognitive, linguistic, and psychosocial development of children with disabilities from birth to 2 years of age.

November 14, 1986 (2677)
Human factors psychologist John Lauber was appointed to the U.S. National Transportation Safety Board, the first psychologist to serve in this capacity. Lauber had previously served at NASA's Ames Research Center.

December 7, 1986 (2678)
The first official meeting of APA Division 46 (Media Psychology) was held in Los Angeles. Stuart Fischoff was the president of the division.

February 4, 1987 (2679)
The APA Board of Directors rejected, 56 to 63, a proposal to reorganize the APA into two to five autonomous assemblies. The proposal was intended to maintain the allegiance of scientist members. The Assembly for Scientific and Applied

Psychology formed as a result, with Charles Kiesler as president. This group formed the nucleus of the American Psychological Society.

February 28, 1987 (2680)
The National Conference on Internship Training in Psychology began in Gainesville, Florida. The conference, cosponsored by the Association of Psychology Postdoctoral and Internship Centers and the Department of Clinical and Health Psychology at the University of Florida, focused on fundamental goals and policies of postdoctoral internship programs.

March 1, 1987 (2681)
The first issue of the *Humanistic Psychologist* was published by APA Division 32 (Humanistic Psychology). The new journal replaced the division's newsletter.

March 3, 1987 (2682)
Psychologists Brian A. Waddell and Lawrence T. Maloney patented a color imaging system that separated ambient lighting from surface reflection to better analyze the surface properties of materials. The researchers won the 1987 National Academy of Sciences Troland Award for this work.

June 13, 1987 (2683)
The first National Conference on Graduate Education in Psychology since 1958 began in Salt Lake City, Utah. Recommendations were made on graduate curriculum, settings, quality, accountability, recruitment and retention, student diversity, and student socialization. The group fully recognized the PsyD and EdD degrees and urged greater diversity in clinical personnel.

June 19, 1987 (2684)
The APA and the Canadian Psychological Associations agreed to semiannual executive meetings.

June 25, 1987 (2685)
The National Medal of Science was presented by President Reagan to Anne Anastasi for her work in differential psychology.

July 1, 1987 (2686)
The APA central office was restructured to create three "directorates," the Science Directorate, directed by Alan Kraut, the Practice Directorate, directed by Bryant Welch, and the Public Interest Directorate, headed by James Jones as interim director.

July 22, 1987 (2687)
President Reagan signed the Stewart B. McKinney Homeless Assistance Act into law. The McKinney Act provided the first comprehensive program to aid homeless

people in the United States. Psychological studies of homelessness and its relation to mental illness, substance abuse, disrupted families, and child development both influenced and resulted from the act.

August 13, 1987   (2688)
The *Journal of Family Psychology*, the journal of APA Division 43, was first published. Howard A. Liddle was editor of the new journal. The APA became the owner of the journal in 1990 and took over publication in 1992.

August 26, 1987   (2689)
The *APA Monitor* announced the availability of PsycPLUS, comprised of abstracts of nonserial materials such as books, films, book reviews, and videotapes.

August 29, 1987   (2690)
Former New York Member of Congress Bella Abzug addressed the convention of the APA. Photos in the *APA Monitor* show that she wore one of her trademark hats. Her topic was "Women and Political Power: Getting It and Keeping It." This was Abzug's second presentation to the APA.

August 29, 1987   (2691)
The first APA Award for Distinguished Career Contributions to Education and Training in Psychology was presented to Wilbert J. McKeachie, of the University of Michigan. The award recognizes continuous contributions made over a lifetime of service.

August 29, 1987   (2692)
The first APA Award for Distinguished Contributions to Education and Training in Psychology was presented to Florence L. Denmark, of the City University of New York. The award recognizes a specific major contribution to education and training.

August 31, 1987   (2693)
The APA convention was addressed by Betty Friedan, author of *The Feminine Mystique* and first woman offered a psychology fellowship at the University of California, Berkeley. Her topic was "The Problem That Has No Name—25 Years Later."

August 31, 1987   (2694)
The mayor of New York City, Edward I. Koch, addressed the APA convention. His speech was titled "Politics and Health Care: For Better and Worse."

August 31, 1987   (2695)
The APA convention was addressed by Ruth ("Dr. Ruth") Westheimer, famous for blunt and humorous advice about sexual behavior delivered on television, radio,

and in the print media. Her topic was "Bringing About Sex Literacy via the Airways."

September 11, 1987 (2696)
The Rhode Island Psychological Association was incorporated.

October 1, 1987 (2697)
St. Elizabeth's Hospital, the nation's oldest federal mental hospital, was transferred from federal to District of Columbia administration. The transfer carried out Public Law 98-621, enacted on November 8, 1984. Construction of St. Elizabeth's was authorized in 1852 and it began official operation in 1855.

October 9, 1987 (2698)
A federal judge upheld the copyright to the MMPI held by the University of Minnesota and National Computer Systems (NCS). They had brought suit against Applied Innovations, Inc., which marketed a computer scoring system that competed with NCS's.

October 26, 1987 (2699)
President Reagan signed a federal law providing up to a $5,000 bonus for American Board of Professional Psychology diplomates in the U.S. Public Health Service.

November 9, 1987 (2700)
The first International Alzheimer's Conference began in Miami Beach, Florida.

November 24, 1987 (2701)
The first issue of the journal *Neuropsychopharmacology* was published.

December 4, 1987 (2702)
The Council for Applied Masters Programs in Psychology, formed in 1986 within the Southeastern Psychological Association, became a national organization at its meeting in Atlanta. Richard D. Tucker was president of the organization at the time.

December 12, 1987 (2703)
The first meeting of the APA Task Force on Women and Depression was held. Ellen McGrath chaired the group, which gathered research and produced an influential report in 1990.

December 29, 1987 (2704)
The U.S. Food and Drug Administration approved the antidepressant drug Prozac (fluoxetine; Eli Lilly) for use. Fluoxetine was discovered in 1972 and clinical trials began in 1976. It seems to work by blocking the reuptake of the neurotransmitter serotonin. A controversy developed about the possibility of higher rates of suicide associated with the use of Prozac.

December 29, 1987 (2705)
The APA sold its headquarters building at 1200 17th Street, NW, Washington, DC to the American Restaurant Association (ARA) for more than $17 million. For the next 5 years the APA rented its office space from the ARA and purchased two buildings in Arlington, Virginia, before moving to the 750 First Street, NE, location.

January 6, 1988 (2706)
The APA agreed to take over publication of the *Clinician's Research Digest* from the Relational Dynamics Institute. The agreement took effect on July 1, 1988. George Stricker was the first editor under APA ownership.

January 7, 1988 (2707)
The use of a fetal tissue transplant to relieve the symptoms of Parkinson's disease was first reported. Neurosurgeon Ignacio Navarro Madrazo of Mexico City's La Raza Medical Center reported in the *New England Journal of Medicine* that he had transplanted brain tissue from a spontaneously aborted fetus into the brain of 35-year-old Leonor Cruz Bello, whose symptoms abated within weeks.

January 15, 1988 (2708)
The U.S. Federal Trade Commission found portions of the APA's Ethical Standards of Psychologists to be illegal restraints of trade. The offending sections restricted the content of advertising and other public statements intended to represent the desirability of services. The APA was ordered to amend its standards on December 16, 1992.

January 20, 1988 (2709)
The U.S. Supreme Court ruled, in *Honig v. Doe*, that schools may not expel children with emotional disorders for more than 10 days without parental consent or court order. The judgment affected the practices of school psychologists and school counselors.

February 8, 1988 (2710)
The National Institute of Mental Health Advisory Council adopted a major new research program directed at causes and treatment of schizophrenia.

February 16, 1988 (2711)
Psychologist Richard C. Atkinson became president of the American Association for the Advancement of Science (AAAS), the first psychologist in 54 years to hold the office. James McKeen Cattell (1924) and Edward L. Thorndike (1934) were earlier presidents of the AAAS.

February 29, 1988 (2712)

The *Newsweek* magazine issue for this date reported the research of Richard Haier relating intelligence to neural activity in the brain as measured by positron emission tomography (PET) scans.

February 29, 1988 (2713)

The *APA Monitor* announced publication of the first issue of *Science Agenda*, the newsletter of the APA Science Directorate.

April 15, 1988 (2714)

A psychologist was accused in the first formal criminal charge of falsifying scientific data. Stephen E. Breuning of the Polk Center in Polk, Pennsylvania, was charged with submitting fraudulent research results in an National Institute of Mental Health grant application for over $200,000. On September 19, 1988, he pled guilty to the charges.

April 25, 1988 (2715)

Congress established the National Center on Child Abuse and Neglect with the passage of Public Law 100-294, the Child Abuse Prevention and Treatment Act. The act created an advisory panel with psychologist members and provided funds for treatment and research support.

May 11, 1988 (2716)

The APA sold *Psychology Today* magazine to Owen Lipstein and T. George Harris for $6.5 million. Negotiations with the new owners, who also published *American Health* and *Mother Earth News*, began on March 5, 1988. In its 5 years of ownership, the APA lost $15,771,000 on *Psychology Today*.

June 27, 1988 (2717)

The Employee Polygraph Protection Act (Public Law 100-347) was signed, prohibiting the use of "lie detectors" in any phase of hiring, advancement, or dismissal of an employee. Some areas, such as national security and drug distribution, were exempted.

July 21, 1988 (2718)

A vote of the APA membership defeated (43% to 57%) a plan to reorganize the APA into three to five semiautonomous societies. Academic and experimental psychologists favored the plan and its defeat added strength to the dissident group that eventually became the American Psychological Society.

August 12, 1988 (2719)

The American Psychological Society (APS) was created from the Assembly for Scientific and Applied Psychology (ASAP), a group promoting the interests of scientific and academic psychology in the APA. Charles Kiesler was the first chair of the ASAP and Janet Taylor Spence the first ASAP president elected by the members that would become the APS. The vote for establishment was 419 to 13.

August 12, 1988 (2720)
Andrew Young, civil rights advocate and mayor of Atlanta, delivered the invited address to the APA's annual meeting in Atlanta.

August 13, 1988 (2721)
The new APA Science Directorate sponsored the first Science Weekend at the APA convention in Atlanta. Selected events were scheduled at nonconflicting times in rooms at a single location.

August 13, 1988 (2722)
Sandra Wood Scarr was presented with the APA's first Award for Distinguished Contribution to Research in Public Policy. Scarr's studies of the effects of environmental enrichment on intelligence and of the effects of the quality of child care are models of the application of behavioral science to important social problems with public policy implications.

August 15, 1988 (2723)
The American Psychological Association of Graduate Students held its first meeting in Atlanta, one day after an organizational symposium and APA Council of Representatives approval. David Pilon and Scott Mesh were elected cochairs of the new body.

August 23, 1988 (2724)
The first issue of the journal *Neuropsychiatry, Neuropsychology, and Behavioral Neurology* was published.

October 28, 1988 (2725)
The National Institute on Deafness and Other Communication Disorders was established by President Reagan's signature on the Health Programs Extension Act.

October 29, 1988 (2726)
The founding meeting of the Human Behavior and Evolution Society was held. Bill Hamilton was elected the first president. The society's constitution was adopted on the last day of its first annual meeting, August 25–27, 1989.

November 18, 1988 (2727)
The first training conference of the APA's AIDS Community Training Project was held in Buffalo, New York. The series of 15 conferences was funded by a grant from the National Institute of Mental Health and administered by the APA.

December 29, 1988 (2728)

The G Place Limited Partnership was formed between the APA and the Trammell Crow Company. The partnership built and managed the APA headquarters building at 750 First Street, NE, Washington, DC. G Place, NE, is the street that borders the south side of the building.

February 13, 1989 (2729)

The Wyoming Psychological Association was incorporated.

February 15, 1989 (2730)

The first electronic mail distribution of the APA Science Directorate Funding Bulletin was sent.

March 10, 1989 (2731)

The APA journal *Psychological Assessment: A Journal of Consulting and Clinical Psychology* was first published. The journal was formed from the assessment content of the *Journal of Consulting and Clinical Psychology*. Alan Kazdin served as editor of both journals for the first year.

March 11, 1989 (2732)

The Pennsylvania Psychological Association dedicated its own building, the first state association to do so.

May 1, 1989 (2733)

In *Price Waterhouse v. Hopkins*, the U.S. Supreme Court decided that discrimination based on gender stereotyping had denied Ann Hopkins a partnership at Price Waterhouse. The case was the first to be influenced by testimony based on psychological research on gender stereotyping. Social psychologist Susan Fiske was the expert witness in the case.

June 5, 1989 (2734)

Raymond Fowler began serving as Chief Executive Officer of the APA. His predecessor was Gary R. VandenBos.

June 9, 1989 (2735)

The first American Psychological Society convention began, in Alexandria, Virginia. George Miller was the first speaker and James McGaugh was the first elected president.

June 27, 1989 (2736)

The petition to create APA Division 48 (Peace Psychology) was submitted. Michael G. Wessells was head of the petitioning group. The first general appeal for signatures was made in a letter by Gregory Marotta-Sims in the *APA Monitor* published May 1, 1984.

July 5, 1989   (2737)

The first five-volume edition of PsycBOOKS was published by the APA. Psyc-
BOOKS was an annotated index to the contents of books in psychology. These
first volumes covered books published in 1988. Volumes covering books of 1987
were published on December 13, 1989. PsycBOOKS information was merged with
Psychological Abstracts beginning with the January 1992 issue.

July 25, 1989   (2738)

A copy of the *American Psychologist* special edition devoted entirely to children
was presented to President George Bush. APA officers Joseph Matarazzo, Raymond
Fowler, and Frances Horowitz, and Senator Nancy Kassebaum made the presentation.

July 25, 1989   (2739)

President George Bush declared the 1990s the "Decade of the Brain," calling
attention to the progress made in understanding, preventing, and treating brain-
related disorders and to the breakthroughs that can be achieved through neuroscience research.

August 7, 1989   (2740)

The first offices of the American Psychological Society first opened, in the words
of its first executive director, Alan Kraut, "above a liquor store in a seedy part of
Northeast DC."

August 8, 1989   (2741)

The first meeting of the board of directors of the American Psychological Society
was held in Irvine, California.

August 11, 1989   (2742)

U.S. Representative Lindy Boggs delivered the keynote address to the APA convention in New Orleans.

August 12, 1989   (2743)

The Council of Undergraduate Psychology Programs was founded in New Orleans.
Margaret Lloyd of Suffolk University headed the group, and Norine L. Jalbert of
Western Connecticut State University succeeded her in 1991.

August 13, 1989   (2744)

The APA Council of Representatives admitted Division 48 (Peace Psychology).

September 26, 1989   (2745)

The antipsychotic drug Clozaril (clozapine; Sandoz Pharmaceuticals) was approved
for use by the U.S. Food and Drug Administration. Clozapine inhibits the action
of the neural transmitters serotonin and dopamine and appears to cause fewer

undesirable side-effects than chlorpromazine and haloperidol. Clozapine was the subject of a *Time* magazine cover story on July 6, 1992.

September 29, 1989   (2746)

The land was purchased for the new APA headquarters building at 750 First Street, NE, Washington, DC.

October 18, 1989   (2747)

Roger Sperry was awarded the National Medal of Science for his research on neurospecificity and hemispheric specialization.

December 2, 1989   (2748)

The ground-breaking ceremony was held for the newest APA headquarters building, on First Street, NE, in Washington, DC. Twelve past presidents, two former chief executive officers, the current chief executive officer, and the 1989 board of directors were present.

December 19, 1989   (2749)

The Agency for Health Care Policy and Research (AHCPR) was established by Congress in Public Law 101-239. The AHCPR administers health care guidelines for prevention, diagnosis, and treatment of illness. Guidelines for the treatment of depression, released on April 14, 1993, were among the initial seven sets of guidelines to be issued.

December 29, 1989   (2750)

The antiobsessional and antidepressant drug Anafranil (clomipramine; CIBA Pharmaceutical) was approved for use by the U.S. Food and Drug Administration. Clomipramine is a tricyclic antidepressant, possibly operating by inhibiting reuptake of the transmitter substances serotonin and, to a lesser extent, norepinephrine.

January 16, 1990   (2751)

The National Conference on Scientist–Practitioner Education and Training for the Professional Practice of Psychology began in Gainesville, Florida. The purpose of the conference was to define the essential characteristics of the scientist–practitioner model that originated with the Boulder Conference of 1949.

January 24, 1990   (2752)

The National Institute of Mental Health Division of Basic Brain and Behavioral Sciences was created from the former Division of Basic Sciences. Seven new branches to support behavioral and neuroscientific research were formed. Stephen Koslow was the acting director.

January 26, 1990   (2753)

The first meeting of the Steering Committee for a National Research Agenda in Psychology began. Initiated by the American Psychological Society, the meeting was attended by representatives of 65 psychological societies.

February 26, 1990 (2754)

By declining to review the cases of *Ben-Shalom v. Stone* and *Woodward v. U.S.*, the U.S. Supreme Court upheld the right of the military to discharge gay or lesbian members of the armed forces.

February 27, 1990 (2755)

In the case of *Washington v. Harper*, the U.S. Supreme Court decided that the state could treat mentally ill prisoners with antipsychotic drugs against their will and without a court hearing. In amicus curiae briefs, the APA opposed this policy and the American Psychiatric Association supported it.

April 13, 1990 (2756)

Eleanor Maccoby delivered the first lecture in the APA Distinguished Scientist Lecture Series to the Southwestern Psychological Association in Dallas. Her topic was gender differences in children. The other inaugural lecturer was Jerome Kagan, whose lecture on childhood fears was first delivered to the Midwestern Psychological Association on May 4.

May 23, 1990 (2757)

The Loebner Prize was established by the Cambridge Center for Behavioral Studies. The prize is given annually to the authors of the computer program that best emulates human behavior.

June 8, 1990 (2758)

The first William James Fellow Awards were made by the American Psychological Society at its annual meeting in Dallas. The recipients were Frances K. Graham and William K. Estes.

June 25, 1990 (2759)

The California Supreme Court delivered its decision in *CAPP v. Rank*. The decision affirmed the right of psychologists to independently admit, diagnose, treat, and discharge mental inpatients, free from psychiatric supervision. Parties to the suit were the California Association of Psychology Providers (CAPP) and Peter Rank, director of the state's Department of Health Services.

June 27, 1990 (2760)

The first International Congress of Behavioral Medicine began in Uppsala, Sweden.

June 29, 1990 (2761)

The APA signed a contract transferring publication of the *Journal of Family Psychology* from Sage Publications to the APA. The journal is the official journal of APA Division 43 (Family Psychology). The actual transfer was dated September 28, 1990.

July 10, 1990 (2762)

The U.S. Department of Labor announced that it would discontinue the use of the General Aptitude Test Battery because of ethnic group differences in scores. An earlier policy to adjust scores for ethnic membership proved problematic. The decision affected 35 state employment services.

August 10, 1990 (2763)

At his last public appearance, B. F. Skinner was presented with the first APA Citation for Lifetime Contributions to Psychology and delivered a spirited address to the audience at the APA convention. Skinner died 8 days later.

August 12, 1990 (2764)

The first business meeting of the Council of Undergraduate Psychology Programs was held in Boston.

October 30, 1990 (2765)

Public Law 101-476 was passed, amending the Education for All Handicapped Children Act (Public Law 94-142). The amendments mandated the use of the term *disability* instead of *handicap* in official usage and expanded the scope of federal support for the education of students with disabilities.

November 5, 1990 (2766)

In the Omnibus Budget Reconciliation Act of 1990, Congress approved Medicare payments for independent psychological services delivered in any setting. The act expanded on similar legislation passed in 1988 and 1989 that opened the door to Medicare support of services delivered without medical supervision or referral.

November 8, 1990 (2767)

The first International Congress of Health Psychology began in Mexico City.

November 13, 1990 (2768)

The first electronic mail distribution of the APA Scientific Psychology Action Network (APA-SPAN) newsletter was sent. APA-SPAN is a grassroots network of scientists and academicians interested in legislation affecting psychology.

November 13, 1990 (2769)

Patrick Suppes was awarded the National Medal of Science by President Bush for his work in the measurement of subjective probability and utility, learning theory, the semantics of natural language, and instructional computing.

November 13, 1990 (2770)

President Bush presented the National Medal of Science to John McCarthy. McCarthy named and defined the field of artificial intelligence, developed the computer language LISP, and applied mathematical logic to computer programs that use commonsense knowledge and reasoning.

December 5, 1990 (2771)

At a news conference, the APA released a report titled "Women and Depression: Risk Factors and Treatment Issues." The report was edited by Ellen McGrath, Gwendolyn Puryear Keita, Bonnie R. Strickland, and Nancy Felipe Russo for the APA's National Task Force on Women and Depression. The report gained widespread media attention.

December 10, 1990 (2772)

The first APA-sponsored Scientific Psychology Forum for science writers and journalists was held at the National Press Club in Washington, DC. Eleven writers attended this first meeting.

December 28, 1990 (2773)

The APA became the owner of the *Journal of Family Psychology*, formerly a publication of APA Division 43 (Family Psychology). The September 1992 issue was the first published entirely by the APA.

February 2, 1991 (2774)

The APA Council of Representatives created the Board for the Advancement of Psychology in the Public Interest (BAPPI). BAPPI replaced both the Board of Social and Ethical Responsibility and the Board of Ethnic Minority Affairs. It was charged with "generation and application of psychological knowledge on issues important to human well being." Melba J. Vasquez chaired BAPPI.

February 8, 1991 (2775)

The APA Council of Representatives voted to admit Division 49 (Group Psychology and Group Psychotherapy). Arthur Teicher headed the petitioning group and was the division's first president pro tem.

February 8, 1991 (2776)

The organizing meeting of the APA Rural Health Caucus was held in Washington, DC. The Rural Health Caucus promotes improvement of psychological research, teaching, and clinical practice in rural communities.

February 22, 1991 (2777)

The first meeting of the APA's Board for the Advancement of Psychology in the Public Interest (BAPPI) was held in Chantilly, Virginia. Melba Vasquez was elected chair and the group chose to focus its first year on "Violence in Society: Research, Prevention, and Treatment."

March 28, 1991 (2778)

The permanent Psychology Exhibition opened at the Ontario Science Centre in Toronto. The 5,000 sq ft (465 sq m) exhibit was a joint product of the Centre, the APA, and the Association of Science-Technology Centers.

April 15, 1991 (2779)
The *Library Journal* named *Psycoloquy*, an electronic journal sponsored by the APA, one of the best new magazines of 1990.

April 23, 1991 (2780)
The Society for Machines and Mentality was founded, and the election of its first officers was announced. William Rapaport was the first president.

June 2, 1991 (2781)
The APA Science Directorate sponsored its first "Science Day" miniconference for representatives and presidents-elect of science-oriented APA divisions. The theme of the 2-day conference was legislative affairs.

June 12, 1991 (2782)
The first free-standing convention of the Society for Personality and Social Psychology (SPSP) was held in Washington, DC. David Sears was the keynote speaker at the meeting, and Kay Deaux was president of the SPSP at the time. The SPSP convention supplements the APA Division 8 program at the annual APA convention.

June 18, 1991 (2783)
The National Conference on Enhancing the Quality of Undergraduate Education in Psychology began at St. Mary's College of Maryland. Margaret Lloyd and Thomas McGovern played significant roles in early conference planning. Seven topics were addressed: curriculum, advising, active learning, faculty development, minority student issues, assessment, and faculty networks.

June 21, 1991 (2784)
The current APA logo was presented to the APA Board of Directors. The logo depicts an asymmetrical Greek letter psi, half drawn in angular lines and half in curves to represent the dual scientific and professional nature of psychology.

July 11, 1991 (2785)
The Ohio legislature passed a law extending hospital privileges to qualified clinical psychologists. Ohio was the sixth state to pass such a law.

August 15, 1991 (2786)
The APA Council of Representatives voted to include student representatives.

August 16, 1991 (2787)
APA President Charles Spielberger presided over the opening ceremonies of the APA Centennial celebration at the 99th Annual Convention in San Francisco.

August 16, 1991 (2788)
The first issue of the *APA Daily News*, the APA's convention newspaper, was published for the APA convention in San Francisco.

August 17, 1991   (2789)
The first APA Award for Distinguished Contributions to the International Advancement of Psychology was presented to Otto Klineberg at the APA convention in San Francisco.

August 30, 1991   (2790)
Neurobiologist Simon LeVay's article "Is Homosexuality Biological?" appeared in *Science*. LeVay's study demonstrated a relation between sexual preference in men and the size of the INAH-3 cluster of cells in the anterior hypothalamus. It was the first study relating sexual preference to a brain center implicated in sexual behavior.

September 10, 1991   (2791)
PSY-PUB, an open access Internet account at the USSR Institute of Psychology, was begun, providing international electronic mail access to Soviet psychologists. Alexandra V. Belyaeva, director of the institute's Vega Laboratory, and Michael Cole, of the University of California, San Diego, were instrumental in inaugurating this communications link.

September 16, 1991   (2792)
George A. Miller was awarded the National Medal of Science by President George Bush. The award recognized Miller's achievements in research on thought, language, and memory.

October 11, 1991   (2793)
The National Science Foundation announced the formation of a separate Social, Behavioral, and Economic Sciences Directorate, created by dividing the former Biological, Behavioral, and Social Science Directorate. Sociologist Cora Marrett was named to head the new division on January 30, 1992.

October 21, 1991   (2794)
A series of public lectures sponsored by the Smithsonian Institution and the APA began. The series, titled New Psychological Findings on the Mysteries of the Life Cycle: From Infancy to Maturity, honored the 100th anniversary of the APA. Speakers were Lewis Lipsitt, Jerome Kagan, John Conger, Amado Padilla, Daniel Levinson, Laura Brown, Anderson Dodd Smith, and Bernice Neugarten.

November 5, 1991   (2795)
The APA announced the formation of a new Public Policy Office to combine the legislative advocacy functions of the APA's Science, Education, and Public Interest directorates. Brian Wilcox was the first director of the office.

November 16, 1991   (2796)
The first full meeting of the APA's Task Force on the "Feminization" of Psychology was held in Washington, DC. The nine-person committee, headed by Dorothy

Cantor, considered issues associated with an increasing proportion of women grad-uates from doctoral programs in psychology. In 1984, 50.1% of new psychologists were women and the proportion has continued to grow.

December 13, 1991 (2797)
The APA and American Red Cross signed a statement of understanding in which the APA offered training services for psychologists to serve in times of disaster. The program certified psychologists nationwide as Red Cross disaster intervention volunteers.

December 28, 1991 (2798)
The first annual meeting of the Society for Machines and Mentality was held in New York City. William Bechtel delivered the keynote address, "Currents in Connectionism." William Rapaport was president of the new organization.

January 3, 1992 (2799)
In its ruling on *Abrahamson v. Gonzalez*, the 11th Circuit Court of Appeals ruled that Florida's law prohibiting unlicensed practitioners from calling themselves psy-chologists was an unconstitutional restriction of free speech.

January 13, 1992 (2800)
In the APA's centennial year, the APA central office staff occupied the association's new building at 750 First Street, NE, Washington, DC.

February 24, 1992 (2801)
The APA and U.S. Department of Health and Human Services announced a program of voluntary participation by psychologists in Head Start schools in the United States. The public service project was part of psychology's continuing involvement in early childhood education and the Head Start program.

March 26, 1992 (2802)
The state of Wisconsin enacted legislation to allow psychologists to admit hospital patients.

May 11, 1992 (2803)
The first Advanced Placement Examinations in psychology were administered by the Educational Testing Service to about 4,000 high school students across the nation. Many colleges and universities award introductory course credit to students with high scores on the Advanced Placement Examination. Essay portions of this examination were scored at Clemson University.

May 18, 1992 (2804)
The APA Traveling Psychology Exhibition made its debut at the Smithsonian Institution's Experimental Gallery in Washington, DC. The exhibit, titled "Psy-

chology: Understanding Ourselves, Understanding Each Other," traveled to nine other cities through 1995.

May 18, 1992   (2805)

In *Foucha v. Louisiana*, the U.S. Supreme Court ruled that a person acquitted of a crime for reasons of insanity could not be held in institutions after regaining his or her mental health just because he or she might still be dangerous. In this particular case, Terry Foucha had been acquitted of charges of armed burglary because of temporary drug-induced mental impairment.

May 18, 1992   (2806)

The U.S. Supreme Court's decision in *Riggins v. Nevada* overturned the murder conviction of David Riggins because the state had forced him to take antipsychotic drugs while he was on trial, thus impairing his ability to testify on his own behalf. The ruling affected the treatment of mentally unstable prisoners during trials.

May 21, 1992   (2807)

The First International Behavioral Neuroscience Conference began in San Antonio.

June 23, 1992   (2808)

Allen Newell was awarded the National Medal of Science by President Bush in a White House ceremony. Newell's work in artificial intelligence was cited in the award presentation.

June 23, 1992   (2809)

Eleanor J. Gibson was awarded the National Medal of Science by President Bush in a White House ceremony. Gibson's lifetime of research and theory in perceptual learning and development led to the award.

July 1, 1992   (2810)

The American Counseling and Development Association changed its name to become the American Counseling Association. Lee J. Richmond was president of the association at the time.

July 8, 1992   (2811)

On the occasion of the centennial of the founding of the APA, a plaque honoring G. Stanley Hall was placed in the wall of the Goddard Library at Clark University.

July 17, 1992   (2812)

The first meeting of the European Society for Philosophy and Psychology began at the Philosophy Institute of the University of Louvain, Belgium.

July 26, 1992 (2813)

The Americans With Disabilities Act of 1990 was signed into law. The act banned employment discrimination against people with physical and mental disabilities and required employers to make accommodations for the capabilities of disabled employees. Assessment, rehabilitation, and industrial/organizational psychologists helped employers comply with the law.

August 3, 1992 (2814)

U.S. Senator Daniel K. Inouye of Hawaii delivered an address to Congress titled "A Tribute to Psychology on the Occasion of the Centennial of the American Psychological Association: A Century of Science and Service." Inouye's remarks honored the APA and extensively described the Traveling Psychology Exhibition at the Smithsonian Institution, supported by the APA.

August 14, 1992 (2815)

Former Surgeon General C. Everett Koop delivered the keynote address to the 100th Annual Convention of the APA. As surgeon general, Koop compiled a record of objective public health advocacy even when the evidence was contrary to political convenience and his own personal preferences. Koop spoke on the changing face of health care in the future.

August 17, 1992 (2816)

The Association for High School Teachers of Psychology was formed at the Washington, DC, convention of the APA.

August 26, 1992 (2817)

President George Bush signed the Animal Enterprise Protection Act of 1992. The act imposed penalties for attacks on animal care facilities by animal rights activists. Instigated by a rash of break-ins and vandalism, the act protected both commercial and academic research facilities.

October 1, 1992 (2818)

The U.S. Substance Abuse and Mental Health Services Administration began operation. The new federal agency was created by Public Law 102-321, which reorganized the former Alcohol, Drug Abuse, and Mental Health Administration. Elaine M. Johnson was the first administrator of the new agency.

October 5, 1992 (2819)

The first International Congress on Behaviorism and the Sciences of Behavior convened in Guadalajara. Fred S. Keller and William N. Schoenfeld were honorary presidents of the meeting.

October 28, 1992 (2820)

The first International Asian Conference in Psychology began in Singapore.

November 14, 1992 (2821)

To commemorate its centennial, the APA sealed a time capsule in the ground floor of its building at 750 First Street, NE, Washington, DC. Among the contents were letters to the future from the president and the chief executive officer of the APA, predictions of the nature of psychology in 2092, convention photos and programs, data on U.S. psychology departments, and centennial souvenirs.

December 16, 1992 (2822)

The U.S. Federal Trade Commission (FTC) ordered the APA to cease enforcement of portions of its Ethical Principles of Psychologists. The order lifted APA prohibitions against truthful advertising that presented comparisons of services, claims of unique services, appeals to emotions or fears, and personal testimonials. The order became final on December 27, 1992.

February 26, 1993 (2823)

APA Division 50 (Psychology of Addictive Behaviors; now called Division on Addictions) was established by the APA Council of Representatives. Herbert Freudenberger chaired the group that petitioned for division status. Members of the Society for Psychologists in Addictive Behavior formed the core of the new division.

March 23, 1993 (2824)

The genetic code for Huntington's disease was identified by a research team headed by James Gusella at Massachusetts General Hospital. The team of researchers at six institutions included Nancy Wexler of Columbia University, herself at risk for the disease. For years, Wexler collected tissue samples from a small village in Venezuela where almost every inhabitant carries the gene.

June 5, 1993 (2825)

The Council on Undergraduate Research, an interdisciplinary organization of science professors, added a Psychology Division at its national meeting. John Batson, of Furman University, was elected chair of the new division.

September 22, 1993 (2826)

The first meeting of the National Academy of Sciences Board on Testing and Assessment was held in Washington, DC. Psychologist Richard Atkinson chaired the board, the first National Academy of Sciences standing committee on this subject. The board was charged with a scientific examination of testing issues in educational and occupational settings.

November 29, 1993 (2827)

A portrait of Sigmund Freud appeared on the cover of *Time* magazine along with the caption, "Is Freud Dead?" The cover article discussed the current status of Freudian thought. This was Freud's fourth appearance on *Time's* cover.

NAME INDEX

Abel, Theodora Mead, 676
Abeles, Norman, 2249
Abelson, Robert P., 1284
Abraham, Karl, 374, 959
Abzug, Bella, 2529, 2690
Ach, Narziss K., 334
Achilles, Paul, 1527
Adams, John, 76
Adkins, Dorothy, 943
Adler, Alexandra, 712
Adler, Alfred, 321, 387, 639, 712, 928,
    959
Adler, Norman T., 2396
Adorno, Theodor W., 1661
Adrian, Edgar, 1366
Affleck, D. Craig, 2155
Agras, W. Stewart, 2538
Aikins, H. Austin, 681
Ainsworth, Mary D. Salter, 843, 970, 1501
Albee, George, 1129, 2355
Albizu-Miranda, Carlos, 1104
Alexander, Franz, 556
Allee, Warder Clyde, 467
Allen, Andrea, 2404
Allen, James E., 1867
Allport, Floyd, 546, 1174
Allport, Gordon, 654, 1221, 1347, 1498,
    1755
Alluisi, Earl A., 1266
Alper, Thelma, 871
Altmann, Margaret, 694
Altmann, Richard, 318
Alvarez, Bernardino, 10
Alzheimer, Alois, 287
Ames, Adelbert, Jr., 405
Ames, Louise Bates, 875
Ammons, Carol H., 1796
Ammons, Robert B., 1796
Amsel, Abram, 1872, 2352
Anastasi, Anne, 877, 1763, 2685
Anderson, Gladys L., 653
Anderson, Harold H., 653

Anderson, John E., 590, 1214, 1532, 1549
Anderson, John P., 1787
Anderson, Nancy, 2357
Anderson, Norman, 2193
Andrews, Judson B., 589
Angell, Frank, 241, 1345
Angell, James R., 311, 838, 880, 1096,
    1310, 1351
Anrep, Gleb V., 1233
Appley, Mortimer, 2048
Archer, E. James, 1947
Argyle, Michael, 2093
Armstrong-Jones, Robert, 714
Arnheim, Rudolf, 1767
Arnold, Magda B., 766, 780, 1501
Aronson, Elliot, 1353, 1919
Asch, Solomon, 854, 1692, 1797
Aserinsky, Eugene, 1741
Astin, Helen, 2278
Atkinson, John W., 1173, 1750, 1869
Atkinson, Richard C., 1298, 2469, 2711,
    2826
Attneave, Fred, III, 1080
Augustinus, Aurelius (St. Augustine), 2
Austin, George A., 1820
Avelino, Andrés, 1752
Axelrod, Julius, 2280
Azrin, Nathan, 1333

Babinski, Joseph, 243, 530
Bacon, Francis, 8
Baer, Donald, 2189
Bagley, W. C., 1866
Bain, Alexander, 113, 465
Baird, John Wallace, 313, 1031
Bakan, David, 1943
Baldwin, Bird T., 1035, 1059, 1091
Baldwin, James Mark, 271, 505, 531, 537,
    569, 599, 611, 724, 770, 774, 798
Ball, Rachel Stutsman, 605
Baltes, Paul B., 2551

Bandura, Albert, 1216, 2006, 2028, 2238, 2308, 2354
Banham, Katharine M., 645
Barber, Theodore X., 1252
Barclay, Allen, 2323, 2533
Bard, Morton, 2633
Bard, Philip, 333
Bardon, Jack I., 1211
Bardwick, Judith, 1371
Bare, John, 2379, 2419
Barker, Roger G., 750, 856
Barnes, T. Cunliffe, 1305
Baron, Robert A., 2475
Barr, Murray, 2004
Bartholow, Roberts, 319
Bartlett, Frederick, 490
Bass, Bernard, 1837
Batson, John, 2825
Batten, Frederick, 290
Baumgarten-Tramer, Franziska, 493
Baumrind, Diana, 2050
Bayley, Nancy, 677, 1670
Bayton, James A., 942
Beach, Frank A., 932, 1654
Beard, George, 309
Beaunis, Henri-Étienne, 806
Bechtel, William, 2798
Beck, Aaron T., 1121
Beck, Samuel J., 629
Beckham, Albert, 649
Beckham, Ruth W., 687
Beebe-Center, John G., 641
Beers, Clifford, 366, 851, 867, 885
Bekhterev, Vladimir M., 231, 1720
Bell, Alexander Graham, 432, 613
Bell, Charles, 72
Bell, J. Carleton, 1866
Bell, J. H., 1270
Bell, Julia, 388
Bellak, Leopold, 1015
Bellugi, Ursula, 1340
Belyaeva, Alexandra, 2791
Bem, Daryl, 2159, 2404
Bem, Sandra L., 1544
Bender, Lauretta, 648, 1475
Benedek, Therese F., 580
Benedict, Ruth F., 500
Benjamin, Ludy T., Jr., 1568
Benne, Kenneth, 1057
Bennett, Chester C., 1954, 1963, 2078
Bennett, George K., 1615, 2084
Bennis, Warren, 1057

Bent, Dale H., 2276
Bentham, Jeremy, 44
Bentler, Peter M., 2557
Bentley, I. Madison, 324, 1002, 1195
Benton, Arthur, 903
Berelson, Bernard, 949
Berger, Hans, 344
Bergh, Henry, 294
Bergin, Allen E., 1055, 1389, 2165
Bergson, Henri, 261
Berkeley, George, 28
Berkowitz, Leonard, 1238
Berliner, Anna, 518, 964
Berlyne, Daniel, 1178, 1941, 2122, 2314
Berman, Joan, 2292
Bernal, Martha E., 1341
Bernard, Claude, 106
Bernays, Martha, 488
Berne, Eric, 1746, 1974
Bernheim, Hippolyte, 157, 530
Bertocci, Peter A., 914
Bessel, Friedrich W., 74, 89, 90, 117
Bettelheim, Bruno, 761
Bevan, William, 1141
Bible, Alan, 2284
Bibring, Grete L., 669
Bichat, Marie F. X., 56, 1906
Bickman, Leonard, 1130, 1508
Bieliauskas, Vytautas, 2560
Bijou, Sidney, 2176, 2377, 2390
Bilak, Myron, 2637
Bills, Arthur G., 1444
Bindra, Dalbir, 1145
Binet, Alfred, 242, 346, 473, 530, 806
Binet, Madeline, 473
Bingham, Walter Van Dyke, 407, 1351, 1496, 1607, 1729, 1759
Bini, Lucio, 1459
Binswanger, Ludwig, 948
Birren, James E., 1058
Bitterman, Morton E., 2085
Blanchard, Phyllis, 614
Blau, Theodore H., 1275
Bleuler, P. Eugen, 237
Block, Jeanne H., 1168
Blue, Yvonne, 1423
Boas, Franz, 250
Boder, David P., 1452
Boggs, Lindy, 2742
Bois, J. S. A., 1828
Bolgar, Hedda, 895
Bolles, Robert C., 2254

Bonaparte, Marie, 426
Bond, Horace M., 793
Bond, Julian, 793
Bonett, Douglas G., 2557
Boring, Edwin G., 491, 808, 1156, 1206,
    1276, 1307, 1316, 1368, 1372,
    1536, 1549, 1806, 1970
Bott, Edward A., 497, 1337, 1501
Boudin, Edward, 1699
Bourne, Lyle E., 2412
Bousfield, Aldridge, 2142
Bousfield, Weston, 2142
Bouthilet, Lorraine, 999
Bowditch, Henry, 156
Bower, Gordon, 1370, 2563
Bowlby, John, 843, 970, 2232
Bowman, Karl, 1433
Brady, Joseph V., 1137, 1817, 1887, 1951,
    2056, 2391
Braid, James, 162
Bray, Charles W., 782, 1326, 1416
Bray, Douglas W., 1074
Brayfield, Arthur H., 993, 2083
Brehm, Jack, 1272
Breland, Keller, 1975
Breland, Marian, 1975
Brentano, Franz, 148, 213, 584
Breuer, Josef, 164, 254, 403, 408, 424,
    427, 430, 431, 572, 1437
Breuning, Stephen, 2714
Bridgman, Percy W., 422, 1262
Briggs, George E., 2348
Briggs, Katharine C., 356, 652
Brill, Abraham A., 353, 901, 930, 1029,
    1108, 1437, 1461
Brimhall, Dean R., 1486
Broadbent, Donald E., 1229, 1966
Broca, Paul, 124, 272, 273
Bronfenbrenner, Urie, 1034
Bronner, Augusta F., 415, 1228
Brotemarkle, Robert A., 1406
Brothers, Joyce, 909
Broverman, Donald, 2255
Broverman, Inge, 2255
Brown, Andrew W., 1406
Brown, Jerry, 2489
Brown, Judson, 1725
Brown, Laura, 2794
Brown, Manuel N., 2024
Brown, Paul, 2179
Brown, Roger, 1201, 2074
Brown, Thomas, 71

Brown, W. Lynn, 1923
Brown-Séquard, Charles-Édouard, 528
Browne, James C., 312
Brožek, Josef, 965
Bruch, Hilde, 775
Brücke, Ernst von, 115
Bruner, Jerome S., 997, 1820, 2044, 2125,
    2419, 2431
Brunswik, Egon, 749
Brush, F. Robert, 2583
Bryan, Alice, 739, 1512
Bryan, William, 269
Bryan, William Jennings, 1208
Bryant, Sophie, 714
Buber, Martin, 379
Buchner, Edward, 773, 774
Buck, Carrie, 1202, 1263, 1270
Bucknill, John C., 215
Buffon, George L., 31
Bugental, James F., 1001
Bühler, Charlotte M., 600
Bühler, Karl, 391
Burnham, John C., 1943
Burnham, William, 225, 511
Buros, Oscar K., 809, 1404
Burt, Cyril, 435, 2458
Burtt, Harold E., 541
Bush, George, 2738, 2739, 2769, 2770,
    2792, 2809, 2817
Bush, Robert, 2016
Bush, Vannevar, 1561
Buss, Arnold, 1962
Butler, Nicholas M., 703
Buxton, Claude E., 1695
Byrne, Donn, 1971

Cabanis, Pierre, 50
Cade, John F. J., 1629
Calkins, Mary Whiton, 183, 281, 552,
    601, 609, 616, 880
Campbell, Angus, 918
Campbell, Donald T., 1025, 1897, 2228
Canady, Herman G., 713, 1762
Candlish, Alexander, 887
Cannon, Walter B., 333, 940, 1334
Cantor, Dorothy, 2796
Cantril, Hadley, Jr., 828, 1476, 1701
Carkhuff, Robert R., 2150, 2244
Carlsmith, J. Merrill, 1899
Carlson, Eric T., 2068
Carmichael, Leonard, 665, 1498, 1549,
    1577

Carnegie, Andrew, 724
Carpenter, Paul, 2489
Carr, Harvey A., 343
Carroll, J. Douglas, 1480
Carter, Jerry, 1674
Carter, Jimmy, 2464, 2536, 2555, 2581
Carter, Rosalynn, 2464, 2468, 2581
Cartwright, Desmond S., 2111
Castaneda, Alfredo, 2447
Cattell, James McKeen, 267, 271, 406,
    429, 441, 452, 455, 463, 465, 475,
    477, 485, 503, 508, 516, 520, 599,
    613, 706, 728, 835, 1048, 1119,
    1527, 2711
Cattell, Psyche, 594
Cattell, Raymond B., 802, 1659
Cerletti, Ugo, 1459
Chapanis, Alphonse, 1030
Chapanis, Natalia P., 1289
Charcot, Jean-Martin, 49, 128, 419, 420,
    470, 471, 489, 529, 530, 593, 595,
    1940
Charles, Don C., 2229
Chase, William G., 1492
Chauncey, Henry, 1622
Chein, Isidor, 941
Chelpanov, Georgy, 954
Chess, Stella, 975
Chin, Robert, 1057, 2645
Chomsky, Noam, 1291, 1829, 2080
Christie, Richard, 1375, 2231
Claiborn, William, 2525
Claparède, Edouard, 342
Clark, Kenneth B., 981, 1693, 2497
Clark, Mamie Phipps, 981, 1049
Clark, Russell A., 1750
Clarkson, Frank, 2255
Cleckley, Herrey, 1838, 1862
Clifton, Rachel, 2119
Cloy, Charles H., 1360
Cobbe, Frances P., 363
Cochran, William G., 1450
Cofer, Charles, 1695, 2048
Coghill, George, 335
Cohen, Jacob, 2221
Cohen, Michael M., 2608
Colby, Martha G., 671
Cole, David L., 2553
Cole, Michael, 2791
Collins, Allan, 2510, 2526
Comte, Auguste, 93, 1860
Conant, James B., 1840

Condillac, Etienne de, 37
Conger, John J., 1116, 2464, 2581, 2794
Conlan, John, 2419
Contini, Renato, 1863
Cook, Stuart W., 958
Cook, T. W., 1588
Coombs, Clyde H., 953
Coons, Wesley H., 2018
Cooper, Franklin, 2175
Copernicus, Nicolaus, 4
Corey, Stephen M., 1866
Costa, Louis, 2506
Cousin, Victor, 83
Cousins, Norman, 2646
Cowen, Emory L., 1224
Craik, Fergus I. M., 2346
Crawford, Meredith P., 923, 1698
Crick, Francis, 1727
Crissey, Marie Skodak, 908
Cronbach, Lee J., 1011, 1655, 1676, 1703,
    1753, 1754, 1795, 1800, 1855,
    2268
Crow, Bruce, 2590
Crowne, Douglas P., 1945
Crozier, William, 570
Cummings, Nicholas, 1183, 1894, 2183,
    2195, 2453, 2532, 2533, 2643
Cunitz, Anita, 2133
Curtis, Quin F., 1664
Cutts, Norma E., 576, 1771
Cuvier, Georges, 55
Cyert, Richard M., 2015

Dahlstrom, Leona, 1158
Dahlstrom, W. Grant, 1158
Dallenbach, Karl, 506, 1498
Daniel, Robert S., 2402
Darley, John G., 910, 2034, 2191
Darrow, Chester W., 1965
Darrow, Clarence, 1208
Darwin, Charles, 54, 102, 121, 135, 136,
    137, 147, 152, 230, 248, 249, 265,
    312
Dashiell, John, 514
David, Henry P., 1166
Davis, Alonzo J., 1764
Davis, Clara M., 1220, 1288
Davis, Frank C., 1446
Deabler, Herdis L., 1813
Dean, Janet, 2093
Dearborn, Walter, 383
Deaux, Kay, 2782

Deese, James, 1128
DeFries, John, 2262
Delabarre, Edmund, 285
Delboeuf, Joseph, 530, 534
DeLeon, Patrick H., 1530
Delgado, Honorio, 577
Dembo, Tamara, 732
Dement, William, 1939
Deming, W. Edwards, 696
Denmark, Florence L., 1355, 2422, 2532,
    2556, 2647, 2692
Dennis, Wayne, 811
Derner, Gordon F., 987, 2453
Descartes, René, 14, 16
Deutch, Helene, 454
Deutsch, Morton, 1094
De Valois, Russell, 1246
Devlin, Tim, 2458
Dewey, John, 262, 675, 1317, 2293
Diamond, Irving T., 1154
Diamond, Shari Seidman, 1600
Diderot, Denis, 36
Dimmick, Forrest L., 1362
Dix, Dorothea L., 99, 210, 221
Dixon, Wilfrid J., 2274
Dodge, Raymond, 329, 1179
Dods, John B., 197
Dodson, John D., 367
Dohrenwend, Barbara S., 1258
Doig, D. N. W., 2018
Doll, Edgar, 527, 830, 1744
Dollard, John, 692, 951, 1481, 1507
Doman, Andrea, 2020
Donaldson, Henry, 240, 511
Donchin, Emanuel, 1401, 2559
Donders, Franciscus C., 112
Doob, Leonard, 1481
Dooley, Lucile, 449
Doren, G. A., 236
Douglas, Robert J., 2162
Douvan, Elizabeth, 2343
Down, John Langdon, 131
Downey, June Etta, 358, 777
Dörken, Herbert, 1207
Dreikurs, Eric, 2199
Dreikurs, Rudolf, 639
Dreistadt, Roy, 2167
Drummond, Edmund, 169
Du Bois-Reymond, Emil, 114
Duffy, Elizabeth, 780
Dumas, Georges, 293
Dunbar, Helen F., 730

Duncker, Karl, 745
Dunlap, Knight, 362
Dunn, Leota M., 1924
Dunn, Lloyd M., 1924
Dunnette, Marvin, 2442
Durkheim, Emile, 245
Dusser de Barenne, Johannes, 1456
Dyk, Ruth B., 1978

Eagleson, Oran W., 911
Ebbinghaus, Hermann, 196, 251
Eberhart, John C., 858
Ebert, Pamela, 2428
Edgerton, J. Wilbert, 1073, 2161
Edison, Thomas A., 402
Edwards, Allen L., 1705, 1779
Edwards, Austin S., 1688
Ehrenfels, Christian von, 258
Eichorn, Dorothy H., 1186
Eisdorfer, Carl, 1327
Eisenhower, Dwight D., 1769, 1871
Eison, James W., 2553
Ekman, Paul, 1386, 2615
Eliot, Charles W., 646
Elliotson, John, 82
Ellis, Albert, 968
Ellis, Henry Havelock, 253
Englehardt, Olga E., 1044
English, Ava C., 578, 1877
English, Horace B., 578, 1448, 1877
Epstein, Robert, 2578
Erickson, Milton H., 717
Erikson, Erik H., 734, 1680
Eron, Leonard D., 1095
Ervin, Sam, 2082, 2083
Escalona, Sibylle K., 994
Espin, Olivia M., 1293
Estes, William K., 1083, 2758
Ewald, Ernst, 220
Ewing, Oscar R., 1671
Eyde, Laurie, 2647
Eysenck, Hans, 1009, 1716

Fabre, Jean Henri, 122, 1809
Fanselow, Michael S., 2532
Faraday, Michael, 81
Faterson, Hanna F., 1978
Fearing, Franklin, 581
Fechner, Gustav T., 96, 202, 308
Feifel, Herman, 998
Feinaigle, Gregor, 52
Feldman, Shammai, 1260

Felix, Robert H., 785, 1583
Fenichel, Otto, 1566
Ferenczi, Sándor, 912, 959
Fernald, Grace M., 307, 395, 1228
Fernald, Mabel, 438
Fernald, Walter E., 186, 193
Fernberger, Samuel, 499, 1217
Ferree, Clarence, 1362
Ferrier, David, 168, 319
Ferster, Charles B., 1157, 1864, 1874, 1951
Festinger, Leon, 1082, 1781, 1854, 1899
Feuerbach, Paul, 66
Fichte, Johann, 53
Fiedler, Fred E., 1150
Findley, Jack, 1951
Fine, Reuben, 2128, 2530
Fischer, Robert P., 1762
Fischhoff, Baruch, 1578
Fischoff, Stuart, 2678
Fisher, Ronald, 539
Fisher, Sarah C., 532
Fiske, Donald W., 1897
Fiske, Susan T., 1715, 2733
Fitts, Paul, 946
Fitzhugh, Parke, 2637
Flanagan, John, 816
Flavell, John H., 1283, 2013
Fleishman, Edwin A., 1254
Flourens, Pierre J. M., 87
Flournoy, Théodore, 342
Foa, Uriel G., 1007
Folling, Ivar, 2004
Forbes, Theodore, 1643
Ford, Gerald, 2439
Fordyce, Wilbert E., 1162
Forel, August, 190
Fowler, Clara E., 338
Fowler, Raymond D., 1335, 2324, 2440, 2483, 2556, 2734, 2738
Fox, Ronald E., 1419
Frank, Jerome D., 890
Franklin, Benjamin, 73, 75
Franks, Cyril M., 2263
Franz, Shepherd Ivory, 351
Frederiksen, Norman, 884
Freedheim, Donald K., 2027, 2249, 2621
Freeman, Frank S., 664, 1867
Freeman, Walter, 1430, 1434, 1528
Freidman, Sanford B., 2610
Freidrich, Max, 396
French, Edward L., 2271

French, John W., 2112
Frenkel-Brunswik, Else, 872, 1661
Freud, Anna, 620, 734, 1662
Freud, Sigmund, 47, 115, 128, 164, 228, 254, 353, 387, 403, 408, 413, 426, 431, 445, 470, 471, 480, 488, 489, 526, 530, 534, 572, 595, 618, 625, 627, 642, 680, 779, 825, 844, 853, 855, 859, 862, 866, 876, 881, 892, 896, 897, 898, 899, 900, 901, 902, 928, 948, 959, 967, 978, 1029, 1086, 1102, 1108, 1155, 1185, 1328, 1377, 1437, 1458, 1461, 1462, 1483, 1488, 1662, 1745, 1812, 2370, 2827
Freudenberger, Herbert, 1244, 2823
Frey, Maximilian von, 211
Frick, Frederick, 1639
Friedan, Betty, 2693
Friesen, Wallace, 2615
Fritsch, Gustav T., 149, 151, 319
Fromm, Erich, 686, 1509
Fromm, Erika, 926
Fromm-Reichmann, Frieda, 533
Frostig, Marianne, 823
Fryer, Douglas, 1447
Fullerton, George S., 259, 681
Fulton, John F., 678
Furby, Lita, 2268
Fushee, Clay, 2204

Gage, Nathaniel L., 2010
Gage, Phineas P., 191
Gagné, Robert M., 1020
Galanter, Eugene, 1931, 2016
Galilei, Galileo, 9, 20
Gall, Franz Joseph, 51
Gallagher, Cornelius, 2318
Gallaudet, Thomas H., 108
Galt, James, 61
Galton, Douglas, 658
Galton, Francis, 119, 198, 337, 509, 516
Galvani, Luigi, 40
Gamble, Eleanor A., 302
Gantt, W. Horsley, 579
Garcia, John, 1042
Gardiner, Jean, 1787
Gardner, Beatrice, 1380, 2121, 2174
Gardner, Howard, 2575, 2600
Gardner, R. Allen, 1380, 2121, 2174
Garfield, James A., 418
Garfield, Sol L., 1055, 1389, 2165

Garner, Wendell R., 1111, 2108
Garrett, Henry E., 603
Gates, Reginald Ruggles, 1585
Gaudet, Hazel, 1476
Gauss, Johann K. F., 69, 1785
Geis, Florence L., 1375, 2231
Geissler, Ludwig R., 1031
Geldard, Frank A., 784
Gendlin, Eugene T., 2009, 2027
Genovese, Kitty, 2046
Gerbrands, Ralph, 808, 1928
Gersoni, Charles, 2333
Gesell, Arnold, 400, 1091
Gessner, Alan, 2637
Ghiselli, Edwin E., 849
Gibbons, Don, 2296
Gibbs, Frederick, 239
Gibson, Eleanor Jack, 925, 1932, 2289, 2809
Gibson, James J., 772, 1673, 2124
Gilad, Benny, 2623
Gilbreth, Lillian M., 380, 2620
Gillette, Annette, 905
Gillie, Oliver, 2458
Glanzer, Murray, 2133
Glaser, Robert, 1110
Gleser, Goldine C., 1753
Glover, John A., 1650
Glueck, Eleanor T., 661
Goddard, Henry H., 296, 830, 832
Goethe, Johann von, 47
Goldiamond, Israel, 2106, 2383
Goldman, George D., 1163
Goldman-Rakic, Patricia S., 1442
Goldstein, Kurt, 385, 691
Goldston, Stephen E., 1343
Golgi, Camillo, 174
Gombrich, Ernst H., 1930
Goodenough, Donald R, 1978
Goodenough, Florence L., 484, 1234, 1236
Goodlet, Carlton B., 980
Goodman, Nelson, 2202
Goodman, Paul, 591
Goodnow, Jacqueline J., 1187, 1820
Goodstein, Leonard, 1248, 2648
Goolishian, Harold A., 1180
Gorham, Donald R., 1989
Göring, Matthias H., 1418
Gosset, William S., 371
Gough, Harrison, 1832
Graf, Herbert, 859, 862

Graham, Clarence H., 815
Graham, Frances K., 1068, 2119, 2758
Graham, Stanley R., 1243
Granit, Ragnar, 2173
Gray, Susan Walton, 972
Green, David M., 1359, 1829, 2130
Green, Hannah, 533
Green, Joe E., 2024
Green, Robert L., 2201
Greenacre, Phyllis, 607
Greene, Ronald R., 1649
Griffith, Coleman R., 588
Grosslight, Joseph H., 1130, 1508
Gruber, Howard, 2584
Gudden, Bernard von, 483
Guetzkow, Harold, 1692
Guggenbuhl, Johann J., 107
Guilford, Joan, 1286
Guilford, Joy Paul, 640, 1210, 1429, 1915, 2157
Guillotin, Joseph I., 75
Guiteau, Charles, 418
Gunther, Anne, 15
Gusella, James, 2618, 2824
Gustad, John W., 1695
Guthe, Carl, 1498
Guthrie, Edwin R., 476
Guttman, Louis, 1005
Guttman, Norman, 1105

Haier, Richard, 2712
Hake, Don, 1420
Hale, George Ellery, 1038
Hall, Calvin S., 882, 1107, 1836
Hall, Edward T., 2114
Hall, G. Stanley, 175, 225, 263, 278, 372,
   381, 396, 399, 411, 423, 436, 444,
   504, 510, 511, 555, 573, 582, 598,
   781, 876, 892, 897, 898, 900, 901,
   990, 1031, 1100, 1140, 2811
Hall, Marshall, 80
Halpern, Florence, 683
Halse, William, 714
Halstead, Ward, 879
Hamilton, William, 79, 2726
Hamon, Joseph, 1704
Hanfmann, Eugenia, 801
Hanson, Harley, 2120
Hardin, Garrett, 2213
Harlow, Harry F., 812, 864, 1698, 1725,
   1895, 2181
Harlow, Margaret K., 1070

Harper, Robert, 2197
Harrington, Lois H., 2634
Harris, Amy, 1746
Harris, Fred, 2302, 2304
Harris, Jesse G., 1219
Harris, Titus H., 1929
Harris, Tom, 1746
Harrower, Molly, 817
Hartley, David, 30
Hartley, Ruth, 916
Hartline, Haldan, 2173
Hartman, James, 2153
Harvey, William, 12, 1848
Haslerud, George M., 831
Hastorf, Albert, 1701
Hathaway, Starke R., 760, 1525
Havemann, Ernest, 1857
Hays, William L., 2029
Head, Henry, 274
Healy, William, 307, 395, 415, 674, 1228
Hebb, Donald Olding, 786, 1501, 1658, 1798
Hecht, Selig, 564
Hefferline, Ralph F., 591, 909
Heidbreder, Edna, 542
Heider, Fritz, 624, 1880
Heider, Grace, 765
Hein, Alan, 2037
Held, Richard, 2037
Helmholtz, Hermann von, 59, 118, 217, 226, 229, 247, 264, 270, 275, 1668
Helson, Harry, 666, 1738
Helson, Ravenna, 1197
Henle, Mary, 963
Henmon, Vivian, 377
Henning, Hans, 461
Henry, Caleb S., 83
Herbart, Johann F., 67, 161, 560, 703
Hering, Ewald, 142
Herrick, Charles, 306
Herrnstein, Richard J., 1325
Hertzog, Herta, 1476
Hess, Walter R., 1657
Hildreth, Gertrude, 1422
Hildreth, Jane D., 1045
Hilgard, Ernest R., 787, 869, 1489, 1536, 1626, 2011, 2206
Hilgard, Josephine R., 821
Hirsch, Jerry, 2606
Hitzig, Eduard, 149, 151, 319

Hobbes, Thomas, 13
Hobbs, Nicholas, 986, 1730, 2601
Hobson, J. Allen, 2479
Hochberg, Julian, 1167
Höffding, Harald, 171
Hoffer, Eric, 2198
Hoffman, Herbert J., 2038
Hoffman, Lois W., 1299
Hoffman, Martin, 1299
Hofmann, Albert, 1533, 1534
Hollingworth, Harry, 398, 904, 931
Hollingworth, Leta Stetter, 482, 1101
Holmes, Oliver W., 1263
Holmes, Thomas H., 2177
Holt, Edwin B., 347
Holt, Henry, 672
Holtzman, Wayne H., 1738, 1751
Homans, George, 1950
Hooker, Evelyn, 852
Hopkins, Ann, 2733
Horner, Matina S., 1485
Horney, Karen, 469, 1793
Hornig, Donald F., 2100
Horowitz, Frances D., 2490, 2738
Horst, Aaron Paul, 1409
Hough, A. J. B., 2001
Hovland, Carl I., 951, 1749
Howard, Alvin, 1875
Howe, Gridley, 186, 193
Hubbard, Gardiner G., 432, 613
Hubbard, L. Ron, 1665, 2140
Hubel, David, 2571
Hughes, John, 2421
Hull, C. Hadlai, 2276
Hull, Clark L., 447, 741, 1529, 1537, 1717
Hume, David, 34
Humphreys, Lloyd, 2055, 2097
Hunt, J. McVicker, 822, 1454, 1736
Hunt, Thelma, 1592, 1718
Hunt, William A., 638, 764
Hunter, Walter S., 523, 1217, 1498
Huntington, George, 199, 2618
Hurvich, Leo, 919, 1106
Husserl, Edmund, 256
Hutchinson, Ronald, 2522, 2543, 2545
Huxley, Thomas Henry, 127, 268

Inhelder, Barbel, 957, 2295
Inouye, Daniel K., 1530, 2533, 2569, 2814
Ireland, William, 141
Irwin, Francis W., 800

Itard, Jean, 65, 95
Ives, Margaret, 751

Jacklin, Carol N., 1040, 2407
Jackson, James S., 1546
Jackson, John Hughlings, 144
Jacobs, Durrand F., 2397
Jacobs, Keith, 2553
Jacobson, Edmund, 512
Jacobson, Lenore, 2187
Jacoby, Walter, 893
Jaensch, Erich R., 434
Jahoda, Marie, 841
Jakobsen, Dr., 1614
Jalbert, Norine L., 2743
James, Maud Merrill, 513
James, William, 143, 163, 282, 323, 440,
    458, 530, 536, 550, 551, 552, 553,
    561, 562, 646, 672, 754, 885, 900,
    901, 1143
Jameson, Dorothea, 919, 1106, 2420
Janet, Pierre, 257, 474, 534, 593, 1399
Janis, Irving L., 951, 1062, 1749, 2320
Jarvik, Murray, 2132
Jastak, Joseph, 2176
Jastak, Sarah, 2176
Jastrow, Joseph, 278, 681
Jenkins, Herbert, 2179
Jenkins, James J., 2403
Jenkins, Martin D., 790
Jenness, David A., 2490
Jennings, Herbert S., 303, 938
Jensen, Arthur, 1169, 2144, 2222
Jessup, Walter, 1337
Joffre, Juan Gilabert, 3
Johansson, Gunnar, 927
Johnson, Buford J., 1324
Johnson, Elaine M., 2818
Johnson, Lyndon B., 2061, 2079, 2181,
    2216
Johnson, Suzanne Bennett, 2637
Johnson, Virginia E., 1196, 2115, 2265
Johnstone, Edward R., 718
Jonas, Gerald, 2334
Jones, Edward E., 1237
Jones, A. Ernest, 387, 853, 901, 934, 959,
    1745
Jones, Harold E., 1670
Jones, James, 2686
Jones, Margaret H., 991
Jones, Mary Cover, 632

Judd, Charles H., 339, 681, 838, 1337
Jung, Carl G., 359, 387, 652, 699, 736,
    746, 779, 825, 844, 853, 881, 896,
    897, 898, 901, 912, 948, 959, 967,
    978, 1367, 1784, 2370

Kagan, Jerome, 1297, 2756, 2794
Kahn, Robert L., 2107, 2490
Kahneman, Daniel, 1387, 1441, 2363
Kanner, Leo, 1403, 1550
Kant, Immanuel, 38, 53, 2381
Kantor, Jacob R., 515
Kardiner, Abraham, 558
Karp, Stephen A., 1978
Kassebaum, Nancy, 2738
Katona, George, 715
Katz, Bernard, 2280
Katz, Daniel, 2066, 2107
Katz, David, 386, 453, 464
Katz, Rosa, 464
Kazdin, Alan, 2731
Keita, Gwendolyn Puryear, 2771
Keller, Fred S., 668, 2065, 2069, 2096,
    2190, 2273, 2513, 2819
Kellerman, Jonathan, 2640
Kelley, Harold H., 951, 1037, 1114, 1749,
    1913
Kelley, Noble H., 710
Kelley, Truman Lee, 448
Kellogg, Luella, 1349, 1378
Kellogg, Winthrop, 1349, 1378
Kelly, E. Lowell, 813
Kelly, George A., 807, 1649, 1790
Kelman, Herbert C., 1255
Kemp, Edward H., 868
Kendall, Edward, 984
Kendler, Howard, 1976
Kendler, Tracy S., 1069, 1976
Kennedy, Edward M., 2391
Kennedy, John F., 2008, 2039, 2040
Kennedy, John L., 960
Kent, Grace, 357, 382
Kepler, Johannes, 11
Kerlinger, Fred N., 2054
Kessler, Jane W., 1117
Kiesler, Charles A., 1390, 2432, 2679,
    2719
Kimble, Daniel P., 2212
King, Irving, 762
King, Martin Luther, Jr., 2166
Kinkade, Robert G., 2392

Kinnebrook, David, 74, 89, 90
Kinsey, Alfred C., 608, 1465, 1602, 1608, 1623, 1638, 1740, 1742
Kintsch, Walter, 1358
Kirk, Roger, 2194
Kirk, Samuel A., 1959, 1985, 2004
Kirkbride, Thomas S., 178
Klaus, Rupert, 972
Klein, Donald, 1343
Klein, Melanie, 421
Kleitman, Nathanial, 1741
Klima, Edward S., 1340
Kline, Nathan, 1010
Klineberg, Otto, 679, 2789
Kluckholn, Florence R., 799
Klüver, Heinrich, 644, 1412
Koch, Edward I., 2694
Koch, Sigmund, 1033, 1896
Koffka, Kurt, 478, 1181, 1396
Kogan, Nathan, 2094
Köhler, Wolfgang, 494, 1181, 1206, 1376, 1393, 1405, 1825
Kolers, Paul A., 1239
Koocher, Gerald P., 1599
Koop, C. Everett, 2591, 2815
Koppitz, Elizabeth M., 1077
Koslow, Stephen, 2752
Koubek, Vlastmil, 2021
Kovacs, Arthur, 2027, 2621
Kraepelin, Emil, 227
Krafft-Ebbing, Richard von, 627
Kraft, Conrad, 1012, 2369
Kramer, Heinrich, 5
Krantz, John C., Jr., 1830
Krapf, Eduardo, 1702
Kraut, Alan, 2686, 2740
Krech, David (Krechevsky, Isadore), 886, 1427
Kretschmer, Ernst, 517
Kries, Johannes von, 214
Kris, Ernst, 688
Kryter, Karl, 1827
Kuder, George Frederick, 1557, 1630, 1633, 1687
Kuhn, Thomas, 1998
Külpe, Oswald, 276, 795
Kutash, Samuel B., 947, 2378

Laborit, Henri, 1683
Lacey, Beatrice C., 988, 1087
Lacey, John I., 988, 1087
Ladd, George Trumball, 165, 496

Ladd-Franklin, Christine, 183, 601
Lamarck, Jean, 41
Lambert, Nadine, 1242
Lambert, Wallace E., 1161
La Mettrie, Julien, 32
Landis, Carney, 638
Landsman, Ted, 1132, 1731
Lange, Carl, 143, 1143
Langer, Ellen, 1601
Langer, Suzanne, 622, 1728
Langfeld, Herbert S., 392, 1217
Langhorne, M. Curtis, 1949, 1970
Lanzer, Ernst, 855
Lanzetta, John T., 1226
Laplace, Pierre S., 45, 57, 103
Lashley, Karl S., 544, 938, 1460, 1520
Latané, Bibb, 2191
Lauber, John, 2677
Laughlin, Philip R., 1484
Lavery, Henry C., 805
Lavoisier, Antoine, 73, 75
Lawton, M. Powell, 2655
Laycock, Thomas, 176
Lazarus, Richard S., 1134
Le Bon, Gustave, 158
Leeper, Robert Ward, 792
Lefcourt, Herbert M., 2117
Lehmann, Alfred G., 252
Lehmann, Harvey, 521
Lehntinen, Laura, 1621
Leibniz, Gottfried Wilhelm, 21, 2126
Leighton, Dorothea C., 874
Lejeune, Jerome, 2004
Lennenberg, Eric, 1126
Lesser, Gerald S., 1240
Leuba, James, 304
LeVay, Simon, 2790
Levelt, Willem, 2546
Levenson, Robert, 2615
Levin, Edith, 2661
Levin, Harry, 1040
Levinson, Daniel J., 1661, 2794
Levinson, Harry, 1131
Levy, Ruth, 1788
Lévy-Bruhl, Lucien, 235
Lewin, Kurt, 549, 792, 1181, 1396, 1582, 1846
Lewis, Frederick H., 1312
Lewis, June, 2316
Liberman, Alvin M., 1039, 2175
Liddle, Howard A., 2688
Liébeault, Ambroise-Auguste, 530

Likert, Rensis, 758, 1961
Lincoln, Abraham, 280
Lindquist, Everet F., 707, 1301, 1516, 1719, 1735, 1921, 2282, 2356
Lindsay, Peter, 2327
Lindsley, Donald B., 780, 857
Lindsley, Ogden, 1152
Lindzey, Gardner, 882, 1107, 1773, 1836
Lippert, Stanley, 1885
Lippmann, Walter, 1156
Lipps, Theodor, 206
Lipsitt, Lewis, 2794
Little, Kenneth B., 1054, 2432
Lloyd, Margaret, 2743, 2783
Locke, John, 18
Lockhart, Robert S., 2346
Locock, Charles, 239
Loeb, Jacques, 255
Loevinger, Jane, 1056
Loewenstein, Sophie, 1184
Logan, Frank A., 1182
Lombroso, Cesare, 146
Lomov, Boris F., 1251, 2319
Long, Beverly, 2464
Long, Howard, 510
Loomer, Harry, 1843
Lord, Frederic M., 955
Lorenz, Konrad, 763, 2372
Lorge, Irving, 352, 803, 1548
Lotze, Rudolf H., 109, 406
Lovell, Joseph, 110
Lowell, Edgar L., 1750
Luce, R. Duncan, 1204, 2016
Luria, Aleksandr R., 735
Lyell, Charles, 230
Lykken, David T., 1280
Lyons, Joseph, 1973

Maccoby, Eleanor E., 1040, 1846, 2141, 2407, 2756
MacCorquodale, Kenneth, 1084
Macfarlane, Jean W., 602
Mach, Ernst, 150
Machiavelli, Niccolò, 2231
Machover, Karen, 740
MacKinnon, Donald W., 744, 1993
MacLeod, Robert B., 1695
Macomber, Lois, 2283, 2295
Madigan, Stephen, 2178
Madrazo, Ignacio Navarro, 2707
Magendie, François, 72
Mahler, Margaret S., 643

Mahoney, Gerald M., 1828
Mahran, Adel, 2180, 2200
Maier, Norman R. F., 737, 1410
Maier, Steven, 2156
Malinowski, Bronislaw, 443, 901
Mallory, Zachariah, 61
Maloney, Lawrence T., 2682
Malthus, Thomas R., 54, 121, 152
Malyon, Alan K., 1503
Mandler, George, 1713, 2559, 2673
Marbe, Karl, 314
March, James G., 1890, 2015
Marlowe, David, 1945
Marotta-Sims, Gregory, 2736
Marquis, Donald, 869, 1489
Marrett, Cora, 2793
Marshall, Henry R., 209
Marshall, Thurgood, 1693
Marston, William M., 586
Martens, Ranier, 2358
Martin, Herman, 1591, 1688
Martin, Lillien J., 205
Martín-Baró, Ignacio, 1526
Marx, Karl, 111
Maskelyne, Nevil, 89, 90
Maslow, Abraham, 864, 1556, 1772, 1936, 2030
Masters, William, 1196, 2115, 2265
Masterson, Jenny, 1221
Matarazzo, Joseph D., 1215, 2496, 2738
Matsumoto, Matataro, 288
Matthews, Charles G., 1321
May, Rollo, 888
Mayer, Ronald, 2088
Mayo, Clara, 1350
Mayo, G. Elton, 409, 1261
McCall, Raymond J., 969
McCandless, Boyd R., 2217
McCarley, Robert W., 2479
McCarthy, Dorothea A., 819
McCarthy, James J., 1959
McCarthy, John, 1268, 2770
McClelland, David C., 1041, 1750, 1967
McClelland, John, 2279
McConnell, James V., 1213, 2513
McCormick, Ernest J., 937, 1865
McCready, Carol, 2588
McCullough, Thomas, 2323
McDougall, William, 331, 725, 1176, 1282
McGaugh, James L., 2490, 2735
McGee, William, 1631

McGeoch, John A., 651, 1352, 1521
McGovern, Thomas, 2783
McGrath, Ellen, 2703, 2771
McGraw, Myrtle, 675
McGuire, William J., 1198
McKeachie, Wilbert J., 1124, 1695, 2691
McKinley, J. Charnley, 760, 1525
McKinney, Fred, 865
McNemar, Quinn, 684, 1644
Mead, George Herbert, 279, 1397
Mead, Margaret, 719
Mednick, Martha T., 1300, 2422
Mednick, Sarnoff A., 1300
Meduna, Ladislas, 1459
Meehl, Paul E., 1092, 1800
Meier, Manfred J., 1306
Meinong, Alexius, 213
Melton, Arthur W., 2544
Melton, Gary B., 1710
Mendel, Gregor J., 120
Menninger, Karl A., 592
Mercer, Jane R., 1188, 2316, 2478
Merrill, Maud M., 513, 1406
Mesh, Scott, 2723
Mesmer, Franz Anton, 39, 64, 70, 73, 75
Meumann, Ernst, 277
Meyer, Adolph, 297
Meyer, Max F., 345
Michael, William B., 2112
Michaels, John, 402
Michotte, Albert E., 417
Miescher, Friedrich, 318
Mikesell, Richard, 2597
Mikulski, Barbara, 2589
Miles, Catherine Cox, 543
Miles, Walter R., 462, 1337, 1498, 1560, 1562
Milgram, Stanley, 1381, 2036, 2050, 2059, 2454
Mill, James, 58
Mill, John Stuart, 100
Miller, George A., 1093, 1639, 1808, 1829, 1931, 2241, 2242, 2735, 2792
Miller, Neal E., 894, 1481, 1507, 2061, 2219, 2310, 2334, 2556, 2583
Miller, Wilfred S., 1618
Millon, Theodore, 2460
Mills, Judson, 1919
Milner, Brenda L., 1065
Mischel, Walter, 1319, 2182, 2550
Mishkin, Mortimer, 1245

Mitchell, Mildred B., 767
M'Naghton, Daniel, 169, 170
Moldawsky, Stanley, 1205
Monahan, John T., 1590, 2537
Moniz, Egas, 355, 1411, 1413
Montessori, Maria, 326, 1008, 2270
Morehouse, Laurence E., 1863
Morgan, C. Lloyd, 207
Morgan, Christiana D., 1539
Morgan, Clifford T., 995, 1089, 1538, 1925, 2045, 2105, 2350
Morgan, Harry, 2243
Morgan, Joseph B., 2490
Morgan, William, 2668
Morgenstern, Oskar, 723, 768
Morin, Stephen F., 1554, 2624
Moro, Ernst, 327
Mote, Frederick A., 850
Mourly-Vold, John, 702
Mowrer, O. Hobart, 839, 1481
Muenzinger, Karl, 466
Müller, Georg E., 200, 205
Müller, Johannes, 97
Müller-Lyer, Franz, 232
Munn, Norman, 742
Munsell, Oliver, 322
Münsterberg, Hugo, 282, 609, 646, 837
Murchison, Carl, 507, 1271, 1276, 1308, 1309, 1317, 1329, 1348, 1394, 1402, 1412
Murchison, Dorothea P., 1414
Murphree, Oddist, 1787
Murphy, Gardner, 617, 1751
Murphy, Lois B., 726
Murray, Henry A., 587, 1477, 1539, 1705
Mussen, Paul H., 1116, 1577
Myers, Charles Roger, 818, 1501, 1596
Myers, Charles S., 341
Myers, Isabel Briggs, 356, 652

Nader, Ralph, 2455
Neale, John M., 2396
Neill, Darryl B., 2167
Neisser, Ulrich, 1292, 2169
Neugarten, Bernice L., 1006, 2794
Newcomb, Simon, 459
Newcomb, Theodore M., 757
Newell, Allen, 1014, 1256, 1804, 1814, 1821, 1829, 1881, 2321, 2654, 2808
Newman, Edwin B., 1312

Newman, Sidney, 2347
Newton, Isaac, 20
Ney, Karl, 1384
Nichols, Charles H., 316
Nie, Norman H., 2276
Nietzsche, Friedrich W., 177
Nisbett, Richard E., 1505
Nissen, Henry, 701
Nixon, Richard, 2284, 2391, 2393
Norman, Donald A., 2073, 2327, 2526
Norman, Ralph D., 1850, 2024
Norsworthy, Naomi, 376
Novick, Melvin R., 1365
Nunnally, Jum C., 1175

Oakes, Ellen, 2436
Ogden, Robert, 375, 1002, 1181
Ohlson, Ron, 2480
Older, Harry, 1827
Olds, James, 1142
Olmedo, Esteban, 2502, 2504
Orne, Martin T., 1269, 1724, 2003, 2025
O'Rouke, Lawrence J., 1147
Orth, Johannes, 180
Ortleb, Ruth, 1649
Osgood, Charles, 1026, 1265, 1783, 1856,
    2025, 2017
Overall, John E., 1989
Owen, Josephine, 503

Pacheco, Alex, 2576
Pacht, Asher R., 1148
Padilla, Amado, 2509, 2794
Page, F. H., 2018
Paine, Harold E., 2024
Paivio, Allan, 2178, 2234, 2300
Palladino, Joseph, 2631
Pallak, Michael S., 1523, 2432, 2648
Palmer, Edward L., 1467, 2248
Pappenheim, Bertha, 254
Paraire, Jean, 1704
Parkinson, James, 49
Pascal, Blaise, 17, 23
Patterson, Gerald R., 1235
Pavlov, Ivan P., 194, 439, 579, 733, 755,
    797, 906, 1112, 1233, 1311, 1393,
    1396, 1399, 1415, 1706, 1912,
    2063, 2246
Payton, Carolyn R., 1203, 2647
Peak, Helen, 685
Pearlstone, Zena, 2134
Pearson, Karl, 234

Peck, Cecil, 1133
Peirce, Charles S., 154, 308, 365, 373
Penfield, Wilder, 557
Penrose, L. S., 1501
Pereire, Jacob, 46
Perkins, F. Theodore, 567
Perloff, Robert, 1113, 2269, 2652
Perls, Fritz, 591, 909
Perls, Laura, 591
Perryman, D. A. R., 1764
Pershing, John J., 1066
Pert, Candace, 2353
Pestalozzi, Johann H., 43, 1571
Peterson, Donald R., 1171
Peterson, John C., 1302
Peterson, Joseph, 384, 929
Peterson, Lloyd R., 1918
Peterson, Margaret J., 1918
Pfaffmann, Carl, 961
Pflüger, Eduard, 132
Pfungst, Oskar, 350, 791
Piaget, Jean, 342, 631, 957, 1283, 1454,
    1721, 2013, 2295
Piéron, Henri, 414, 1136
Pillsbury, Walter B., 336, 838
Pilon, David, 2723
Pinel, Philippe, 42, 84, 85, 86, 1870
Pinter, Rudolf, 457
Piotrowski, Zygmunt A., 778
Plateau, Joseph A. F., 98
Plato, 1
Poffenberger, Albert T., 472, 1362
Polyak, Stephan, 535
Popplestone, John, 2103
Portenier, Lillian G., 547
Porter, Natalie P., 2532
Porteus, Stanley D., 437, 830, 1667
Posner, Michael I., 1428, 2411
Post, Harry H., Jr., 2480
Postman, Leo, 1063, 1725, 1990
Pratt, Carroll, 1498
Premack, David, 1212
Pressey, Sidney, 519, 1222, 1279, 1572,
    1587
Preyer, Wilhelm T., 160, 416
Pribram, Karl H., 1078, 1931
Price, Melvyn, 2436
Prince, Morton, 219, 338, 660, 662, 663,
    814, 824, 913, 1214, 1223, 2066
Proxmire, William, 2522, 2545
Pugh, Edward N., 2622
Purkinje, Jan, 77, 1449

Putnam, James J., 934
Putnam, Tracy, 239

Quételet, Adolphe, 91, 2406

Rahe, Richard H., 2177
Ramón y Cajal, Santiago, 208, 1712
Randall, Lowell O., 1853
Randolph, Jennings, 2632
Rank, Otto, 445, 959
Rapaport, David, 939
Rapaport, William, 2780, 2798
Ratliff, Floyd, 1081
Rauschenbach, Emma, 746
Rawlins, Maxine, 2664
Ray, Isaac, 101
Rayner, Rosalie, 1103
Razran, Gregory, 708
Reagan, Nancy, 2652
Reagan, Ronald, 2632, 2685, 2687, 2699, 2725
Rebelsky, Freda Gould, 2273
Redfield, William, 192
Redl, Fritz, 738, 1700, 1707
Reese, Ellen, 2102
Reich, Wilhelm, 642, 1392, 1737, 1841
Reid, Thomas, 33
Reiff, Robert, 2110, 2131
Reitman, Walter, 2252
Renouvier, Charles, 323
Renshaw, Samuel, 568, 1589
Rescorla, Robert, 1490, 2143
Resnick, Robert J., 1500, 2548
Restle, Frank, 1253
Révész, Géza, 386, 453
Reynolds, George S., 1952
Rhine, Joseph Banks, 619, 1451
Ribot, Théodule Armand, 155, 468
Richards, James B., 212
Richardson, Myron W., 1409
Richet, Charles, 201
Richmond, Lee J., 2810
Richter, Curt P., 604
Rieber, Robert, 2584
Riecken, Henry, 1781
Riesen, Austin H., 1610
Riesman, David, 1776
Rigby, Marilyn K., 1249
Riggs, Lorrin A., 950

Rioch, Margaret, 840
Risley, Todd, 2189
Roback, Abraham A., 545
Roberts, Shearley Oliver, 915
Robinson, Edward, 585
Robinson, Frances, 1699
Robinson, Halbert B., 1330
Robinson, Nancy Mayer, 1330
Robinson, Saul B., 2035
Rock, Irvin, 1149
Rodin, Judith, 1547, 2564
Roe, Anne, 788
Rogers, Carl R., 721, 1684, 1825, 1826, 1987, 2025, 2336
Rogers, Henry, 187
Rohrer, John, 1593
Rokeach, Milton, 1075, 1933, 2043
Rolando, Luigi, 60
Romanes, George J., 188
Rook, Lawrence, 25
Roosevelt, Theodore, 878, 883
Rorschach, Hermann, 456, 1079, 1098, 1120
Rosanoff, Aaron, 382
Rosencrantz, Paul, 2255
Rosenhan, David, 2349
Rosenthal, Robert, 2137, 2187
Rosenzweig, Mark R., 1153, 2116, 2593
Ross, Dorothea, 2006
Ross, Sheila, 2006
Rotter, Julian B., 1023, 2113
Rousseau, Jean-Jacques, 35
Rowan, Carl, 2669
Rowles, Frederick H., Jr., 1923
Royce, Josiah, 224, 552
Rubin, Edgar John, 487
Ruckmick, Christian, 486, 945
Ruiz, Rene, 1303
Rulon, Phillip J., 1719, 1735, 2356
Russell, Roger W., 982
Russo, Nancy Felipe, 2771
Rymarkiewiczowa, Dorota, 1575

Sachs, Hanns, 410, 959
Sakel, Manfred J., 690
Saks, Michael J., 1598
Samuels, Richard, 2547
Sanchez, George I., 833
Sanchez, Pedro Troncoso, 1752
Sanders, Joseph R., 1922, 1942

Sanford, Edmund C., 263, 511, 563, 597, 850
Sanford, Fillmore H., 973, 1674, 1780
Sanford, R. Nevitt, 1661
Sanvold, Kenneth, 2436
Sapir, Edward, 442
Sarason, Seymour B., 1076, 1713
Sarton, George A. L., 451
Sartre, Jean-Paul, 810
Saxe, Leonard, 1605
Scarr, Sandra Wood, 1424, 2457, 2722
Schachter, Stanley, 1138, 1781, 1903, 1996
Schafer, Roy, 1159
Schaie, Klaus Warner, 1274
Schank, Roger, 2510
Scheerer, Martin, 691
Schein, Edgar, 2025
Schiffer, Jerome, 1787
Schildkraut, Joseph J., 2101
Schjelderup, Harald, 1611
Schlesinger, Kurt, 2395
Schlosberg, Harold, 769, 1469, 1758, 1766
Schneider, Stanley F., 1144
Schneirla, Theodore C., 737, 1410
Schoenfeld, William N., 2819
Schopenhauer, Arthur, 78
Schumann, Friedrich, 283
Schur, Max, 1488
Schuster, Charles R., 1318
Schwesinger, Gladys, 1515
Scopes, John, 1200, 1208
Scott, John Paul, 2002
Scott, Walter Dill, 310, 720
Scott, William, 1225
Scripture, Edward Wheeler, 286, 288, 728
Scudder, Samuel H., 432
Sears, David, 2782
Sears, Pauline Snedden, 870
Sears, Robert R., 873, 1040, 1481, 1594, 1846
Seashore, Carl E., 291, 838, 880, 1035, 1139, 1866
Seashore, Harold G., 1615
Sechenov, Ivan M., 133, 295, 1818
Séguin, Edouard O., 104, 368
Seligman, Martin E. P., 1522, 2156
Sells, Saul, 1738
Selye, Hans, 842, 1421, 1823
Sessions, Robert S., 1473
Seward, Georgene H., 722

Seward, John P., 804
Sexton, Virginia Staudt, 1021, 2389
Shaffer, Laurance F., 759
Shainess, Natalie, 1000
Shakow, David, 700, 1616, 1627
Shankweiler, Donald, 2175
Shannon, Claude E., 1639
Sharnik, John, 2243
Shaw, Marvin E., 1881
Sheldon, William H., 667
Shepard, Roger N., 1295
Sherif, Carolyn Wood, 1146
Sherif, Muzafer, 829
Sherman, Julia, 2422
Sherman, Mandel, 1315
Sherrington, Charles S., 244, 1366
Shiffrin, Richard M., 2580
Shinn, Millicent Washburn, 246
Shneidman, Edwin, 1060
Shoben, Joe, 1973
Shock, Nathan W., 836
Shore, Milton, 2456
Sidis, Boris, 301
Sidowski, Joseph B., 2203
Siegel, Alberta E., 2320
Siegel, Max, 1067
Siegel, Sidney, 1004
Siegmann, Philip J., 2087
Siipola, Elsa, 861
Silverstein, Charles, 2351
Simon, Eric, 2353
Simon, Herbert A., 1014, 1256, 1804, 1814, 1821, 1829, 1881, 1890, 2321, 2556, 2654
Simon, Theodore, 346, 806
Simoneit, Max, 1614
Simpkins, Gary, 2241
Sinclair, Upton, 1282
Singer, H. Douglas, 1395
Singer, Jerome, 1996
Skinner, Burrhus F., 776, 1083, 1084, 1152, 1157, 1273, 1305, 1363, 1369, 1423, 1440, 1445, 1470, 1559, 1565, 1620, 1634, 1686, 1826, 1864, 1987, 2047, 2136, 2151, 2216, 2218, 2307, 2309, 2318, 2445, 2513, 2763
Skinner, Deborah, 1565
Skinner, H. Clay, 1663
Skinner, Yvonne, 1423
Slater-Hammel, Arthur T., 2146

Small, Willard S., 325, 704
Smirnov, A. A., 1907
Smith, Anderson D., 2794
Smith, M. Brewster, 1085
Smith, Patricia Cain, 1050
Smith, W. G., 725
Smith, William D., 2394
Snedecor, George W., 1450
Snyder, Solomon, 2353
Solomon, Richard L., 1072
Spaner, Fred E., 2168
Spearman, Charles, 284
Spence, Janet Taylor, 1170, 1733, 2719
Spence, Kenneth, 848, 1825
Spencer, Herbert, 116
Spencer, Lyle M., 1984
Spencer, William A., 2109
Sperling, George, 1388, 1948, 2014
Sperling, Sally E., 2490
Sperry, Roger, 966, 2208, 2572, 2747
Spielberger, Charles D., 1259, 2787
Spinoza, Baruch de, 19
Spitz, René, 495
Spock, Benjamin, 1581, 2628
Spranger, Eduard, 425
Sprenger, Johann, 5
Spurzheim, Johann, 68, 138
Stalnaker, John M., 752
Stammeyer, Eugene, 2020
Stanger, Ross, 1426
Stanley, Julian C., 1025
Starbuck, Edwin, 292
Starr, Henry E., 1314
Staton, Thomas F., 1764
Steinem, Gloria, 2495
Steiner, Gary, 949
Steiner, Matilda, 817
Steinfeld, Julius, 1438
Steingarten, Karen, 2637
Stekel, Wilhelm, 959
Stellar, Eliot, 1089, 2391
Stephenson, William, 731
Stern, L. William, 330
Sternbach, Leo, 1853, 1926
Sternberg, Saul, 1382, 2123
Stevens, S. Smith, 834, 1660, 1685, 1691,
     1748, 1849
Stevenson, Harold, 2556
Stewart, Dugald, 48
Stewart, Judith, 2637
Stoddard, George D., 650

Stogdill, Ralph M., 789
Stolz, Lois M., 559
Stone, Calvin P., 566, 1670
Stouffer, Samuel A., 1513, 1647
Stout, George F., 266
Strang, Ruth, 615
Stratton, George M., 289, 647
Strauss, Alfred A., 1621
Stricker, George, 1432, 2706
Strickland, Bonnie R., 1435, 2771
Strong, Edward K., Jr., 450, 2306
Stroop, John R., 1391
Stroud, James B., 1866
Strupp, Hans H., 1125, 2128
Studdert-Kennedy, Michael, 2175
Stumpf, Carl, 184, 954
Suci, George, 1265, 1856
Sue, Derald, 2345
Sue, Stanley, 1543, 2345
Sullivan, Harry Stack, 565
Sully, James, 714, 725
Sumner, Francis C., 621, 1100
Sundberg, Norman, 1997
Super, Donald E., 917, 1699
Suppes, Patrick, 1135, 2769
Sutich, Anthony, 1936, 1957, 2030
Swets, John A., 1281, 1829, 2130
Symonds, Johnnie P., 1439
Szapocznik, José, 1612
Szasz, Thomas, 1934
Szondi, Lipot, 583

Taft, William H., 944
Tangri, Sandra S., 1300
Tannenbaum, Percy, 1265, 1783, 1856
Tarbell, Horace S., 636
Tarde, Gabriel, 172
Taub, Edward, 2576
Tausk, Victor, 1086
Taylor, Dalmas A., 1383, 2417
Taylor, Franklin, 1827
Taylor, Janet, 1170, 1733
Teicher, Arthur, 2775
Teitelbaum, Philip, 1287
Tepas, Donald I., 2312
Teplin, Linda A., 1679
Teplov, Boris M., 633
Terenius, Lars, 2353
Terman, Lewis M., 372, 513, 543, 1013,
     1122, 1156, 1194, 1277, 1729,
     1759

Teuber, Hans-Lukas, 1018
Theaman, Milton, 1019
Thibaut, John W., 1037, 1114, 1913, 2067
Thigpen, Corbett, 1838, 1862
Thomas, Alexander, 975
Thomas, Charles W., II, 1227, 2201
Thomas, Ernestine, 2201, 2267, 2290
Thomasius, Christian, 29
Thompson, Clara, 596
Thompson, Godfrey, 412
Thompson, James D., 2145
Thompson, Richard F., 1331, 2109, 2158, 2418, 2604
Thompson, Vaida, 2366
Thorndike, Edward L., 352, 747, 803, 962, 1032, 1119, 1339, 1373, 1548, 2711
Thorndike, Robert L., 921
Thorne, Frederick C., 1555
Thurstone, Louis L., 498, 655, 1408, 1409, 1652, 1904
Thurstone, Thelma G., 655
Tijo, Joe Hin, 2004
Tinbergen, Nikolaas, 847, 2372
Titchener, Edward B., 298, 302, 630, 771, 777, 891, 977, 1260, 1271
Tolman, Edward C., 466, 479, 1195, 1342, 1354
Tomes, Henry, 1364
Tomkins, Silvan, 935
Tourette, Gilles de la, 222
Town, Clara H., 1406
Tracy, Carol, 2574
Treisman, Anne, 1407
Troland, Leonard T., 525, 1346, 2622, 2682
Troll, Lillian E., 996
Trow, William Clark, 612, 1511, 1866
Truax, Charles, 2150
Truman, Harry S, 1561, 1583, 1646, 1666
Tryon, Robert C., 711
Tucker, Ledyard R., 920
Tucker, Richard D., 2702
Tulving, Endel, 1264, 1991, 2134
Turner, Henry, 575
Turvey, Michael, 2396
Tversky, Amos, 1387, 1441
Twedt, Dik, 1944
Twitmyer, Edwin B., 348, 733
Tyler, Leona E., 826, 1997, 2306

Underwood, Benton J., 985
Utter, Robert S., 2024
Uzgiris, Ina, 1454

Valentine, Charles W., 393
Valentine, Willard, 796, 1532
Van Gieson, Ira, 628
Vandenberg, Steven, 2262
VandenBos, Gary R., 1541, 2648, 2734
Vasquez, Melba J., 2774, 2777
Veluz, Jean, 1704
Vernon, Philip, 1347
Vernon, William H. D., 1640
Viteles, Morris, 659
Vives, Juan Luis, 6
Vogel, Susan, 2255
Von Békésy, Georg, 673, 1969, 2337
Von Euler, Ulf, 2280
Von Frisch, Karl, 492, 2372
Von Neumann, John, 723, 768
Von Wartensleben, Gabriele Grafin, 689
Vroom, Victor H., 2049
Vygotsky, Lev S., 634

Waddell, Brian A., 2682
Wagner von Jauregg, Julius, 233, 1043
Wagner, Allen R., 1490, 2410
Wald, George, 2173
Walk, Richard D., 1932
Walker, Lenore, 1524
Wallace, Alfred Russel, 121, 248, 249
Wallach, Hans, 794
Wallach, Michael, 2094
Wallin, J. E. Wallace, 922, 1052
Wallon, Henri, 389
Walter, Jr., Paul, 1850
Walters, Richard, 2028
Warden, Carl, 540
Wardrop, James, 129
Warner, Lucien, 693
Warner, Susan, 2553
Warren, Howard C., 299, 599, 770, 1191, 1313, 1322, 1337, 1416, 1468
Warren, Neil, 1635
Washburn, A. L., 940
Washburn, Margaret Floy, 332, 777, 1344, 2289
Watson, Goodwin, 1426, 1427, 2071
Watson, James, 1727

Watson, John B., 345, 378, 716, 860, 938, 956, 977, 983, 1047, 1090, 1103, 1118, 1176, 1190, 1209, 1858, 2513
Watson, Robert I., 889, 1943, 2031, 2068, 2099
Watts, James, 1430, 1434, 1528
Waugh, Nancy C., 2073
Webb, Wilse, 2025
Weber, Ernst, 88
Wechsler, David, 623, 1482
Wedgwood, Josiah, 135
Weinberg, Richard A., 2457
Weinstein, Sidney, 1964, 1979
Weiss, Albert P., 394
Weiss, Stephen, 2496, 2609
Weisskopf-Joelson, Edith, 924
Welch, Bryant, 2686
Welles, G. Orson, 1476
Wellner, Alfred M., 1357, 2397, 2430
Wells, Frederick, 446
Wells, H. G., 1476
Welsh, George S., 1158
Wenger, Marion A., 846
Werner, Heinz, 538
Wertheimer, Max, 397, 795, 926, 1181, 1189, 1567
Wertheimer, Michael, 1257
Wesman, Alexander G., 1615
Wessells, Michael G., 2736
West, James E., 878
West, Joseph V., 1787
Westheimer, Ruth, 2695
Wever, Ernest G., 782, 1326, 1416
Wexler, Nancy, 2824
Wheeler, Raymond, 567
Wherry, Robert J., 783
Whipple, Guy M., 370, 880, 1002, 1866
White, Robert W., 1636, 1920
White, William Alanson, 320, 1323
Whitehouse, Frederick, 1886
Whitely, John M., 2227
Wickens, Delos D., 2253
Wiener, Norbert, 610
Wiens, Arthur N., 1241
Wiesel, Torsten, 2571
Wiggins, Jack G., 1218
Wilberforce, Samuel, 268
Wilbur, Harvey B., 218, 401
Wilcox, Brian, 2795
Williams, Allen, 2192

Williams, Gertrude J., 2317
Williams, Henry S., 501
Williams, Juanita H., 1160
Williams, Roger K., 974
Willis, Virgil, 2503
Wilson, Charles R., 2020
Wilson, John T., 976
Wilson, Woodrow, 1028
Wineman, David, 1700, 1707
Winer, Ben James, 1986
Winner, Ellen, 2598
Wiseman, Frederick, 2405
Withey, Stephen B., 1061
Witkin, Herman A., 1017, 1978
Witmer, Lightner, 300, 574, 635, 637, 756, 1586, 1819
Wohlwill, Joachim, 1285
Wolf, Montrose, 2188, 2189
Wolfe, Harry Kirke, 251, 485
Wolfe, John B., 1775, 1794
Wolff, Werner, 1702
Wolfle, Dael, 820, 1498, 1563, 1570, 1604, 1674, 1694, 1695
Wolman, Benjamin, 2090
Wolpe, Joseph, 989, 1876, 2239
Wood, Scott W., 2488
Woodrow, Herbert, 433
Woodward, Samuel B., 179
Woodworth, Robert S., 315, 769, 827, 838, 1119, 1322, 1337, 1466, 1469, 1758, 1766, 1824
Woolley, Helen T., 354
Worcester, Dean A., 522
Wrenn, C. Gilbert, 1699, 1757
Wright, Herbert F., 856
Wright, Howard E., 863
Wright, John D., 364
Wright, Logan, 1385
Wright, Mary J., 992
Wright, Rogers H., 1250, 2211, 2299
Wundt, Wilhelm, 139, 140, 148, 223, 247, 251, 252, 275, 308, 360, 361, 390, 396, 399, 406, 441, 452, 455, 463, 465, 475, 477, 485, 518, 574, 876, 954, 964, 1540
Wyatt, Gail E., 1552

Yarrow, Leon J., 1127
Yerkes, Robert M., 367, 907, 1028, 1036, 1038, 1051, 1165, 1195, 1393, 1498, 1517, 1549

Young, Andrew, 2720
Young, Paul T., 571, 1195
Young, Thomas, 59
Yule, George, 328

Zachry, Carolyn, 606
Zajonc, Robert, 1172, 2089
Zeigarnik, Bluma W., 697

Zener, Karl, 753
Zigler, Edward F., 1320
Zilboorg, Gregory, 554
Zimbardo, Philip G., 1374, 2301
Zimet, Carl N., 1230
Ziskin, Jay, 2199, 2235
Zubin, Joseph, 695
Zuckerman, John V., 1071
Zwaardemaker, Hendrick, 238

SUBJECT INDEX

Abrahamson v. Gonzalez, 2799

Acadia University, 1640

Accreditation, 1406, 1594, 1627, 1675, 1699, 1734, 1835, 2258, 2264, 2344, 2636

Acta Psychologica, 386, 453

Adapin, 2245

Addiction. *See* Division Index: Divisions 28 and 50

Addiction Research Center, 1294

Addington v. Texas, 2518

Adelphi University, 987, 1163

Adelphi University Institute of Advanced Psychological Studies, 987

Adult development. *See* Division Index: Divisions 7 and 20

Advanced Placement Examination in Psychology, 2803

Advertising. *See* Division Index: Divisions 23 and 46

Aesthetics. *See* Division Index: Division 10

African American psychology. *See* Division Index: Divisions 9 and 45

Agency for Health Care Policy and Research, 2749

Aging. *See* Division Index: Divisions 7 and 20

Aid to Families With Dependent Children law, 936

AIDS, 2566, 2727

Air Force Interdisciplinary Behavioral Sciences Conference, 1850

Ake v. Oklahoma, 2638

Alabama Psychological Association, 1764, 2033

Alaska Psychological Association, 2154, 2480, 2523, 2543

Alcohol, Drug Abuse, and Mental Health Administration, 2384

Allonal, 1474

Allport-Vernon Scale, 1347

Alprazolam, 2573

Alzheimer's Conference, 2700

Alzheimer's disease, 287

American Association for the Accreditation of Laboratory Animal Care, 2076

American Association for the Advancement of Psychotherapy, 1595

American Association for the Advancement of Science, 182, 187, 192, 1122, 1464, 1925, 2428, 2711

American Association for the Study of Mental Imagery, 2521

American Association for Applied Psychology, 472, 1447–1448, 1478, 1493, 1497, 1511, 1536

American Association of Clinical Psychologists, 482, 1052, 1091

American Association of Guidance and Development, 1115

American Association of State Psychology Boards, 1922, 1942, 1954, 1963, 2449, 2473, 2636. *See also* Association of State and Provincial Psychology Boards

American Association of Suicidology, 1060

American Association of University Professors, 1048

American Association of University Women, 1056

American Association on Mental Deficiency, 368–369, 1457, 2277

American Biodyne, 2643

American Board of Examiners in Professional Psychology, 1584, 1604

American Board of Professional Psychology, 710, 1584, 1604, 2304, 2699

American Board of Psychiatry and Neurology, 1395

American College Test, 1921

American Council on Education, 1619

American Counseling Association, 2810

American *Imago*, 410
American Institute for Psychoanalysis, 469
American Institutes for Research, 816
American Journal of Clinical Hypnosis, 717
American Journal of Orthopsychiatry, 1332
American Journal of Psychology, 504
American Journal of Psychotherapy, 1595
American Medical Association, 1910
American Men and Women of Science, 728, 835
American Mental Health Counselors Association, 2524
American Personnel and Guidance Association, 2524
American Philosophical Association, 682, 727
American Philosophical Society, 977
American Psychiatric Association, 101, 178–179, 204, 305, 589, 827, 2351, 2373, 2539, 2666, 2755
American Psychoanalytic Association, 934
American Psychological Association. *See* APA
American Psychological Association of Graduate Students (APAGS), 2723
American Psychological Foundation, 1736
American Psychological Foundation Distinguished Contributions to Education in Psychology Award, 2273
American Psychological Foundation Distinguished Scientific Writing Award, 1857
American Psychological Foundation Distinguished Achievement Award, 2302
American Psychological Foundation Gold Medal, 1824
American Psychological Foundation National Media Award, 1857, 2243
American Psychological Society, 2679, 2718–2719, 2735, 2740–2741, 2753, 2758
American Psychological Society William James Fellow, 2758
American Psychologist, 999, 1549, 1553, 1564, 1570, 2333, 2505, 2738
American Psychology–Law Society, 2199, 2235, 2552. *See also* Division Index: Division 41
American Psychopathological Association, 913

American Red Cross, 2797
American Social Science Association, 670
American Society for Psychical Research, 458–459
American Society of Clinical Hypnosis, 717
American Soldier, 1513, 1647
American Vocational Guidance Association, 1115
Americans With Disabilities Act, 2813
Amitriptyline, 1955
Amobarbital, 1778
Amoxapine, 2554
Amytal, 1778
Anafranil, 2750
Analysis of variance, 539
Animal Enterprise Protection Act, 2817
Animal Learning and Behavior, 2352
Animal psychology, 56, 122, 188, 190, 207, 240, 255, 303, 367, 467, 492, 523, 540, 566, 570, 590, 693–694, 701, 704, 711, 737, 763, 847, 907, 932, 1123, 1137, 1142, 1349, 1378, 1380, 1520, 1654, 1809, 1887, 1923, 2174, 2604. *See also* Division Index: Divisions 3 and 6
Animal subjects, 123, 294, 363, 1195, 2076, 2127, 2576, 2650, 2817. *See also* Ethics: Experimental
Animal Welfare Act, 2127, 2650
Anna O. case, 254, 403, 408, 424, 427, 430–431
Annual Review of Psychology, 1670
Antivivisectionism, 363
APA (General), 573, 727, 2355, 2577, 2684, 2730, 2796–2797
APA Ad Hoc Committee on Minority Affairs, 2502
APA amicus curiae briefs, 1977, 2659, 2755
APA annual meeting, 582, 601, 656, 837, 1002, 1336, 1518. *See also* APA convention
APA anonymous review, 2333
APA Award for Distinguished Career Contributions to Education and Training in Psychology, 2691
APA Award for Distinguished Contribution to Research in Public Policy, 2722
APA Award for Distinguished Contributions to Education and Training in Psychology, 2692

APA Award for Distinguished Contributions to Psychology in the Public Interest, 2497

APA Award for Distinguished Contributions to the International Advancement of Psychology, 2789

APA Award for Distinguished Professional Contributions, 721, 2336

APA Award for Distinguished Scientific Contributions, 721, 1825

APA Board of Directors, 1646, 2679

APA Board of Ethnic Minority Affairs, 1364

APA books, 1771, 1873

APA budget, 657

APA buildings, 1674, 1708, 1709, 1711, 1972, 2000, 2005, 2017, 2021–2022, 2100, 2477, 2705, 2728, 2746, 2748, 2800, 2821

APA centennial, 2787, 2811, 2814, 2821

APA Central Office, 2441

APA China visit, 2556

APA Citation for Lifetime Contributions to Psychology, 2763

APA Committee on Animal Research and Ethics, 1195

APA Committee on Lesbian and Gay Concerns, 2540

APA Committee on Methods of Teaching Psychology, 880

APA Committee on Physical and Mental Tests, 657

APA Committee on Research Support, 2490

APA Committee on Scientific and Professional Ethics, 1473

APA Committee on Training in Clinical Psychology, 1616

APA Committee on Women in Psychology Leadership Awards, 2647

APA Conference on Patterns and Levels of Professional Training, 2362

APA Congressional Science Fellow, 2428

APA convention, 681, 1053, 1363, 1826, 1858, 1916, 2166, 2198, 2240, 2242, 2272, 2337, 2455, 2474, 2495, 2528–2529, 2569, 2589, 2591, 2628, 2646, 2669, 2690, 2693–2695, 2720, 2788, 2815. See also APA annual meeting

APA Council of Representatives, 2291, 2355, 2603, 2786

APA *Daily News*, 2788

APA directorates, 2686

APA Distinguished Award for an Early Career Contribution to Psychology in the Public Interest, 1546

APA Distinguished Contribution for Applications of Psychology Award, 2369

APA Distinguished Scientist Lecture Series, 2756

APA Distinguished Scientific Award for Early Career Contributions to Psychology, 2396

APA divisions: For entries with subject matter related to APA divisions, see the APA Division Index. The following entries relate to the histories of the divisions.

APA Division 1, 2673

APA Divisions 1–19, 1549

APA Division 2, 1249, 2402, 2553

APA Division 3, 1645, 1964, 1979

APA Division 4, 1408

APA Division 6, 1645, 1964, 1979, 1995

APA Division 12, 1052, 1091, 1873, 2009, 2128, 2168, 2325

APA Division 16, 1609, 2602

APA Division 17, 2227, 2501

APA Division 20, 1569, 1572, 1587

APA Division 21, 1827

APA Division 22, 1878, 1883, 1886

APA Division 23, 1944

APA Division 24, 1973, 1994

APA Division 25, 2047, 2056

APA Division 26, 889, 1943, 2088, 2099

APA Division 27, 2098, 2110, 2129, 2131

APA Division 28, 2120, 2132

APA Division 29, 2009, 2027, 2128, 2168, 2338, 2621

APA Division 30, 2180, 2200, 2206

APA Division, 31, 1617, 2072, 2192, 2196, 2207, 2211

APA Division 32, 2296, 2305

APA Division 33, 2277, 2323, 2339

APA Division 34, 2347, 2366

APA Division 35, 2343, 2357, 2367

APA Division 36, 2365, 2389, 2434

APA Division 37, 2456, 2462

APA Division 38, 2493, 2496

APA Division 39, 2530

APA Division 40, 2506, 2531

APA Division 41, 1590, 2199, 2235, 2537, 2552

APA Division 42, 2547, 2561

APA Division 43, 2597, 2629

APA Division 44, 2567, 2624, 2630

APA Division 45, 2664, 2670

APA Division 46, 2582, 2661, 2671, 2678

APA Division 47, 2668, 2672

APA Division 48, 2736, 2744

APA Division 49, 2775

APA Division 50, 2823

APA dues, 2653

APA Education and Training Board, 2032

APA ethical standards, 1473, 1714, 1730, 2397, 2708, 2822. See also Ethics: Experimental, Ethics: Professional

APA Ethnic and Cultural Affairs Office, 2502, 2504

APA Ethnic Minority Affairs Office, 2491

APA Experimental Publication System, 2237

APA G. Stanley Hall Lecture Series, 2550

APA History of Psychology Group, 1943. See also Division Index: Division 26

APA, Incorporated, 1192–1193, 1199

APA journal policy, 2225, 2470, 2512

APA journals, 907, 2298, 2465

APA lecture series, 2794

APA library, 2544

APA logo, 2784

APA Master Lectures, 2395

APA media forum, 2772

APA Minority Fellows, 2417

APA Minority Fellowship Program, 1383

APA Monitor, 2505

APA National Media Award, 2334

APA National Media Grand Prix Award, 2334

APA Office of Cultural and Ethnic Affairs, 2491

APA Presidential Citation, 2581, 2634, 2652

APA Psychology Defense Fund, 2543

APA Psychology Exhibition, 2778

APA Public Policy Office, 2795

APA public service messages, 2641

APA Publication Office, 1070

APA reorganization, 472, 820, 1448, 1535–1536, 1549, 1563, 2679, 2718

APA Rural Mental Health Caucus, 2776

APA Science Agenda, 2713

APA Science Day, 2781

APA Science Directorate Funding Bulletin, 2730

APA Science Weekend, 2721

APA Scientific Psychology Forum, 2772

APA staff, 1045

APA Student Affiliate Organization, 2590

APA student travel scholarships, 2338

APA Task Force on the Feminization of Psychology, 2796

APA Task Force on the Status of Women in Psychology, 1916, 2278

APA Task Force on Victims of Crime and Violence, 2633

APA Task Force on Women and Depression, 2703, 2771

APA tax status, 1487

APA Tennis Tournament, 2399

APA Traveling Psychology Exhibition, 2804, 2814

APA-SPAN, 2768

APAGS, 2723. See also American Psychological Association of Graduate Students

Apparatus, 805, 808, 1053, 1222, 1928, 2057, 2203

Applied Behavioral Science Symposium, 2486

Applied psychology, 330. See also Division Index: Divisions 14 and 21

Aprobarbital, 1474

Archives de Psychologie, 342

Archives of General Psychiatry, 1910

Archives of the History of American Psychology, 2103

Arizona Psychological Association, 1656, 1663, 2075

Arizona State University, 2069

Arkansas Psychological Association, 1787, 2251

Armed services. See Division Index: Division 19

Army Alpha Test, 446, 1051, 1156

Army Beta Test, 457, 1051

Army General Classification Test, 1496, 1607

Artificial intelligence, 2139

Arts. See Division Index: Division 10

Arvynol, 1801

Asendin, 2554

Asian American Psychological Association, 1543, 2345, 2452, 2645
Assembly for Scientific and Applied Psychology, 2679, 2719
Assessment. *See* Division Index: Divisions 5 and 12
Association for Behavior Analysis International, 2383, 2488, 2541
Association for Computing Machinery, 2139
Association for Consumer Research, 1113, 2269
Association for High School Teachers of Psychology, 2816
Association for Humanistic Psychology, 1001, 2030
Association for the Advancement of Behavior Therapy, 2263
Association for the Advancement of Psychology, 2375, 2380, 2413, 2435
Association of American Psychologists, 2375, 2380
Association of Black Psychologists, 1227, 2201, 2394
Association of Consulting Psychologists, 1422, 1439, 1447
Association of Gay Psychologists, 2368
Association of Lesbian and Gay Psychologists, 1554
Association of Medical Officers of Asylums and Hospitals for the Insane, 215
Association of Psychologists of Nova Scotia, 2018
Association of Psychology Postdoctoral and Internship Centers, 2680
Association of State and Provincial Psychology Boards, 1922, 1942, 1954, 1963. *See also* American Association of State Psychology Boards
Association of Women in Psychology, 2278, 2292, 2437
Associationism, 34, 58, 100. *See also* Division Index: Division 24
Asylum Journal, 167, 215
Atarax, 1810
Ativan, 2476
Autism, 1403, 1550, 2359
Aventyl, 2058
Aviation psychology, 1486. *See also* Division Index: Divisions 19 and 21

Baker v. Owen, 2466
BAPPI. *See* Board for the Advancement of Psychology in the Public Interest

Bard College, 1702
Barefoot v. Estelle, 2613
Battle of Behaviorism debate, 1176
Bayley Scales of Infant Development, 677
Behavior analysis. *See* Division Index: Division 25
Behavior Analyst, 2488
Behavior Genetics, 2262
Behavior modification, 1152, 1333, 2341, 2377, 2390, 2429
Behavior Research Methods, Instruments, and Computers, 2203
Behavior Theory in Practice, 2102
Behavior Therapy, 2263
Behavioral economics, 715
Behavioral economics conference, 2623
Behavioral Neuroscience, 2604, 2606
Behavioral Science, 999, 1807
Behaviorally Anchored Rating Scales, 1050
Behaviorism, 378, 776, 956, 977, 1470. *See also* Division Index: Division 25
Bellevue Psychiatric Hospital, 1433
Ben-Shalom v. Stone, 2754
Benadryl, 1574
Bender Visual Motor Gestalt Test, 648, 1077, 1475
Bennington College, 757
Benton Visual Retention Test, 903
Bethany College, 1664
Bicêtre asylum, 42, 84–86, 272
Biofeedback, 512
Biofeedback conference, 2467
Biopsychology, 87, 124, 151, 191, 240, 272–273, 306, 315, 351, 528, 544, 786, 857, 893, 966, 988, 1078, 1087, 1287, 1289, 1331, 1352, 1401, 1442, 2353, 2739. *See also* Division Index: Divisions 6 and 40
Black mental health symposium, 2446
Black Students Psychological Association, 2241, 2267, 2290
Blue Cross case, 2364
Blue Shield of Virginia v. McCready, 2588
BMD computer program, 2274
Board for the Advancement of Psychology in the Public Interest (BAPPI), 2491, 2774, 2777
Boston University, 1057, 2078, 2575
Boulder Conference, 858, 1653, 2751
Bowen v. City of New York, 2662
Brain, 168

Brandeis University, 1970
Briggs v. Elliott, 1693
Brigham Young University, 929
British Columbia Psychological Association, 1579
British Journal of Educational Psychology, 393
British Journal of Psychology, 331, 341
British Psychological Society, 331, 714, 725, 2077
Brown University, 285
Brown v. Board of Education, 981, 1049, 1693, 1765
Bryn Mawr College, 304, 508
Buckley Amendment, 2408
Bulletin of the Psychonomic Society, 2350
BuSpar, 2675
Buspirone, 2675
Bystander intervention, 2046

California F Scale, 872, 1661
California Personality Inventory, 1832
California Psychological Association, 1635, 1852, 1898
California School of Professional Psychology, 1183, 2183, 2226, 2275, 2335
California State Psychological Association, 1635
California State University, Los Angeles, 1958
Cambridge Center for Behavioral Studies, 2578, 2757
Canadian Board of Examiners in Professional Psychology, 1632
Canadian Psychological Association, 497, 818, 992, 1464, 1501, 1558, 1579, 1603, 2684
Canadian psychology, 1510, 2001, 2018
CAPP v. Rank, 2759
CAPPS. *See* Council for the Advancement of the Psychological Professions and Sciences
Carbamazepine, 2184
Caribbean Center for Advanced Studies, 1104
Carleton College, 2379
Carnegie Foundation for the Advancement of Teaching, 1619
Carnegie Institute of Technology, 407, 1052
Carnegie Institution, 724
Case Western Reserve Mental Development Center, 1117

Catalog of Selected Documents in Psychology, 2315, 2614
Cattell Developmental Scales, 594
Cattell Fund, 1527
Center for Cognitive Studies, 997, 2125
Central Intelligence Agency, 1937, 2025, 2472
Central limit theorem, 103
Centrax, 2459
CHAMPUS. *See* Civilian Health and Medical Program of the Uniformed Services
Character and Personality, 1361
Cheiron, 889, 2205
Chicago Conference on Professional Preparation of Clinical Psychologists, 2092
Chicago Institute of Psychoanalysis, 556
Chicago Juvenile Psychopathic Institute, 307, 395, 415, 674, 1228
Chicano psychology symposium, 2447
Child Abuse Prevention and Treatment Act, 2715
Child advocacy, 2408, 2520, 2709
Child care, 936, 1916
Child Conference for Research and Welfare, 892
Child development. *See* Division Index: Divisions 7, 33, and 37
Child Development, 1324
Child services. *See* Division Index: Divisions 18, 27, and 37
Childhood Society of Great Britain, 658
Children's Television Workshop, 1240, 1467, 2248
China (People's Republic of China), 2556
Chloral hydrate, 1504
Chlorazepate, 2332
Chlordiazepoxide, 1853, 1926, 1929
Chlormezanone, 1893
Chlorpromazine, 1683, 1704, 1760
Chlorprothixene, 1892
Christian Association for Psychological Studies, 1761, 1842, 1911
City University of New York, 2692
Civil Rights Act, 2051
Civilian Health and Medical Program of the Uniformed Services, 2266, 2525, 2549
Clark University, 225, 263, 511, 573, 876, 892, 896, 897–899, 901–902, 1100, 1317, 1662, 2811

Clemson University, 2803
Clever Hans, 350, 791
Clinical child psychology, 653
Clinical neuropsychology. *See* Division Index: Divisions 6, 28, and 40
Clinical Psychologists Group of the District of Columbia, 1580
Clinical psychology, 300, 574, 637, 1586. *See also* Division Index: Division 12
Clinical Social Work Conference on Family Therapy, 2516
Clinical training, 446, 481, 700, 1144, 1406, 1594, 1616, 1627, 1653, 1675, 1835, 2092, 2264, 2325, 2344, 2362, 2492, 2517, 2636, 2683, 2751
Clinician's Research Digest, 1432, 2706
Clomipramine, 2750
Clonazepam, 2423
Clozapine, 2745
Clozaril, 2745
Cognitive development, 1187, 1283, 1297
Cognitive psychology, 112, 610, 997, 1063, 1080, 1083, 1093, 1167, 1229, 1239, 1253, 1256, 1264, 1268, 1281, 1292, 1295, 1298, 1358, 1359, 1370, 1382, 1387, 1428, 1441, 1480, 1492, 1639, 1804, 1808, 1814, 1820–1821, 1829, 1881, 1976, 1991, 2139, 2321, 2510, 2521, 2526, 2654, 2757, 2770, 2780, 2798, 2808
Cognitive Psychology, 2252
Cognitive Science Society, 2510, 2526
College Entrance Examination Board, 698, 709, 1232, 1619
Colorado Conference on Graduate Education in Clinical Psychology, 1653
Colorado Psychological Association, 1956, 2592
Colorado State University, 1992
Columbia University, 354, 376, 601, 888, 945, 956, 1048, 1519, 1642
Commitment, 2518. *See also* Patient rights
Community mental health centers, 2008, 2040, 2568
Community mental health conference, 2078
Community psychology. *See* Division Index: Divisions 18, 27, and 37

Compazine, 1844
Comparative psychology. *See* Division Index: Division 6
Computer application, 1268, 1335, 1719, 1735, 2139, 2274, 2312–2313, 2649, 2674, 2698, 2730, 2757, 2768, 2779
Concept Formation Test, 801
Conference of State Psychological Societies, 1617. *See also* Division Index: Division 31
Conference on Applied Social Psychology, 2658
Conference on Morale, 1493, 1497
Conference on Prevention, 2515
Conference on Professional and Social Issues in Psychology, 2072, 2196. *See also* Division Index: Division 31
Conference on Urban Mental Health, 2617
Confidentiality, 2503
Conflict resolution. *See* Division Index: Divisions 9 and 48
Connecticut Psychological Association, 1551, 1560, 1562, 1573
Connecticut Society for Mental Hygiene, 867
Connecticut State Psychological Society, 1551, 1573
Consumer psychology. *See* Division Index: Division 23
Contemporary Psychology, 1806
Cornell University, 241, 656, 1050, 1181, 1363, 1694–1695
Corporal punishment, 2466
Corporation of Psychologists of the Province of Quebec, 1822, 1828
Council for Applied Masters Programs in Psychology, 2702
Council for Exceptional Children, 1151, 1164
Council for the Advancement of the Psychological Professions and Sciences, 1218, 2299, 2364, 2375, 2413, 2435
Council of Chairmen of Graduate Departments of Psychology, 2032, 2055, 2097
Council of Graduate Departments of Psychology, 2032, 2055, 2097

Council of Teachers of Undergraduate Psychology, 2197
Council of Undergraduate Psychology Departments, 2197
Council of Undergraduate Psychology Programs, 2743, 2764
Council on Undergraduate Research, 2825
Counseling of women, 2501
Counseling Psychologist, 2227
Counseling psychology. *See* Division Index: Division 13
Counselor training, 1699, 1734
Cumulative recorder, 1928
Current Research Summaries, 2298

Dalmane, 2260
Dantol, 1479
Dartmouth College, 1426, 1701
Deafness, 108
Dearborn Group Tests of Intelligence, 383
Debriefing, 2059
Decade of the Brain, 2739
Delaware Psychological Association, 1988
Desipramine, 2060
Desoxyn, 1542
Desryl, 2579
Detroit Edison v. National Labor Relations Board, 2508
Developmental disabilities. *See* Division Index: Division 33
Developmental psychology. *See* Division Index: Divisions 7, 20, and 37
Developmental Psychology, 2217
Developmental Test of Visual Perception, 823
Devereux Schools, 2443
Diagnostic and Statistical Manual of Mental Disorders, 1503, 2351, 2373, 2539, 2666
Diana v. State Board of Education, 2414
Diazepam, 2042
Differential Aptitude Test, 1615
Dilantin, 1723
Dimethacol, 2104
Diphenhydramine, 1574
Directory of Psychological Service Centers, 1739
Disabled services, 130. *See also* Division Index: Division 22
Disabled access, 2505, 2813

Disabled student services, 2326, 2439, 2676, 2765. *See also* Division Index: Division 33
Disaster relief, 2797
District of Columbia Psychological Association, 1315, 1580, 1592, 1718, 2020, 2284
DNA, 318, 1727
Doctor of Mental Health degree, 2492
Donald and Gua Study, 1349, 1378
Doriden, 1777
Down's Syndrome, 131
Downey Will-Temperament Tests, 358
Doxepin, 2245
Draw-A-Man Test, 484, 1236
Draw-A-Person Test, 740
Dreaming, 702, 1939, 2479
Drug treatment center, 216, 1294
Drugs. *See* Division Index: Divisions 6, 28, and 50
DSM. *See Diagnostic and Statistical Manual of Mental Disorders*
Duke University, 645, 1361
Dulles Conference, 2491
Durham v. U.S., 1768
Duty to protect law, 2651

Eastern Branch of the APA, 1417, 1460
Eastern Psychological Association, 626, 747, 1322, 1417, 1460
Economic psychology. *See* Division Index: Divisions 8, 14, and 23
Education and credentialing conference, 2449
Educational and Psychological Measurement, 1502
Educational Psychologist, 1511
Educational psychology. *See* Division Index: Division 15
Educational Psychology Newsletter, 1511
Educational Research Act, 1769
Educational Testing Service, 1431, 1619, 1622, 2282, 2455, 2803
Edwards Personal Preference Survey, 1705, 1779
Elavil, 1955, 2091, 2482
Electroconvulsive shock therapy, 1459, 2596
Electroencephalogram, 344
Electronic journals, 2730, 2768
Emmy von N. case, 526, 534

Emory University, 1591
Emotion, 312, 333, 586, 641, 780, 1386
Empiricism, 18
Employment Retirement Income Security Act (ERISA), 2642
Endep, 1955
Endorphins, 2353, 2421
Engineering psychology. See Division Index: Division 21
Enkephalin, 2421
Environmental psychology. See Division Index: Divisions 21 and 34
Epilepsy, 144, 239, 557, 1384
Equal Rights Amendment, 2294, 2433, 2474
Equanil, 1791
Ergonomics. See Division Index: Division 21
ERISA decision, 2642
Eskalith, 2259
Ethchlorvynol, 1801
Ethics: Experimental, 123, 294, 363, 1195, 2050, 2059, 2076, 2127, 2301, 2386, 2391, 2405, 2576, 2650, 2714. See also Animal subjects
Ethics: Professional, 1473, 1714, 1730, 2084, 2342, 2397, 2450, 2708, 2822. See also APA ethics policy, patient rights
Ethnic Affairs, 2502, 2504
Etraphon, 2091
Eugenics, 845, 1177, 1202, 1263, 1270, 1585
Evaluation. See Division Index: Division 5
European Society for Philosophy and Psychology, 2812
Exercise psychology. See Division Index: Division 47
Experiential education conference, 2400
Experimental analysis of behavior. See Division Index: Division 25
Experimental laboratories. See Laboratories
Experimental psychology. See Division Index: Division 3
Experimental social psychology. See Division Index: Division 8
Expert testimony, 1977, 2613

Factor analysis, 412
Family services. See Division Index: Divisions 27 and 37

Family therapy conference, 2516
Family psychology. See Division Index: Division 43
Federal Aviation Administration, 2204
Federal Employees Health Benefit Act, 2393
Federation of Behavioral, Psychological, and Cognitive Sciences, 2559
Feeble-Minded Club, 718
Fisk University, 915
Florida Presbyterian College, 2167
Florida Psychological Association, 1960, 2523, 2637, 2799
Fluoxetine, 2704
Fluphenazine, 1917
Flurazepam, 2260
Focus On Behavior television series, 2034
Ford Foundation, 2422, 2447
Ford v. Wainwright, 2665
Fordham University, 1417
Forensic psychology. See Division Index: Division 41
Foucha v. Louisiana, 2805
Frankfurt Psychoanalytic Institute, 686
Freedom of choice, 2266
Freedom of choice laws, 1500, 2195, 2364, 2393, 2398, 2448, 2489, 2548, 2588, 2616, 2619, 2642, 2759, 2766, 2785, 2802
Fuller Theological Seminary Graduate School of Psychology, 2344
Functionalism, 165, 262, 311, 343. See also Division Index: Division 24

G Place Limited Partnership, 2728
Gainesville conference, 2680, 2751
Gay and lesbian psychology. See Division Index: Divisions 9 and 44
Gay Psychologists' Caucus, 2368
General adaptation syndrome, 1421, 1823
General Aptitude Test Battery, 2762
General psychology. See Division Index: Division 1
George Washington University, 1430, 1592, 1698
Georgetown University, 2467
Georgia Psychological Association, 1591, 1613, 1688
Gerbrands Corporation, 1928, 2057
German Institute for Psychological Research, 1418

Gerontology. *See* Division Index: Division 20

Gesell Institute of Child Development, 400, 875

Gestalt psychology, 258, 375, 397, 478, 494, 549, 624, 689, 1189, 1567

Glutethimide, 1777

Goodenough Intelligence Test for Kindergarten–Primary, 1234

Göring Institute, 1418

Government service. *See* Division Index: Division 18

Graduate Education in Psychology conference, 1130, 1508, 2683

Graduate Record Examination, 1681

Graham-Kendall Memory for Designs Test, 1068

Griggs v. Duke Power Co., 2287

Group psychology. *See* Division Index: Divisions 8 and 49

Group psychotherapy. *See* Division Index: Divisions 12, 29, and 49

Guilford Award (Psi Chi), 2167

Halazepam, 2570

Halcion, 2599

Halderman v. Pennhurst State School, 2481

Haldol, 2152

Haloperidol, 2152

Halstead Battery of Neuropsychological Tests, 879

Handicapped services. *See* Disabled services

Harvard Medical School, 669

Harvard Psychological Clinic, 219

Harvard University, 156, 282, 381, 383, 440, 536, 552, 561, 587, 609, 616, 646, 672, 808, 837, 997, 1206, 1240, 1477, 1520, 1601, 1620, 1820, 2125

Hawaii Psychological Association, 1643, 1982, 2160

Hawthorne effect, 1261

Head Start, 726, 972, 2053, 2079, 2601, 2801

Health Insurance Association of America, 2448

Health psychology. *See* Division Index: Divisions 38 and 47

Health psychology conference, 2609

Healy-Fernald tests, 307, 395

Hedonism, 13

Henmon-Nelson Test of Mental Ability, 377

High school psychology, 2379, 2494

High schools, 1840

Highgate Asylum for Idiots, 185

Hispanic Journal of Behavioral Sciences, 2509

Hispanic psychology. *See* Division Index: Division 45

History of psychology. *See* Division Index: Division 26

Hogg Foundation for Mental Health, 1495

Homelessness, 2687

Homosexuality, 2351, 2373, 2666, 2754, 2790. *See also* Division Index: Division 44

Honig v. Doe, 2709

Horney Clinic, 1793

Hospital staff privileges, 2489, 2616, 2619, 2759, 2785, 2802

House-Tree-Person Test, 2560

Howard University, 649

Human Behavior and Evolution Society, 2726

Human factors, 462, 868, 946, 960, 2204, 2511, 2677. *See also* Division Index: Divisions 19, 21, and 34

Human factors, 1885

Human Factors and Ergonomics Society, 1863

Human Factors Research Symposium, 1958

Human Factors Society, 1863, 1885

Human participants protection, 2386, 2391. *See also* Ethics: Experimental

Human Relations, 1625

Human Resources Research Office (HumRRO), 1698, 1726, 2595. *See also* Human Resources Research Organization

Human Resources Research Organization (HumRRO), 923. *See also* Human Resources Research Office

Humanistic Psychologist, 2681

Humanistic psychology, 2062. *See also* Division Index: Division 32

HumRRO, 923, 1698, 1726, 2595

Huntington's disease, 199, 2618, 2824

Hutchinson v. Proxmire, 2543, 2545

Hydroxyzine, 1810, 1879

Hypnosis. *See* Division Index: Division 30

Hypnotic testimony, 2612

Idaho Psychological Association, 2023, 2657

Illinois Psychological Association, 2026

Illinois Test of Psycholinguistic Abilities, 1959

Illuminator, 173

Imipramine, 1859, 1902

Independent practice. *See* Division Index: Division 42

Indiana Psychological Association, 1453, 2224

Indiana State University, 2631

Indiana University, 269, 1465, 2674

Individual differences, 74, 89–90, 117. *See also* Division Index: Division 5

Indoklon, 1830

Industrial psychology. *See* Division Index: Division 14

Ingraham v. Wright, 2466

Innocent VII, Pope, 5

Insanity defense, 169–170, 418, 502, 1768, 2611, 2638, 2665, 2805

Institute for Behavioral Research, 2576

Institute for Child Guidance, 1267

Institute for Juvenile Research, 1228

Institute for Personality and Ability Testing, 1659

Institute for Sex Research, 1602

Institute of Electrical and Electronics Engineers, 1829

Institute of Child Behavior and Development, 1035

Institute of Human Relations, 311, 1296, 1345

Institute of Psychology, 1510

Institute on Teaching Psychology to Undergraduates, 2499

Instituto Psicologico de Puerto Rico, 1104

Instrumentation. *See* Apparatus

Insulin shock therapy, 690, 1433, 1438

Intelligence, 242, 330, 346, 372, 473, 513, 623, 713, 802, 806, 1046, 1145, 1169, 1188, 1325, 2144, 2222, 2712. *See also* Division Index: Division 5

Inter-Society Color Council, 1362

Interamerican Congress of Clinical Psychology, 2401

Interamerican Congress of Psychology, 7, 1752

Interamerican Society of Psychology, 1702

Intercollegiate Psychological Association, 1642

International Asian Conference in Psychology, 2820

International Association for the Scientific Study of Mental Deficiency, 2170

International Behavioral Neuroscience Conference, 2807

International Congress of Behavioral Medicine, 2760

International Congress of Health Psychology, 2767

International Congress of Psychiatry, Neurology, and Psychology, 853

International Congress of Psychoanalysis, 866, 967, 1155

International Congress of Psychology, 128, 529, 1310–1311

International Congress on Behaviorism and the Sciences of Behavior, 2819

International Congress on Hypnotism, 530

International Congress on Mental Health, 1702

International Congress on Mental Hygiene, 1323

International Council of Psychologists, 1512, 1514–1515

International Council of Scientific Unions, 2593

International Journal of Clinical and Experimental Hypnosis, 1724

International Psychoanalytic Association, 912

International psychology, 2789

International relations. *See* Division Index: Division 48

International Society for Developmental Psychobiology, 2215

International Society for the History of the Behavioral and Social Sciences, 2205. *See also* Cheiron

International Society for the Study of Behavioral Development, 2297

International Union of Psychological Science, 1696–1697, 2593

Intersociety Constitutional Convention, 1535

Iowa Child Welfare Research Station, 291, 1035, 1360

Iowa Psychological Association, 1637, 1831, 2385

Iowa Tests of Basic Skills, 707, 1301, 1398, 1516, 1719
Iproniazid, 1843
Isocarboxazid, 1909

Jackson v. Indiana, 2329
James I, 15
Janimine, 1902
Jean Piaget Society, 2283, 2285, 2295
Jenkins v. U.S., 1977
Job Descriptive Index, 1050
Johns Hopkins University, 92, 278, 399, 423, 436, 444, 459, 798, 860, 938, 979, 1047
Joint Commission for the Accreditation of Hospitals, 2619
Jones v. U.S., 2611
Journal of Abnormal and Social Psychology, 824, 1214, 1223, 2066
Journal of Abnormal Psychology, 219, 824, 1223, 2066
Journal of Applied Behavior Analysis, 2188
Journal of Applied Behavioral Science, 2071
Journal of Applied Psychology, 1031
Journal of Black Psychology, 2394
Journal of Clinical Child Psychology, 2317
Journal of Clinical Psychology, 1555
Journal of Comparative and Physiological Psychology, 1070, 1123, 2604, 2606
Journal of Comparative Psychology, 1123, 2606
Journal of Conflict Resolution, 1255
Journal of Consulting and Clinical Psychology, 1439, 2731
Journal of Consulting Psychology, 1439
Journal of Counseling Psychology, 1757, 2333
Journal of Educational Psychology, 370, 1866
Journal of Experimental Psychology: Animal Behavioral Processes, 2410
Journal of Experimental Psychology: Human Perception and Performance, 2411–2412, 2580
Journal of Experimental Psychology: Learning, Memory, and Cognition, 2412, 2580
Journal of Experimental Psychology, 299, 2410–2412
Journal of Experimental Social Psychology, 1037, 2067
Journal of Family Psychology, 2688, 2761, 2773

Journal of General Psychology, 507, 1271
Journal of Genetic Psychology, 555
Journal of Humanistic Psychology, 1936, 1957
Journal of Nervous and Mental Disease, 349
Journal of Neurophysiology, 1456
Journal of Parapsychology, 1455
Journal of Personality and Social Psychology, 219, 1223, 2066, 2512
Journal of Personality, 1361
Journal of Psychology, 1412, 1414
Journal of Self Psychology, 1936
Journal of Social Psychology, 507, 1317
Journal of the American Psychoanalytic Association, 1722
Journal of the Asian American Psychological Association, 2507
Journal of the Experimental Analysis of Behavior, 1157, 1874
Journal of the History of the Behavioral Sciences, 889, 2031, 2068
Journal of Verbal Learning and Verbal Behavior, 1990
Journal Supplement Abstract Service, 2315
Jury selection, 2659
Juvenile court, 674
Juvenile Psychopathic Institute, 307, 395, 674

Kaimowitz v. Michigan Department of Mental Health, 2360
Kansas Psychological Association, 1302, 1792, 2153
Kennedy Foundation, 2004
Kent-Rosanoff Free Association Test, 357
Kentucky Psychological Association, 1628, 2667
Klonopin, 2423
Klüver-Bucy syndrome, 644
Knox College, 2197
Kuder Preference Record, 1557, 1633, 1687

Laboratories, 139, 156, 163, 231, 269, 281, 390, 396, 436, 440, 514, 537, 1206, 1337, 1540
Larry P. v. Wilson Riles, 2414, 2535
Laws and legal decisions, 62, 126, 130, 195, 210, 221, 305, 340, 428, 524, 674, 748, 845, 936, 944, 1064, 1099, 1177, 1290, 1496, 1583, 1769, 1770, 1799, 1841, 1867,

1871, 1884, 2008, 2039–2040,
2051, 2053, 2082, 2127, 2138,
2195, 2204, 2261, 2266, 2279,
2281, 2294, 2342, 2359, 2364,
2382, 2386, 2391, 2393, 2398,
2408, 2414, 2439, 2448, 2485,
2489, 2503, 2555, 2568, 2592,
2596, 2616, 2650–2651, 2660,
2676, 2687, 2699, 2715, 2717,
2739, 2749, 2762, 2765–2766,
2785, 2802, 2813, 2817
Learning, 194, 196, 231, 281, 325, 348,
476, 490, 651, 693, 792, 804, 848,
894, 985, 1042, 1083, 1128, 1149,
1182, 1212, 1325, 1370, 1947. *See
also* Division Index: Division 3
Learning Disabilities Act, 2261
Learning disability, 1985
Learning disorders conference, 2443
Legal decisions. *See* Laws and legal decisions
Legal psychology. *See* Division Index: Division 41
Librium, 1853, 1926, 1929, 2482
Licensure, 1802, 1867, 1922, 2473, 2524,
2653, 2799
Licensure law (state laws), 1560, 1562,
1575, 1628, 1688, 1690, 1731,
1787–1788, 1811, 1837, 1845,
1847, 1852, 1900, 1914, 1956,
1960, 1988, 2012, 2019, 2023–
2024, 2026, 2033, 2052, 2070,
2075, 2086, 2118, 2135, 2149,
2153–2155, 2160–2161, 2172,
2186, 2224, 2233, 2236, 2250,
2256, 2284, 2286, 2311, 2322,
2331, 2340, 2361, 2385, 2444,
2451, 2471, 2523
Licensure laws, 1073, 1506, 1531, 1981
Life span development conference, 2229
Limbitrol, 2482
Linguistics, 622, 1026, 1126, 1128, 1161,
1201, 1291, 1340, 2080
Lithane, 2259
Lithium, 1629
Lithium carbonate, 1010, 2259
Lithonate, 2259
Little Albert study, 1103
Little Hans case, 859, 862
Lobotomy, 1411, 1413, 1430, 1434, 1528,
1597
Lockhart v. McCree, 2659

Loebner Prize, 2757
London Psycho-Therapeutic Society, 705
Lorazepam, 2476
Louisiana Psychological Association, 1837,
2052, 2214
Loxapine, 2415
Loxitane, 2415
Loyalty oaths, 479, 1646, 1677
Loyola University, 2553
LSD, 1533–1534, 2138
Ludiomil, 2558
Ludwig II, 483
Luminal, 1479

MacArthur Prize, 2575
Maine Psychological Association, 2172
Malleus Maleficarum, 5
Man, A Course Of Study (MACOS),
2379, 2419, 2431
Maprotiline, 2558
Maritime Psychological Association, 1640
Marplan, 1843, 1909
Marsilid, 1843
Maryland Psychological Association, 1845
Massachusetts Institute of Technology,
1748, 1829
Massachusetts Psychological Association,
2311
Max Planck Institute, 2035, 2546, 2551
Mayo Clinic, 984
McCarthy Scales of Children's Abilities,
819
McGill University, 1501
McKinney Act, 2687
Measurement Research Center, 1735
Mechanism, 32
Media psychology. *See* Division Index: Di-
vision 46
Medicare, 2766
Mellaril, 1905
Memory, 196, 585, 735, 985, 1264, 1382,
1442, 1492, 2123, 2133, 2403. *See
also* Division Index: Divisions 3
and 6
Memory & Cognition, 2348
Menninger Clinic, 592
Menninger conference, 2328
Mental deficiency congress, 2170
Mental health, 428, 748, 952, 1927. *See
also* Division Index: Divisions 12,
17, and 27
Mental Health Act, 2555

Mental health commission, 2464, 2468, 2487

Mental health conference, 2371, 2617

Mental health insurance, 1894, 2195, 2448, 2485, 2577, 2642–2643, 2766

Mental hospitals, 3, 10, 61–63, 92, 99, 105, 126, 145, 153, 159, 166–167, 173, 189, 195, 203–204, 210, 216, 221, 316–317, 404, 481, 548, 1016, 1177, 1491, 1927, 2152, 2427, 2518, 2520, 2697

Mental hygiene, 225, 297, 320, 366, 851, 867, 1323. *See also* Division Index: Divisions 12 and 17

Mental retardation, 181, 185–186, 193, 212, 218, 236, 260, 368, 524, 636, 1177, 1202, 2008, 2039, 2281, 2324, 2416, 2481. *See also* Division Index: Division 33

Mental retardation: Institutions, 185, 193, 212, 236, 2481

Meprobamate, 1791

Merrill-Palmer Scales for Children, 354

Mesoridazine, 2257

Methamphetamine, 1542

Methaqualone, 2104

Methylphenidate, 1803

Methyprylon, 1782

Metropolitan Life Insurance Co. v. Massachusetts, 2642

Mexican Psychoanalytic Institute, 686

Michigan Psychological Association, 1914

Michigan State University, 2201

Mid-America Conference for Teachers of Psychology, 2631

Midwestern Association for Behavior Analysis, 2383, 2541

Midwestern Psychological Association, 568, 729, 1278, 1304, 1425, 1444, 2756

Military psychology. *See* Division Index: Division 19

Miller Analogies Test, 1618, 1624

Millon Clinical Multiaxial Inventory, 2460

Mills v. Rogers, 2586

Miltown, 1791

Mind, 113

Minnesota Multiphasic Personality Inventory (MMPI), 760, 1158, 1525, 2082, 2084, 2698

Minnesota Psychological Association, 1690, 2565

Mississippi Psychological Association, 1813, 2041, 2118

Missouri Psychological Association, 1774, 2471

MKULTRA, 1937. *See also* Central Intelligence Agency

Moban, 2374

Model licensure legislation, 1802

Molindone, 2374

Montana Psychological Association, 1968, 2286

Moody v. Albemarle Paper Co., 2426

Moray House Tests, 412

Morgan State College, 790

Moscow Institute of Psychology, 954

Mother's aid laws, 936

Motion picture, 1862, 2102

Motivation, 315, 571, 800, 1142, 1145, 1173, 1178, 1220, 1288. *See also* Division Index: Division 3

Multivariate Behavior Research, 2111

Myers-Briggs Type Indicator, 356, 652

Nardil, 1908

National Academy of Sciences, 154, 280, 332, 365, 373, 525, 706, 754, 925, 933, 990, 1032, 1096, 1106, 1139, 1165, 1179, 1277, 1344, 2289, 2420, 2622, 2682, 2826

National Aeronautics and Space Administration, 2472

National Association for Nursery Education, 559

National Association for the Protection of the Insane and Prevention of Insanity, 401

National Association for Retarded Children, 2004

National Association of School Psychologists, 2185, 2223, 2230, 2288. *See also* Division Index: Division 16

National Association of School Psychologists Newsletter, 2230

National Center on Child Abuse and Neglect, 2715

National Committee for Mental Hygiene, 1678

National Computer Systems, 2698

National Conference on Enhancing the Quality of Undergraduate Education in Psychology, 2783

National Conference on Internship Training in Psychology, 2680

National Conference on Scientist-Practitioner Education and Training for the Professional Practice of Psychology, 2751

National Conference on the Undergraduate Curriculum in Psychology, 1694

National Council of Schools of Professional Psychology, 987, 2453

National Council of Women Psychologists, 739, 1512, 1514–1515

National Defense Education Act, 1871

National Education Association, 774

National Herbart Society, 703

National Hispanic Psychological Association, 1303

National Hospice Organization, 2498

National Institute of Child Health and Human Development, 1999, 2007

National Institute of Education, 2330

National Institute of Mental Health, 785, 858, 1144, 1343, 1552, 1583, 1648, 1799, 2163, 2328, 2384, 2417, 2422, 2429, 2607, 2710, 2714, 2727, 2752

National Institute of Social Science, 670, 1231

National Institute on Aging, 836, 1327

National Institute on Alcohol Abuse and Alcoholism, 2384, 2607

National Institute on Deafness and Other Communication Disorders, 2725

National Institute on Drug Abuse, 1318, 2384, 2607

National Institute on Neurological Disease and Stroke, 1672, 1682, 2210

National Institutes of Health, 1545

National Medal of Science, 776, 812, 877, 894, 925, 966, 1014, 1093, 1135, 1256, 1268, 2061, 2181, 2216, 2654, 2685, 2747, 2769–2770, 2792, 2808–2809

National Mental Health Association, 885, 979, 1678, 1732, 1935

National Mental Health Bell, 1732

National Mental Health Foundation, 1678

National Press Club, 2772

National Register of Health Service Providers in Psychology, 1218, 1230, 1357, 2387–2388, 2430, 2449, 2635–2636

National Research Agenda in Psychology, 2753

National Research Council, 1022, 1024, 1088, 1097, 1660

National Science Foundation, 976, 1561, 1666, 1871, 2312, 2379, 2469, 2793

National Society for the Study of Education, 703

National Training Laboratory, 1582, 1606, 2071

Nativism, 38

Navane, 2164

Nebraska Psychological Association, 2155, 2461

Nebraska Symposium on Motivation, 1725, 1743

Nembutol, 2409

Neurasthenia, 309

Neurological Institute of New York, 887

Neurology, 419

Neuropsychiatry, Neuropsychology, and Behavioral Neurology, 2724

Neuropsychology. *See* biopsychology, Division Index: Divisions 6, 28, and 40

Neuropsychopharmacology, 2701

Nevada Psychological Association, 2012

New England Psychological Association, 1949, 1970, 2038

New Hampshire Psychological Association, 831, 1847, 2627

New Jersey Psychological Association, 2135

New Jersey School of Applied and Professional Psychology, 947, 2378

New Jersey State Psychological Services, 922

New look (perception), 886

New Mexico Psychological Association, 1833, 2024

New York Academy of Sciences, 626

New York Branch of the APA, 626, 747, 1322, 1417, 1460

New York Psychiatric Society, 1027, 1097

New York Psychoanalytic Society, 353, 930

New York Psychoanalytical Institute, 558

New York Psychological Association, 1811, 1867

New York Society for the Prevention of Cruelty to Children, 364

New York University, 2205
Newman awards (Psi Chi), 2532
Newspaper, 167, 173, 203
Nobel prize, 174, 194, 201, 233, 244, 261, 355, 422, 492, 673, 763, 797, 847, 966, 1014, 1043, 1366, 1413, 1657, 1727, 1969, 2173, 2280, 2337, 2372, 2571–2572
Noctec, 1504
Noludar, 1782
Norpramin, 2060
North American Society for the Psychology of Sport and Physical Activity, 2146, 2148, 2358
North Carolina Psychological Association, 1073, 1631, 1641, 2161, 2514
North Dakota Psychological Association, 1888, 2149
Northwestern University, 729, 1170
Nortriptyline, 2058
Nova University, 2590
Nowicki-Strickland Children's Locus of Control Scale, 1435

O'Connor v. Donaldson, 2427
Obscenity, 340
Ohio Psychological Association, 1649, 2331
Ohio School Psychology Association, 2185
Ohio State University, 796, 1478
Oklahoma Psychological Association, 1593, 2086, 2436
Old Saybrook Conference, 2062
Ontario Psychological Association, 818, 1596
Ontario Science Centre, 2778
Orap, 2626
Oregon Health Sciences University, 1215
Oregon Psychological Association, 1980, 2019, 2361
Organizational psychology. See Division Index: Division 14
Oxazepam, 2081

Pamelor, 2058
Parapsychological Association, 1851
Parapsychology, 619, 1136, 1282, 1451, 2472
PARC decision. See Pennsylvania Association for Retarded Children v. Commonwealth of Pennsylvania
Parham v. J. R., 2520

Parkinson's disease, 49, 2707
Parmate, 1953
Parsons v. State, 502
Patient rights, 305, 401, 845, 952, 1177, 1202, 1263, 1270, 2329, 2360, 2427, 2481, 2518, 2534, 2586–2587, 2596, 2660, 2662–2663, 2665, 2755, 2805–2806. See also Ethics: Professional
Paxipam, 2570
Peabody Picture Vocabulary Test, 1924
Peace Corps, 1085, 1203
Peace psychology. See Division Index: Division 48
Pedagogical Seminary, 555
Peer review, 2525, 2549, 2607
Pennsylvania Association for Retarded Children v. Commonwealth of Pennsylvania, 2326
Pennsylvania Psychological Association, 1576, 1946, 2322, 2340, 2732
Pentobarbital, 2409
People v. Kirk L. Hughes, 2612
Perception, 77, 98, 129, 200, 259, 289, 313, 329, 405, 417, 434, 453, 487, 506, 647, 666, 673, 772, 794, 925, 927, 950, 1039, 1063, 1080, 1111, 1141, 1149, 1167, 1239, 1388. See also Division Index: Divisions 3 and 6
Perception and Psychophysics, 2105
Permitil, 1917
Perphenazine, 1839
Personality psychology. See Division Index: Division 8
Personalized system of instruction, 668, 2065, 2069, 2096
Personnel Psychology, 1630
Pertofrane, 2060
Phenelzine, 1908
Phenergan, 1689
Phenobarbital, 1479
Phenomenology, 256
Phenytoin, 1723
Philosophical psychology. See Division Index: Divisions 1 and 24
Phrenology, 51, 68, 138, 805, 1338
Physiological psychology. See Division Index: Division 6
Pimozide, 2626
Piperacetazine, 2220
Placidyl, 1801

Political psychology, 125, 918, 1284. *See also* Division Index: Divisions 9 and 48
Polygraphy, 586, 2717
Pornography, 2279
Porteus Maze Test, 437, 1667
Position Analysis Questionnaire, 937
Postdoctoral education in clinical psychology conference, 2328
Pragmatism, 154, 163
Prazepam, 2459
Price Waterhouse v. Hopkins, 2733
Primary Mental Abilities Battery, 655
Princeton University, 1701
Prisons, 1335, 2301, 2341, 2377, 2390, 2440
Private practice. *See* Division Index: Division 42
Problem solving, 745, 1650
Prochlorperazine, 1844
Professional Association of German Psychologists, 1614
Professional psychology, 947, 969, 1129, 1171, 1218, 1243, 1250, 1385, 1419, 1584, 1603–1604, 1922, 1942, 1954, 1963, 2183, 2226, 2275, 2335, 2344, 2378, 2387–2388, 2463, 2533. *See also* Division Index: Divisions 18, 29, 31, and 42
Professional Psychology: Research and Practice, 2249
Professional Psychology, 2249
Professional School Psychology, 2602
Professional standards, 2342
Profoundly mentally retarded research conference, 2416
Prolixin, 1917
Promethazine, 1689
Protriptyline, 2171
Prozac, 2704
Psi Beta, 2542, 2574
Psi Chi, 1304, 1312, 1440, 1882, 2167, 2532
PSY-PUB, 2791
PsycBOOKS, 2737
Psychiatric Foundation, 1678
Psychiatry, 86, 101, 105, 178–179, 204, 227, 233, 237, 297, 305, 320, 344, 382, 589, 592, 627–628, 648, 690, 775, 785, 827, 1010, 1027, 1043, 1097, 1332, 1395, 1403, 1413, 1433, 1503, 1910, 2588, 2613, 2666, 2759
Psychoanalysis, 625. *See also* Division Index: Division 39
Psychoanalytic Institute of Southwest Germany, 533
Psychoanalytic Quarterly, 1356
Psychoanalytic Review, 971
Psychobiology. *See* Biopsychology, Division Index: Division 6
Psychological Abstracts Direct Access Terminal, 2303
Psychological Abstracts, 1109, 1217, 1247, 1400, 1549, 2087, 2163, 2303, 2737
Psychological assessment. *See* Division Index: Divisions 5 and 12
Psychological Assessment, 2731
Psychological Association of Alberta, 2001
Psychological Bulletin, 271, 299, 770, 1109, 1472, 1549, 2333
Psychological calendar, 743
Psychological clinic, 637, 756, 1586
Psychological Corporation, the, 759, 1048, 1119
Psychological Documents, 2614
Psychological Index, 1400
Psychological Insight Test, 871
Psychological Monographs, 299
Psychological museum, 1452
Psychological Record, 1471
Psychological Register, 1309
Psychological Reports, 1796
Psychological Review Company, 1191, 1313, 1468
Psychological Review, 271, 299, 599
Psychological Round Table, 1436
Psychologists Association of Alberta, 2001
Psychologists for Social Responsibility, 2585
Psychologists Interested in Religious Issues (PIRI). *See* APA Division 36 and Division Index: Division 36
Psychologists Interested in the Advancement of Psychotherapy, 2009, 2168. *See also* Division Index: Division 29
Psychologists League, 1443
Psychology and Aging, 2655
Psychology of women. *See* Division Index: Division 35
Psychology Press, 2031

Psychology Society, 1938
Psychology magazine, 2465
Psychology Today magazine, 2603, 2605, 2716
Psychology Today radio program, 1351
Psychology Today television program, 2644
PsychoMath Stud Poker System, 1494
Psychometric Society, 1408–1409, 1493
Psychometrics, 29, 119, 284, 435, 498, 509, 640, 684, 707, 731, 758, 809, 877, 920–921, 953, 955, 1005, 1009, 1011, 1175, 1286, 1496, 1499, 1659, 1763, 2685. *See also* Division Index: Division 5
Psychonomic Science, 2045
Psychonomic Society, 995, 1925, 2105, 2174, 2203, 2312, 2348, 2352
Psychopath, 460
Psychopharmacology. *See* Division Index: Divisions 6, 28, and 50
Psychophysics, 88, 96, 98, 200, 202, 259, 834, 1111, 1748
Psychosomatic medicine, 556
Psychosurgery, 2360, 2376
Psychotherapy research, 1873. *See also* Division Index: Divisions 12, 29, and 49
Psychotherapy: Theory, Research, and Practice, 2027, 2621
Psychotherapy, 2621
PsycINFO, 2237, 2303, 2313, 2614, 2649, 2689
PsycLIT, 2649, 2674
Psycoloquy, 2779
PsycPLUS, 2689
PsyD degree, 1171
Public Law 94-142, 2439, 2676, 2765
Public opinion polling, 125
Public policy, 62, 428, 524, 748, 858, 952, 986, 1141, 1390, 1530, 1677, 2051, 2522, 2559, 2577, 2662, 2774, 2777, 2795. *See also* Division Index: Divisions 9, 18, and 27
Public service, 2797, 2801
Public service, psychologists in. *See* Division Index: Division 18
Public service messages, 2594, 2641
Publication Manual of the APA, 999, 1290, 1532
Purdue University, 2583

Quaalude, 2104
Quality control, 1519
Quebec Psychological Association, 1558, 1822, 1828, 1981
Quide, 2220

Radio, 1351, 1476, 2641
Rat Man case, 855
Rational–emotive therapy conference, 2424
Rationalism, 14
Regional psychological associations, 1425
Rehabilitation Act, 1099
Rehabilitation psychology. *See* Division Index: Division 22
Reinforcement, 1233
Religion. *See* Division Index: Division 36
REM sleep, 1741
Rennie v. Klein, 2534
Research Center for Group Dynamics, 1625
Reserpine, 1137, 1747, 1817
Restoril, 2562
Rhode Island Psychological Association, 2233, 2696
Riggins v. Nevada, 2806
Ritalin, 1803
Rivers v. Katz, 2663
Roane State Community College, 2553
Rorschach Institute, 1463
Rorschach Test, 456, 629, 778, 817, 1098, 1120, 1463
Rosemead Graduate School of Psychology, 2463
Royal Academy of Sciences (France), 27
Royal Society (Great Britain), 25–26
Rural mental health, 2776
Russia, 1868, 1907, 2209, 2319, 2791
Russian Academy of Pedagogical Sciences, 1834
Russian Psychological Society, 1834, 1868, 1907
Rutgers Psychological and Mental Hygiene Clinic, 1314
Rutgers—The State University, 947, 1205, 1314, 2378, 2623

Sally Beauchamp case, 338, 660, 662–663
Salpêtrière asylum, 22, 24, 86, 134, 419, 471

Salt Lake City conference, 1130, 1508, 2683

Saskatchewan Psychological Association, 1983

Scandinavian Meeting of Psychologists, 1611

Schedule of Recent Experience, 2177

Schizophrenia, 237, 2710

Scholastic Aptitude Test, 1232

School psychology. *See* Division Index: Division 16

School psychology conference, 1771

School Psychology Digest, 2288

School Psychology Quarterly, 2602

School Psychology Review, 2288

Science Research Associates, 1984

Science, 402, 432, 613

Scientology, 1665

Scopes trial, 1200, 1208

Secobarbital, 1669

Seconal, 1669

Selective Service System, 1499

Sensation, 97, 142, 183, 211, 214, 220, 238, 302, 461, 506, 525, 564, 581, 782, 784, 815, 850, 919, 961, 1081, 1106, 1154, 1246, 1359. *See also* Division Index: Divisions 3 and 6

Serax, 2081

Serentil, 2257

Serpasil, 1747

Sesame Street, 1240, 1467, 2248

Sexist language, 2437

Sigma Xi, 501

Sinequan, 2245

Sixteen Personality Factor Questionnaire (16PF), 802, 1659

Smithsonian Institution, 2794, 2804

Social facilitation, 546

Social psychology. *See* Division Index: Division 8

Social science, 76

Social Scientists Against Nuclear War, 2584

Social Work, 1805

Societies of Mental Hygiene, 979

Society for Behavioral Pediatrics, 2608, 2610

Society for Computers in Psychology, 2312

Society for Community Research and Action. *See* APA Division 27, Division Index: Division 27

Society for Developmental and Behavioral Pediatrics, 2610

Society for Machines and Mentality, 2780, 2798

Society for Neuroscience, 2310

Society for Personality and Social Psychology, 2782

Society for Personality Assessment, 1463

Society for Psychologists in Addictive Behavior, 2823

Society for Psychophysiological Research, 1965

Society for Research in Child Development, 1324, 1379

Society for Research on Adolescence, 2656

Society for the Experimental Analysis of Behavior, 1874

Society for the Prevention of Cruelty to Animals, 123, 294

Society for the Psychological Study of Social Issues (SPSSI), 1426–1427. *See also* APA Division 9 and Division Index: Division 9

Society of Behavioral Medicine, 2500, 2538

Society of Experimental Psychologists, 771, 777, 945, 1497

Society of Experimental Psychologists Warren Medal, 782, 1416

Society of Experimental Social Psychology, 2095

Society of Multivariate Experimental Psychology, 2111

Society of Psychologists in Management, 2639

Sociology, 93

South Carolina Psychological Association, 1789, 2186

South Dakota Psychological Association, 1816, 2444, 2484, 2523

Southeastern Psychological Association, 1775, 1794

Southern Illinois University, 710

Southern Society for Philosophy and Psychology, 773–774, 798, 1425, 1775

Southwestern Psychological Association, 1738, 1751, 1780

Space psychology, 1923, 1951

Special education. *See* Division Index: Division 33

Special education act, 1884

Spencer Foundation, 1984
Sport psychology. *See* Division Index: Division 47
Sport psychology association, 2146, 2148, 2358
SPSS computer program, 2276
St. Elizabeth's Hospital, 210, 221, 316, 548, 1016, 1491, 2697
St. Mary's conference, 2783
Standards for Educational and Psychological Testing, 2112
Stanford University, 205, 241, 566, 2301, 2447
Stanford-Binet Intelligence Test, 1046
State licensure laws. *See* Licensure law
State mental health care, 524
State Psychological Association Affairs. *See* Division Index: Divisions 31 and 42
State-Trait Anxiety Inventory, 1259
Statistics, 17, 23, 45, 57, 69, 91, 103, 125, 234, 284, 328, 371, 412, 448, 539, 684, 707, 783, 920, 955, 1004, 1365, 1450, 1644, 1986, 2029, 2221, 2274. *See also* Division Index: Division 5
Stelazine, 1889
Stoelting Company, 486
Stress, 842, 1134, 1421, 1823, 2177
Strong Vocational Interest Blank, 450
Structuralism, 298
Substance abuse. *See* Division Index: Divisions 28 and 50
Sudden Infant Death Syndrome Act, 2382
Suicide, 245
Sunset laws, 2154, 2523
Surmontil, 2519
Swiss Psychoanalytic Society, 1079
System of Multicultural Pluralistic Assessment (SOMPA), 1188, 2316, 2478
Systems of psychology. *See* Division Index: Division 24

T-groups, 1582, 1606
t test, 371
Talks to Teachers (William James), 561
Taractan, 1892
Tarasoff v. Regents of the University of California, 2247, 2450, 2651
Tavistock Institute of Human Relations, 1625

Teaching machines, 1222, 1279
Teaching of psychology. *See* Division Index: Division 2
Teaching of psychology conference, 1695
Teaching of Psychology, 2402
Technicolor, 525, 1346
Tegratol, 2184
Televised violence, 2320
Television, 865, 1467, 2034, 2243, 2248, 2320, 2405, 2454, 2594, 2644. *See also* Division Index: Division 46
Temazepam, 2562
Temple University, 2283, 2295
Tennessee Psychological Association, 1132, 1731, 1756
Testing standards, 657, 838, 1003, 1156, 1365, 1496, 1676, 2082–2083, 2112, 2287, 2414, 2426, 2508, 2535, 2762, 2826
Texas Psychological Association, 1751, 2064, 2236
Thayer Conference (school psychology), 1771
Thematic Apperception Test, 587, 924, 935, 1015, 1173, 1539
Theoretical psychology. *See* Division Index: Divisions 1 and 24
Thesaurus of Psychological Index Terms, 2392
Thioethamyl, 1778
Thioridazine, 1905
Thiotixene, 2164
Thorazine, 1683, 1704, 1760
Three Faces of Eve, 1838, 1862
Three Mile Island disaster, 2511
Thyroid hormone, 984
Thyroxine, 984
Tofranil, 1859, 1902
Tolman Hall, 2011
Tomkins-Horn Picture Arrangement Test, 935
Trancopal, 1893
Transactional analysis, 1746
Transactional Analysis Journal, 1974
Transnational Family Research Institute, 1166
Tranxene, 2332
Tranylcypromine, 1953
Trazodone, 2579
Triavil, 2091
Triazolam, 2599
Trifluoperazine, 1889

Triflupromazine, 1861
Trilafon, 1839, 2091
Trimipramine, 2519
Turner's syndrome, 575

University of Aberdeen, 2421
University of Akron, 2103
University of Alabama, 773
University of Berlin, 1405
University of California, 1677
University of California, Berkeley, 246,
    479, 632, 744, 849, 1122, 1186,
    1285, 1638, 2011, 2247, 2492
University of California, Irvine, 2447
University of California, Los Angeles,
    2504
University of Chicago, 716
University of Copenhagen, 252
University of Florida, 2680
University of Geneva, 957
University of Georgia, 2428
University of Göttingen, 161
University of Graz, 213
University of Hawaii, 1643
University of Heidelberg, 223, 275
University of Illinois, 588, 1171, 1210,
    1659, 2055, 2097, 2358, 2499
University of Iowa, 1337, 2356
University of Kazan, 231
University of Leipzig, 139, 360–361, 390,
    485, 1540
University of London, 714
University of Louisville, 710
University of Louvain, 2812
University of Maryland, 863
University of Massachusetts, 2269
University of Michigan, 671, 1807, 2691
University of Minnesota, 590, 687, 1440,
    1525, 2698
University of Mississippi, 1775
University of Montreal, 645
University of Nebraska, 251, 485
University of Nevada, 2121
University of North Carolina, 514
University of Ottawa, 1510
University of Paris, 155, 414, 468
University of Pennsylvania, 267, 300, 348,
    520, 582, 635, 637, 756, 1547,
    1586
University of Saskatchewan, 1588
University of Texas, 2258
University of Toronto, 537

University of Vienna, 413, 689
University of Western Ontario, 992
University of Wisconsin, 1070, 1321
University of Würzburg, 180, 276, 314,
    334, 391, 795
University of Wyoming, 358, 547
University of Zurich, 736
U.S. Department of Health, Education,
    and Welfare, 2386
U.S. Alcohol, Drug Abuse, and Mental
    Health Administration, 2818
U.S. Army, 2595
U.S. Army Medical Corps, 110
U.S. Children's Bureau, 944
U.S. Department of Education, 2536
U.S. Institute of Peace, 2632
U.S. National Transportation Safety
    Board, 2677
U.S. Navy, 764, 2472
U.S. Office of Education, 2264
U.S. Public Health Service, 94, 1294,
    1545
U.S. Public Health Service Division of
    Mental Hygiene, 1648
U.S. Substance Abuse and Mental Health
    Services Administration, 2818
U.S. v. 40 Barrels and 20 Kegs of Coca-
    Cola, 398, 904, 931
U.S. v. Bennett, 340
U.S. v. Brawner, 1768
USSR Institute of Psychology, 2319
Utah conference, 2683
Utah Psychological Association, 1900,
    2438

Vail conference, 2362, 2517
Valium, 1926, 2042
Vanderbilt University, 2601
Vermont Conference on Primary Preven-
    tion of Psychopathology, 2425
Vermont Psychological Association, 2147,
    2451
Vesprin, 1861
Veterans Administration, 767, 1133,
    1484, 1594, 1616
Victimization, 2633–2634
Vienna Psychoanalytic Society, 928
Vineland laboratory, 718, 832
Vineland Social Maturity Scale, 527, 1744
Vineland Training School, 296, 830, 922
"Virginia Blues" case, 1500, 2543, 2548

Virginia Psychological Association, 1575, 1815, 1901, 2625
Virginia Tech Symposium, 2486
Vistaril, 1879
Visual Aural Digit Span Test, 1077
Visual Psychology, 568
Vivactil, 2171
Vocational Rehabilitation Act, 1064

Wake Forest University, 514
Walter Reed General Hospital, 1059
"War of the Worlds," 1476
Washington State Psychological Association, 1788
Washington v. Harper, 2755
Washington-Baltimore Branch of the APA, 1315, 1580
Washoe (chimpanzee), 1380, 2121, 2174
Watson symposium, 2513
Wechsler Adult Intelligence Scale, 1786
Wechsler Intelligence Scale for Children, 1651
Wellesley College, 281, 302, 616
Wellesley Role-Orientation Scale, 871
West Virginia Psychological Association, 1664, 1762, 2256
West Virginia University, 1664, 2229
Western Philosophical Association, 682
Western Psychological Association, 1122, 1425, 1446
White House Conference on Aging, 1671
White House Conference on Children, 878, 883

White House Conference on Education, 1770
Wide Range Achievement Test, 2176
"Wild Boy of Avyron," 65, 95
Wilderness psychology conference, 2527
William Alanson White Institute, 596, 686
William James Book Award, 2673
Wisconsin Psychological Association, 969, 2250
Wisconsin School of Professional Psychology, 969
Women's studies conference, 2422
Woodward v. U.S., 2754
World War I, 367, 398, 457, 1024, 1028, 1036, 1038, 1051, 1066
World War II, 1376, 1405, 1486, 1493, 1497–1498, 1506, 1513, 1517–1518, 1531, 1535, 1607, 1614, 1647
Worm Runner's Digest, 1213
Wright State University, 1419, 2533
Wyatt v. Stickney, 2324, 2440
Wyoming Psychological Association, 1875, 1891, 2070, 2729

Xanax, 2573

Yale University, 288, 311, 1076, 1296, 1310, 1345, 1520, 1560
Yerkes laboratories, 1520, 2405
Youngberg v. Romeo, 2587

CALENDAR INDEX

*Numbers refer to entry numbers, which appear
in the upper right-hand corner of each entry.*

January 1, 203, 387, 520, 602, 682, 1190, 1191, 1218, 1247, 1894, 2504–2505, 2539, 2651

January 2, 419, 668, 700, 1054, 1192, 1684, 2177

January 3, 356, 769, 1092, 1162, 1480, 1950, 2043, 2321, 2799

January 4, 613, 1004, 1437, 1623, 1754, 1836

January 5, 683, 927, 1219, 1624, 1722, 1895, 2347

January 6, 226, 266, 815, 1530, 1723, 2706

January 7, 816, 859, 1570, 1869, 2707

January 8, 121, 459, 536, 721, 1055, 1163, 2284, 2409

January 9, 71, 378, 476, 508, 555, 744, 1193, 1317, 1353, 1354, 1438, 1837, 2410

January 10, 410, 908, 1516, 1973, 2560

January 11, 163, 298, 537, 638, 669, 1248

January 12, 43, 271, 623, 658, 1076, 1249, 1571, 1643, 1724, 1896

January 13, 168, 1625, 2065, 2440, 2800

January 14, 180, 799, 2580, 2601

January 15, 164, 372, 770–771, 1194, 1703, 1725, 1805, 1838, 2044, 2708

January 16, 101, 148, 1131, 1272, 1371, 2751

January 17, 396, 881, 1644, 2107, 2178, 2216, 2348, 2635

January 18, 563, 882, 1110, 1782, 2285, 2374, 2540

January 19, 90, 93, 165, 319, 1294, 1455, 1704, 2066, 2349, 2375, 2602

January 20, 92, 104, 169, 231, 307, 338, 1974, 2217, 2411–2412, 2709

January 21, 460, 494, 722, 1111, 2108, 2376

January 22, 8, 126, 195, 556, 2006, 2218, 2603

January 23, 62, 839, 1028, 1174, 1626, 1975, 2252, 2561

January 24, 196, 320, 723, 840, 1112, 1132, 1250, 1318, 2441, 2752

January 25, 817, 883, 1372, 1870

January 26, 442, 557, 841, 842, 973, 1594, 2179, 2413, 2753

January 27, 603, 772, 1220, 1595, 1871, 2045, 2581

January 28, 291, 388, 670, 724, 1251, 1355, 1783, 2109–2110

January 29, 130, 495, 1252, 1398, 1685, 1755, 1976, 2462

January 30, 278, 1295, 2007, 2652

January 31, 1338, 1951, 2111, 2219, 2350, 2653

February 1, 175, 1175, 1273, 1274, 1726, 2143, 2180, 2636

February 2, 253, 745, 1195, 1339, 1806, 2067–2068, 2442, 2506, 2774

February 3, 1093, 1113, 2220, 2253–2254

February 4, 1094, 2679

February 5, 57, 232, 411, 701, 1176, 2008, 2414, 2541, 2542, 2582

February 6, 149, 207, 1056, 1686

February 7, 321, 1872, 1977

February 8, 379, 564, 639, 773, 928, 1756, 2351, 2710, 2775–2776

February 9, 432, 884, 1077, 2112

February 10, 212, 1005, 1373, 2069

February 11, 538, 800, 929, 1006, 1196, 1502, 2604

February 12, 102, 818, 930, 2637

February 13, 420, 1197, 1543, 1807, 2181, 2221, 2729

February 14, 54, 220, 746, 1784, 2377

February 15, 9, 44, 227, 461, 725, 909, 1029, 1296, 1386, 1456, 1596, 1687, 1757, 2113, 2378, 2730

February 16, 119, 197, 1114, 1133, 1553, 2711

February 17, 539, 1198, 2144, 2255, 2256

February 18, 80, 150, 328, 624, 702, 974, 2605

February 19, 4, 885, 1572, 2070

February 20, 292, 329, 339, 604, 684, 910, 1399, 1414

February 21, 565, 1340, 1688, 1727, 1952–1953, 2222, 2443, 2507

February 22, 78, 91, 671, 1319, 2777

February 23, 747, 1785–1786, 2009, 2463

February 24, 3, 774, 956, 1926, 2620–2621, 2801

February 25, 433, 1007, 1078, 1115, 1297, 1439, 2114, 2415

February 26, 349, 434, 843, 1164, 2182, 2352, 2444, 2638, 2754, 2823

February 27, 254, 279, 1116, 1839, 2257, 2286, 2562, 2755

February 28, 509, 566, 703, 985, 1481, 1489, 1573, 2680

February 29, 1008, 1415, 1927, 2712–2713

March 1, 477, 940, 975, 1320, 1758, 1840, 1928, 1978, 2010, 2681

March 2, 302, 1253, 1787, 2563

March 3, 221, 280, 340, 435, 748, 801, 844, 860, 1134, 1275, 1597, 2682

March 4, 73, 510, 819, 1009, 1574, 2071

March 5, 151, 820, 941, 1057, 1387, 2508

March 6, 6, 170, 293, 365, 2379, 2380

March 7, 233, 640, 976

March 8, 79, 436, 1598, 1627, 2145–2146, 2287

March 9, 51, 567, 845, 1117, 1645, 1728, 2353, 2606, 2639

March 10, 568, 1221, 1254, 1440, 2147, 2731

March 11, 171, 583, 704, 775, 1457, 1897, 2183–2184, 2732

March 12, 28, 172, 569, 821, 846, 1929, 2640, 2654–2655

March 13, 341, 521, 986, 1321, 1599, 2011, 2046, 2072, 2148, 2149

March 14, 614, 911, 1199, 1930, 1979, 2223

March 15, 389, 861, 1118, 1458–1459, 1661, 2224, 2509

March 16, 931, 1441, 1931, 2543

March 17, 335, 685, 1030, 1031, 1135, 1600, 1898, 2510

March 18, 308, 478, 540, 749, 1255, 1899, 1954

March 19, 641, 822, 1256, 1298, 1729, 1841, 2583

March 20, 776, 802, 1136, 1177, 1222, 1257, 1646, 1900, 2047, 2225

March 21, 522, 659, 1705, 1788, 1932, 1980–1981, 2185–2186, 2416, 2544, 2656

March 22, 523, 1010, 1531, 2354

March 23, 45, 686, 726, 1374, 1647, 2226, 2322, 2824

March 24, 342, 390, 642, 1079, 2545

March 25, 687, 1080, 1299, 1601, 1628, 1759, 2012

March 26, 1258, 1575, 1760, 2802

March 27, 234, 412, 886, 2288, 2641, 2657

March 28, 1137, 1259, 1388, 1842, 2417, 2511, 2546, 2778

March 29, 462, 496, 1576, 1629, 1689, 2464

March 30, 134, 281, 366, 421, 625, 862–863, 912, 1554

March 31, 14, 413, 727, 750, 823, 1300, 1933, 2073, 2150

April 1, 12, 87, 173, 705, 824, 864, 1223, 1460, 1648, 1789, 1934, 2227, 2355, 2512

April 2, 1982, 2187

April 3, 511, 615, 977, 1375, 1400–1401, 2013, 2151

April 4, 99, 144, 156, 777, 865, 1058

April 5, 13, 198, 660, 887, 942, 2074, 2513

April 6, 58, 943, 1200, 1808, 1843, 2258–2259, 2323, 2356

April 7, 255, 443–444, 1761, 1809, 1955, 2260

April 8, 256, 303, 463, 1602, 1844

April 9, 103, 199, 304, 464, 944, 987, 1416, 1873, 1901

April 10, 235, 751, 1276, 1730–1731, 1874

April 11, 49, 272, 322, 497, 584, 825, 988, 1417, 1532, 2014, 2115, 2658

April 12, 661, 1322, 1503, 1603, 1810, 1875, 2152, 2188–2190

April 13, 932, 1341, 1732, 2261, 2514, 2756

April 14, 105, 110, 479, 1201, 1342, 1706, 1983, 2048

April 15, 108, 245–246, 397, 728, 847, 957, 1138, 1202, 1260, 1356, 1790, 1845, 2015, 2153, 2418, 2714, 2779

April 16, 945, 1533, 1902

April 17, 157, 236, 605, 752, 958, 1059, 1301, 1876, 2262, 2381, 2483

April 18, 273, 373, 585, 706, 778, 1032–1033, 1811, 1956, 2324–2325, 2465

April 19, 63, 96, 729, 779, 803, 933, 1343, 1534, 1577, 2466

April 20, 42, 606, 978, 989, 1034, 1224, 1662, 1957, 2116

April 21, 184, 294, 350, 422, 888, 990, 1035, 1225, 1578, 1762, 1877, 2075

April 22, 38, 445–446, 512, 672, 753, 1011, 1036, 1095, 1442, 1663, 2263, 2382

April 23, 754–755, 991, 1604, 1690, 1763, 1812, 1903, 2228, 2564, 2780

April 24, 65, 437, 465, 804, 1226–1227, 1846, 2154, 2419, 2445, 2484

April 25, 480, 524, 805, 1012, 1165, 1178, 1261, 1277, 1302, 2191, 2515, 2715

April 26, 33, 185, 525, 541, 688, 866, 1139, 1262, 1418, 1649, 2420, 2485, 2607

April 27, 22, 116, 626, 1813, 1984, 2117, 2289, 2486–2487, 2516

April 28, 466, 806–807, 1096, 1119, 1140, 1376, 1791, 1904, 2517

April 29, 309, 323, 330, 1344, 1792, 2446

April 30, 69, 237, 343, 481, 513–514, 662, 1037–1038, 1097, 1179, 1733–1734, 2076, 2229, 2518, 2622

May 1, 24, 181, 208, 310, 423, 526, 542, 1081, 1443, 2230, 2264, 2383, 2488, 2733

May 2, 70, 527, 627, 913, 1263, 1303, 1402, 1504, 1691, 1707, 1814, 1878, 2155, 2421

May 3, 374, 607, 689, 1482, 1555, 2016, 2077, 2231, 2489

May 4, 67, 127, 1764, 2078, 2608

May 5, 111, 946, 1180, 1228, 1323, 1664, 2290, 2326–2327, 2659

May 6, 228, 780, 848, 867, 1229, 1556, 1630, 1793, 1935

May 7, 34, 158, 438, 1444, 1557, 2291–2292

May 8, 186, 247, 311, 1082, 1631, 2232, 2293

May 9, 586, 868, 934, 1345, 1490, 1665, 2118, 2156, 2357

May 10, 187, 238, 643, 781, 826, 889, 1039, 1304, 1377, 1666, 1936, 2192

May 11, 239, 1278, 1419, 1815, 2490, 2716, 2803

May 12, 240, 628, 947, 1816

May 13, 587, 914, 1060, 1203

May 14, 229–230, 730–731, 782, 1692, 2358, 2384, 2467, 2491

May 15, 216, 528, 1040, 1324, 1650, 1708, 1985, 2447

May 16, 783, 1141, 1204, 1461, 1579, 1709, 1847, 2157, 2233

May 17, 1667, 1765, 2294

May 18, 663, 2079, 2328, 2448, 2804–2806

May 19, 53, 204, 312, 2080, 2119

May 20, 100, 188, 543, 784, 992, 1041, 1325, 1848, 1937

May 21, 109, 286, 313, 344, 915, 1580, 2807

May 22, 1, 588, 993, 1279, 1326, 1581, 1794, 2234, 2623

May 23, 39, 439, 808, 1693, 1795, 2120, 2609, 2660, 2757

May 24, 380, 447, 570, 1061, 2017, 2158, 2468

May 25, 189, 267, 448, 482, 644, 959, 979, 2265

May 26, 367, 398, 571, 645, 916, 948, 960, 1062, 1264, 1766, 2295

May 27, 112, 351, 391, 961, 1098, 2018

May 28, 732, 1166, 1558, 1632–1633, 1879, 1905, 2385

May 29, 498, 785, 1357, 1535, 2019–2020, 2159

May 30, 257, 890, 1142, 1205, 1358, 2386–2387

May 31, 1265, 1445, 1536, 2422, 2610

June 1, 282, 1505, 2235, 2388, 2469, 2565

June 2, 305, 949, 1099, 1143, 1346, 1559, 1767, 2661–2662, 2781

June 3, 673, 1230, 1735, 2642

June 4, 499, 707–708, 935, 1144, 1206, 1462, 1710, 1986, 2081, 2423, 2584

June 5, 50, 467, 500, 1880, 2049, 2389, 2566, 2624, 2734, 2825

June 6, 115, 357, 368, 589, 690, 962, 1120, 1463, 1958, 2424

June 7, 132, 369, 424, 544, 733, 1063, 1359, 2082, 2329

June 8, 1634, 1736, 1817, 1938, 2083, 2160, 2758

June 9, 2470, 2547, 2735

June 10, 153, 616, 646, 691, 1347, 1939, 2050, 2084, 2663

June 11, 46, 113, 950, 1145, 1266, 1940, 1987–1988, 2085

June 12, 299, 370, 827, 951, 1042, 1605, 2519, 2585, 2782

June 13, 59, 159, 371, 483, 590, 1906, 1989, 2683

June 14, 287, 809, 1043, 1100, 1517, 1849, 2236

June 15, 129, 217, 345, 501, 734, 1013–1014, 1348, 1818, 2021, 2359

June 16, 123, 283, 828, 891, 1231, 1506, 1606, 2449, 2548

June 17, 709, 1083, 1181, 1796, 1850, 2296

June 18, 248, 324, 399, 1280, 1305, 1635, 1711, 2586–2587, 2783

June 19, 17, 545, 1281, 1378, 1518, 1851, 2051, 2684

June 20, 258, 1327, 1797, 1959, 2520

June 21, 400, 810, 2121, 2588, 2784

June 22, 331, 869, 1015, 1101–1102, 1544, 1960

June 23, 608, 1232, 1941, 2161, 2266, 2330–2332, 2492, 2521, 2808–2809

June 24, 88, 1379, 1582, 1907

June 25, 1636, 2425–2426, 2625, 2664, 2685, 2759

June 26, 381–382, 1084–1085, 1146, 1349, 1403, 1483, 2427, 2522, 2665

June 27, 425, 1064, 1694–1695, 2717, 2736, 2760

June 28, 35, 124, 300, 849, 952, 1420, 2022, 2086, 2162, 2666

June 29, 468, 572, 1464, 1908, 2087, 2428, 2611, 2761

June 30, 268, 1491, 1607, 2163

July 1, 21, 249, 401, 674, 936, 1016, 1147, 1267, 1507, 1519–1520, 1545, 1637, 1768, 1909, 2023–2024, 2122, 2267, 2333, 2450–2451, 2523–2524, 2549, 2686, 2810

July 2, 426, 1148, 1608, 2643

July 3, 402, 1086, 1583

July 4, 160, 1421, 2297

July 5, 870, 2612, 2737

July 6, 375, 892, 2613

July 7, 174, 205, 893, 994, 1149, 1207, 2088

July 8, 241, 573, 591, 617, 1404, 1712, 1798, 2811

July 9, 250, 295, 756, 1465, 2429

July 10, 346, 647, 917, 1167, 1208, 1668, 2360, 2762

July 11, 242, 1508, 2785

July 12, 106, 427, 1233, 1638, 1990, 2390–2391

July 13, 358, 1150, 1282, 1380, 1737

July 14, 97, 963, 2268, 2614, 2667

July 15, 26, 1065, 1422, 1696, 2430

July 16, 94, 735, 1328, 1852, 2052, 2089

July 17, 213, 736, 1168, 1306, 1910, 2812

July 18, 403, 414, 574, 1066, 1121, 1911

July 19, 383, 629, 1484, 1560–1561, 1651, 1669, 1697, 1819, 2298, 2299

July 20, 60, 200, 1670

July 21, 336, 995, 2431, 2718

July 22, 74, 120, 209, 415, 592, 786, 953, 1067, 1087, 1182, 1423, 1466, 2361, 2687

July 23, 737, 980, 1234, 1329, 1492

July 24, 125, 392, 618, 757, 871, 981, 1235, 1738, 2164, 2567

July 25, 95, 332, 787, 1183, 2362, 2392, 2525, 2738–2739

July 26, 359, 1739, 1769–1770, 1853, 2813

July 27, 1698, 2363

July 28, 64, 206, 502, 630, 1485, 1713, 1799, 2471

July 29, 593, 829, 1236, 2452

July 30, 1546, 1800, 2393

July 31, 2193, 2626

August 1, 41, 133, 337, 404, 675, 964, 1068, 1609–1610, 1714, 1801, 1881

August 2, 89, 594, 1017, 1209, 2237

August 3, 276, 428, 894, 1639, 2814

August 4, 138, 274, 1069, 1122, 1389, 1584

August 5, 142, 758, 1611, 2123

August 6, 484, 529, 1184, 1360, 1820

August 7, 1018, 1123, 2472, 2740

August 8, 515, 530, 1070, 1424, 1912, 1961, 2741

August 9, 161, 631, 648, 1283, 1821, 2627

August 10, 710, 918, 1151, 1493, 2090, 2763

August 11, 75, 516, 1152, 1237, 1238, 1467, 2238, 2300, 2453, 2742

August 12, 449, 759, 850, 1521–1522, 2719–2720, 2743, 2764

August 13, 503, 1468, 1494, 1671, 2526, 2568, 2688, 2721–2722, 2744

August 14, 296, 965, 1239, 1390, 2025, 2239, 2301, 2815

August 15, 851, 1381, 1391, 1612, 1672, 2026, 2432, 2723, 2786

August 16, 107, 139, 393, 2787–2788

August 17, 485, 558, 1537, 2364, 2789, 2816

August 18, 259, 450, 872, 1962, 2124, 2668

August 19, 405, 895, 1652, 1715, 1913, 2334

August 20, 788, 966, 1653, 1673, 2053, 2527

August 21, 347, 896, 1019–1020, 1914, 1991, 2644

August 22, 546, 760, 937, 1240, 1405, 1771, 2027, 2125, 2645, 2669

August 23, 55, 547, 1103, 1406, 2091, 2589, 2590, 2646, 2724

August 24, 325, 1124, 1169, 1740, 2126, 2127, 2591, 2628, 2647, 2670–2672

August 25, 84, 1125, 1307, 1772–1773, 2394, 2473, 2673

August 26, 52, 140, 201, 1044, 1392, 1446, 1774, 2028–2029, 2365, 2454, 2569, 2629–2630, 2689, 2817

August 27, 1425, 1613, 1854, 2092, 2269, 2493–2494

August 28, 47, 575, 761, 1509, 1822, 1915, 2030, 2194–2195, 2335, 2474, 2495

August 29, 18, 277, 692, 789, 897, 1170, 1308–1309, 1614, 1882, 2240, 2433, 2496–2497, 2690–2692

August 30, 30, 548, 982, 1021, 1330, 1382, 1447, 1562, 1699, 1963, 2093–2094, 2165, 2366–2368, 2395, 2790

August 31, 118, 210, 314, 326, 352, 451, 873, 1942, 2196–2198, 2270, 2369, 2396, 2693–2695

September 1, 135, 190, 632, 811, 830, 954, 1310, 1426, 1448, 1469, 1495, 1992, 2031, 2166, 2199, 2241, 2242, 2550–2551

September 2, 85, 852–853, 874, 1311, 1407, 1449, 1470, 1802, 1823–1825, 1855–1858, 1883, 2032, 2054, 2095, 2200–2201, 2336, 2434–2435, 2528–2529, 2592

September 3, 1427, 1585, 1916, 1943, 2167, 2243, 2302, 2337, 2455, 2530–2531, 2552–2553

September 4, 486, 711, 1268, 1312, 1408, 1486, 1741, 1826–1828, 1993–1995, 2128–2129, 2271–2272, 2303–2304, 2338, 2397, 2532

September 5, 136, 531, 1409, 1487, 1586, 1964–1965, 2096–2097, 2168, 2273, 2305–2306, 2339

September 6, 487, 898, 1331, 1563, 1587, 1674, 1675–1676, 1775, 1859, 1884, 1944, 2098, 2130–2132

September 7, 31, 899, 967, 1241, 1313, 1471, 1564, 1654, 1677, 1945, 2055, 2099, 2398, 2648

September 8, 218, 384, 1361–1362, 1472–1473, 1615, 1946, 2056

September 9, 40, 549, 595, 676, 693, 712, 738, 900, 1383, 1547, 1917, 2436

September 10, 76, 154, 284, 901–902, 1171, 1363, 1616, 2244, 2791

September 11, 86, 739, 790, 919, 1548, 1617, 1829, 2696

September 12, 740, 762, 1153, 1284, 1393–1394, 1428, 1549, 2133–2134, 2169–2170

September 13, 191, 297, 488, 550, 1350, 1678, 2475, 2593

September 14, 348, 831, 854, 1429, 1430, 1538, 1742, 1860, 2533–2534

September 15, 288, 394, 832, 1071, 1210, 1523, 1966

September 16, 469, 1045, 1104, 1496, 1618, 1861, 2033, 2057, 2274, 2615, 2792

September 17, 532, 791, 1154, 1364, 1918, 2370, 2674

September 18, 275, 1862

September 19, 920, 1046, 1126, 1885, 2399

September 20, 182, 192, 1022, 1047, 1830, 2135, 2307

September 21, 649, 1365, 1488, 1655, 1947–1948, 2275

September 22, 81, 921, 2554, 2826

September 23, 576, 1743, 1919, 2245

September 24, 983, 996, 1656, 2308, 2570

September 25, 285, 792, 1744, 1863, 1886, 2276

September 26, 194, 289, 577, 1155, 2202, 2246, 2745

September 27, 968, 1285, 1776, 2171, 2594

September 28, 152, 176, 260, 677, 1286, 1550, 1565, 1967, 2136, 2277

September 29, 290, 376, 452, 551, 619, 938, 1887, 2034, 2675, 2746

September 30, 37, 504–505, 939, 1127, 2203–2204, 2476, 2595

October 1, 193, 360, 453, 552, 578, 855, 922, 997, 1048, 1450, 2035, 2697, 2818

October 2, 147, 1072, 1831

October 3, 553, 596, 1524, 1996, 2278, 2309

October 4, 429, 597, 833, 1451, 1510, 2616

October 5, 36, 2205, 2477, 2498, 2819

October 6, 214, 306, 416, 694, 2206–2207

October 7, 1551, 2172, 2456, 2555

October 8, 517, 650, 1588, 1745, 2371, 2400, 2676

October 9, 454, 651, 695, 713, 1287, 1640, 1832, 1920, 1968, 2208, 2401, 2571–2572, 2698

October 10, 15, 741

October 11, 470, 664, 1314, 2457, 2793

October 12, 61, 301, 353, 2137, 2631

October 13, 417, 923, 1474, 1679, 1746, 1888–1889, 2279, 2556, 2617

October 14, 98, 696

October 15, 72, 177–178, 489, 1997, 2036–2037, 2209, 2280

October 16, 179, 598, 903, 969, 1269, 1315, 1998, 2100, 2138, 2535, 2573

October 17, 315, 1105, 1351, 1475–1476, 1999, 2536

October 18, 261, 406, 652, 1049, 1288, 2173, 2747

October 19, 333, 559, 1270, 1680, 1969, 2632

October 20, 262, 407, 471, 490, 506, 904, 1088, 1395, 1970

October 21, 633, 1242, 1890, 2402, 2794

October 22, 202, 1023, 1864

October 23, 472, 491, 533, 560, 653, 1641, 1865, 2038, 2340

October 24, 579, 714, 1211, 1971, 2039, 2210, 2437, 2458

October 25, 455, 1156, 1289, 1452, 1891, 2000, 2341

October 26, 1212–1213, 2174, 2649, 2699

October 27, 141, 561, 1185, 1366, 1657, 2001, 2247, 2310

October 28, 7, 1050, 1681, 2725, 2820

October 29, 82, 166, 334, 430, 609, 875, 1431, 1589, 1619, 1747, 1949, 2726

October 30, 222, 1477, 1525, 2281, 2342, 2537, 2765

October 31, 812, 2040, 2282

November 1, 167, 269, 678, 1073, 1089, 1157–1158, 1511, 1590, 2101

November 2, 10, 679, 1367, 1384, 1497, 2596

November 3, 1477, 1498

November 4, 680, 793, 834, 998, 2597

November 5, 473, 634, 2102, 2574, 2766, 2795

November 6, 354, 385, 715, 1316, 1432, 2058

November 7, 114, 763, 999, 1074, 1332, 1499, 1921

November 8, 456, 580, 1410, 1539, 2618, 2767

November 9, 665–666, 697, 1214, 1526, 1777, 2311, 2403, 2499, 2700

November 10, 16, 223, 251, 263, 764, 1453, 1892, 2248, 2312, 2557

November 11, 56, 264, 654, 1512, 2139

November 12, 742, 955, 1215, 1411, 1433, 1716, 2313, 2438

November 13, 2, 162, 1748, 2768–2770

November 14, 66, 145, 1700, 2041, 2677, 2821

November 15, 215, 534, 813, 1024, 1658, 2042, 2103, 2314, 2598–2599

November 16, 211, 418, 457, 1106, 1368, 2796

November 17, 243, 698, 1369, 2478, 2575, 2600

November 18, 131, 146, 431, 1186, 1749, 2059, 2727

November 19, 667, 716, 1717, 1922, 2500

November 20, 224, 361, 440, 492, 1025–1026, 1718, 2060

November 21, 362, 441, 1434, 1893, 2249

November 22, 48, 1090, 1682, 2343, 2404

November 23, 23, 835, 1172, 1591, 1701, 2104, 2211, 2315, 2576

November 24, 19, 265, 316, 581, 1435, 1527, 2175, 2501, 2701

November 25, 1187, 1866

November 26, 493, 610, 635, 1243–1244, 1333

November 27, 244, 355, 377, 1107, 1412, 1750, 2061

November 28, 25, 83, 794, 2062

November 29, 128, 395, 924, 1833, 2316, 2439, 2827

November 30, 474, 636, 765, 795, 1528, 2002, 2479, 2633–2634

December 1, 183, 970, 1108, 1271, 1290, 1620, 1659, 2558

December 2, 363, 796, 1000, 1454, 2212, 2577, 2748

December 3, 225, 507, 620, 1751

December 4, 143, 1216, 1540, 1592, 1923, 2003, 2702

December 5, 717, 971–972, 1188, 1396, 1436, 1621, 1719, 1803, 2344, 2405, 2771

December 6, 1027, 1385, 1593, 1778, 2004, 2140

December 7, 611, 621, 718, 925, 1291, 2105, 2559, 2678

December 8, 327, 1292, 1513–1514, 2141

December 9, 5, 386, 743, 1334

December 10, 699, 1566, 1752, 2063, 2250, 2372, 2480, 2619, 2772

December 11, 408, 599, 612, 655, 856, 1642, 1683

December 12, 797, 1293, 1753, 1867, 1972, 2317, 2703

December 13, 535, 1245, 2213, 2538, 2797

December 14, 562, 1128, 1159, 1834, 2345, 2406, 2459

December 15, 876, 1246, 1515, 1660, 1804, 1924, 2176, 2251, 2283, 2318, 2373, 2502

December 16, 117, 719, 1500, 1541, 1779–1780, 2142, 2319, 2822

December 17, 77, 317, 905, 1160, 1189, 1352, 2005, 2214

December 18, 155, 458, 2064, 2503

December 19, 270, 877, 1567, 1622, 2749

December 20, 600, 622, 720, 1129, 1397, 1702, 2460

December 21, 122, 219, 518, 1478, 1781

December 22, 27, 766, 878, 1335, 1552, 2578

December 23, 318, 857, 1479, 2481–2482, 2650

December 24, 1051, 1720, 1721, 1868, 2579

December 25, 20, 32, 475, 554, 767, 836, 926, 984, 1001

December 26, 409, 858, 1568, 2346, 2407

December 27, 11, 137, 582, 601, 798, 837–838, 1075, 1413, 1569, 2461

December 28, 364, 519, 656, 681, 768, 906, 1052–1053, 1130, 1217, 1529, 2773, 2798

December 29, 252, 637, 657, 907, 1002–1003, 1091, 1336, 2704–2705, 2728, 2750

December 30, 814, 1109, 1337, 1370, 1501, 2215

December 31, 29, 68, 879, 880, 1161, 1173, 1542, 1835, 1925, 2106, 2320, 2408

APA DIVISION INDEX

Numbers refer to entry numbers, which appear
in the upper right-hand corner of each entry.

Division 1: General Psychology, 1, 2, 4, 7, 9, 25–27, 36, 41, 76, 102, 135, 136, 138, 147, 182, 187, 192, 198, 224, 248, 249, 265, 268, 269, 280, 299, 322, 337, 373, 402, 432, 444, 458–459, 466, 497, 499, 501, 504, 505, 507, 511, 529, 531, 536, 537, 550, 551, 553, 562, 573, 578, 582, 584, 599, 601, 619, 621, 626, 646, 656–657, 670, 702, 714, 724–725, 727–729, 739, 743, 747, 754, 773–774, 787, 796, 798, 805, 820, 837, 842, 865, 933, 954, 976, 990, 999, 1002–1003, 1022, 1033, 1045, 1053, 1088, 1109, 1122, 1136, 1179, 1191, 1193, 1199, 1200, 1208, 1217, 1231, 1247, 1249, 1260, 1271, 1278, 1282, 1290, 1296, 1304, 1309–1310, 1312–1313, 1315, 1322, 1336–1337, 1351, 1376, 1400, 1412, 1414, 1417, 1425, 1436, 1443–1444, 1446, 1448, 1451, 1455, 1460, 1464, 1468, 1471–1472, 1473, 1487, 1494, 1501, 1510, 1518, 1527, 1532, 1535–1536, 1540, 1549, 1553, 1558, 1561, 1563–1564, 1570, 1579–1580, 1588, 1592, 1596, 1603, 1611, 1614, 1618, 1640, 1642, 1665–1666, 1670, 1674, 1695–1697, 1702, 1706, 1708–1709, 1711, 1714, 1718, 1729–1730, 1736, 1738, 1751–1752, 1775, 1780, 1794, 1796, 1806–1807, 1809, 1825, 1829, 1834, 1841, 1851, 1855, 1857, 1858, 1868, 1877, 1882, 1896, 1907, 1916, 1925, 1937–1938, 1949, 1970, 1972, 1981, 1983, 1992, 2000–2001, 2003, 2005, 2011, 2017–2018, 2020–2022, 2025, 2032, 2034, 2038, 2050, 2055, 2059, 2077, 2087, 2097, 2100, 2115, 2163, 2167, 2197, 2209, 2225, 2237, 2240, 2242, 2265, 2272, 2291, 2298–2299, 2302–2304, 2313, 2315, 2319, 2333, 2355, 2375, 2379–2381, 2386, 2391–2392, 2396, 2399, 2413, 2428, 2432, 2435, 2437, 2441, 2465, 2469–2470, 2477, 2505, 2528, 2544–2545, 2550, 2556, 2559, 2569, 2574, 2583, 2590, 2593–2594, 2603, 2605, 2614, 2640, 2643–2644, 2648–2649, 2673–2674, 2679, 2684, 2686, 2689, 2702, 2705, 2711, 2713–2714, 2716, 2718–2719, 2723, 2728, 2730, 2734–2735, 2737, 2740–2743, 2746, 2748, 2753, 2764, 2768, 2772, 2774, 2777, 2779, 2781, 2784, 2786–2789, 2791, 2793, 2795, 2800, 2804, 2811, 2814, 2820–2821

Division 2: Teaching of Psychology, 191, 468, 563, 612, 681, 764, 865, 880, 929, 1124, 1130, 1144, 1213, 1230, 1249, 1304, 1355, 1440, 1508, 1568, 1677, 1694–1695, 2032, 2055, 2065, 2069, 2096–2097, 2190, 2197, 2273, 2402, 2419, 2431, 2494, 2499, 2532, 2542, 2553, 2574, 2631, 2691–2692, 2743, 2764, 2783, 2803, 2816, 2825

Division 3: Experimental Psychology, 14, 20, 47, 74, 79, 87–90, 96, 98, 112–113, 117–118, 123–124, 132–133, 139–140, 143, 151, 156, 184, 194, 196, 200, 202, 211, 223, 229, 231–232, 241, 247, 251, 253, 259, 263, 269–270, 275–276, 278, 281, 283, 285–286, 289, 294–295, 298, 302, 304, 313–315, 324–325, 329, 332, 336, 343, 347–348, 352, 360–363, 365, 370, 375, 378, 384–386, 390–392, 396–399, 405, 414, 417, 423, 434, 436, 439–440, 442, 447, 453, 462, 466, 468, 476, 478–479, 485, 487, 490–491, 494, 499, 506, 514, 540, 567–568, 571, 577–579, 585, 597, 603–604, 608, 610, 630, 634, 638, 644, 647, 651, 668, 685, 691, 693, 697, 704, 708, 716, 732–733, 741–742, 745, 753, 755, 766, 769, 771–772, 776–777, 780, 784, 786–787, 791–792, 794–795, 797, 800, 803–804, 808, 812, 822, 828, 831, 834, 839, 842, 848, 861, 865, 869, 884, 886, 891, 894, 904, 906, 925, 927,

931, 950–951, 953, 963, 966, 974, 976, 985, 988, 991, 997, 1010–1014, 1017, 1020, 1032–1033, 1039, 1042, 1047, 1058, 1063, 1068–1069, 1072, 1080, 1083–1084, 1087, 1089, 1092–1093, 1103, 1105, 1111–1112, 1128, 1135, 1141, 1143, 1145, 1149, 1153–1154, 1165, 1167, 1170, 1173, 1178, 1182, 1186–1187, 1195–1196, 1206, 1209, 1212–1213, 1216, 1220, 1229, 1233, 1239, 1252–1253, 1256, 1261, 1264, 1266, 1268–1269, 1281, 1292, 1295, 1298, 1308, 1311, 1316, 1318–1319, 1325, 1339–1340, 1344, 1352, 1354, 1358–1359, 1362, 1368, 1370, 1372–1373, 1382, 1387–1388, 1391, 1393–1394, 1396, 1407–1408, 1415–1416, 1428, 1441, 1445, 1454, 1465–1466, 1469, 1480, 1489–1490, 1492, 1521–1522, 1529, 1537, 1547–1548, 1578, 1589, 1602, 1608, 1623, 1626, 1639, 1645, 1654, 1660, 1673, 1685–1686, 1691, 1706, 1713, 1717, 1720, 1725, 1741, 1743, 1748, 1750, 1758, 1766, 1798, 1804, 1808, 1814, 1818, 1820–1821, 1824–1825, 1849, 1855, 1858, 1864, 1872, 1881, 1887, 1896, 1912, 1918, 1923, 1925, 1931–1932, 1939, 1947–1948, 1951, 1965–1966, 1976, 1990–1991, 2003, 2014, 2016, 2037, 2045, 2048, 2050, 2057, 2059, 2061, 2063, 2073, 2076, 2080, 2105, 2108–2109, 2111, 2115, 2119, 2122–2124, 2127, 2130, 2133–2134, 2137, 2139, 2142–2143, 2156, 2169, 2175, 2178, 2181, 2189, 2203, 2216, 2219, 2234, 2238, 2246, 2252–2253, 2289, 2300, 2312, 2321, 2327, 2334, 2346, 2348, 2350, 2352, 2354, 2363, 2403, 2410–2412, 2420, 2428, 2469, 2486, 2490, 2510–2511, 2521, 2526, 2532, 2546, 2563–2564, 2575–2576, 2580, 2623, 2641, 2650, 2654, 2685, 2701, 2711, 2713, 2721, 2724, 2752, 2757, 2758, 2769–2770, 2778–2781, 2792, 2798, 2807–2809, 2817, 2825

Division 4: 1408

Division 5: Evaluation, Measurement, and Statistics, 17, 23, 29, 45, 51, 57, 68, 69, 89, 91, 103, 119, 125, 146, 234, 242, 267, 284, 292, 328, 330, 346, 356–358, 370–372, 376–377, 383, 406, 412, 429, 433, 435, 437, 441, 448, 452, 455–456, 457, 463, 473, 475, 477, 482, 484, 498, 503, 508–509, 513, 516, 520, 527, 539, 583, 594, 603, 605, 613, 623, 629, 640, 648, 652–653, 655, 659, 667, 676–677, 684, 691, 695–696, 698, 706–707, 709, 711, 713, 740, 752, 759–760, 768, 778, 783, 790, 802, 805–806, 809, 813, 816, 819, 823, 826, 828, 835, 838, 841, 849–850, 871, 877, 903, 910, 920–921, 924, 935, 943, 953, 955, 1004–1005, 1009, 1011, 1013, 1025, 1027–1028, 1036, 1041, 1046, 1048, 1051, 1056, 1066, 1074–1075, 1077, 1092, 1097–1098, 1104, 1119–1120, 1135, 1147, 1156, 1158, 1169, 1175, 1188, 1204, 1232, 1234, 1236, 1241–1242, 1253, 1281, 1286, 1301, 1335, 1365, 1398, 1404, 1409, 1424, 1429, 1431, 1441, 1450, 1454, 1463, 1475, 1480, 1482, 1486, 1496, 1499, 1502, 1516, 1519, 1525, 1539, 1557–1578, 1607, 1615, 1618–1619, 1622, 1624, 1633, 1644, 1651–1652, 1655, 1659, 1667, 1676, 1681, 1687, 1705, 1719, 1733, 1735, 1753, 1763, 1779, 1785–1786, 1795, 1800, 1832, 1897, 1904, 1915, 1921, 1924, 1986, 1989, 1993, 2016, 2029, 2054, 2082–2084, 2111–2112, 2157, 2176, 2182, 2194, 2221–2222, 2268, 2274, 2276, 2282, 2287, 2306, 2316, 2356, 2406, 2414, 2426–2457, 2458, 2460, 2478, 2535, 2557, 2560, 2595, 2685, 2698, 2731, 2762, 2803, 2813, 2826

Division 6: Physiological and Comparative Psychology, 11–12, 31, 40–41, 49–51, 55–56, 59–60, 72, 77, 80, 87, 97, 106, 109, 114–115, 118, 120, 122–123, 127, 129, 131, 137, 142, 149, 156, 160, 165, 168, 174, 176, 183–184, 188, 190, 199, 207–208, 211, 214, 217, 220, 226, 229–230, 238–240, 244, 255, 264–265, 273–274, 294–295, 303–304, 306, 313, 318–319, 333, 335, 342, 344–345, 350–351, 363, 367, 386, 388, 419, 461, 467, 472, 486, 492, 496, 512, 518, 523, 525, 528, 535, 540, 544, 564, 566, 568, 570, 575, 581, 586, 633, 641, 644, 665–666, 673, 678, 693–695, 701, 704, 711–712, 731, 735, 737, 742, 760, 763, 772, 782, 786, 797, 815, 831, 846–847, 850, 857, 879, 882, 893, 904, 907, 919, 931–932, 938, 940, 961, 964, 966, 976, 982–984, 988, 995, 1018, 1042, 1044, 1065, 1068, 1070,

1072, 1078, 1081, 1087, 1089, 1105–1106, 1123, 1126, 1137, 1142, 1153–1154,
1165, 1195, 1213, 1245–1246, 1280, 1287, 1289, 1294, 1305–1306, 1321, 1326,
1331, 1334, 1340, 1346, 1349, 1352, 1359, 1362, 1366, 1378, 1380, 1401, 1407,
1410, 1421, 1442, 1449, 1456, 1474–1475, 1479, 1504, 1520, 1533–1534, 1538,
1542, 1574, 1585, 1610, 1645, 1654, 1657, 1658, 1668–1669, 1689, 1712, 1727,
1741, 1747, 1777–1778, 1782, 1791, 1801, 1809–1810, 1817, 1839, 1844, 1848,
1861, 1879, 1889, 1893, 1905–1906, 1908–1909, 1917, 1923, 1926, 1951, 1953,
1964–1965, 1969, 1975, 1979, 1995, 2002, 2014, 2037, 2042, 2060, 2076, 2081,
2085, 2091, 2104, 2108, 2116, 2119, 2121, 2127, 2152, 2158, 2162, 2173–2174,
2208, 2212, 2215, 2220, 2254, 2257, 2260, 2262, 2280, 2310, 2332, 2337, 2346,
2353, 2372, 2374, 2395, 2405, 2409, 2415, 2418, 2421, 2459, 2476, 2479, 2482,
2558, 2562, 2564, 2570–2573, 2575–2576, 2579, 2596, 2599, 2604, 2606, 2615,
2618, 2622, 2626, 2650, 2675, 2682, 2707, 2711–2712, 2717, 2721, 2726, 2739,
2747, 2752, 2790, 2824

Division 7: Developmental Psychology, 35, 43, 95, 160, 175, 242–243, 246, 251, 260,
271, 290, 327, 330, 340, 342, 354, 364, 372, 381, 389, 391, 400, 411, 416, 433,
464, 473, 478, 484–485, 495, 513, 519, 521, 538, 543, 547, 555, 559, 567, 590,
594, 598, 600, 602, 605, 611, 631–632, 634, 637–639, 645, 658, 661, 665, 671,
675, 677, 687–688, 719, 726, 732, 734, 742, 750, 762–763, 765, 781, 806, 811,
813, 819, 822, 836, 843, 846, 870, 873, 875, 878, 883, 892, 905, 908, 915–916,
925, 936, 943–944, 957, 970, 972, 975, 990–992, 994, 1008, 1034–1035, 1040,
1058, 1068–1070, 1095, 1116, 1127, 1139, 1151, 1164, 1168, 1186–1187, 1194,
1201, 1220, 1228, 1234, 1236, 1240, 1267, 1274, 1277, 1283, 1288, 1297, 1324,
1327, 1348–1349, 1360, 1379, 1424, 1454, 1467, 1571–1572, 1577, 1581, 1650–
1651, 1667, 1680, 1710, 1721, 1727, 1744, 1759, 1846, 1895, 1932, 1978, 1999,
2013, 2028, 2044, 2116, 2125, 2141, 2176, 2181, 2215, 2217, 2229, 2232, 2270,
2283, 2285, 2295, 2297, 2407, 2551, 2575, 2601, 2608, 2610, 2628, 2656, 2715,
2722, 2738, 2756, 2794, 2801, 2809

Division 8: Personality and Social Psychology, 51, 66, 125, 158, 172, 235, 245, 250, 289,
311–312, 331, 392, 442–443, 467, 500, 517, 532, 546, 549, 558, 565, 581, 585–
587, 608, 617, 621, 624, 653–654, 667, 679, 685–686, 692, 713, 719, 723, 726,
732, 744, 750, 757–759, 768, 779, 789, 799, 802, 805, 807, 812, 828–829, 839,
854, 856, 863–864, 870–873, 882, 886, 915–916, 918, 935, 942, 949, 951, 958,
973, 992, 997, 1001, 1005, 1007, 1009, 1015, 1023, 1025–1026, 1037, 1040–
1041, 1044, 1049, 1061–1063, 1075, 1082, 1085, 1092, 1094–1095, 1104, 1107,
1114, 1116, 1121, 1124, 1138, 1146, 1158, 1161, 1169, 1172, 1174, 1197–1198,
1201, 1214, 1216, 1221, 1223, 1225–1226, 1237–1238, 1259, 1265, 1269, 1272,
1284, 1299–1300, 1317, 1319, 1345, 1347, 1353, 1355, 1361, 1374–1375, 1381,
1383, 1387, 1390, 1397, 1402, 1435, 1465, 1476–1477, 1481, 1485, 1507, 1509,
1513, 1523, 1526, 1544, 1546–1547, 1600–1602, 1608, 1623, 1625, 1647, 1659,
1661, 1680, 1692, 1701, 1705, 1713, 1715, 1733, 1749, 1750, 1755, 1772–1773,
1776, 1781, 1783, 1790, 1797, 1832, 1836, 1846, 1854, 1856, 1860, 1869, 1880,
1899, 1903–1904, 1913, 1919–1920, 1933, 1941, 1945, 1950, 1962, 1967, 1971,
1993, 1996, 2006, 2028, 2036, 2046, 2049–2051, 2066–2067, 2074, 2089, 2093,
2095, 2113–2114, 2117, 2159, 2182, 2187, 2191, 2193, 2198, 2213, 2279, 2301,
2308, 2320, 2354, 2404, 2407, 2454, 2475, 2512, 2522, 2550, 2564, 2615, 2623,
2658–2659, 2717, 2722, 2733, 2782

Division 9: Society for the Psychological Study of Social Issues, 99, 105, 340, 364, 411,
679, 685, 713, 738, 744, 750, 790, 793, 822, 829, 833, 841, 852, 872, 890, 911,
918, 936, 941, 944, 951, 958, 980–981, 991, 1007, 1026, 1034, 1056–1057, 1061–
1062, 1075, 1085, 1094–1095, 1146, 1150, 1161, 1168, 1203, 1227, 1238, 1255,
1284, 1341, 1345, 1350, 1353, 1355, 1374–1377, 1381, 1383, 1386, 1424, 1426–

1427, 1505, 1513, 1526, 1530, 1544, 1546, 1554, 1582, 1590, 1598, 1600–1601, 1605–1606, 1646, 1648, 1661, 1677, 1679, 1693, 1710, 1715, 1755, 1765, 1933, 2051, 2144, 2166, 2198, 2222, 2228, 2241–2242, 2279, 2287, 2301, 2320, 2341, 2419, 2431, 2433, 2454, 2457, 2466, 2474, 2502, 2504, 2529, 2540, 2584–2585, 2589, 2591, 2611, 2628, 2632–2633, 2638, 2659, 2662, 2665, 2687, 2690, 2720, 2733, 2774, 2777, 2789

Division 10: Psychology and the Arts, 184, 206, 209, 252, 288–289, 291, 359, 392, 607, 622, 753, 1111, 1139, 1178, 1197, 1567, 1728, 1767, 1930, 1993, 2094, 2202, 2314, 2598, 2600

Division 12: Clinical Psychology, 3, 5, 10, 15, 29, 42, 49, 61–63, 84–86, 92, 94, 99, 101, 105, 126, 144–146, 153, 155, 159, 166–167, 169–170, 173, 178–179, 189–191, 195, 199, 203–204, 210, 215–216, 219, 221–222, 225, 227–228, 233, 237, 239, 245, 253, 257, 293, 297, 300–301, 305, 309, 316–317, 320, 348–349, 354, 358, 366, 382, 388, 401, 404, 415, 418, 421, 428, 433, 446, 449, 456, 460, 471, 474, 481, 483, 489, 502, 512, 517, 524, 548, 554, 572, 574, 580, 583, 587, 589, 591– 593, 596, 602, 614, 628–629, 635, 637–639, 641, 643, 645, 648–649, 653, 660, 662–663, 676, 683, 695, 700, 705, 710, 722, 730, 744, 748, 756, 759–760, 764, 775, 778–779, 785, 801, 813–814, 817–819, 824, 827, 842–843, 851, 853, 855, 858, 867, 870, 874, 876, 885, 887, 890, 895, 905, 910, 912–913, 916, 922, 924, 926, 930, 935, 947, 952, 959, 969, 973, 979, 987, 989, 998–999, 1009–1010, 1015–1016, 1019, 1027–1028, 1036, 1052, 1054–1055, 1059–1060, 1066–1067, 1070, 1073, 1076, 1091–1092, 1095, 1097–1098, 1104, 1116–1117, 1121, 1125, 1129–1130, 1132–1134, 1144, 1148, 1152, 1158–1159, 1162–1163, 1166, 1170– 1171, 1175, 1177, 1180, 1182–1183, 1196, 1205, 1207, 1211, 1215, 1218–1219, 1221, 1223–1224, 1227, 1230, 1235, 1241, 1248, 1250, 1259, 1263, 1275, 1289, 1293, 1300, 1303, 1306, 1314, 1323, 1330, 1332–1333, 1335, 1357, 1364, 1385, 1389, 1403, 1406, 1411, 1418, 1420–1421, 1430, 1432–1433, 1435, 1438–1439, 1447, 1459, 1474, 1478–1479, 1484, 1491, 1495, 1499–1500, 1504, 1506, 1508, 1522, 1524–1525, 1528, 1531, 1539, 1541–1543, 1545, 1550, 1552, 1554–1555, 1574, 1583–1584, 1586, 1594, 1599, 1603–1604, 1616, 1627, 1629, 1632, 1636, 1648, 1653, 1669, 1675, 1678, 1683, 1689, 1704, 1716, 1723, 1732, 1739, 1747, 1760, 1768, 1777–1778, 1782, 1791, 1801, 1803, 1810, 1819, 1823, 1830, 1835, 1839, 1843–1844, 1853, 1859, 1861–1862, 1870, 1873, 1876, 1879, 1889, 1892– 1894, 1902, 1905, 1908–1909, 1917, 1926–1927, 1929, 1934–1935, 1940, 1953, 1955, 1977, 1997, 2008–2009, 2027, 2040, 2042–2043, 2058, 2060, 2081, 2090– 2092, 2104, 2112, 2128, 2150, 2152, 2156, 2164–2165, 2168, 2171, 2183–2184, 2195, 2220, 2226, 2239, 2245, 2247, 2249, 2255, 2257, 2259–2260, 2264, 2266, 2275, 2317, 2325, 2328–2329, 2332, 2335, 2342, 2344, 2349, 2359–2360, 2362, 2371, 2374–2376, 2382, 2388, 2393, 2398, 2401, 2409, 2415, 2423, 2425, 2429– 2430, 2446, 2448, 2450, 2453, 2459–2460, 2463–2464, 2467–2468, 2476, 2482, 2485, 2487, 2489, 2492, 2517–2519, 2520, 2525, 2533–2534, 2539, 2543, 2549, 2554, 2558, 2562, 2568, 2570, 2573, 2577, 2579, 2581, 2586–2588, 2596, 2599, 2607, 2611, 2613, 2616–2618, 2621, 2626, 2638, 2660, 2662–2663, 2665–2666, 2675, 2680, 2683, 2697, 2699–2700, 2703–2704, 2706–2707, 2710, 2731, 2745, 2749–2751, 2755, 2759, 2766, 2797, 2802, 2805–2806, 2818, 2822

Division 13: Consulting Psychology, 170, 380, 502, 512, 645, 649, 710, 731, 778–789, 816, 852, 917, 937, 1067, 1071, 1074, 1091, 1113, 1131, 1158, 1190, 1248, 1275, 1371, 1422, 1439, 1447, 1478, 1506, 1525, 1531, 1603–1604, 1615, 1630, 1632, 1768, 2082–2084, 2306, 2463, 2508, 2511, 2731, 2751, 2797, 2822

Division 14: Industrial and Organizational Psychology, 282, 288, 310, 341, 380, 407, 409, 450, 493, 518, 541, 549, 659, 696, 715, 723, 758, 768, 783, 788–789, 816, 849, 869, 884, 917, 921, 923, 937, 964, 993, 1030, 1044, 1050, 1057, 1071, 1074,

1113, 1131, 1141, 1147, 1150, 1248, 1254, 1256, 1261, 1371, 1447, 1486, 1519, 1531, 1557, 1582, 1584, 1604, 1606, 1607, 1615, 1630, 1632–1633, 1647, 1687, 1729, 1863, 1890, 1961, 1966, 2015, 2049, 2082–2084, 2107, 2145, 2426, 2442, 2508, 2595, 2620, 2623, 2639, 2717, 2762, 2826

Division 15: Educational Psychology, 6, 43, 52, 67, 108, 161, 251, 262, 277, 291–292, 326, 339, 370, 377, 381, 383, 393, 395, 457, 485, 510, 519, 522, 560–561, 569, 606, 612, 615, 623, 650, 655, 664, 672, 703, 707, 726, 752, 793, 803, 830, 833, 846, 878, 883–884, 908, 916, 921, 943, 962, 972, 1008, 1011, 1020, 1046, 1076, 1110, 1188, 1222, 1240, 1279, 1301, 1320, 1330, 1398, 1431, 1467, 1511, 1516, 1548, 1571, 1606, 1612, 1619, 1622, 1650, 1693, 1703, 1719, 1735, 1754, 1765, 1769, 1770, 1840, 1866, 1871, 1921, 1924, 1984, 2010, 2035, 2053, 2079, 2112, 2144, 2187, 2190, 2248, 2261, 2270, 2282, 2293, 2330, 2356, 2400, 2408, 2466, 2535–2536, 2738, 2769, 2801, 2824, 2826

Division 16: School Psychology, 65, 326, 377, 574, 576, 606, 612, 615, 623, 635, 703, 740, 756, 806, 823, 905, 972, 1067, 1076, 1115, 1211, 1242, 1586, 1609, 1621, 1744, 1771, 1819, 1840, 1866, 1871, 1884, 1959, 1985, 2185, 2223, 2230, 2258, 2271, 2288, 2408, 2414, 2439, 2443, 2466, 2517, 2536, 2602, 2709

Division 17: Counseling Psychology, 225, 253, 307, 446, 450, 547, 554, 575, 587, 591, 606, 608, 615, 661, 740, 759, 785, 788, 823, 826, 851, 865, 885, 910, 917, 968, 979, 993, 1001, 1031, 1115, 1121, 1132, 1134, 1170, 1224, 1228, 1235, 1267, 1361, 1465, 1495, 1556, 1584, 1602, 1608, 1623, 1633, 1638, 1659, 1692, 1699, 1734, 1740, 1742, 1757, 1761, 1772, 1799, 1802, 1823, 1840, 1842, 1871, 1894, 1911, 2106, 2112, 2115, 2140, 2156, 2177, 2183, 2195, 2226–2227, 2244, 2264, 2275, 2306, 2331, 2333, 2335, 2342, 2362, 2371, 2384, 2388, 2424, 2448, 2463–2464, 2467, 2485, 2487, 2489, 2501, 2517, 2524, 2533, 2539, 2566, 2581, 2607, 2617, 2634, 2641, 2680, 2695, 2749, 2751, 2771, 2810, 2818, 2822

Division 18: Psychologists in Public Service, 62, 94, 204, 221, 316, 428, 548, 748, 751, 840, 858, 952, 998, 1016, 1060, 1133, 1147–1148, 1280, 1294, 1335, 1343, 1491, 1512, 1515, 1530, 1616, 1679, 1739, 1805, 2301, 2324, 2341, 2360, 2376, 2377, 2390, 2440, 2497, 2617, 2634, 2660, 2687, 2699, 2755

Division 19: Military Psychology, 110, 310, 407, 446, 610, 633, 764, 767, 800, 816, 850, 868, 921, 923, 942, 946, 960, 1020, 1024, 1028, 1036, 1038, 1051, 1059, 1066, 1133, 1156, 1484, 1486, 1493, 1496–1499, 1512–1513, 1517, 1607, 1647, 1698, 1726, 1850, 1863, 1923, 1951, 2472, 2549, 2595, 2754

Division 20: Adult Development and Aging, 287, 632, 836, 864, 875, 996, 998, 1006, 1058, 1140, 1186, 1274, 1327, 1482, 1545, 1556, 1569, 1572, 1587, 1671, 1786, 1920, 2229, 2498, 2607, 2655, 2700

Division 21: Applied Experimental and Engineering Psychologists, 339, 341, 394, 398, 462, 472, 610, 696, 731, 767, 834, 868, 923, 937, 946, 960, 1012, 1030, 1229, 1251, 1266, 1346, 1486, 1827, 1850, 1863, 1865, 1885, 1923, 1951, 1958, 2071, 2204, 2312, 2369, 2511, 2677, 2682

Division 22: Rehabilitation Psychology, 108, 382, 693, 735, 1018, 1028, 1064, 1099, 1484, 1878, 1883, 1886, 2505, 2725, 2739, 2813

Division 23: Consumer Psychology, 942, 1113, 1944, 2269, 2455

Division 24: Theoretical and Philosophical Psychology, 1–2, 6, 8–9, 13–14, 16, 18–19, 21, 28, 30, 31–34, 37–38, 44, 47–48, 53–54, 58, 67–68, 71, 78–79, 81, 83, 93, 100, 111, 113, 116, 121, 127, 148, 150, 154, 163, 165, 171, 177, 180, 202, 213, 224, 228, 230, 235, 256, 258, 261, 266, 276, 279, 298, 308, 311, 314, 323, 334, 343, 345, 365, 397–398, 422, 425, 447, 478–479, 494, 515, 532, 536, 542, 550, 560, 622, 634, 666, 682, 689, 715, 727, 749, 754, 780, 810, 914, 956, 969, 977, 998, 1021, 1033, 1056, 1096, 1112, 1176, 1189, 1216, 1262, 1281, 1291, 1342, 1354, 1626, 1639, 1658, 1717, 1836, 1881, 1896, 1973, 1994, 1998, 2080, 2126, 2231, 2308, 2381, 2780, 2812, 2827

Division 25: Experimental Analysis of Behavior, 279, 347–348, 352, 362, 378, 394, 476, 515, 519, 632, 668, 716, 733, 776, 808, 860, 909, 956, 977, 983, 989, 1032, 1047, 1069, 1083–1084, 1090, 1103, 1105, 1118, 1152, 1157, 1162, 1176, 1190, 1209, 1212, 1222, 1233, 1273, 1279, 1305, 1325, 1330, 1333, 1341, 1363, 1369, 1397, 1420, 1423, 1440, 1445, 1470, 1559, 1565, 1620, 1634, 1686, 1826, 1858, 1864, 1874, 1876, 1928, 1934, 1952, 1975, 1987, 2047, 2056–2057, 2065, 2069, 2096, 2102, 2106, 2136, 2151, 2179, 2188–2190, 2216, 2218, 2238–2239, 2263, 2307, 2309, 2318, 2341, 2377, 2383, 2390, 2429, 2445, 2488, 2500, 2513, 2541, 2578, 2763, 2819

Division 26: History of Psychology, 1–2, 9, 36, 51, 83, 117, 202, 247, 275, 308, 360–361, 390, 399, 413, 423, 436, 440, 444, 451, 465, 491, 499, 515, 542, 545, 596, 617, 727, 770–771, 787, 818, 889, 898, 901, 945, 963, 965, 1021, 1054, 1107, 1141, 1181, 1192, 1257, 1260, 1276, 1307, 1311, 1316, 1325, 1329, 1338, 1399, 1405, 1415, 1452, 1568, 1662, 1896, 1943, 2031, 2068, 2088, 2099, 2103, 2205, 2787, 2821

Division 27: Society for Community Research and Action, 205, 297, 366, 785, 851, 856, 867, 885, 972, 979, 986, 1035, 1073, 1076, 1129, 1224, 1258–1259, 1323, 1343, 1364, 1495, 1546, 1599, 1679, 1799, 1805, 2008, 2040, 2053, 2078–2079, 2098, 2110, 2129, 2131, 2371, 2384, 2425, 2464, 2468, 2487, 2515, 2555, 2568, 2581, 2617, 2662, 2687, 2715, 2727, 2797, 2801

Division 28: Psychopharmacology and Substance Abuse, 233, 329, 641, 904, 931, 982, 1137, 1294, 1318, 1474, 1479, 1504, 1533–1534, 1542, 1545, 1574, 1669, 1689, 1723, 1747, 1760, 1777–1778, 1782, 1791, 1801, 1803, 1810, 1817, 1830, 1839, 1843–1844, 1853, 1859, 1861, 1879, 1889, 1892–1893, 1902, 1905, 1908–1909, 1917, 1926, 1929, 1953, 1955, 2042, 2058, 2060, 2081, 2091, 2101, 2104, 2120, 2132, 2138, 2152, 2164, 2171, 2184, 2220, 2245, 2257, 2259–2260, 2310, 2332, 2374, 2409, 2415, 2423, 2459, 2476, 2482, 2519, 2534, 2554, 2558, 2562, 2570, 2573, 2579, 2599, 2626, 2652, 2675, 2701, 2724, 2745, 2750, 2818

Division 29: Psychotherapy, 15, 22, 42, 86, 92, 101, 126, 134, 145, 159, 166, 178–179, 189, 210, 215–216, 219, 221, 225, 237, 257, 297, 301, 305, 320, 338, 357, 401, 481, 483, 579, 589, 592, 628–629, 662, 663, 690, 700, 705, 712, 751, 761, 775, 778–779, 807, 814, 821, 827, 840, 853, 888, 890, 913, 926, 968, 989, 1009, 1015–1016, 1019, 1027, 1043, 1055, 1060, 1073, 1097–1098, 1102, 1120–1121, 1125, 1130, 1133, 1144, 1148, 1173, 1180, 1196, 1205, 1207, 1218, 1224, 1230, 1241, 1243–1244, 1289, 1293, 1303, 1357, 1364, 1377, 1389, 1395, 1418–1419, 1432, 1463, 1484, 1500, 1506, 1508, 1531, 1541, 1583, 1595, 1599, 1636, 1716, 1746, 1832, 1838, 1862, 1873, 1876, 1894, 1910, 1927, 1938, 1974, 1989, 2009, 2027, 2101, 2128, 2165, 2168, 2177, 2183, 2195, 2226, 2238–2239, 2263, 2266, 2275, 2328, 2335–2336, 2338, 2387–2388, 2393, 2397, 2424–2425, 2427, 2430, 2446, 2448–2449, 2453, 2467–2468, 2485, 2489, 2503, 2515, 2538–2539, 2555, 2568, 2613, 2621, 2636, 2651, 2680, 2697, 2749, 2759, 2766

Division 30: Psychological Hypnosis, 39, 64, 70, 73, 75, 82, 128, 157, 162, 197, 201, 257, 420, 474, 530, 534, 595, 717, 787, 821, 1252, 1269, 1724, 2180, 2200, 2206, 2612

Division 31: State Psychological Association Affairs, 700, 710, 818, 831, 973, 1019, 1073, 1132, 1207, 1215, 1218, 1250, 1302, 1357, 1453, 1495, 1551, 1558, 1560, 1562, 1573, 1575–1576, 1579, 1588, 1591, 1593, 1603, 1613, 1617, 1628, 1631, 1635, 1637, 1641, 1643, 1649, 1656, 1663–1664, 1688, 1690, 1731, 1739, 1756, 1762, 1764, 1774, 1787–1789, 1792, 1802, 1811, 1813, 1815–1816, 1822, 1828, 1831, 1833, 1837, 1845, 1847, 1852, 1867, 1875, 1888, 1891, 1898, 1900–1901, 1914, 1922, 1942, 1946, 1954, 1956, 1960, 1963, 1968, 1980–1983, 1988, 2012, 2019, 2023–2024, 2026, 2033, 2041, 2052, 2064, 2070, 2072, 2075, 2086, 2118, 2135,

2147, 2149, 2153–2155, 2160–2161, 2172, 2186, 2192, 2196, 2207, 2211, 2214, 2224, 2233, 2236, 2250–2251, 2256, 2284, 2286, 2311, 2322, 2331, 2340, 2361, 2375, 2385, 2436, 2438, 2444, 2451, 2461, 2471, 2473, 2480, 2484, 2514, 2523, 2565, 2592, 2616, 2619, 2625, 2627, 2637, 2642, 2653, 2657, 2667, 2696, 2729, 2732, 2776, 2785, 2802

Division 32: Humanistic Psychology, 256, 379, 591, 600, 654, 721, 810, 864, 888, 914, 969, 1001, 1132, 1509, 1556, 1582, 1684, 1772, 1936, 1957, 1987, 2030, 2062, 2296, 2305, 2336, 2681

Division 33: Mental Retardation and Developmental Disabilities, 22, 24, 46, 65, 85, 95, 104, 107–108, 130–131, 134, 141, 181, 185–186, 193, 212, 218, 236, 239, 260, 296, 368–369, 376, 385, 388, 395, 438, 457, 482, 527, 576, 623, 636, 645, 676, 687, 718, 748, 761, 765, 830, 832, 845, 879, 903, 908, 952, 975, 986, 1018, 1077, 1101, 1117, 1151–1152, 1164, 1202, 1242, 1270, 1314, 1320, 1330, 1333, 1403, 1457, 1476, 1621, 1884, 1959, 1985, 2004, 2008, 2039, 2170, 2176, 2261, 2277, 2281, 2323–2324, 2326, 2339, 2416, 2439, 2443, 2481, 2601, 2676, 2709, 2725, 2739, 2765, 2813

Division 34: Population and Environmental Psychology, 152, 750, 856, 958, 1085, 1166, 1285, 1578, 2093, 2213, 2347, 2366, 2527

Division 35: Psychology of Women, 449, 469, 547, 552, 580, 601, 609, 616, 722, 726, 739, 799, 841, 964, 996, 1000, 1021, 1056, 1160, 1184, 1197, 1203, 1293, 1299–1300, 1350, 1355, 1371, 1375, 1435, 1485, 1512, 1514–1515, 1524, 1544, 1552, 1793, 1916, 2272, 2278, 2292, 2294, 2333, 2343, 2357, 2367, 2422, 2433, 2437, 2470, 2474, 2495, 2501, 2529, 2532, 2589, 2647, 2690, 2693–2694, 2703, 2733, 2756, 2771, 2796

Division 36: Psychology of Religion, 5, 292, 304, 411, 1021, 1389, 1761, 1842, 1911, 2365, 2389, 2434

Division 37: Child, Youth, and Family Services, 99, 205, 291, 307, 364, 415, 661, 674, 687, 738, 761, 811, 878, 883, 892, 936, 944, 986, 1035, 1117, 1151, 1164, 1184, 1228, 1235, 1267, 1275, 1360, 1581, 1599, 1700, 1707, 1710, 1805, 1999, 2007, 2039, 2053, 2382, 2439, 2456, 2462, 2520, 2536, 2676, 2715, 2722, 2765

Division 38: Health Psychology, 556, 775, 965, 1131, 1162, 1220, 1244, 1258–1259, 1288, 1343, 1421, 1435, 1522, 1530, 1554, 1601, 1823, 2039, 2493, 2496, 2498, 2500, 2538, 2566, 2591, 2609, 2646, 2680, 2727, 2760, 2767, 2815

Division 39: Psychoanalysis, 22, 134, 164, 228, 237, 254, 321, 353, 359, 374, 387, 403, 408, 410, 413, 421, 424, 426–427, 430–431, 445, 454, 456, 469, 470–471, 480, 488–489, 495, 518, 526, 533, 556, 558, 566, 572, 577, 580, 592, 595–596, 607, 618, 620, 625, 627, 642–643, 652, 669, 680, 686, 688, 699, 730, 736, 738, 746, 825, 839, 844, 853, 855, 859, 862, 866, 876, 881–882, 895–900, 902, 912, 926, 928, 930, 934, 939, 948, 959, 967, 971, 978, 1000, 1015, 1029, 1079, 1086, 1108, 1116, 1155, 1159, 1163, 1184–1185, 1205, 1243–1244, 1250, 1328, 1356, 1367, 1392, 1418, 1437, 1458, 1461–1462, 1483, 1488, 1509, 1566, 1662, 1680, 1700, 1707, 1722, 1737, 1745, 1784, 1793, 1812, 2370, 2530, 2827

Division 40: Clinical Neuropsychology, 49, 128, 132, 144, 157, 174, 191, 199, 208, 231, 240, 243, 272, 273, 287, 290, 306, 327, 335, 342, 355, 382, 385, 419, 557, 593, 678, 695, 735, 817, 857, 879, 887, 903, 966, 982, 1010, 1018, 1043, 1065, 1137, 1215, 1306, 1318, 1321, 1366, 1384, 1395, 1401, 1411, 1413, 1430, 1433–1434, 1438, 1456, 1459, 1474, 1479, 1504, 1528, 1542, 1574, 1597, 1629, 1657, 1669, 1672, 1682–1683, 1689, 1704, 1712, 1723, 1747, 1760, 1777–1778, 1782, 1791, 1801, 1803, 1810, 1830, 1839, 1843–1844, 1853, 1859, 1861, 1879, 1889, 1892–1893, 1902, 1905, 1908–1909, 1917, 1926, 1929, 1953, 1955, 2042, 2058, 2060, 2081, 2091, 2101, 2104, 2109, 2116, 2138, 2152, 2164, 2171, 2184, 2208, 2210, 2220, 2245, 2257, 2259, 2260, 2280, 2310, 2332, 2353, 2360, 2374, 2376, 2409,

2415, 2423, 2459, 2476, 2482, 2506, 2519, 2531, 2554, 2558, 2562, 2570, 2573, 2579, 2596, 2599, 2618, 2626, 2675, 2700–2701, 2704, 2707, 2712, 2724, 2739, 2745, 2750, 2790, 2807, 2824

Division 41: American Psychology–Law Society, 66, 101, 146, 169–170, 305, 415, 418, 460, 502, 524, 586, 674, 710, 760, 845, 1148, 1243, 1270, 1386, 1590, 1598, 1600, 1646, 1679, 1710, 1715, 1768, 1977, 2138, 2199, 2235, 2247, 2287, 2324, 2329, 2360, 2364, 2377, 2390, 2426–2427, 2433, 2440, 2450, 2508, 2518, 2520, 2522, 2537, 2552, 2586–2587, 2611–2613, 2633, 2638, 2651, 2659, 2660, 2663, 2665, 2709, 2714, 2733, 2755, 2805–2806

Division 42: Psychologists in Independent Practice, 592, 683, 947, 987, 1019, 1129, 1163, 1171, 1183, 1205, 1207, 1215, 1244, 1385, 1419, 1447, 1478, 1500, 1541, 1560, 1562, 1575, 1616, 1628, 1688, 1690, 1731, 1787–1788, 1802, 1811, 1813, 1816, 1828, 1833, 1837, 1845, 1847, 1852, 1867, 1900, 1914, 1956, 1960, 1988, 2012, 2019, 2023–2024, 2026, 2033, 2052, 2070, 2075, 2086, 2118, 2135, 2149, 2153–2155, 2160–2161, 2172, 2186, 2224, 2233, 2236, 2250, 2256, 2284, 2311, 2322, 2331, 2340, 2342, 2361, 2378, 2385, 2398, 2444, 2451, 2463, 2471, 2473, 2503, 2523, 2525, 2543, 2547–2548, 2561, 2588, 2616, 2619, 2635, 2642, 2653, 2708, 2766, 2785, 2799, 2802, 2823

Division 43: Family Psychology, 936, 1180, 1218, 1235, 1524, 1612, 2516, 2597, 2629, 2688, 2761, 2773

Division 44: Society for the Psychological Study of Lesbian and Gay Issues, 852, 1289, 1503, 1554, 2351, 2368, 2373, 2540, 2566–2567, 2624, 2630, 2666, 2754, 2790

Division 45: Society for the Psychological Study of Ethnic Minority Issues, 10, 63, 195, 317, 404, 500, 621, 793, 863, 874, 911, 915, 918, 958, 980, 981, 1049, 1100, 1169, 1188, 1227, 1255, 1293, 1303, 1341, 1350, 1364, 1383, 1526, 1543, 1546, 1552, 1612, 1693, 1702, 1755, 1765, 2051, 2144, 2166, 2201, 2222, 2241, 2267, 2287, 2290, 2316, 2345, 2394, 2414, 2417, 2446–2447, 2452, 2457–2458, 2478, 2491, 2497, 2502, 2504, 2507, 2509, 2535, 2645, 2664, 2669–2670, 2720, 2762, 2774

Division 46: Media Psychology, 125, 518, 720, 964, 1118, 1238, 1240, 1351, 1467, 1477, 1749, 1857, 2006, 2102, 2243, 2248, 2334, 2582, 2641, 2661, 2671, 2678, 2695

Division 47: Exercise and Sport Psychology, 588, 1210, 2146, 2148, 2358, 2400, 2483, 2668, 2672

Division 48: Peace Psychology, 890, 1026, 1255, 1493, 1497, 1517, 1611, 2584–2585, 2632, 2736, 2744

Division 49: Group Psychology and Group Psychotherapy, 549, 1582, 1606, 1746, 2775

Division 50: Addictions, 216, 329, 941, 1137, 1275, 1294, 1333, 2384, 2652, 2818, 2823

ABOUT THE AUTHOR

Warren R. Street received his PhD in experimental psychology in 1967 from the Claremont Graduate School. He has served on the faculty of Central Washington University since that time and is now professor of psychology. He was a cofounder and director of the university's William O. Douglas Honors College, an honors program based on a 4-year great books reading regimen. Dr. Street, who describes himself as a compulsive collector of dates of events in the history of psychology, compiled the historical notations that appeared in the American Psychological Association 1992 Centennial Calendar. In addition to his research and teaching interest in the history of psychology, he has written on the application of the principles of behavior analysis to the traditional problems of social psychology.